'Managing behaviour is fundamental to teaching: teachers should read first. Roland Chaplain's writ rare combination of rigorous research knowledge translated into exemplary classroom practice. His work with trainee teachers on behaviour management continues to be at the cutting edge. Most of all, Chaplain's expertise is built on a deep understanding of the psychological and social factors that are a daily reality for teachers and their pupils.'

**Professor Dominic Wyse**, Institute of Education, University College London

'Roland Chaplain has a highly-developed insight into the reasons why students exhibit challenging behaviour, based upon wider ranging empirical studies and personal expertise and experience. This is the basis for developing a clear range of strategies and proven approaches that teachers can employ to manage and challenge students' behaviour. They will help to create an effective, positive and purposeful learning environment, where student behaviour allows teachers to teach without disruption. There is a very clear focus upon coping strategies and improvements to teacher well-being, allowing teachers to become resilient and better able to deal with challenging situations and behaviour. As well as considering the role of the individual, their expectations, skills and strategies, Roland Chaplain takes a broader view to consider how school organisation and the role of school leaders can be influential in creating a school climate where learning comes first and is not impacted by poor behaviour. I wholeheartedly recommend this book for initial teacher trainees, for those who are more experienced but wish to refresh their knowledge and skills, but also leaders who are looking to create a more positive climate for behaviour within their schools.'

**Martin Barwise**, Assistant Headteacher, Jack Hunt School, Peterborough, and SCITT Co-Director, Teach East

'This second edition is not just another book of "tips for teachers"; Roland Chaplain's straight-talking approach also sets a critical eye on "quick fix" solutions and pseudo-science. Adopting a fresh and evidence-based perspective allows him once again to address this complex subject in a clear, informed and practical way. If you only have one book on behaviour management make it this one!'

**Dr Phil Kirkman**, Deputy Head of Education and Social Care/ Principal Lecturer, Anglia Ruskin University

# Teaching without Disruption in the Secondary School

What is the most effective way of managing pupils' behaviour?

The effective management of pupils' behaviour has long been a principle concern, not only for classroom teachers, but for all involved with the management of schools. Motivating pupils and preventing disruption whilst developing positive relationships and promoting well-being can be difficult for any teacher.

Roland Chaplain is the behaviour management specialist on the PGCE courses at Cambridge University, which topped the teacher training rankings and was named the 'pre-eminent individual provider' in the 2017 Good Teacher Training Guide. This book reflects the behaviour management element of the course considered 'excellent' and 'highly distinctive' by Ofsted. The materials are also used on school-based CPD courses and consultancy work.

Fully updated to include recent changes in government policy, this second edition highlights the importance of behaviour management training for trainee and qualified teachers. Readers are provided with evidence-based training and personal development materials along with case studies and examples of how to apply research to practice.

Topics include:

- a theoretical framework based on what works in managing behaviour and how to apply it in school
- whole-school and leadership roles in developing effective strategies to anticipate and eliminate disruption
- enhancing teachers' efficacy, professional skills, coping and well-being
- how socio-emotional development and stress affect adolescent behaviour and well-being
- developing pupils' self-control and self-regulation
- understanding and supporting pupils who have emotional, behavioural and mental health difficulties
- a step-by-step guide to developing an effective personalised classroom management plan.

The book is enhanced throughout with evidence from contemporary educational and psychological research to support the advice and guidance offered. Each chapter includes thought-provoking and reflective materials for teachers and trainers, as well as readings for Masters level activities. Experienced and trainee teachers, school leaders and ITT providers will find this an indispensable guide.

**Roland Chaplain** is a chartered psychologist, educational consultant and behaviour management specialist in the Faculty of Education, University of Cambridge, UK. He has experience as a teacher, headteacher and senior lecturer in Psychology.

# Teaching without Disruption in the Secondary School

A Practical Approach to Managing Pupil Behaviour

Second Edition

Roland Chaplain

LONDON AND NEW YORK

Second edition published 2018
by Routledge
2 Park Square, Milton Park, Abingdon, Oxon OX14 4RN

and by Routledge
711 Third Avenue, New York, NY 10017

*Routledge is an imprint of the Taylor & Francis Group, an informa business*

© 2018 Roland Chaplain

The right of Roland Chaplain to be identified as author of this work has been asserted by him in accordance with sections 77 and 78 of the Copyright, Designs and Patents Act 1988.

All rights reserved. No part of this book may be reprinted or reproduced or utilised in any form or by any electronic, mechanical, or other means, now known or hereafter invented, including photocopying and recording, or in any information storage or retrieval system, without permission in writing from the publishers.

*Trademark notice*: Product or corporate names may be trademarks or registered trademarks, and are used only for identification and explanation without intent to infringe.

First edition published by RoutledgeFalmer 2003

*British Library Cataloguing-in-Publication Data*
A catalogue record for this book is available from the British Library

*Library of Congress Cataloging-in-Publication Data*
Names: Chaplain, Roland, author.
Title: Teaching without disruption in the secondary school: a practical approach to managing pupil behaviour / Roland Chaplain.
Description: Second edition. | New York: Routledge, 2017.
Identifiers: LCCN 2017014358| ISBN 9781138690684 (Hardback) | ISBN 9781138690691 (Paperback) | ISBN 9781315536781 (Ebook)
Subjects: LCSH: School discipline—Great Britain. | High school students—Great Britain—Discipline.
Classification: LCC LB3012.4.G7 C53 2018 | DDC 373.1102—dc23
LC record available at https://lccn.loc.gov/2017014358

ISBN: 978-1-138-69068-4 (hbk)
ISBN: 978-1-138-69069-1 (pbk)
ISBN: 978-1-315-53678-1 (ebk)

Typeset in Bembo
by codeMantra

To the loving memory of my dear son, Roland, who will never get to read this book – and to Felix and Elysia who hopefully will (when they are old enough to read).

# Contents

*List of figures* x
*List of tables* xii
*Preface* xiii
*Acknowledgements* xvii

Introduction 1

1 Theory, research and behaviour management 6

2 Stress, coping and well-being 29

3 Teacher thinking and pupil behaviour 57

4 Professional social skills 79

5 Whole-school influences on behaviour management 105

6 Leadership and positive behaviour 126

7 Classroom climate: the physical and socio-psychological environment 142

8 Classroom structures: the role of rules, routines and rituals in behaviour management 163

9 Managing difficult behaviour 182

10 Classroom management planning 210

*References* 237
*Index* 267

# Figures

| | | |
|---|---|---|
| i.1 | Multilevel model of behaviour management | 2 |
| i.2 | Layered questions about behaviour management | 3 |
| 1.1 | ABC model of behaviour | 8 |
| 1.2 | Triadic reciprocity – the relationship between personal factors, the environment and behaviour | 20 |
| 2.1 | The cognitive architecture of BOSS and EMPLOYEE systems | 38 |
| 2.2 | Interactive model of coping | 42 |
| 2.3 | Individual Coping Analysis (ICAN) | 50 |
| 3.1 | A simplified model of the teacher expectancy-confirmation process | 62 |
| 4.1 | Elements of social competence | 80 |
| 4.2 | Information loss in classroom communication | 87 |
| 4.3 | A hierarchy of social skills used in teaching | 91 |
| 4.4 | Facial code – emotion signalled through facial expression | 92 |
| 4.5 | The business gaze | 95 |
| 4.6 | The social gaze | 95 |
| 4.7 | A model for developing assertive behaviour | 102 |
| 5.1 | A simple systems model | 115 |
| 5.2 | Communication networks | 119 |
| 5.3 | Person-environment fit | 123 |
| 7.1 | Potential effects of classroom environment and climate on pupils' thinking, emotions and behaviour | 143 |
| 7.2 | Traditional classroom layout – (a) individual desks and (b) dyads | 147 |
| 7.3 | Coffee bar layout | 150 |
| 7.4 | Nightclub layout | 150 |
| 7.5 | Open circle and horseshoe layouts | 151 |
| 8.1 | A developmental perspective on classroom management comparing early and later encounters with a class | 170 |
| 9.1 | Generalised temporal sequence for the development of behaviour disorders | 195 |

| | | |
|---|---|---|
| 9.2 | An example of a progressive intervention for a pupil with EBD | 200 |
| 9.3 | Outline of a behavioural intervention | 202 |
| 9.4 | Frequency graph showing number of occurrences of negative and positive behaviour recorded each day for eight days | 203 |
| 10.1 | Chapter 10 outline | 211 |
| 10.2 | All about me questionnaire | 218 |
| 10.3 | Normal distribution of pupils | 219 |
| 10.4 | Stages in developing a behavioural intervention to address an inefficient routine | 227 |
| 10.5 | Reinforcement schedule | 228 |

# Tables

| | | |
|---|---|---|
| 1.1 | Using classical conditioning to establish a basic routine behaviour | 10 |
| 1.2 | Positive and negative reinforcement | 13 |
| 1.3 | Types and categories of reinforcer | 13 |
| 1.4 | Positive and negative punishments | 17 |
| 1.5 | Procedural steps in self-instruction training used with individual pupil or group of pupils | 26 |
| 2.1 | Everyday BOSS and EMPLOYEE coping in school | 40 |
| 2.2 | Matching social support to specific stressors | 45 |
| 2.3 | Coping styles | 50 |
| 2.4 | Individual Coping Analysis (ICAN) | 51 |
| 3.1 | Implying personality from limited information | 68 |
| 3.2 | Explanations for Lee's misbehaviour | 73 |
| 4.1 | A simplified script for a lesson | 86 |
| 4.2 | Some examples of professional skills used by teachers | 88 |
| 5.1 | A simple systems analysis of inputs, processes and outcomes | 116 |
| 7.1 | Explaining the causes of success and failure | 155 |
| 8.1 | Evaluating classroom routines at the start of a lesson | 180 |
| 9.1 | DSM-V Diagnostic criteria for ADHD, ODD and CD | 189 |
| 9.2 | Relative seriousness of anti-social behaviours | 201 |
| 9.3 | Categories of irrational teacher 'must' statements | 206 |
| 10.1 | Assess your behaviour management efficacy | 214 |
| 10.2 | Evaluating sources of social support | 214 |
| 10.3 | Evaluating classroom routines | 225 |

# Preface

Since the first edition, and despite there having been many changes to legislation and a shift to trainee teachers spending increasing amounts of time in schools to learn from experience, behaviour management remains a significant ongoing concern for teachers at all levels. A recent YouGov survey found that pupils are losing up to 38 days of teaching each year because of low-level disruption in classrooms – something many teachers have come to accept as normal (Ofsted, 2014).

Disruption has grabbed the attention of successive government departments, not least because of the numbers of teachers leaving the profession who cite problems managing behaviour as a reason for doing so. Behaviour management training, or lack of it, is one of the reasons why teachers have these difficulties. A major contributing factor is the low priority given to teaching trainees research-based approaches to behaviour management whose effectiveness has been established. As a result, many trainees pick up ideas along the way in a grab-bag fashion as tips for surviving that might work for some people, but which are often contradictory. Hence we end up with patchy quality which might be 'good enough' or 'not good enough' behaviour management. What constitutes mediocre, good or outstanding behaviour management is largely subjective, as is the degree to which it is due to a teacher's personal ability or other factors. What is clear is that even teachers who are considered to be 'very good' in one school, are not guaranteed that they will be so in another.

There have been two government working parties over the last five years concerned with improving behaviour management training in initial teacher training. They were created to determine how best to train teachers to be more effective at managing behaviour and provide some consistency in their knowledge and practice base. I was invited to contribute to both. The first, organised by Charlie Taylor and published in 2012, produced a description of the knowledge, skills and understanding of that trainees need in order to be able to manage pupil behaviour. These include: personal development; understanding the influence of school systems; classroom management strategies; managing challenging behaviour and theoretical knowledge. The contents of this book and its predecessor focus on these and other areas.

The second working party, the Carter review of initial teacher training (ITT), published in 2015, again identified behaviour management training as a priority. As a result, behaviour management now forms part of the core curriculum for ITT (DfE, 2016). Whilst the reviews are interesting, their findings were familiar rather than novel. What is needed is more time being dedicated to training in methods which have been shown to work.

During my time as a senior lecturer at the University of Cambridge, I designed and continue to teach the in-house Behaviour Management Training and Support (BMaTS) programme to all Postgraduate Certificate in Education (PGCE) trainees. The quality of the programme has been highlighted in Ofsted inspections and consistently in newly qualified teacher (NQT) satisfaction surveys. Ofsted considered it to be 'highly distinctive training and support' (2008) and later commented that it

> ... has led to a marked improvement in trainees' confidence and outcomes for trainees' practice in the classroom ... very positive trainee satisfaction levels and the excellent above sector responses to the NQT surveys.
> (2011)

The contents of this book largely reflect the programme, with the exception of the additional individual support that I offer trainees during and after the course. In addition to training preservice teachers, I have also maintained my contact with teachers, leaders and teacher trainers through my work as a freelance consultant, delivering professional development courses in schools in the UK.

This second edition of *Teaching without Disruption in the Secondary School* is fully updated in line with changes to legislation and official guidance, practice in school, research into behaviour management and cognate findings drawn from various disciplines – notably psychology and neuroscience. All of the chapters in this second edition have been substantially revised and two new chapters added. The first makes explicit the research-based evidence and theoretical frameworks which inform my approach. The second new chapter teaches readers how to use the various chapters to produce an effective behaviour management plan for use with pupils of different ages and developmental levels.

Behaviour management is influenced by many factors, but the psychological level is the crossroad where all these factors join. It is an individual's appraisal and interpretation of themselves and their situation that holds the key to understanding why they behave the way they do, as well as why they think others behave the way they do. I am a firm believer that teachers are more effective in managing behaviour if they are reflective, analytical and think strategically about their practice, which should be informed by research-based evidence.

The need to be critical in differentiating between authentic research and nonsense, is highlighted in distinguishing between science and pseudoscience. For example, neuroscience has gained prominence in education and has produced interesting findings, which add to our understanding of human development, some of which are discussed in this book. However, some 'brain science' serves as an example of how something labelled 'scientific research', but which is not, can find its way into classrooms. Whilst interest in the brain and understanding how it functions might improve schooling, offering potentially exciting opportunities, caution is advised. One danger of applying neuroscience to schooling uncritically is reductionism – that everything is explainable at the neuron level. Of more concern is that the ill-informed adoption of so-called brain science has seen the rise of neuromyths. This has led to the growth and sale to schools of unevaluated, alleged 'brain-based' programmes which are not supported by research but sold through slick marketing. Something I have always encouraged in all my students at Cambridge for over two decades, is a healthy scepticism towards what they hear and read, encouraging them to examine their assumptions and acknowledge the constraints of research methods and practical advice. A healthy scepticism does not mean being cynical or doubting the validity of everything, it means judging the validity of a claim based on empirical evidence and its critiques. That being the case, I hope it is clear that this is not a book of tips for teachers, merely drawing on my experience as a teacher, headteacher or psychologist. Nonetheless, reflecting on those experiences and the many hours I continue to spend observing and supporting teachers has informed my teaching, my research and what I deem to be important in training teachers how to manage behaviour, something I have now done for over 25 years. My goal has always been to help teachers develop their knowledge, skills and coping strategies to support their well-being and the effectiveness of their teaching and hence the quality of schooling for pupils. There are many approaches to managing behaviour, and each has its own strengths and limitations. Which approach is considered most appropriate by an individual teacher or school depends on a range of interlinked organisational and individual factors (school ethos, beliefs, relationships and the personal characteristics of those who work and study there). There is no single right way of doing things, but choice should be made on measured effectiveness. Adopting a research-based approach means you can determine its origins, that is: what was done, under what circumstances and its theoretical basis. Formal research is required to be rigorous and reviewed before publication – 'good' ideas and tips are not, however intuitively correct or easy they sound. In several chapters of this book I demonstrate how some popular beliefs and practices in teaching have been shown to be completely contrary to what the objective evidence has shown to be correct, but which are still practiced. The effectiveness of the approaches I recommend are backed up by hundreds of research studies, so the reader can scrutinise and determine who was involved, what was done and what happened.

I hope the various contents of this book will be read with an eye to the superordinate goal of improving the quality of behaviour management in schools and in doing so improve the quality of teaching, learning and the well-being of teachers and pupils.

I have used the term 'pupil' rather than student, child, adolescent or young person except where the latter are included in a quote or is being used in a non-school context.

I have attempted to avoid the overuse of the pronoun 'he' except when referring to specific cases where the sex of a teacher is a man, or where a pupil is a boy. The intention is to represent both sexes equally.

In some places I have suggested those readers interested in analysing their verbal and nonverbal behaviour might make video recordings of themselves teaching. If you are making video or other image capture in the classroom, data protection and child safety procedures must be followed.

So if all your pupils behave impeccably, are highly motivated, extremely successful in all subjects and well-adjusted; your colleagues are always caring and supportive; you have all the resources you could ever wish for, and your school organisation and senior staff are infallible – congratulations! If not read on, there is something in this book for you.

# Acknowledgements

I am indebted to the many people who have shaped my thinking and influenced the content of this book. Thanking everyone personally would take a book in itself.

I am especially grateful to the thousands of pupils, students, trainee and qualified teachers, headteachers and psychologists that I have worked with, taught, interviewed, supported or who have graciously afforded me their time just to talk about behaviour in schools during my career. Some asked not to be named, so I resolved to use pseudonyms throughout. Some of the quotes and case studies were taken from interviews, not all of which were published, so they do not appear in the references, but I thank them for sharing their thoughts.

I extend my appreciation to Helen Pritt, Fiona Burbage, Emilie Coin and the staff at Routledge for their encouragement and support.

Last, but most definitely not least, my wonderful wife Sandra, without whose encouragement and support, this book would not exist. Her extraordinary patience and attention to detail when working through endless revisions, sorting out my computer files, deciphering my notes and the critical feedback she provides me with is invaluable.

# Introduction

As with the first edition, this second edition is structured around a multilevel model of behaviour management (see Figure i.1). The model represents a top-down approach, advocating progressive focusing, in other words, it reflects on how the organisation overseen by senior leaders impacts on behaviour management in general, on classroom management and on how a school deals with challenging behaviour. The school's values and expectations should be communicated through the school's behaviour policy. So a well-designed behaviour policy, operated throughout the school day, provides the framework for what goes on inside classrooms and other areas inside and outside the school grounds. Where the policy is working correctly (i.e. well thought-out, supported and operated consistently by all staff) it should eliminate many low-level disruptive behaviours almost routinely, making life easier for teachers and providing them with more time to teach. The behaviour policy should also provide the fundamental principles for day-to-day classroom management, including how teachers deal with challenging behaviour. However, this does not mean that teachers should not enjoy distinctiveness in how they operate their classrooms. Far from it, the whole-school framework provides the continuity, but should run alongside the distinctiveness of different teachers and phases to construct the school's identity. In effect, the school climate and individual classroom climates will inevitably have differences, but they will operate within a common organisational culture. There has to be means of ensuring consistency between the three levels in order to minimise confusion for pupils and staff, so a monitoring and evaluation process is needed (see Figure i.1).

Figure i.2 provides an overview of the types of questions this book seeks to answer, these are nested in the various layers of the multilevel model. A brief examination of Figure i.2 reveals how the various levels are interrelated and overlap. Whole-school activity is shown as encompassing classroom management and individual work with difficult pupils, the behaviour policy providing the framework and direction for behaviour management at these levels. The personal level questions refer to the teacher, and this level is shown as overlapping the other three levels, highlighting the centrality of the teacher in the overall plan.

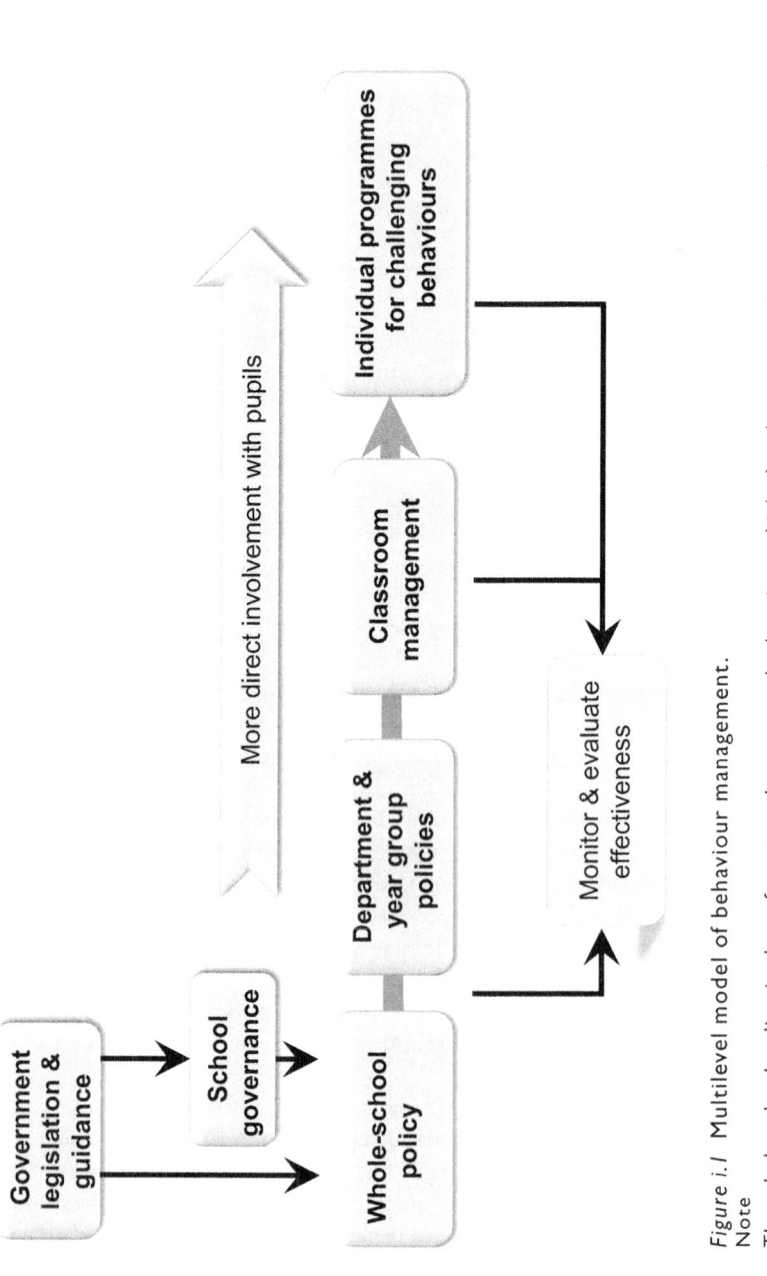

*Figure i.1* Multilevel model of behaviour management.
Note
The whole-school policy is the reference value or standard against which the classroom management and intensive strategies are compared. As the management function moves from left to right the level of intrusiveness and direct teacher control over the pupil increases

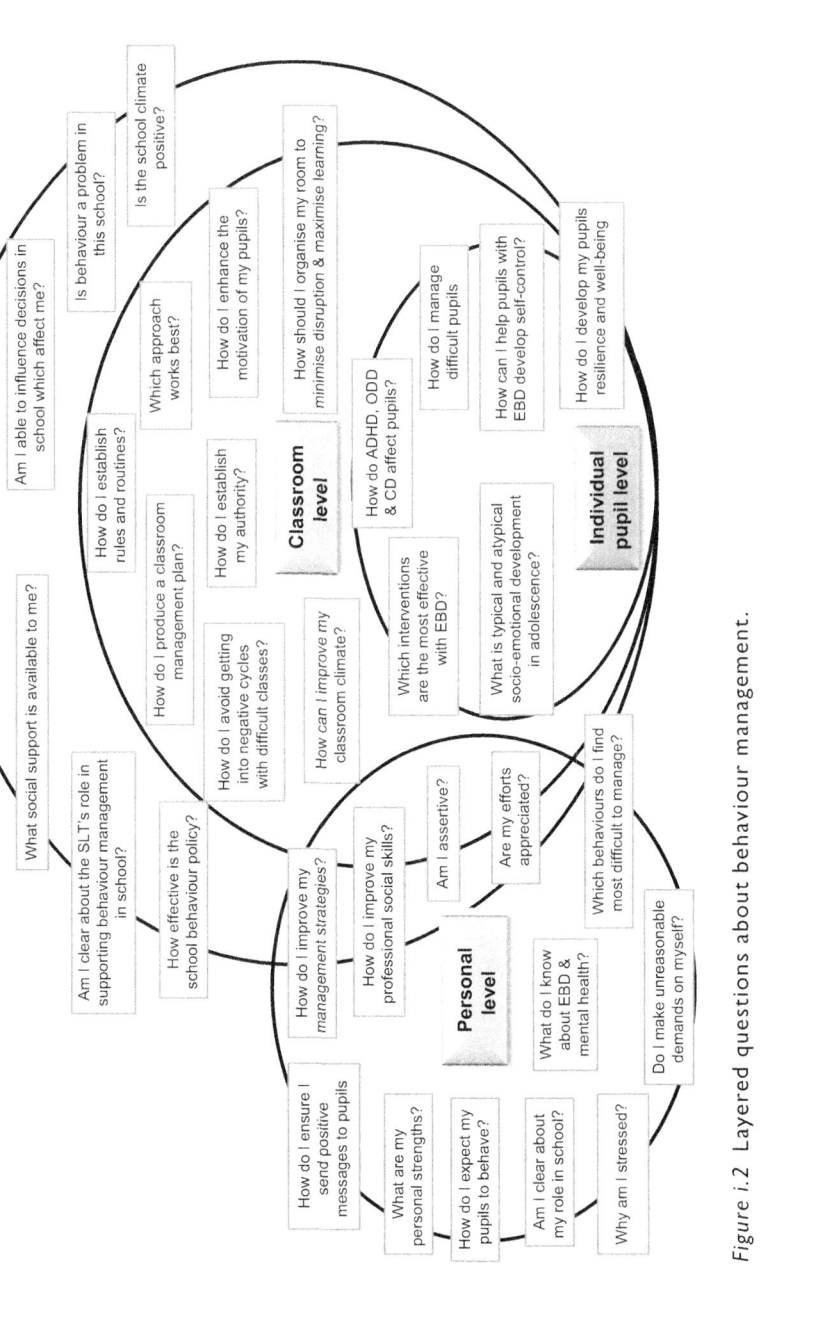

Figure i.2 Layered questions about behaviour management.

The book begins by first describing the evidence-based framework for the various chapters and then, the teacher as the focus, before moving to organisational factors and leadership; then it looks at classroom climate, rules and routines, followed by pupils with emotional and behaviour difficulties, and finally how to integrate the above into your classroom management plan. Whilst most of the book concerns various aspects of behaviour management, some chapters focus specifically on classroom management.

Chapter 1 describes the evidence base for the methods proposed throughout the remaining chapters. Cognitive-behavioural approaches are chosen because of their long history of effectiveness in managing behaviour and developing self-regulation in pupils. Care is taken to explain some of the common misunderstandings about fundamental assumptions of the theories and models, as well as the meanings of the key terms used. Some of these terms, whilst familiar in everyday language, have specific technical meanings in cognitive-behavioural approaches.

Chapters 2, 3 and 4 focus on developing teacher self-awareness, self-knowledge and professional skills. Chapter 2 focuses on how to improve teacher well-being through understanding how the coping process operates. Teacher stress and pupil misbehaviour are positively correlated, but the mechanisms that differentiate effective copers from ineffective copers are often not understood or are oversimplified. Various examples are used to explain why we might become stressed and, more importantly, how to improve coping and enhance well-being. Chapter 3 looks at the teacher expectancy-confirmation cycle, illustrating the ways in which teachers form impressions about pupils and how this affects teacher behaviour, which in turn can unwittingly influence pupil behaviour in a negative way. The theme of Chapter 4 also concerns teacher effects. Here, attention shifts to developing and using professional social skills to convey authority, enhance assertiveness and produce positive teacher-pupil relationships. Attention is drawn to the complexities of nonverbal behaviour and how such behaviours influence how others see us, what we think about ourselves and how we interpret the reciprocal behaviour of others.

Chapters 5 and 6 focus on understanding the school as an organisation and its influence on behaviour management in general, as well as in the classroom. Chapter 5 highlights the relationships between the behaviour policy, school climate and communication, and how each connects to behaviour. The importance of achieving a balance between organisational needs and individual goals with respect to considering person-school fit and the effects on staff well-being is also discussed. Chapter 6 looks at the role of the head and senior leadership team in developing and maintaining effective behaviour management. Changes to the nature of leadership in schools in recent years is also considered with reference to distributed leadership, as well as an examination of how teachers might be best supported in managing pupil behaviour.

Classroom management issues are the subject of Chapters 7 and 8. Having discussed the school's organisational climate earlier, the focus in Chapter 7 shifts to classroom climate – including both the physical and socio-emotional elements and their effects on pupils' behaviour, motivation, relationships and well-being. How to manipulate the physical environment to create optimal conditions for different types of learning and prosocial behaviour is the starting point for Chapter 7. The latter part of this chapter focuses on the social psychological effects of classroom climate on pupils' motivation, emotions and behaviour.

Chapter 8 examines how rules, routines and rituals influence the quality of social and learning behaviour in the classroom. Establishing effective rules and routines in early encounters with a class to minimise disruption and maximise time on learning cannot be overemphasised. Making pupil logistics and mundane tasks automatic minimises the need for the teacher to be continually engaged in thinking about and actively directing these behaviours, which wastes valuable teaching time.

In Chapter 9, the difficult issue of managing and supporting pupils who have emotional and behavioural difficulties (EBD) is addressed. The inclusion of pupils with EBD and mental health issues (e.g. attention deficit hyperactivity disorder (ADHD), conduct disorder (CD), etc.) has made additional demands on the management skills of regular classroom teachers. Mental health issues have been flagged as a growing problem among children. Hence, in addition to considering EBD in general, an in-depth look is made at the three most common mental health disorders among pupils – ADHD, CD and oppositional defiant disorder (ODD). The difficulty with using labels such as ADHD is that they represent clusters of behaviours. Shifting focus from these clusters to understanding the specific presenting behaviours of a particular pupil (e.g. talking out of turn) makes designing an in-class intervention more possible. The chapter includes interventions which can be operated at both the whole-class and individual levels. A least-restrictive intervention model is provided, starting by looking at modifying the classroom environment to produce the desired behaviours, followed by whole-class strategies and finishing with individual programmes.

The final chapter (Chapter 10) draws on material from the previous nine chapters to illustrate how to use them to build a classroom management plan. Beginning with self-awareness and understanding your pupils and your school, focus then shifts to developing proactive, reorientation and reactive strategies, and how to put them into action. The chapter ends by discussing how to develop pupil self-regulation and social competence and how to organise your classroom to support pupils with EBD, notably those with attention and impulsivity difficulties.

Despite the interconnectedness of the chapters, you may wish to concentrate on those chapters that relate to the specific aspects of behaviour management that you most wish to develop. By reading the whole book, however, you can best appreciate the important links between the different areas, without which a complete understanding cannot be achieved.

# Chapter 1

# Theory, research and behaviour management

Rigorously researching what works best in respect of managing pupil behaviour should be routine in education. Judging the validity of a claim that one approach is better than another should be based on objective empirical research, not what sounds like a good idea. Unfortunately, that is not always the case in reality. Many books on managing behaviour often contain statements like 'this book avoids dry/boring/complex theory and research' and go on to say that the book is based on common sense and on the author's experience as a teacher. Out-of-hand rejection of theory and research in this way demonstrates ignorance of what a theory is. These authors' collections of anecdotes, good ideas and tips collectively constitute their *implicit theory* of how to manage behaviour in class. As discussed in Chapter 3, we all have our own implicit theories about a range of phenomena, including intelligence (Blackwell *et al.*, 2007) and personality (Baudson and Preckel, 2013), and we all have theories about behaviour (Geeraert and Yzerbyt, 2007).

'Practical people' often believe that 'the facts' (i.e. their experience) speak for themselves – but they don't. Facts are interpreted, and the interpretation relies on implicit theories that go beyond the facts to give them meaning. Despite their limitations, personal theories might work satisfactorily for some people most of the time, but those theories may prove wrong, inappropriate or disastrous for someone else. Should the 'tip' you are given not work for you, what do you conclude and what do you do next? Picking up ideas as you go along may work for gardening, but I consider teaching to be a profession, and being professional should include having the particular knowledge and skills necessary to do your job. Just because behaviour management training has had a low profile in teacher education should not mean that the research evidence available about what works best should be ignored.

The term 'evidence-based practice', increasingly used in education, means adopting methods based on sound theoretical principles and supported by empirical research. It applies to all areas of pedagogy, including behaviour management as the DfE recommendations for behaviour management training made clear:

> Theoretical knowledge: trainees should know about scientific research and developments, and how these can be applied to understanding, managing and changing children's behaviour.
>
> (DfE, 2012)

Whilst there are a number of established theories, models and frameworks available with contrasting views on how to manage behaviour, I have chosen to focus on those supported by the strongest empirical evidence. If you wish to know more about other models, Porter (2006) provides a useful overview of seven contrasting approaches.

The cognitive-behavioural approaches, models and methods that follow are housed in empirical evidence drawn from educational, psychological and neuroscientific research about behaviour management and wider aspects of human behaviour. Applied correctly, they will provide you with a framework on which to organise your classroom management planning to quickly establish and maintain your authority as a teacher, develop pupils' engagement with learning, build effective classroom relationships, create the conditions for teaching and learning and help develop pupils' self-control and social competence.

Behavioural approaches focus solely on observable behaviour, whereas cognitive-behavioural approaches focus on both observable (overt behaviour) and thinking and emotions (covert behaviour). Behavioural approaches change behaviour by reinforcement and/or punishment. Cognitive approaches change the behaviour by changing the thinking (and emotions) behind the behaviour, actively trying to persuade people to think differently. It follows that cognitive-behavioural approaches (CBA) combine the two in different proportions, depending on the specific approach. CBA have been shown to be effective in decreasing disruptive behaviour in the classroom (Sukhodolsky and Scahill, 2012); to improve pupils' self-control (Feindler *et al.*, 1986) and to have lasting effects (Lochman, 1992).

The following descriptions of the theories and models have been simplified to make them more accessible and usable in the classroom. Numerous references are included throughout the chapter for anyone wishing to develop an in-depth knowledge.

## Behavioural approaches (BA)

The basic premise of these approaches is that all behaviour, including unacceptable behaviour, is learned through reinforcement and deterred by punishment. Elements of BA are evident in all schools, where pupils receive

# 8  Theory, research and behaviour management

rewards (e.g. praise, tokens, or having tea with the head, etc.) for behaving as required or sanctions (e.g. detention) for misbehaving. Unfortunately, in many instances, because the principles underpinning the approach are misunderstood, they are ineffective, or their effectiveness is limited.

BA offer a scientific approach to behaviour management, since they are based on structured observation, manipulating the environment and measurement of behaviour. There are three areas of focus: what occurs before a behaviour (antecedent) or what starts it off; the behaviour itself; and what follows or keeps it going (consequence), from which a hypothesis is created and tested (see Figure 1.1). For example, Miss Jones has difficulty getting pupils to stop talking so that she can give out instructions. She decides to introduce an incentive for speeding up responses to her request for pupils to stop talking and face her when she claps her hands. She claps her hands (antecedent) and the first five pupils who stop talking immediately (behaviour) receive a sticker (consequence). She repeats this process until satisfied that the routine is established. The objective being for the class to complete the task competently and quickly.

Whilst behaviourists recognise that something goes on inside the brain (covert behaviour), they argue that we can only theorise about *what* the

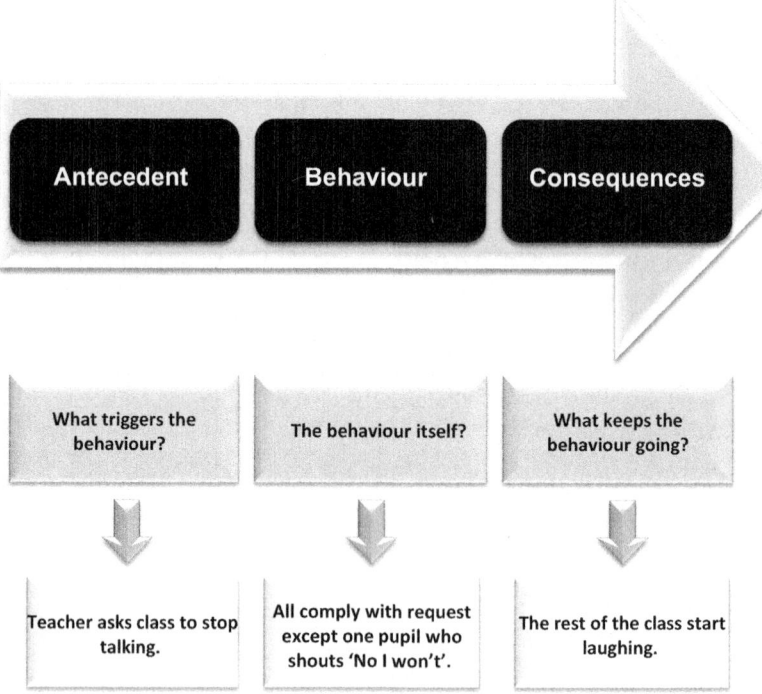

*Figure 1.1* ABC model of behaviour.

individual is thinking and how their previous history *might* have influenced that behaviour. This focus on the measurement of overt behaviour is not limited to behaviourists. Other approaches in psychological and educational research also rely on measuring behaviour to support their theories. Cognitive psychologists might compare time taken to complete a maths task and infer how different metacognitive strategies are advantageous or disadvantageous in problem-solving. Neuroscientists measure performance on a task whilst mapping brain activity using scanning equipment, inferring which brain regions might be associated with specific behaviour.

Neuroscience has provided information about the effect of rewards, punishment and motivation on brain activity, elements central to the behavioural approach. For example, dopamine, a neurotransmitter, helps control the brain's reward and pleasure centres, notably through pathways between the limbic system and the forebrain (Thompson, 2000). It also enables individuals to prioritise rewards and to take action to approach them. At the very moment your brain recognizes something it likes (e.g. food), it will make you *think* it is good and will encode that information and remember that you liked it (Galván, 2013). Research has also demonstrated that the substantial behavioural changes during adolescence are largely believed to be driven by rewards, including monetary, novel and social rewards, and by extension, the reward-sensitive dopamine system (Galván et al., 2006; Van Leijenhorst et al., 2010). This helps explain why, if a teacher picks the right reward and correct rate of rewarding, he/she is able to manipulate behaviour and engagement with learning since it is associated with pleasure and reward. A reward does not need to be present to have an effect, as dopamine can be released in anticipation or triggered by association with a stimulus, e.g. a teacher opening a drawer that contains *desirable* stickers, which are associated with a particular behaviour.

Competent teachers can make managing pupils (including those others find difficult) look comparatively easy. Teacher A walks into a room and gives a disappointed look at those pupils who are misbehaving, and those pupils all stop talking, sit down and face the front. New teacher B repeats the same behaviour, but the noise continues – begging the question why? There may be a number of possible explanations, one being a lack of association between stimulus (teacher B's expression) and the required response and/or the consequences of not doing so – an association that needs to be established and reinforced over time to become automatic.

The two most familiar origins of behavioural approaches are classical and operant conditioning.

### Classical conditioning

Classical conditioning is the most basic form of associative or automatic learning in which one stimulus brings about a response.

The Nobel Prize winner Ivan Pavlov, known for his research with dogs (and children), is less well-known as being one of the most influential neurophysiologists of his century (Pickehain, 1999). Pavlov believed dogs were hard-wired to salivate in response to food (a natural response), but he trained them to salivate at the sound of a bell (an unnatural response). He noticed that the dogs in the laboratory would begin to salivate in anticipation of food, for example, when an assistant entered the laboratory at feeding time or when they heard the 'click' made by the machine that distributed the food – both unnatural responses. So he began ringing a bell at the same time he provided the food to teach an association between the unnatural and natural stimulus. Initially, the bell was a neutral stimulus, i.e. it did not produce a salivary response. However, after repeated pairings between bell and food, the bell in the absence of food provided the trigger for the dogs to salivate. This relationship is known as contiguity – an association between two events that occur closely together in time. Association learning can be observed in all classrooms. Pupils learning to respond in a particular way to unnatural stimuli, e.g. lining up when a bell is rung.

Humans have a distinct advantage over dogs – that is, language, which means that the desired behaviour can initially be stated explicitly – e.g. stand up, sit down, stop talking, or line up – then replaced with more subtle nonverbal triggers such as gestures (e.g. the teacher claps or raises their hand) to initiate the required behaviour (see Table 1.1).

Competent teachers spend the first couple of weeks with a new class establishing routines and teaching their pupils to associate particular cues with specific behavioural requirements in their classrooms (Leinhardt et al., 1987). Trainee teachers taking over classes in which routines are established and efficient can find it daunting, especially if the pupils do not respond to their signals in the same way as they do for the regular teacher. It is essential, therefore, to understand how such behaviours are established and how to develop these routines quickly in order to help a novice teacher feel in control.

Table 1.1 Using classical conditioning to establish a basic routine behaviour

| Stage | Teacher behaviour | Pupil behaviour |
| --- | --- | --- |
| Stage 1<br>No routine in place | Claps<br>Tells pupils to face her | ➤ Pupils don't face her<br>➤ Pupils face her |
| Stage 2<br>Establishing routine | Tells pupils to face her whilst clapping | ➤ Pupils face her |
| Stage 3<br>Routine established | Claps | ➤ Pupils face her |

## Operant conditioning

The second approach is operant conditioning (OC). The basic premise of OC is that any behaviour that is followed by reinforcement is likely to be repeated. If a pupil blows a raspberry and the class laughs, she is likely to do so again – laughter being the reinforcer. In contrast, behaviour followed by punishment is less likely to be repeated. OC owes much to the work of B.F. Skinner (1974) who explained learning in terms of the relationship between stimulus, response and reinforcement. For Skinner, a stimulus or response should be defined by *what it does*, rather than how it looks or what it costs; in other words, a functional definition of behaviour. Definitions need not be fixed in advance; a definition can be selected according to what works (Skinner, 1961). OC is a pragmatic approach to specifying behaviour based on a functional definition, meaning that activities should be designed to produce orderly results. For Skinner, the emphasis should always be on *positive reinforcement of required behaviour* rather than on punishment of undesirable behaviour.

Operant conditioning is used in all schools. For example, verbally supporting a pupil (consequence) for completing a task (behaviour) when asked (stimulus) *may* increase the likelihood that he/she will continue to make an effort, in order to gain more verbal support. However, this depends on the degree to which a pupil values that consequence. Being praised publicly may not be seen as rewarding by some pupils, who would rather just have a quiet word or a thumbs up from that teacher (Burnett, 2001). Other pupils will not respond to verbal support but will respond to tangible rewards, e.g. stickers. Other pupils are self-reinforcing, in effect they reward themselves for their successes – i.e. they complete tasks because they enjoy it. Put simply, any behaviour that is followed by *something* that an individual finds pleasurable, is likely to be repeated and becomes learned. *Anything* that follows a behaviour to keep it going or strengthens it is termed a 'reinforcer'.

Difficulties in school often result from pupils being inappropriately reinforced for unacceptable behaviour – an action known as negative reinforcement (not to be confused with punishment). The following case study illustrates negative reinforcement.

### Case study

From Year 7, Craig had never enjoyed English nor had he experienced much success in the subject. Now in Year 9, he would often not pay attention to Mr Smith, his English teacher, and would frequently disturb other pupils. When Craig's disruptive behaviour became unacceptable to Mr Smith, he would send him to Mrs Wills, the head of year, where he would stay until the end of the English lesson. As Mrs Wills was invariably

> busy, she would give Craig jobs, such as tidying an equipment cupboard or sorting papers, which Craig did enthusiastically. These behaviours – misbehaving in English class and getting sent to the head of year – became ritualised behaviour for all involved and proved hard to break.

There are four points I would make about this case study. First, it is not acceptable for a pupil to be spending time off legitimate learning tasks (however important the equipment cupboard might be). Second, the reinforcer in this case (tidying the store cupboard) was preferable to having to spend time learning English, despite teachers informing Craig of the importance of English to his future. It is a reinforcer because it is perpetuating the undesirable behaviour. Third, the ritual provided a coping strategy for all three individuals. Fourth, the habitual nature of the process made it difficult for people to stand back and think out alternative ways of dealing with the problem, so they had become locked into a negative cycle.

Negative cycles can become automatic, destructive and accepted as 'normal' behaviour. Many such cycles occur initially by chance and often none of the parties involved are aware of its development. A class observing a negative cycle developing between a teacher and a pupil frequently collude to focus attention away from their own misbehaviour. Pupils regularly in trouble are often automatically blamed, sometimes even in their absence. Making a conscious effort to change what has become a negative ritual can have significant effects. Being more polite when you think the group is rude and ignorant, or using humour when you would routinely use a reprimand can produce positive effects. Changing the ritual is, in effect, changing the link between stimulus, response and reinforcer.

### *Rewards and reinforcement*

Rewards and sanctions are referred to in school behaviour policies and in government publications (e.g. DfE, 2014a) and, as such, they represent a loose connection to behavioural approaches – loose because behaviourists distinguish between the terms 'reward' and 'reinforcement'. Rewards vary between both schools and classrooms. A reward (e.g. certificates, house points, special activities) is something that is given to someone to denote an accomplishment. On the other hand, reinforcement is an effect, which must lead to an increase in a specific behaviour (Maag, 2001) and not all 'rewards' do. A reinforcer is anything that initiates or sustains a behaviour, and it can be positive or negative (see Table 1.2).

Reinforcers must be something pupils like, value or find interesting, and they can include the mere pleasure of engaging with a task for its own intrinsic sake or self-reinforcement. Whilst some pupils will make extra effort to behave as required in order to gain a pencil others will not, but they may do so for the 'privilege' of sharpening pencils for their teacher. For some pupils,

Table 1.2 Positive and negative reinforcement

| Type of reinforcement | Description | Outcomes | Example |
|---|---|---|---|
| Positive reinforcement | Add or increase a pleasant stimulus | Behaviour is strengthened | Giving a pupil a prize after she gets an A on a test |
| Negative reinforcement | Reduce or remove an unpleasant stimulus | Behaviour is strengthened | Allow pupils to miss homework to watch a 'special' TV show increases the likelihood that they will request this again |

just being in a particular teacher's classroom is sufficient to motivate them to engage with learning and behave as that teacher requires. House points or merits given for behaving as required are potential reinforcers for some, but not all pupils. So you need to know your pupils: what they like and do not like; what their interests are both in and out of school; what types of lessons and which subjects they find most and least interesting and so on. Knowing this provides you with information to initiate and sustain engagement with their learning. A simple way of finding this out is to use the 'All about me' questionnaire (see Chapter 10), which is quick and easy to administer to a class and can be reviewed at your leisure.

Reinforcers are divided into primary (e.g. food) or secondary (e.g. stickers) (see Table 1.3) and they range from tangible (e.g. food) to abstract (e.g. praise). However, praise can be both effective and ineffective, so it needs to be used thoughtfully. Burnett and Mandel (2010) found that general, non-targeted praise was the type of praise most frequently used by teachers (77% of lessons) despite general praise being shown *not* to be predictive of a positive classroom environment or of having a positive relationship with a teacher (Burnett, 2002). Over several decades, many researchers (e.g. Brophy, 1981; Gable et al., 2009; Lannie and McCurdy, 2007) have found that praise is ineffective

Table 1.3 Types and categories of reinforcer

| Type | Category | Examples |
|---|---|---|
| Primary reinforcers | Edible | Food |
| | Sensory | Music |
| Secondary reinforcers | Tangible | Stickers |
| | Special activities | Computer time |
| | Responsibilities | Monitor |
| | Social | Verbal feedback |

unless contingent on a specific behaviour. A statement such as 'Filip, I am impressed by the way you are working on your drawing', is more effective than a vague statement such as 'great job'. Praise can also negatively affect learning. Hyland and Hyland (2006) found that around 50% of teachers' feedback was praise, but also noted that premature and gratuitous praise confused pupils and discouraged persistence, especially when they began to fail on a task. The most harmful effect of praise is that it can feed learned helplessness (Chapter 7) because pupils come to depend on being praised in order to engage with their learning. Providing pupils with feedback without praise led to more engagement and effort than feedback with praise (Kessels *et al.*, 2008).

With social behaviour, Loveless (1996) found praise was most effective when it was delivered immediately and enthusiastically, when it involved eye contact with a pupil, when it *specified* behaviour and when a range of praise statements were used (Burnett, 2002). However, when a teacher says 'well done' to different pupils, despite intending to communicate the same sentiment to them all, because vocal tones differ on each occasion, praise may be interpreted subjectively. In contrast, giving someone a token does not suffer from this subjective effect (Kazadin, 1977).

Some schools use the same reward for the same behaviour *ad infinitum* despite even the most attractive reward losing its impact or value over time. Whilst the initial novelty may attract the desired behaviour, any reward loses its effectiveness if used repeatedly over time. Think of your favourite food and imagine having it for every meal, every day, for a month – would you not welcome a change? The important message here is to review and vary reinforcers over time (Stafford *et al.*, 2002).

### Getting pupils to manage their own behaviour

The long-term objective should be to move pupils from external reinforcement towards regulating their own behaviour. However, the time this takes will vary depending on a range of factors, not least the level of self-control your pupils have when you begin teaching them. In the early stages, external reinforcement should be continuous, gradually moving to intermittent over time, and *always* contingent on a pupil or group displaying the required behaviour; otherwise, it will be less effective. The easiest way to manage this in a planned way is to produce a reinforcement schedule (see Figure 10.5). A schedule has two broad elements, continuous and intermittent reinforcement. Continuous reinforcement is where reinforcement is provided whenever the target behaviour occurs. Intermittent reinforcement is where reinforcement is provided after *some* behaviours, but not every time.

Whilst continuous reinforcement is commonly used to establish new behaviours, intermittent reinforcement is used to maintain previously learned behaviours (Cooper *et al.*, 2007). To establish a new behaviour or routine, or to motivate a disengaged class, it is usual to begin by using a regular reinforcement system (Alberto and Troutman, 2013) to encourage them to engage with learning. If at this stage teachers are inconsistent in their reinforcement of the behaviour they require, pupils become uncertain of what is expected of them (Evertson *et al.*, 2003). However, once initial learning has been achieved through continuous reinforcement, intermittent reinforcement produces stronger learning (Cameron, 2002). Consider for example, how people are motivated to continue putting money into a slot machine, even though they do not know when they will win – but know that it is possible.

There are four basic forms of intermittent reinforcement:

- *Fixed-ratio reinforcement schedule*—Reinforcement is provided after a 'fixed' number of correct responses (e.g. completing five maths problems).
- *Variable-ratio reinforcement schedule*—Reinforcement frequency will 'vary', e.g. a teacher will reinforce following one correct response, then after three correct responses, then five, then two and so on.
- *Fixed-interval reinforcement schedule*—Reinforcement will be available after a specific period of time (e.g. staying on task for five minutes).
- *Variable-interval reinforcement schedule*—Specific varying periods of time must be met before reinforcement becomes available (e.g. sometimes after five minutes on task, sometimes after ten minutes).

Sometimes different schedule regimes are operated concurrently and in conjunction with different reinforcers, so verbal support may be used at fixed intervals, whereas tokens (e.g. stickers) are used on a more variable schedule. The sooner reinforcement is given following performance of the desired behaviour, the greater the effect on that behaviour since 'those responses that precede the reinforcer most closely in time are strengthened the most' (Donahoe and Dorsel, 1999: 273). Not doing so results in a weak association between behaviour and consequence. Finally, reinforcers should not cost a lot of money, nor require a lot of staff time or effort to administer (Rhode *et al.*, 1996).

Ignoring an undesirable behaviour *may* result in reducing or stopping it (extinction), depending upon what is reinforcing the behaviour. If receiving attention for misbehaving is reinforcing, then starving the pupil of that attention may reduce it. On the other hand, it may result in pupils using more extreme behaviour to gain attention, which cannot be ignored.

## *Rewards and pupil motivation*

Some argue that pupils should not be rewarded for behaving in a socially acceptable way. However, there is considerable empirical evidence that teachers who do not offer rewards to pupils for behaving as required run the risk of creating a negative classroom climate, and increased antagonism towards school (Colvin, 2004; Evertson *et al.*, 2003; Kauffman, 2008).

The positive effects on GCSE performance of using extrinsic motivation, in the form of financial and non-financial incentives for low-attaining pupils, was demonstrated in a recent field study. Burgess *et al.* (2016) measured the performance of 10,600 pupils taking GCSEs at more than 60 secondary schools. They found that although the incentives had limited impact on stronger students, underachieving pupils improved their exam grades and pass rates by up to 10%.

Deci *et al.* (1999) had argued that extrinsic rewards for *learning* reduces the motivation to learn for its own sake. Other researchers have demonstrated that rewards can increase intrinsic motivation (Cameron *et al.*, 2005). In their analysis of 145 studies, Pierce *et al.* (2003) found that *contingent* rewards, i.e. *only* given for completing a *specific* task to a required standard, had a positive effect on intrinsic motivation, which was maintained or enhanced when the rewards were given for meeting a specific criterion. A few very rare circumstances where rewards were not effective were when: 1) the pupil was already highly engaged with a task, 2) the reward was a tangible item, and 3) the reward was given without reference to a specific behaviour. When these three conditions occurred, output decreased – but this did *not* happen when the reward was unexpected. There is now acceptance among most researchers that motivation is driven by both intrinsic and extrinsic elements at any given time, and both forms can occur simultaneously (Covington and Müeller, 2001).

Chance, commenting on whether it is right or wrong to reward pupils for positive behaviour in school said:

> ...If it is immoral ... to pat students on the back for a good effort, to show joy at a student's understanding of a concept, or to recognise the achievement of a goal by providing a gold star or a certificate – if this is immoral, then count me a sinner.
>
> (1993: 788)

To maximise the effect and approach of this process in an objective way, you should plan your reinforcement schedule in advance and monitor effectiveness, adjusting the rate of reinforcement in response to measured effect.

## Punishment

Many schools prefer to use terms like 'sanctions' or 'consequences', considering the term 'punishment' to have negative connotations (Robertson, 1996). For pupils on the receiving end, the semantics are less important than the actions. Unfortunately, many schools employ more punishment-based practices (e.g. classroom exclusion and suspensions), than rewards for positive behaviour (Maag, 2001). Despite perhaps making schools seem safer by removing those pupils who exhibit the most severe challenging behaviours, such measures fail to teach these pupils how to behave in more socially acceptable ways (ibid.).

In behavioural approaches, punishment has a technical definition that describes a relationship between specific *mis*behaviour and a consequence which must reduce the likelihood of its reoccurrence (Alberto and Troutman, 2013). As with reinforcement, punishment can be positive or negative (see Table 1.4).

Actions in response to unacceptable behaviour are not punishment just because someone thinks the consequence is unpleasant. To qualify as punishment a response should be *contingent* on the demonstration of a particular behaviour and result in that behaviour decreasing. Furthermore, to be most effective, punishment should occur as near to the behaviour as possible to help the recipient to associate the link between the two. Punishing pupils by putting them in detention on Friday for something they did on Monday morning does not meet this criterion. Furthermore, psychological and neuroscientific research has shown that adolescents tend to focus on the present, giving little thought to how their actions will affect their future outcomes (e.g. Bettinger and Slonim, 2007; Gruber and Yurgelun-Todd, 2005; Steinberg *et al.*, 2009).

A punishment is only ever a punishment if it reduces or stops the undesirable behaviour – if it does not do so, it is not a punishment. For example, if a teacher repeatedly sends a pupil out of class for refusing to work and the pupil continues to misbehave, then sending out is not a punishment. Whilst the miscreant's absence provides respite for teacher and class, it is doing nothing to teach her/him the required behaviour (Maag, 2001). The pupil has probably learnt an association between the misbehaviour and being allowed to wander round outside the classroom. Since the pupil is avoiding the aversive experience, he/she is likely to continue misbehaving to achieve his/her aim – this is negative reinforcement (see Table 1.2).

Punishment is much more readily accepted in schools for many reasons, as it can terminate unacceptable behaviour quickly. However, it is often only temporary and only in the presence of the punisher, e.g. the familiar practice in some schools of a senior member of staff sitting in with an NQT for 'support', resulting in better behaviour until the senior member

Table 1.4 Positive and negative punishments

| Type of punishment | Description | Outcomes | Example |
| --- | --- | --- | --- |
| Positive punishment | Present or add an unpleasant stimulus | Behaviour is weakened | Giving a pupil extra homework after she misbehaves in class |
| Negative punishment | Reduce or remove a pleasant stimulus | Behaviour is weakened | Preventing a pupil going to football practice because of misbehaviour |

leaves. Behaviour management based on punishment is preferred to positive reinforcement since the latter is more time-consuming and more complex (Axelrod, 1996). Nonetheless, you would (I assume) find it odd if I were to say the most effective way to motivate pupils to engage with your academic subject is to punish anyone who produced the wrong answer. And yet that is how many teachers operate in respect of social behaviour – pupils are expected to behave, and if they do not they are punished. I am not suggesting that pupils who misbehave should not be punished; however, it is not the way to teach pupils how to behave. The best that punishment achieves is how to avoid punishment.

The brain uses separate systems to process rewards and threats (punishment), which affects subsequent behaviour – rewards facilitating learning, threats inhibiting it. There are also developmental differences in the effects of reward and punishment on brain activity that are age-related. Crone et al. (2005, 2014) found that children responded disproportionately to punishment. They argued that, whilst reward is more effective than punishment, the latter is less effective with younger and developmentally delayed children, because failure is more complicated and requires more effortful thinking to understand than success. It necessitates more deliberate conscious activity to pursue causal explanations for failure, and younger pupils are still developing the mechanisms that control this.

In sum, positive reinforcement of pupils for completing required tasks is more effective in improving the overall behaviour of all pupils in classrooms. It is proactive and aims to teach pupils what they should do – that is, they should behave in a socially responsible way. In contrast, punishment teaches them what they should *not* do. Many behaviourists believe that behavioural approaches represent the only way to maintain control over pupils' learning (Alberto and Troutman, 2013). It is the teacher who manipulates the environment to bring about behaviour change in the pupil (Wheldall and Merrett, 1984). However, in some settings, pupils are involved in the process.

Teachers should adopt approaches where the weight of evidence from research support it, and behavioural approaches have received solid support in the literature for decades (e.g. Fabiano *et al.*, 2009; Stage and Quiroz, 1997).

## Cognitive behavioural approaches (CBA)

CBA utilise behavioural methods to change overt behaviour alongside self-directed change of covert behaviours (cognition) (Larson and Lochman, 2003). CBA are not informed by a single coalesced theory. They are represented by a loose collection of models and methods arranged around the premise that emotions and associated behaviours result from a transaction between the environment and a pupil's interpretation and appraisal of it – which can be positive or negative (Friedberg and McClure, 2002). The following sections examine a number of the theories, models and methods.

A large number of studies have demonstrated CBA effectiveness in managing disruptive and aggressive behaviours in schoolchildren. For reviews, see Ho et al., 2010; Mennuti et al., 2012; Sukhodolsky et al., 2004; Weisz and Kazdin, 2010.

CBA utilise two interacting approaches – cognitive and behavioural – to produce tailored responses to address a behaviour issue (Kendall, 2000). They can be operated at the group level (whole class) or individual level (aggressive pupil). The behavioural element addresses the environmental effects (e.g. seating arrangements) and/or skills deficits (e.g. social skills). Cognitive elements address either cognitive deficiencies (e.g. underdeveloped impulse control) or cognitive distortions (e.g. misinterpreting social cues) (Kendall and MacDonald, 1993).

The balance between cognitive and behavioural elements used depends on the developmental level of the pupil. Given the emphasis on language in cognitive approaches, pupils with limited language development will require a larger behavioural element. Another consideration is that cognitive elements rely on an established positive relationship between teacher and pupils since they require active interaction in a safe and trusting environment in order to empower pupils (Beck, 1995). Finally, pupils need to have the motivation to change.

What distinguishes CBA from purely behavioural approaches is that, whilst acknowledging the power of direct reinforcement on behaviour, people are able to learn by observing others being rewarded for their behaviour, which they then imitate in anticipation of being likewise rewarded. Furthermore, it is accepted that there exists a reciprocal relationship between behaviour, the environment and cognition, so CBA extend the behavioural approach to recognise internal processing and personal agency. The interconnection between your thoughts, feelings, physical sensations and actions means that getting locked into negative thoughts and feelings can draw you into a negative behavioural cycle.

## Social cognitive theory

Bandura (2001) argued that direct reinforcement of behaviour could not explain all forms of learning. Whilst experiencing reinforcement and punishment directly plays an important role in motivation and learning, observing others being reinforced or punished can also be motivating and bring about behaviour change. Bandura (1986) proposed a social cognitive theory (SCT), with emphasis on social influence alongside external and internal reinforcement and highlighting the importance of self-reflection and self-regulation in determining ongoing behaviour. As Bandura and Locke put it, in SCT 'people function as anticipative, purposive, and self-evaluating proactive regulators of their motivation and actions' (2003: 87).

Bandura proposed a reciprocal relationship between personal factors (e.g. cognition), behaviour, and environmental factors (e.g. school), all of

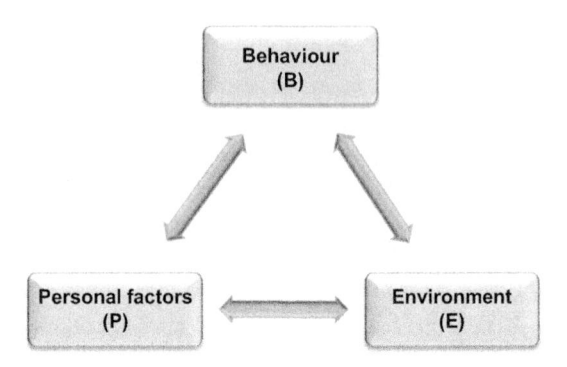

*Figure 1.2* Triadic reciprocity – the relationship between personal factors, the environment and behaviour.

which influence each other bi-directionally, something he called triadic reciprocal determinism (see Figure 1.2). In doing so, he challenged previous explanations, which he referred to as unidirectional, i.e. human behaviour is generated from *either* internal processes or external processes.

However, he did not suggest that all three factors have equal weight, nor that they all operate simultaneously. Personal factors: including what people think, feel, believe and expect; their goals; and their physical make-up influence how they behave. Their behaviour is then responded to by others (the environment), which may lead to them thinking or feeling differently about themselves (positively or negatively). The same behaviour praised in one context may receive admonishment in another – shouting on a football field is likely to be viewed differently to shouting in a library. People also display different social reactions to others, depending on their social status. For example, a pupil who has a reputation as being aggressive will likely provoke different reactions from peers and teachers than someone considered shy or withdrawn. Sometimes their reputation can affect their environment without them saying or doing anything. Changing a single element of the triad can have a knock-on effect on the other elements. For example, changing your teaching style (E) may result in increased on-task activity of a usually disruptive pupil (B), which may lead to that pupil enjoying learning and success (P). Alternatively, taking action to get a pupil to think differently about behaviour (P) may lead to a change in their behaviour (B), which may change the classroom climate (E).

## Self-efficacy

Bandura (2001) argued that through personal agency individuals can influence and regulate their own behaviour (self-regulation) and their environment in a focused, goal-directed way. Personal agency is an individual's belief in their capability to originate and direct actions. It is influenced by the belief that you have the capability to complete tasks (self-efficacy). Research over the last 40 years has demonstrated that pupils' self-efficacy is a powerful predictor of achievement, how much effort they expend, how long they persist and their resilience in the face of adversity (Pajares and Urban, 2006). Pupils who doubt, or are uncertain about their capabilities, are most likely to disengage from learning and engage in disruptive behaviour.

Self-efficacy can be measured at different levels, from the specific (your beliefs about your ability to teach science) to more global (your beliefs about your ability to influence school policy). It is dynamic and influenced by context. Consider the difference between being asked to teach a class which you believe is likely to be extremely difficult to manage, with one where you believe the pupils are extremely well-behaved. Self-efficacy is not the same as self-esteem, which is the degree to which you like yourself. Teachers often try to boost the self-esteem of pupils who are struggling using general praise e.g. 'You did really well'. Whilst soothing children who appear upset with comments believed to enhance self-esteem seems natural, they do not promote self-efficacy. Levels of self-efficacy depend on four factors: mastery experiences (past experiences), vicarious experiences (modelling by others), verbal persuasion (feedback, teaching), physiological feedback (emotional state) (Bandura, 1997).

- *Mastery experiences*, according to Bandura:

    > Enactive mastery experiences are the most influential source of efficacy information because they provide the most authentic evidence of whether one can muster whatever it takes to succeed. Success builds a robust belief in one's personal efficacy. Failures undermine it, especially if failures occur before a sense of efficacy is firmly established.
    >
    > However, some difficulties and setbacks serve a beneficial purpose in teaching that success usually requires sustained effort.
    >
    > (1997: 80)

    Coping with setbacks provides opportunities for learning how to turn failure into success by refining people's capabilities to have improved control over important events and resilience.
- *Vicarious experiences*, or observing others who are similar to oneself succeeding on a task, can reinforce a belief that we too can influence our environment.
- *Verbal persuasion*, for example feedback, should be frequent and focused and not general praise, as discussed earlier. Comparisons should be made to the pupils' own not peers' performance to develop mastery thinking.
- *Emotional state* (and trait) can have a profound impact on self-efficacy. In social contexts, the presence of others can be facilitatory or inhibitory.

The latter is often linked to high aversive arousal, which can be debilitating, for example, being observed teaching an unfamiliar subject. The opposite being the case with a subject in which you have expertise. Emotional experiences include the interpretation and appraisal of a physiological state (sweating, tense) which is influenced by the situation. Emotional self-efficacy involves taking ownership of one's feelings and understanding that emotions are subjective and do not reflect objective facts. Many emotions reflect social labels, so modelling and teaching pupils to regulate their emotions and express emotions appropriate to the circumstance in a socially acceptable way is important.

Self-efficacy is not the same as confidence. Bandura stated that 'Confidence is a nondescript term that refers to strength of belief but does not necessarily specify what the certainty is about' (1997: 382). Outcome expectations are also important in SCT because they influence people's decisions about what action to take and what to withhold. Where outcome expectations are salient, individuals are likely to make an effort but avoid doing so where they are not. Self-efficacy beliefs influence how individuals regulate their own behaviour. Shonkoff and Phillips (2000) consider self-regulation to be the foundation of children's development influencing all aspects of behaviour. Self-regulation is the basis for choice, decision making and for control of higher cognitive processes. Unfortunately, some pupils will not have fully developed these self-regulatory skills by the time they reach secondary school.

### Modelling behaviour

Bandura promoted the concept of vicarious reinforcement – whereby an individual, observing someone being rewarded for behaving in a particular way (modelling) encodes that relationship and then copies the behaviour in anticipation of achieving a similar outcome. In a classroom, a pupil observing another pupil receiving positive comment from the teacher for raising their hand to ask a question, may well copy that behaviour (assuming they value the positive comment from the teacher) in anticipation of being similarly reinforced. Pupils also learn unacceptable behaviours in the same way. A pupil, observing a classmate causing others to laugh by being rude to the teacher, may well present similar behaviour to get the class to laugh. It follows then that adults should be aware of what they are modelling to pupils, both intended and unintended.

Aggressive behaviour is a case in point. Bandura *et al.* (1961) showed how aggressive behaviour can be reinforced through observational learning. He went on to claim that exposing children to antisocial models in the media, home, local community and school should be of concern to responsible adults.

Bandura and colleagues carried out a series of classic experiments with children using a Bobo Doll (an inflatable toy standing around 150cm high, made of plastic and usually painted to look clown-like. It is bottom-weighted, so if hit, it falls over but returns immediately to an upright position). In his experiments, children observed adults hitting the Bobo Doll. In one experiment (Bandura et al., 1961) a group of boys and girls observed an adult in a playroom punching a Bobo Doll and hitting it with a mallet. Later, the children, along with the control group, were left in a room full of toys including a Bobo Doll. Children, both boys and girls, who had seen an adult assaulting a Bobo Doll were more aggressive towards the doll (especially those who witnessed same sex adult models) than the control group who had not witnessed the aggression. A second experiment (Bandura et al., 1963) followed a similar theme, except that the children observed videos of the adult aggression to the doll. In one video, the adult was rewarded after assaulting the doll; in a second, the adult was punished after doing so and in the third, the adult received neither punishment nor reward. Following the videos, the children were left in a room full of toys including a Bobo Doll. Children, both boys and girls, who had seen the adult being rewarded showed the highest levels of aggression, whereas those who had seen the adult being punished showed less aggression than either of the other conditions. Bandura carried out many variations of the experiment (e.g. using a live clown) and found similar results. As with all psychological research, the work was criticised for using an experimental method as opposed to 'real' life representation of violence (Wortman et al., 1998). However, debates about the influence of exposure to violence on children and young people's behaviour – in the home, community and through violent media – continue. A wealth of research findings confirm that children (mainly boys) exposed to media violence have increased probability of aggression (Anderson et al., 2003). Eron et al. (1972) found relationship between having viewed television violence during early childhood and aggressive and antisocial behaviour ten years later.

Longitudinal studies of children's development, using large samples, have consistently shown that the peak age for aggression is between the age of three and four years – the best time to intervene and prevent the development of chronic aggression (Tremblay, 2007). Although most children learn to regulate their emotions and begin developing a repertoire of socially acceptable coping responses from then on, some do not even by secondary school (see also Chapter 9).

Condon (2002) argued that advertising for violent movies, television shows, video games, and music CDs deliberately targets young audiences who develop aggressive and violent scripts (Bushman and Huesmann, 2006). Cognitive scripts provide a blueprint of what is likely to happen, how to respond and likely outcomes. To understand scripts, think about the sequence of events when going into a restaurant: being greeted, directed to a table, offered a menu etc. Children exposed to violent images develop cognitive scripts which are stored in the memory and act as guides to social problem-solving (Abelson, 1981). As a result, they failed to develop non-aggressive coping strategies to deal with frustration and regulation of their thoughts and feelings. This limited and aggressively loaded repertoire of responses was linked to persistent long-term aggressive behaviours and beliefs (ibid.).

Children and adolescents have an innate tendency to imitate the behaviour of people they observe (Hurley and Chatter, 2004), action which neuroscientists attribute to 'mirror neurons' (Rizzolatti et al., 1996). Observing violence can be arousing as defined by physiological measures such as heart rate, blood pressure etc. This arousal makes the activation of an established coping strategy more likely, which, in the case of those with aggressive tendencies, often leads to more aggression (Berkowitz, 1993). Following arousal, the residual negative emotion (mild anger) can later make responses to minor events more exaggerated through excitation transfer (Zillmann et al., 1981), i.e. they react even more aggressively.

In sum, pupils who observe aggressive behaviour are likely to reproduce aggressive behaviour (e.g. Anderson et al., 2003), and repeated viewing of violent images desensitises attitudes towards violence. Desensitisation is a process where emotional arousal is lowered, in this case, when exposed to aggression. Based on physiological measures (heart rate and respiration), Staude-Müller et al. (2008) found that individuals exposed to violent, as opposed to non-violent, video games were found to have lower levels of emotional arousal when subsequently exposed to further violent images.

However, whist modelling has been shown to have negative outcomes, it is also an effective way of teaching pupils how to behave both academically and socially. But to ensure its effectiveness requires attention to the following four elements of modelling which make behaviour change most likely (Bandura, 1997):

- *Attention*—Attention is influenced by many factors (e.g. emotional significance; distinctiveness; complexity). Pupils easily distracted can have problems with observational learning.
- *Retention*—The ability to remember what you have observed, along with the ability to store the information, requires mental imaging, cognitive organisation and symbolic representations of the modelled behaviour. So, an individual constructs a cognitive model of what he/she has observed and then rehearses it mentally to produce an enduring mental model – essential if the behaviour is to be repeated in the absence of the model. Hence, to ensure behaviour modelled to your class is sustained in your absence requires the pupils to have developed such a model.
- *Reproduction*—Copying and practicing motor components and integrating them in order to develop the skills, patterns and sequences required to reproduce the observed behaviour.
- *Motivation*—There must be a desire to perform the task for intrinsic or extrinsic value based on previous success (reinforcement), expectation of receiving reinforcement or seeing someone else being reinforced for demonstrating that behaviour.

Modelling is more likely to be copied when performed by someone you trust and with whom you have a positive relationship. Using modelling as a teaching tool in a planned way, a teacher is able to demonstrate correct social protocols when speaking, and through nonverbal behaviours (gesture, posture, personal space, etc.) to indicate positive and negative responses and emotional reactions. At the same time teachers should be aware of the potential negative effects of modelling by antisocial peers who model and 'reward' antisocial and delinquent behaviour (Patterson *et al.*, 1990).

## Inner speech and self-regulation

The basic premise in cognitive approaches is that people's difficulties are rooted in their beliefs, expectations, interpretations and evaluations of their worlds (Corey, 1986). Distorted interpretations lead to negative thinking, negative emotions and behaviour difficulties. Negative thinking is likely to generate self-defeating behaviours ('I'm useless, so why bother trying') and CBA work toward changing this inner speech and thus behaviour. CBA focus on promoting positive feelings through using language to alter cognitive processes (e.g. perception, beliefs and social problem-solving) which in turn change behaviour. Distorted cognitive processes, such as faulty social information processing, contribute to the maintenance of behavioural problems.

There are various forms of CBA to address negative and distorted cognition and self-defeating behaviour including: conflict resolution; anger management; social problem-solving; self-instructional training – which are used in the treatment of disruptive behaviour disorders (Beck and Fernandez, 1998). All are based on the belief that as pupils progress through school they should be capable of regulating their emotions, delaying gratification, being reflective in their decision making, and developing their social competence to cope with different social contexts.

One approach, self-instruction training (SIT), is used to train pupils to develop self-control using modelling and guided self-talk. SIT has proved to be effective in increasing prosocial behaviour (Camp *et al.*, 1977) and decreasing distractibility, aggressiveness, and restlessness (Kendall, 1982; Kendall and Zupan, 1981). The emphasis is on teaching children *how* to think rather than *what* to think. In SIT, the emphasis is on teaching children how to use verbal mediation to initiate and guide behaviour. Meichenbaum (1977) developed a five-stage model of SIT (see Table 1.5) which has proven successful in helping children to control their own behaviour (e.g. impulsivity). Manning (1991) provides a detailed account of the processes, including classroom applications. SIT owes much to the Russian psychologists Vygotsky and Luria, who theorised how the origins of thought are in 'external processes of social life, in the social and historical forms of human existence' (Luria, 1981: 25). For Vygotsky, children are born with some inherited capabilities, such as perception, attention, memory and basic emotions, which are

*Table 1.5* Procedural steps in self-instruction training used with individual pupil or group of pupils

| Step | Behaviour |
| --- | --- |
| 1. Cognitive modelling | Adult models the behaviour whilst saying aloud what they are doing |
| 2. Overt external guidance | The behaviour is copied by the pupils with overt adult guidance |
| 3. Overt self-guidance | The behaviour is performed by the pupils whilst saying the instructions out loud |
| 4. Faded overt self-guidance | The behaviour is performed by the pupils whilst whispering instructions |
| 5. Covert self-guidance | The behaviour is performed by the pupils with silent self-guidance – speech is internalised |

transformed through socialisation and education to generate higher-order mental functions. A child begins with a focus on concrete stimuli in their immediate environment then moves towards self-formulated goals through the development of self-regulatory skills.

Luria (1971) proposed that children's behaviour is subject to Pavlov's 'rule of force' (the strongest stimulus will win), and the child responds to its carer's speech like any other stimulus. As the child develops, speech becomes the dominant force – provided there is no conflict between mother's speech and the child's activity, in which case the latter will win. Pupils who have established verbal control over their behaviour are able to follow verbal requests even in the presence of other potentially distracting environmental stimuli. However, some pupils in secondary schools will find this difficult, notably those with attention deficits. Prior to establishing such control, there is a *zone of potential development* wherein the child may exercise control using their own overt speech. Finally, an older child will utilise covert or inner speech to control their 'voluntary behaviour' (Luria, 1961). Vygotsky (1978) proposed that every function in a child's psychological development occurs twice. First, at the social level (or interpsychological) and second, within the child (or intrapsychological). The interpsychological involves the transmission of socio-cultural tools (e.g. language) from others to the child, which he/she adopts initially to serve solely as social functions or ways to communicate needs. Vygotsky believed that the internalisation of speech led to higher thinking skills (e.g. planning, decision making and self-control) or the ability to guide our actions in the service of a particular goal. There is considerable empirical evidence to support Vygotsky's claims about the development of verbal self-regulation being mediated through social interaction (Winsler *et al.*, 2009).

*Executive functioning and impulse control*

Executive functioning (EF) sometimes used interchangeably with self-regulation (or BOSS, Chapter 2) is a catchall term that refers to higher-order, 'supervisory' mental structures, which control complex thoughts and behaviour. These structures enable individuals to maintain focus and solve problems in the presence of distractions and involve working memory, planning and goal-setting. Carlson and Moses (2001) considered EF development to be the growing ability to inhibit inappropriate behaviour, whilst Case (1996) felt it was how well an individual could draw on various types of information to plan and monitor their actions.

EF is a theorised cognitive system, but evidence from neuroimaging now suggests that EF is intimately connected with the frontal lobes of the brain. According to Luria (1973), EF development is driven by maturation of the prefrontal cortex in the first five years of life. Vocabulary is strongly connected to executive function (Hongwanishkul *et al.*, 2005), and research evidence highlights a relationship between poor language skills and physical aggression. Given the interpersonal nature of aggression, it is little wonder that language skills are particularly important for regulating social interaction (Séguin *et al.*, 2009). Individuals at any age, with limited language skills are more likely to have a limited linguistic and behavioural repertoire, so they resort to physical aggression when under pressure. EF, or lack of it, plays an important role in the development of behaviour disorders (Castellanos *et al.*, 2006; Sonuga-Barke, 2005; Seguin *et al.*, 2004).

In typical social development, individuals learn to regulate their impulses and delay gratification through internalised self-statements. This is a natural process when a child is raised in a social facilitatory environment, where carers take the time to direct and correct behaviour, which eventually becomes internalised. In atypical development (e.g. impulsive-aggressive individuals), the inability to regulate behaviour is often because of distorted social information processing whereby neutral social signals are misinterpreted as being potential threats (Choe *et al.*, 2015). Impulsive-aggressive children and adolescents can be very demanding, leading to carers seeking respite, which can lead to children spending too much time isolated, playing computer games, for instance. Where the games are violent, the negative effects are exacerbated. Video games, whilst providing instant and continuous reinforcement (i.e. no need to delay gratification), lack social interaction and subsequently the development of inner speech – self-instruction training can be used to correct this.

Whilst emphasising the salience of language in the transmission of cultural knowledge, Vygotsky (1962) also recognised that some things are better learned through observation. He saw the ability to imitate as an important sign that a child was developmentally ready to understand a particular task (in the same way, Bandura viewed the role of modelling in social development).

In sum, the approaches reviewed above all acknowledge the importance of external and internal forces on behaviour but differ in the way they believe these forces operate. All have proven effective at changing behaviour but differ in their fundamental assumptions about where to begin with an intervention. In deciding which to adopt at any one point depends on the nature of the behaviour problem and developmental level of target pupils (e.g. language level, social development, self-awareness) and the quality of the teacher–pupil and pupil–pupil relationships. Teachers should adopt approaches which have the strongest level of empirical evidence to support them. CBA have received solid and consistent support for many decades.

## Annotated further reading

Porter, L. (2006). *Behaviour in schools: theory and practice for teachers*. Buckingham: Open University Press.

Porter describes a range of theories and approaches relating to managing behaviour. She discusses their underlying philosophy, understanding of childhood, practical application and case studies and highlights the assumptions, effectiveness and different goals of each.

## Further reading to support M level study

Martella, R., Nelson, J., Marchand-Martella, N., and O'Reilly, M. (2012). *Comprehensive behavior management* (2nd ed.). Thousand Oaks, CA: Sage.

### *Part I: Introduction to behaviour management*

The first part of this book reviews eight different classroom management models and offers a critique of both positive and negative features of each model. All eight models have their origins, however tenuous, in psychological theories or their author's interpretation of those theories in terms of how they might apply to managing behaviour in the classroom. Whilst all eight models have positive elements and are used in some schools, several have little (if any) evidence to support their effectiveness beyond sounding like a nice idea.

# Chapter 2

# Stress, coping and well-being

The primary focus of this chapter is how to maintain and enhance teacher well-being and resilience by developing effective strategies to cope with perceived stressors. Well-being has two components: feeling good and functioning effectively, whereas resilience is the ability to cope with stress and adversity.

Armchair conjecture suggests that teacher stress has negative effects on well-being, but the evidence shows this is not inevitable. Being subjected to excessive demands and feeling unable to cope can make some people ill, but stress can also be a motivator – the spice of life! By understanding how the stress and coping process works, teachers can develop proactive and less cognitive-demanding coping strategies. As with stress and coping, definitions of well-being are wide-ranging and often nebulous. In this chapter, the focus is on psychological well-being, which is experienced as a positive emotional state, the product of maintaining a balance between situational factors, organisational factors and personal factors – all of which are developed throughout the book.

## Stress in schools

Over 30 years ago, the International Labour Organisation (1982) highlighted teacher stress as a 'steadily growing problem'. Almost 20 years later, the National Union of Teachers argued that 'Stress is one of the biggest problems facing teachers today' (NUT, 2000). In a comparative survey of all professions, the Health and Safety Executive (HSE) found teaching was the most stressful occupation (HSE, 2000). The HSE later classified stress as health-related and issued guidance to employers (HSE, 2001) requiring them to ensure that their employees' health is not harmed by work-related stress. The HSE went on to produce guidelines for developing the competencies required for managers to prevent and reduce stress at work and support their staff. These were: consideration; integrity; managing emotions; communication, empowerment and problem solving; managing conflict; sociability and empathy – interestingly the very qualities necessary to produce a positive classroom environment. Thus, the onus is on managers and employers to make sure that their staff are sufficiently resilient and supported to cope with the pressures of their work.

Labelling teaching as a stress-ridden profession can be destructive for both experienced and prospective teachers. Doing so can create self-fulfilling prophecies if

> ... teachers read frequent reports that teaching is stressful and start to believe it. As a result perhaps, normal upsets that are part of most jobs become mislabelled as chronic, inherent stressors, and a vicious circle begins that results in a higher incidence of self-reported stress.
> (Hiebert and Farber, 1984: 20)

Occupational stress continues to attract the interest of many research and professional groups, with hundreds of articles appearing in journals aimed at teachers, psychologists and health professionals. There is extensive evidence established over many years which has repeatedly identified pupil behaviour as a major contributor to teacher stress, affecting the well-being of both trainee and qualified teachers (e.g. Chaplain, 1996a, 2008; Hart, 1987; Head et al., 1996; Tsouloupas et al., 2010; Zeidner, 1988). In almost every study of newly qualified teachers, behaviour management and discipline have been identified as the toughest, most persistent problems (Gavish and Friedman, 2010). Stressed teachers also tend to use more severe discipline methods and are less positive towards their pupils (Bibou-Nakou et al., 1999), creating a negative classroom climate.

Their concern continues to be an issue, as Taylor pointed out: 'The greatest fear trainee teachers have is that they won't be able to manage behaviour' (TTA, 2012). Unfortunately, trainee teacher stress, associated with problems managing behaviour, does not decline as they progress through their in-school experiences (Burn et al., 2003; Capel, 1997), which may well contribute to the high numbers of trainees failing to complete their training (Smithers and Robinson, 2000) and to those who leave teaching within a few years (Jarvis, 2002). Kyriacou and Kunc, discussing the issue of trainee and teacher attrition reported that, 'in England, about 40% of those who embark on a training course (on all routes) never become teachers, and of those who do become teachers, about 40% are not teaching 5 years later' (2007: 1). They also found that teachers leaving the profession within a few years of qualifying identified disruptive pupils as a key concern – an observation which remains unchanged (e.g. Wilshaw, 2015). Merrett and Wheldall (1992) suggested that the low priority given to teaching trainees' classroom management skills was a major contributor to stress levels and an unacceptable omission. This continues to be the case despite evidence that training teachers in classroom management (including knowledge and practice based) brings about changes in teacher behaviour which lead to improved pupil behaviour and positive and successful classroom environments (e.g. Allen and Blackston, 2003; Sawka *et al.*, 2002).

A teacher's ability to cope with stress is not just down to their personal qualities. Resilience and well-being – that is, how people cope, respond to and thrive when faced with stress and adversity – are influenced by the culture of the organisation in which they work. Levels of stress are affected by the interaction between the individual and the organisation, which is multi-level in nature. Stress at the organisational and structural level can result from: ineffective management (Torrington and Weightman, 1989); lack of communication; poor working environment; excessive workloads (Kyriacou, 2001); staffing levels; lack of support; time pressures and lack of resources; job demands; role strain, role ambiguity and role conflict (Bacharach *et al.*, 1986); or, in more global terms, through negative organisational culture. A negative school culture can threaten a teacher's self-worth, self-efficacy and authority, generating feelings of isolation and undermining their well-being (Johnson *et al.*, 2010). They (Johnson *et al.*, 2010) identified four processes evident in those schools that are successful in promoting teacher resilience:

> (a) a sense of belongingness and social competence, (b) educative, democratic, and empowering processes, (c) formal and informal transition and induction processes, and (d) develop a professional learning community.
> 
> (2010: 539)

Most organisational stressors are not peculiar to schools and can be found in any workplace. At the interpersonal level, lack of *perceived* support from colleagues and senior staff can make coping more difficult, since social support correlates negatively with stress. According to Sarason *et al.* (1990) the higher the level of perceived social support, the lower the level of stress. Believing support is available, prepared and capable of helping in the form of materials, lesson cover, advice or just an adult to have a chat with can combat feelings of isolation and uncertainty.

Murray-Harvey *et al.* (2000) reported that mentors supervising trainee teachers had two contrasting functions – first, as principal coping strategy (support, advice) and second, paradoxically, as a potential stressor, because of the supervisor's role in assessing trainee performance. As Merrett and Wheldall (1992) concluded, the chances of a trainee finding him/herself in a welcoming school, with supportive teachers, cooperative pupils and a skilled, well-informed and appropriately experienced mentor were uncertain, adding to the stresses of joining the profession.

The perceived quality of interpersonal relationships with pupils can be both the greatest source of job satisfaction but also a major source of stress. As Klassen *et al.* pointed out, 'Teaching is a unique occupation in its emphasis on establishing long-term meaningful connections with the clients of the work environment (i.e. pupils) at a depth that may not be found in other professions' (2012: 151). They concluded that emotional involvement with pupils in the classroom is driven by teachers' basic psychological need for relatedness and where this is undermined by conflict, it causes stress (ibid.). Teachers are required to engage in direct continuous social interaction with pupils and their emotions, but with strict rules governing teachers' own emotional reactions in such interactions. Consider, for example, dealing with an aggressive, threatening or challenging pupil whilst containing your own frustration or anger at being on the receiving end of abuse – something demanding what Morris and Feldman called the 'effort, planning, and control needed to express organisationally desired emotions during interpersonal transactions' (1996: 987). Teacher-pupil conflict can reduce teachers' efficacy beliefs and, worse, lead to helplessness, negatively affecting teachers' socio-emotional well-being (Spilt et al., 2011). Pupils' disruptive behaviour can undermine a teacher's sense of efficacy, leading to them to question their ability to teach (Lambert et al., 2009).

Whilst positive feedback from pupils raises levels of job satisfaction, negative feedback can make excessive demands on coping, notably when having to spend time managing disruptive pupils at the expense of teaching (Kalker, 1984). Baumeister et al. (2001) reported that negative experiences (e.g. negative emotions; negative feedback) have a greater impact and are more powerful than positive ones. Negative information is processed more thoroughly in the brain than positive information, so leaves a stronger emotional footprint and has a greater potential long-term effect on well-being.

Many studies of occupational stress fail to acknowledge pressures beyond school, which can significantly influence coping and well-being. Galloway et al. (1985) reported that one in six teachers questioned said they suffered extreme stress from their families, and one in seven reported stress from financial worries. The interplay between home and work was shown in a study by Syrotuik and D'Arcy (1984), who found levels of social support from spouses were inversely related to stress among individuals with high-pressure jobs. Despite the stressful nature of their jobs, social support from spouses or partners could buffer negative work effects. However, expectations of teachers in terms of commitment, preparation and marking outside school hours, which encroaches on personal lives, along with poor career and salary structures, has the potential to create disharmony in some households and leave people feeling unsupported.

Personal resources or vulnerabilities either facilitate or impede coping. An individual with appropriate resources and weak constraints develops adaptive coping strategies, which results in having a healthier psychological and physical well-being (Jerusalem, 1993). Nonetheless, as teachers progress through their careers, factors considered responsible for stress change. Some have suggested that stress in training should be regarded as a normal part of teacher development (Murray-Harvey et al., 2000). Others suggest that new entrants to the profession will experience more stress than their older and/or more experienced colleagues (Coates and Thorensen, 1976). Whilst new entrants may well experience some anxiety as they adjust to a new role, more experienced teachers have been found to experience stress in relation to their career and perceived obsolescence (Chaplain, 1996a; Laughlin, 1984). At the beginning of their careers, teachers' concerns are directed inward to issues concerned with survival and protecting the self, which has been linked with stress (Chaplain and Freeman, 1996). In contrast, experienced teachers tend to be more pupil-focused, concerned with empowering and developing them holistically (Fuller, 1969). Smilansky (1984), however, found that *more* competent teachers reported higher levels of stress since they felt more pressured to ensure higher levels of performance, which could be difficult to live up to. Hence, just as concerns change with age and experience, so do stressors.

At the personal level, a range of dispositional characteristics have been shown to influence levels of stress and well-being. Individual characteristics implicated in these processes include: type A personality (Cinelli and Zeigler, 1990), self-efficacy (Schwartzer, 1992), locus of control (Steptoe and Appels, 1989), extraversion (Hills and Norvell, 1991), self-esteem (Brockner, 1988), sense of humour (Martin and Dobbin, 1988), assertiveness (Bruan, 1989), and hardiness (Funk, 1992). However, the ability to predict coping based solely on these characteristics has been challenged because accurately isolating and measuring single characteristics and controlling for the effects of overlaps between some of the constructs is problematic (Burchfield, 1985; Schaubroeck and Ganster, 1991). It is well established that individual differences can affect how people approach or cope with stress, but there is no complete explanation of the stress and coping process.

In conclusion, stress or the ability to cope cannot be explained solely in terms of organisational effects, although certain organisations do generate stressful conditions, whilst others are supportive. Similarly, it cannot be explained purely in terms of interpersonal relationships or individual characteristics. Nonetheless, certain 'types' of individuals appear more prone to stress than others. Separating individual differences from context is unwise because of the transactional nature of stress. The balance between the two – the associated emotional state and the coping strategies used – moderates the level of an individual's well-being.

## What is stress?

Contemporary definitions of stress and coping highlight the centrality of a psychological dimension (e.g. Folkman, 2013)

In doing so, account is taken of how individuals interpret their worlds differently, which affects their experience of stress and how they cope. Within most psychologically based definitions, cognitive appraisal is seen as an important element (ibid.). Hence, the degree to which something in our lives is stressful (or not stressful) depends on how we perceive or interpret it and to what extent we appraise it as a potential or actual threat, along with what resources we perceive are available to help us to cope with it. An imbalance between perceived stress and resources determines whether we consider ourselves stressed, distressed or coping.

To understand the relationship between stress, coping and pupil behaviour many psychologists refer to an interactive or transactional model of stress. Lazarus (1966) argued that an event could only be considered stressful if perceived as such by an individual. He emphasises the importance of mental activity (cognition) in what he refers to as 'transactions' with the environment – individuals both *influence* and *respond* to their environments. Stress is experienced when the magnitude of stressors exceeds the person's ability to resist them. In response, the coping individual either changes themselves or their environment (or both) in order to counter the stressors. This relationship is interdependent, dynamic and reciprocal.

A number of developments and changes have been made to Lazarus's original model, both in terms of stress generally and more specifically in respect of teaching (e.g. Sutherland and Cooper, 1991). It is to a cognitive model of stress and coping, developed by Freeman and Chaplain (Chaplain and Freeman, 1996; Freeman, 1988) that I now turn to explore stress and coping in schools.

## Thinking, feelings and behaviour

Stress is about thinking (cognition), feelings (emotions) and behaviour. Someone who is stressed will have thought about and interpreted an event, experienced some emotions and will probably behave differently than normal. Whereas Lazarus emphasised the role of thinking (cognition) and its 'transaction' with the environment in his explanation of stress, Kyriacou highlights the emotional component of the process:

> The experience by a teacher of unpleasant emotions such as frustration, anxiety, anger and depression, resulting from aspects of his or her work as a teacher.
>
> (1997: 156)

Chaplain and Freeman incorporated all three elements, highlighting the role of individual differences and changes over time:

> Stress is a negative feeling state which has both psychological and physical components. It is experienced as an assault on 'self'. Stress is not consistent between individuals, nor stable over time.
>
> (1996: 40)

What constitutes an assault to the self is down to the interpretation of the individual teacher. For example, it could be perceived as being directed toward a teacher's professional self – that their teaching competence is being questioned; or their social self – being made to look stupid in front of others; or personal self – a comment about their looks. The self is comprised of, in part, a set of goals that are apparent in ongoing behaviour, many of which are experienced socially. Stress can result from these shared experiences being interrupted (Millar *et al.*, 1988). An example of this is when disruptive pupils disturb the shared goals of teachers and 'on task' pupils, increasing coping demands on both parties.

In neurological terms, any potential threat to 'self' is perceived by and symbolised in several neural regions (including the amygdala) which are believed to make up a basic 'neural alarm system'. This system is considered responsible for perceiving and producing a coordinated response to stressful events (Eisenberger, 2012). In contrast to stress, teacher well-being is associated with a positive feeling state and minimally requires two crucial ingredients – positive affect or pleasure and a sense of meaningfulness or engagement in life, the neural mechanisms of which are believed to be distributed about the brain including hotspots in the limbic system (Berridge and Kringelbach, 2011).

Comparing the psychological components of both definitions of stress and well-being highlights the importance of the interpretation and appraisal process, which is central to experiencing different emotions (Power and Dalgleish, 2007).

Cognition, emotion and behaviour are interlinked; consider, for example, a pupil continually disrupting a lesson, whose disruptions the teacher *interprets* as deliberate and directed towards her. She may initially feel anger toward the pupil, which is likely to be mediated through body position, facial expression and language. Anger, a moral emotion, is a response to personal offence which results from attributing blame to another person for a wrongdoing (Power and Dalgleish, 2007). If later, on reflection, she concludes that the lesson could have been better prepared and more interesting, her emotional reaction might be guilt or shame, which are social emotions (ibid.). Cognition and emotion are not the only mental activities that influence what is perceived as a stressor, as there is another member of the psychological trilogy – motivation. Who or what we blame for our stress affects the degree to which we persevere with a task (Hewstone, 1989). If, for example, a teacher attributes a pupil's misbehaviour to internal, unchangeable and uncontrollable causes (e.g. genetic), she may see little value in persevering to change that pupil's behaviour.

## Levels of coping

How we cope depends on how we interpret and appraise potential stressors and resources and how that appraisal makes us feel and behave. Alternatively, how we feel can affect what we select to appraise and give attention to in the first place. If we are feeling sad or depressed, we are likely to attend to negative behaviours, and if we are feeling happy, we are more likely to attend to positive behaviours (Calder and Gruder, 1988).

Not all coping results from deliberate attention (conscious activity); some is carried out automatically or unconsciously (Kihlstrom, 1999). One measure of an individual's competence is the degree to which they can cope or solve problems with minimal conscious attention, i.e. 'automatically' (Power and Brewin, 1991). Automaticity is demonstrated by competent individuals who, with seemingly little effort, solve problems or sustain coping with difficult situations over time, hence, are resilient. In contrast, the less competent individual would need to engage more deliberately with a problem in order to find a solution, which is a slower and more inefficient process.

A coping teacher is able to integrate cognitive, emotional and physical activity to manage a class apparently without effort. Her body language, what she says and how she says it project confidence and authority. Expressing appropriate emotions, interacting with pupils, focusing primarily on positive features but quickly perceptive to changes such as early indicators of pupils 'sliding' off task or unacceptable behaviour, and responding with a little fine tuning here and there to keep pupils engaged with learning. Yet, in the same school there may be colleagues who seem to have to work flat out, are hurried and overwhelmed and who struggle to maintain a reasonable level of order. How might we explain these differences, given that they share a similar environment and are similarly trained? Can it be put down to personal qualities, and are these qualities inherent or learned? Some people have attributes, such as their physical build, manual dexterity or social skills, which are well-suited to particular activities. Others appear able to organise and reflect on their thinking more easily than others. Some seem to flourish in environments that others feel sick even thinking about. These and other differences highlight the multiplicity of factors involved in trying to unravel how people differ in their response to pressure and how to support them when their responses are ineffective.

People can start to improve their coping skills by redefining the way in which they view the world and how they interact with it. By analysing their resources, developing their knowledge and skills; seeking appropriate support and reflecting upon how they perceive and solve problems, they can extend their repertoire of coping skills. If these skills are effective and practiced (overlearned) they can become automatic, reducing the amount of mental energy required to use them.

A number of cognitive and motor skills, initially carried out deliberately or consciously, can be made automatic through overlearning, after which we have no direct introspective access (conscious awareness). For example, learning to drive a car begins with focused thinking, even talking aloud to guide behaviour until automatic. Once established, we cannot reflect *directly* on the procedures or mental operations involved. Asking an experienced competent teacher how he manages behaviour so easily and effortlessly often results in him finding it hard to explain, because many of his actions are habitual – often resulting in the conclusion that he must have special qualities. However, in reality he will have learnt, memorised, redefined and modified, incorporating what he has been taught and observed, initially in a very deliberate and planned way before, over time, it became automatic. Understanding the history of their learning experiences and identifying how they influenced the final behaviour, thinking and emotional reactions become extremely difficult.

## A dual-process model of coping

Chaplain and Freeman (1996) offer an architecture to explain how: coping occurs at two levels; coping teachers differ from those who are not coping; and the various personal, situational and organisational and interpersonal dimensions might influence the coping process (see Figure 2.1). In this model, understanding how levels of thinking interact with the different mediating factors is the key to understanding stress and coping. The following section considers some of these issues.

The model presents two levels of thinking that reflect different theorised systems, explained by reference to a metaphor of the functional relationship between executives and workers in an organisation or, BOSS (executive system) and EMPLOYEE (automatic system). These terms were adopted from Hampson and Morris (1989) and share features of other dual process models in social and cognitive psychology (e.g. Evans, 2008) that inform our judgements, decisions and behaviour. References to other variants can be found elsewhere in this volume.

In simple terms, employee systems operate at the *non-conscious* automatic level, for example, perception and memory. They are fast and include routine processes that rely on mental shortcuts (heuristics) whose operations we find hard to explain but use continually in routine everyday activities. Examples of non-conscious processes include a range of actions developed by teachers over time and carried out without having to think about them. Triggered by a cue that is salient to the current context, stored knowledge and/or emotional reactions associated with that cue are automatically accessed, e.g. a teacher using facial expression and eye contact to redirect potential disruptive behaviour. The learning of this association is through repeated practice over a long time (Evans, 2008). Once activated, these knowledge structures and associated emotions, can further affect an individual's thoughts, feelings or overt behaviours; e.g. the first time a novice teacher experiences a defiant pupil refusing to work may invoke an ineffective response, since they have not acquired the requisite knowledge and developed effective responses. Even having acquired a new response, a teacher may regress to a previous automatic ineffective response when under pressure if the new response is not overlearned.

38  Stress, coping and well-being

In contrast, higher level cognitive activities (e.g. planning) are controlled by BOSS systems that require *conscious* intentional activity and are slow, flexible and responsive to novelty (see Figure 2.1); e.g. organising an educational trip to London for 30 Year 9 pupils would require considerable planning. The two systems, the theory suggests, usually interact seamlessly to determine behaviour, but sometimes compete. The head cancelling your non-contact time for the third week in a row may make you want to give her a piece of your mind, but an upcoming promotion may make you think twice!

Whether a person becomes consciously aware of an event depends on the level of attention BOSS systems pay to incoming information, their active knowledge of that information and their current state. In the classroom, how we respond to the behaviour of a particular pupil amongst the mass of information reaching our ears, eyes and nose will be influenced by: previous experience; how we are feeling; whether we have been primed (positively or negatively) in advance; which behaviours we are generally sensitised to; plus any other things

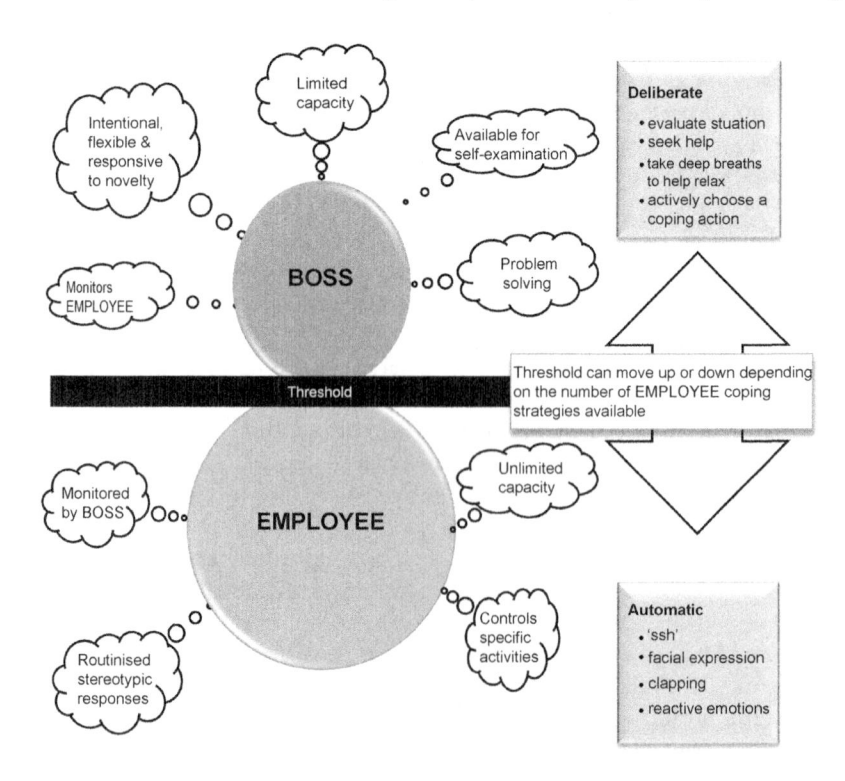

*Figure 2.1* The cognitive architecture of BOSS and EMPLOYEE systems.
Note
The size of the two systems in the diagram symbolises the relative capacity of each – EMPLOYEE having the more extensive capacity but only dealing with routinised behaviour. The threshold distinguishes the two different types of coping and changes depending on internal and external conditions. If you are feeling unwell (internal) you may be preoccupied with your health, which takes up BOSS processing capacity limiting its availability for other problem-solving activity.

demanding our attention. Whilst it is possible to close our eyes and concentrate on sounds, smells and bodily sensations, these sensations usually encroach minimally on conscious awareness. When the executive system (BOSS) takes in information, it restructures and re-organises it and decides whether to process it further, store it or discard it. This manipulation of information occurs at many levels, from simple images to how we represent the world.

The point at which coping changes from BOSS to EMPLOYEE and vice versa is called the *threshold* (Freeman, 1988). The coping teacher has a large repertoire of automatic coping responses, so he has a high threshold, hence the longer it takes before having to engage in conscious coping, minimising demands on BOSS. The poor coper has a low threshold, requiring them to make more regular demands on BOSS in order to cope. The threshold is dynamic for both effective and ineffective copers. Various issues can influence its upward or downward movement. Consider the following example of a teacher's working day (see Table 2.1).

The example illustrates how levels of coping can fluctuate over even short periods of time. Feeling good in your personal life is no guarantee of feeling likewise at work and vice versa, but each can influence the other quite markedly.

BOSS is also responsible for monitoring EMPLOYEE systems – to make sure everything is working OK. If you thought you saw your partner in the street and asked them what they fancied for lunch only to discover that you were speaking to a stranger, you might decide to visit an optician, as one of your EMPLOYEE systems is not functioning correctly. In the present model, stress is experienced when BOSS systems decide we are *not* coping, usually when overlearned non-conscious coping strategies have been identified as unsuccessful (an example is provided in Figure 2.2).

Automatic coping is the norm, since most people cope with various difficulties with little or no apparent conscious regard for them. To cope effectively, people tend to select activities that they enjoy and in which they are usually successful. However, it usually becomes painfully obvious if our strategies and actions are not working as we become alerted to feeling stressed, i.e. not coping. We might pause, try to select carefully what we say, take deep breaths to control our heart rate to mask signs of anxiety, and look for support from others. In this way, coping becomes an intention of which we are fully aware (i.e. BOSS level). BOSS, however, has limited processing capacity and so is more restricted in the number of procedures it can carry out at any one time. Try multiplying 54 by 13 in your head whilst reading this page to see what I mean! Hence, overreliance of BOSS to cope with trivia leaves people feeling unable to think about other important issues.

The best copers tend to have a large repertoire of automatic coping strategies (EMPLOYEE), relieving pressure on BOSS. Poor copers and novices are more aware of having to make a conscious effort to cope (i.e. extensively use BOSS) because they have a limited number of effective overlearned automatic strategies. Making a conscious effort to cope and find ways to 'survive' minor disruptions reduces available processing capacity in BOSS.

Table 2.1 Everyday BOSS and EMPLOYEE coping in school

| Time | Event | Appraisal | Coping or not coping | Emotional state |
|---|---|---|---|---|
| 0800 | Start the day on a high, having just received a tax rebate. | Life is great! Now I can afford a new iPad – will take my husband out this evening for a meal! | Coping. | Happy. |
| 1130 | Have a great morning and my classes are really responsive. One or two pupils are a little excitable but I deal with them quickly. | Teaching is really satisfying pupils are enthusiastic and this is a topic I enjoy teaching. | Normal coping mode mainly automatic (EMPLOYEE). | Happy. |
| 1315 | During lunch find a group of pupils playing with matches in the cloakroom. Two boys become verbally abusive in front of a large group of pupils. | I am very unhappy with this behaviour. Arguing and threatening when caught is pushing the limits and especially embarrassing in public. | Coping but requiring more BOSS level thinking to resolve conflict and deal with aggression. Feeling stressed. | Irritated and angry. |
| 1400 | Report incident to head who arranges to meet with the pupils and myself at 4.00 pm to discuss situation. | Could have done without meeting at that time, as I have to pick up my husband from work. | Coping (still using BOSS) with pupil problem but have to negotiate with my husband to alter pick up time. Head is likely to keep me there until 5.00 pm. Not normally a problem – I could tell him about my date, but I am applying for promotion. | Frustrated. |

(Continued)

| | | | |
|---|---|---|---|
| 1430 | The deputy head asks me (again) to keep an eye on her class (a regular occurrence when she is 'teaching'). | I am getting sick of this. It is becoming more regular and although I am next door, she has a number of difficult pupils in her class who take some watching – she has no consideration for others. Tonight's date looks like it will be a disaster. | Struggling a little to cope (still using BOSS), quite annoyed at pupils, colleagues and deputy head – I feel really put upon. | Angry. |
| 1530 | Boys involved in incident come to the classroom and apologise. I give them a number of jobs to complete over the next week and tell them I will be speaking with their parents, which they accept without an argument. | Feeling a little better, don't need to go through drawn out discussion with head. Just need to avoid him or he will end up telling me his life story if I tell him I have dealt with the situation. I will send him an email. | Can get back to winding up this lesson (using EMPLOYEE). Pupils respond well to this routine. I can also go back to thinking about spending my windfall, having a nice meal and start smiling again. | Relieved and happy. |

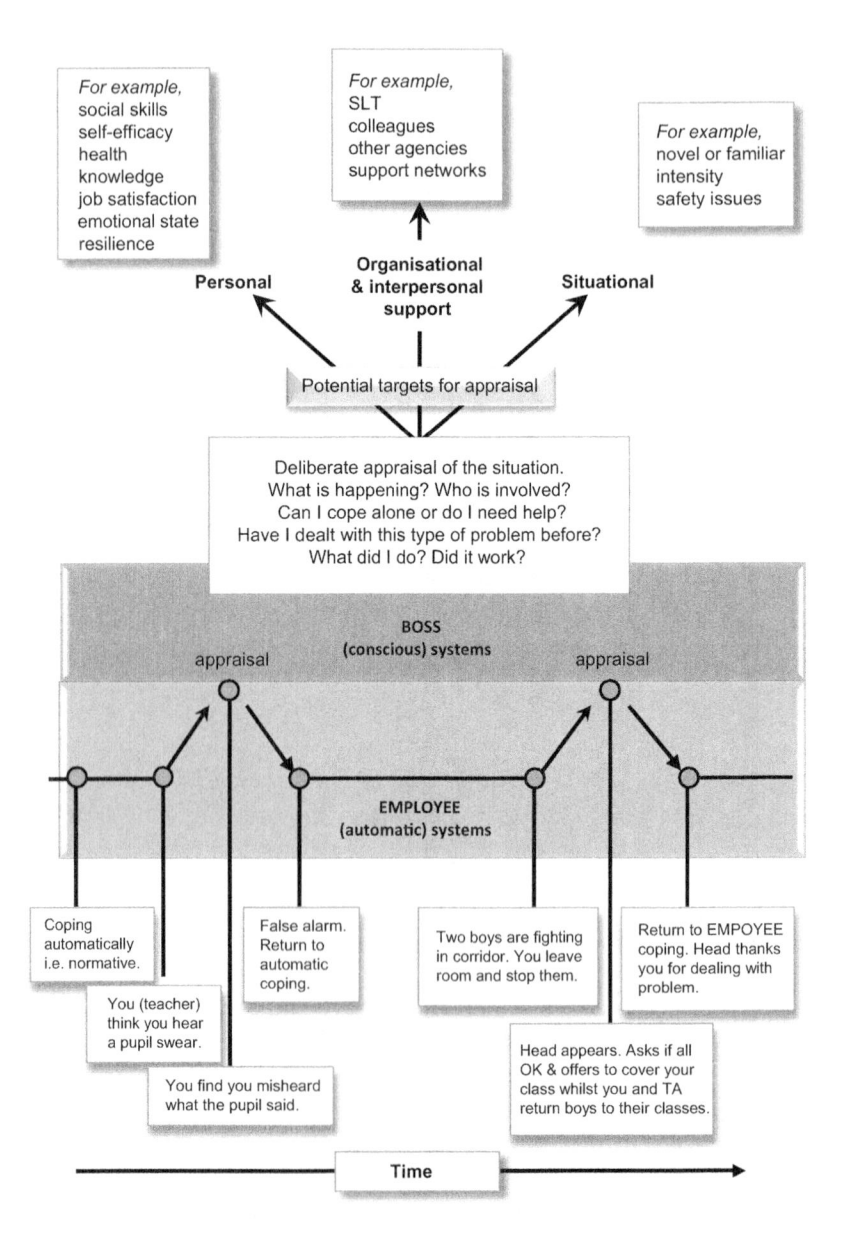

*Figure 2.2* Interactive model of coping.

Note

The figure shows how coping might move between conscious (BOSS) and automatic (EMPLOYEE) over a short period of time. Only two events are shown, but in reality there will be multiple things being coped with simultaneously in EMPLOYEE mode. It is only when we become aware that something is not how it should be that we activate BOSS mode. How we then cope depends on our appraisal of the nature of the event and whether we believe we have the resources available (personal, interpersonal, organisational) to cope.

In the classroom, the poor coper is aware that they are not managing their pupils' behaviour and have to make a conscious effort to solve more 'crises', limiting attention to thinking about teaching, making lessons less interesting and making matters worse.

Whilst poor copers will have automatic responses to managing behaviour, they are usually ineffective; e.g. overuse of avoidance or arguing with pupils. Many of these responses, developed in childhood, continue into adulthood but remain unchanged and immature, e.g. shouting, bullying, running away and sulking. Since these responses are activated automatically, people are unaware that they are using them unless they take time to consciously reflect, appraise and modify them, which is difficult during a lesson!

I have on a number of occasions observed teachers trying to reduce the noise level in their classes by repeatedly using commonly recognised instructions, such as 'Be quiet' or 'Stop talking', but they are seemingly unaware that the pupils are not taking a blind bit of notice. Despite this, they carry on, often increasing the frequency and/or volume to little or no avail. When told about this, they often do not believe it until they see themselves on video. Other behaviours can result in similar outcomes, e.g. shouting, clapping, blowing whistles and so on. This is not to suggest that such techniques do not work for many teachers. I certainly support maximising triggers to cue routines or responses from pupils, provided they are working – which means monitoring pupils' responses, not making assumptions. Many behaviours and expressions that come naturally and which are used automatically often work well; however, they can become inappropriate or redundant. Again, monitoring can be enlightening and helpful in developing new ways of working.

Amongst a large staff group it is probable that some will, at times, use immature ineffective strategies in order to cope, but until they become aware of doing so, and take action to extend their repertoire, effective coping will likely not be forthcoming. For some, this will only occur after they have become angry or dealt with a situation badly. Therefore, some automatic coping strategies create more stress and upset, *not* because we intended to use them *but* because they were activated before we became aware of them.

In sum, a lack of coping at EMPLOYEE level usually comes to BOSS's attention through cognitive appraisal or feedback from others. Therefore, coping precedes stress, since stress is awareness of not coping. At that point, BOSS systems take over and plan how to deal with the problem and monitor/control emotional functioning. EMPLOYEE functions continue to be monitored by BOSS as long as it is not overloaded. New ways of dealing with novel situations, if practiced, can become EMPLOYEE strategies.

### *Appraising stressful events*

What is actually appraised will vary from event to event and from individual to individual. What constitutes a threat will differ: from class to class, pupil to pupil and where in school or when the event is taking place. Dealing with an aggressive Year 10 pupil in a hidden area of the school car park whilst surrounded by a group of his friends *may* be perceived as more threatening than dealing with him in a corridor with a colleague nearby.

Figure 2.2 shows the three principal sources of stress, i.e. perceived personal inadequacy, external impediments and situational threats that are the usual targets for appraisal. Within these three headings, the range of possibilities is almost limitless because of the interplay between individual and context. What follows are some not-exhaustive examples of the potential influence different factors may have on coping.

### Situational variables

The first response after becoming aware that you are not coping is usually to consider the immediate situation to confirm: whether you have read and understood it correctly, to what extent it poses a threat, and the degree to which it is novel or familiar to you. If it is novel, then you may at first be alarmed or shocked as to why it has occurred, and the initial emotional reaction may require you to consider how to react. Coping with the unexpected can result in people reacting inappropriately when emotions are running high, because they have not previously considered or rehearsed how to cope with it. However, it is also possible to mishandle the familiar since a teacher and a pupil(s) may have fallen into a ritualised negative cycle, which is reinforcing the undesired behaviour. Always making a disruptive pupil work with a TA may be something the pupil quite enjoys, providing him/her with an incentive to misbehave! The message here is twofold – on the one hand, anticipating possible changes and being proactive in preparing for how to deal with them; on the other, reviewing the strategies you use regularly but knowing that they may be creating problems for you.

### Organisational variables

Organisational support can provide a framework for supporting teachers dealing with managing behaviour. However, a classroom teacher, unless in a management role, may have limited control over a number of organisational variables. Nonetheless, teachers are likely to cope more effectively with behaviour management if they:

- believe that the school's rewards and sanctions are effective and that they are empowered to make full use of them all;
- perceive the leadership team as supportive, available and committed to professional development in respect of behaviour management and minimising unnecessary pressure on teachers;
- work in a school with a strong social identity which acts as a buffer to stress;
- perceive colleagues are willing and in a position to offer appropriate social support;

- are provided with necessary resources;
- have pleasant working conditions – preferably spacious, well-ventilated/heated/decorated rooms;
- believe communication systems are appropriate, accessible and effective;
- work at a school that encourages open, non-judgemental discussion of stress and behaviour management, as opposed to viewing stress as a personal weakness on the part of a teacher; and
- receive positive feedback for their efforts.

### Interpersonal variables

Relationships with colleagues, managers and pupils can provide support or raise stress levels. A number of researchers have proposed that social support is a buffer to stress (e.g. Cobb, 1976; Frese, 1999). In his study of trainee teachers, Chan (2002) suggested that social support might be regarded as a resource or protective factor and *could* also serve as a buffer that mitigates the effects of stress. However, other researchers have questioned the role of social support in helping people cope. Stansfeld *et al.* (1997), for example, suggested that social support did not act as a buffer for stress. Such contradictions highlight the complex and multi-dimensional nature of social support in terms of structure and function and how it changes over time (Kahn and Antonucci, 1980) and therefore differs in its power to alleviate stress. Cassidy (1999) suggests that having a social network is more important than functional social support. Different types of social support (emotional, instrumental, esteem, intergroup; see Table 2.2) are believed to operate as buffers, if matched to specific types of stress (Cohen and Wills, 1985).

*Table 2.2* Matching social support to specific stressors

| Type of social support | Function | Type of stress buffered |
| --- | --- | --- |
| Emotional | Someone to turn to for comfort | Unexpected events which are usually emotionally charged e.g. pupil being violent in class |
| Instrumental | Practical advice and tangible support | Expected events e.g. preparing to teach a difficult class |
| Esteem | Recognition of effort or competence being valued by others | Stress following prolonged period of pressure e.g. taking a difficult pupil into your class to relieve pressure on other teachers |
| Inter-group | Colleagues with shared professional interests | Sharing teaching methods, developing new initiatives to support teachers and pupils |

The importance of making this distinction was made clear by Cutrona and Russell, 'we encourage researchers to distinguish between tangible and informational forms of support and between expressions of caring and respect for competence as distinct types of emotional support' (1990: 360). Again, it is understanding the interaction between an individual and their environment and how this changes that holds the key to understanding stress and coping.

### *Personal variables*

Personal characteristics are often proposed as a key to effective coping, and much popular advice on coping with stress suggests, for example, developing: a healthy lifestyle, assertiveness, skills and knowledge, self-efficacy and the like – some of which are discussed elsewhere in this book. However, whilst the value of individual strengths is salient, it is equally important to remember that a teacher exists within a complex hierarchy of nested systems (Bronfenbrenner, 1979), some of which he/she has direct control over, whilst others are more abstract. A wide variety of personal characteristics have been found to relate to levels of stress (see Figure 2.2) but the focus in this chapter is on self-efficacy.

Self-efficacy is an individual's beliefs about their capabilities to execute and regulate important events in their lives, which influences a person's choice of what they undertake or avoid (Bandura, 1981). If you do not believe that you have the capability or status to manage an aggressive, challenging pupil, why bother trying? However, individuals with high self-efficacy take on challenges and persist longer when faced with a problem.

In respect of stress and coping, Maier *et al.* (1985) argued that it is not stressful life conditions that determine whether an experience will be detrimental but the degree to which an individual *believes* they are capable of coping with the stressor. People experience lower levels of anxiety from threats they believe they can control. High self-efficacy then acts as a buffer to negative stress and fosters positive appraisals of difficult situations (Carver and Scheier, 1988).

Self-efficacy is considered to be both a (personality) trait (Barfield and Burlingame, 1974) and a state, i.e. a response to a specific situation (Ashton and Webb, 1986). The development of self-efficacy is complex and begins in childhood through self-appraisal skills which inform self-knowledge and self-regulation. As an individual gets older, self-efficacy continues to be influential in how he/she copes with various life transitions (e.g. home to school, school to work, job to job) and feedback from significant others. Self-efficacy results from the interaction between: personal factors (e.g. physical, psychological); behaviour (e.g. verbal, nonverbal) and environmental factors (e.g. social, situational).

Self-efficacy can be general or specific to particular activities (such as teacher-efficacy). Teachers' efficacy beliefs have a critical influence on their performance and motivation (Bandura, 1997). High efficacy teachers tend to be more relaxed and more trusting of pupils, experience less disruption in class and behaviour management is more positive and more successful (Tschannen-Moran and Woolfolk Hoy, 2007).

However, whilst individual teacher efficacy is important, so too is collective teacher efficacy which Goddard *et al.* (2000) define as teachers' beliefs about the collective (not individual) capability of a staff group to influence pupil outcomes. In other words, the degree to which the staff of a school believe their efforts will result in positive outcomes for pupils. Klassen (2010) argues that support intended to assist teachers in managing pupil behaviour should not be solely directed at developing individual capabilities, but also address building collective beliefs about managing pupil behaviour, i.e. the mindset of the staff as a group. In his study of teachers' attributions for misbehaviour, Miller (2003) highlighted the role of the collective staff group (staffroom culture) in contextualising individual teachers' beliefs about their ability to manage children's behaviour successfully.

Mastery experiences are the most important contributor to the development of efficacy beliefs amongst both novice and experienced teachers (Tschannen-Moran and Woolfolk Hoy, 2007). Other contributors include observing others, emotion regulation and advice from others (Bandura, 1997). The latter is particularly susceptible to the prevalent attitudes that a school's staff collectively hold and communicate about how to cope with certain groups of children. This can influence the beliefs of individual teachers (Jordan and Stanovich, 2003), especially early in their careers.

Teacher efficacy operates at the personal and institutional level in schools, and the effects on teachers' performance and well-being are well established in the literature as Bandura pointed out:

> Many teachers find themselves beleaguered day in and day out by disruptive and non-achieving pupils. Eventually their low sense of efficacy to fulfil academic demands takes a stressful toll. Teachers who lack a secure sense of institutional efficacy show weak commitment to teaching, spend less time in subject matters in their areas of perceived inefficacy, and devote less overall to academic matters.... They are especially prone to occupational burnout ... a syndrome of reactions to chronic occupational stressors that include physical and emotional exhaustion, depersonalisation of the people one is serving and feelings of utility concerning personal accomplishments.
>
> (1995: 20)

Organisational conditions that undermine teachers' professional self-efficacy include limited professional development, heavy workloads, poor prospects and an unsatisfying imbalance between their work life and personal life (McAteer-Early, 1992).

Teachers with a low sense of self-efficacy are vulnerable to difficult situations because they often have low expectations, experience strong negative emotional reactions, feel criticism is directed at their self-worth, tend to accept criticism for failure more readily than praise for success and worry about their level of competence. Worry is a cognitive characteristic of anxiety, which is correlated with rumination. Both are associated with defective problem-solving, cognitive rigidity and difficulty shifting attention away from negative stimuli (Hazlett-Stevens, 2001). Worry is concerned with preparing for anticipated threats in the future, especially those events whose outcomes are uncertain and likely result in negative outcomes (Sibrava and Borkovec, 2006). Rumination focuses on past events, which often has a negative impact on self-worth, leading individuals to conclude all is hopeless and giving up is the only option. justifying inactivity (Lyubomirsky and Nolen-Hoeksema, 1993).

These negative cognitive processes and related behavioural responses can have a knock-on effect on pupils, creating an overall negative classroom environment. Gibson and Dembo (1984) found that teachers who have high instructional efficacy empower their pupils to master their learning, whereas those with low efficacy undermine their pupils' efficacy and cognitive development.

Low self-efficacy can be improved by attention to issues at personal, interpersonal and institutional levels. For example, forcing yourself to take recuperative breaks from emotionally taxing work by not always taking work home all the time and stopping ruminative thinking. Bandura (1997) and Rosenthal and Rosenthal (1985) suggest that those who do not work this way and who convince themselves that there is no time to rest, or feel they are too tired after work to engage in leisure pursuits do not usually welcome such advice. Bandura (1997) recommends a guided mastery programme to help them gain control of their lives to alleviate pressure. However, this is not likely to be sufficient since the difficulties are not just at the individual level, as previously discussed, and so intervention is also required to prevent organisational demands undermining teachers' efficacy. Teachers need some control over matters that affect their working lives and ownership of schooling as well as classroom process. In appraising their effectiveness, teachers should focus primarily on those features over which they have control. Being realistic about what you can and cannot control, acquiring knowledge about how to manage behaviour and mastering the requisite skills rather than relying on 'luck' may seem obvious. However, this is often not the case, especially among inexperienced teachers. For example, Weinstein (1988) found that trainee teachers had unrealistic optimism in thinking that the problems others experienced managing pupil behaviour would not be a problem for them. Furthermore, Emmer and Aussiker (1990) found that even when trainee teachers had experienced difficulty managing classes, they still held unrealistic beliefs about their capability to manage behaviour.

## Balancing stressors and resources to improve well-being

In order to develop new ways to enhance coping and well-being, Chaplain and Freeman (1996) developed the individual coping analysis (ICAN) model (see Figure 2.3). It is used to analyse the (im)balance between stressors and resources to provide a basis for developing new ways of doing things, including raising self-efficacy.

The analysis is intended to be ongoing, not just a one-off activity, since stressors and resources can change roles over time, stressors becoming resources and vice versa because of changes to ourselves and our environment. One example of this might be professional commitment or enthusiasm. Teachers are expected to be committed to their work, and indeed many interviewers are looking for evidence of this when making appointments. In practice, demonstrating one's commitment or enthusiasm often includes: completing work outside official hours (e.g. marking, preparation); supplementing equipment from personal funds, supporting trips and sports activities beyond the working week. If this commitment leads to success in gaining a job or promotion, then it might be considered a resource. However, if this commitment leads to a teacher spending more and more time at work or engaged in work-related activities and less and less time at home or with their friends and family, it can lead to difficulties at the personal and/or interpersonal level (i.e. become a stressor). In the case of the latter, if those close to you feel marginalised and neglected, then there is a danger of losing valuable social support. As one teacher sadly informed me:

> I get home from work by around 5.00 pm absolutely tired out. Then I often have two or three hours of marking or preparation to do. Meals at home tend to be convenience or take away. I used to really enjoy cooking and doing the garden but it doesn't happen anymore. My husband also works hard but can't understand why I have to spend so much additional time preparing and marking. He says I am turning him into a 'curriculum widower'. We never even manage to get to the gym together now, despite planning to do so. I really love teaching but this is not helping my marriage at all.
>
> (Rachel)

Disruption in teachers' personal lives can result in difficulties coping at school and vice versa, hence the need to keep personal and professional lives in balance. It is not difficult to find yourself in a ritual of behaviour that fails to acknowledge the thoughts and feelings of others. Generating time to stand back and evaluate your situation is one way to avoid this.

Where the two circles meet in Figure 2.3 is where coping takes place. One might argue that coping invariably occurs, but some forms of coping

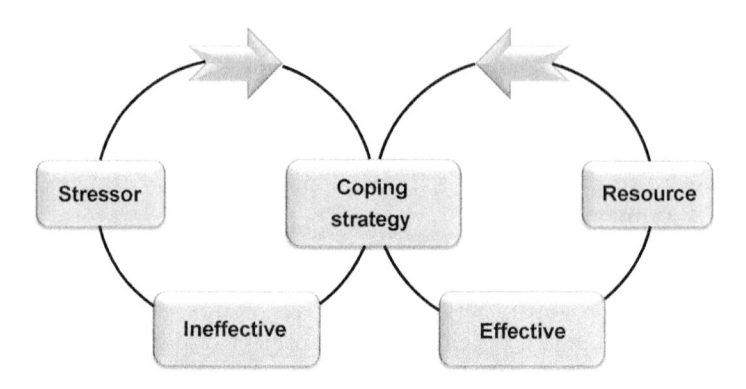

*Figure 2.3* Individual Coping Analysis (ICAN).

are more effective than others under certain circumstances, but not in others. For example, an event may be so painful to take on board that initially you ignore it or pretend everything is OK, even if it is not. However, doing so as a long-term or regular strategy is likely to lead to further problems. At the same time, always confronting your problems head-on and immediately can also be counterproductive since it is likely to prove exhausting and lead to other difficulties, such as being seen as being aggressive (see Table 2.3). Some forms of coping have their own logic, such as initially deflecting a problem with a view to making space and time to solve it more directly later. A simple example might be overhearing a pupil swearing and opting not to intervene until the situation is more easily dealt with, perhaps when there is no audience. There is no right or wrong way of coping effectively (beyond legal and professional requirements); it depends on the individual and the social context. Coping is not simply a matter of either/or – that we cope or we do not. In some instances for example, we might use a coping strategy which is initially effective and subsequently disastrous. There can also be unintended consequences. Improving your coping requires reflecting on the strategies you are using, identifying your favoured approach and if necessary proactively planning and learning new strategies, to cope with current or future potential stressors, which Lazarus and Folkman (1984) called 'anticipatory coping'.

*Table 2.3* Coping styles

|  | Active | Passive |
| --- | --- | --- |
| Direct | Confront the problem | Avoid the problem |
| Indirect | Seek advice on how to deal with the problem | Smoke or drink more |

You will no doubt be familiar with preparing for particular social encounters – an interview, for example – and trying to anticipate what is likely to be asked and how you will respond and rehearsing what you will say. However, rehearsing coping strategies should go beyond what to say, to include how to say it, along with nonverbal communication, something we are less aware of when communicating.

Since all behaviour can be expressed in terms of the interaction between ourselves, stressors and resources, it follows that the evaluation of our coping strategies is central to understanding whether or not we are dealing with our stressors in the most effective way. Using the layout in Table 2.4, you can carry out a number of evaluations. For example, if you are concerned about the behaviour of a particular class or pupil, you could consider how:

- the behaviour which is causing you concern, is influenced by the stressors and resources of the pupils;
- you normally cope with their behaviour and how this may affect their coping strategies and stressors;
- others cope with this group;
- whole-school policies interact with what is going on in your classroom;
- much support is available.

It is not sufficient to merely list stressors and resources. It is essential that you take time to examine the interaction between you and the various factors

*Table 2.4* Individual Coping Analysis (ICAN)

| Resource (support) | | Difficulty (stressor) |
|---|---|---|
| I am a good teacher and I enjoy teaching. | **Self** | I do not feel confident teaching pupils with ADHD. |
| They are always prepared to listen to my problems. | **Friends** | They want me to go out every night and I cannot. |
| I find teaching pupils with SEN very rewarding. | **Pupils** | I find some pupils apathetic. |
| Most are happy to share ideas for lessons. | **Colleagues** | Some are inconsistent in dealing with disruptive pupils, which creates problems for me. |
| The school is fortunate in having lots of good resources. | **School organisation** | There is a lack of structure. |
| The head is an excellent teacher and very supportive. | **Management** | The deputy undermines my authority by coming into my room and disciplining pupils when it is not necessary. |

involved. You, and other colleagues may all be aware of particular difficulties but cope with them in very different ways despite seemingly having similar resources (training, lifestyle and working in the same organisation). To make new strategies automatic requires overlearning – doing so can increase your coping repertoire and improve your well-being.

## A note on pupil stress, coping and well-being

It would be remiss of me not to mention how adolescent pupils experience stress, given that managing their behaviour plays such an important role in teachers' stress coping and well-being. Dunham (1989) reported that, whilst teacher stress tended to be a high-profile concern for researchers, 'stress amongst pupils has generally aroused less specific concern' (1989: 16). What limited research exists comes to similar conclusions, that the pressure of academic work (that is, exams, revision and homework) are the main sources of stress for pupils (e.g. Kyriacou and Butcher, 1993; Owen-Yeates, 2005). The latter study added coursework as a stressor, something absent in previous studies but that reflected a shift in examination formats.

Adolescence is often referred to as a time of 'storm and stress' – a conceptualisation not without its critics (Casey et al., 2010). Nonetheless, it is recognised as a period in which adolescents frequently experience intense negative affect linked to mood swings, risky behaviour and emotional volatility. The speed and magnitude of these changes can exceed the socio-emotional coping capacity of many young people and the resultant phenomenon of adolescent stress is now widely acknowledged (Byrne et al., 2007). Adolescence is also marked by an increase in the frequency of various mental health problems (Compas and Reeslund, 2009), often related to increases in risk-taking behaviour (Reyna and Farley, 2006).

Compas and Reeslund (2009), argued that the healthy development of adolescents can be put at risk through exposure to stressful events, both in and out of school, but they also acknowledged individual differences. These differences result from the interplay of individual and environmental susceptibilities and resources, and the individual's range of coping strategies. The type of coping strategies adopted by an adolescent is predictive of the likely effects of stressors on his/her psychological health, well-being and resilience.

Most studies of adolescent stress and coping have tended to focus on life and/or traumatic events and their effects on functioning (e.g. Sandberg and Rutter, 2008). Such research looks at the psychological effects on stressful events such as exposure to violence, abuse, neglect, and marital conflict (Cicchetti and Toth, 2005). Life events such as the arrival of a step-parent, divorce, and teasing are often associated with anxiety, which is in keeping with the wider observation that most life events are associated with high anxiety. This is especially the case where an individual has an external locus of control, which is the tendency to expect that outcomes are the result of external forces (e.g. luck) rather than one's own behaviour or competence. External locus of control has been linked to high levels of anxiety in children (Gale et al., 2008) and increased anxiety in the context of a stressful event, such as an important examination at school (Edwards et al., 2010). Exposure to extreme stressors during children's development has long-lasting neurobiological effects and increased risk of mood, anxiety and aggressive disorders (Shaw, 2003). Whilst the majority of pupils will not have been exposed to extreme events, everyday hassles in their lives can be interpreted and appraised by them as being of similar magnitude (Chaplain, 1996b). These daily hassles include those most reported by teachers as being stressful including, the disruptive behaviour of other pupils (Bradshaw et al., 2010).

Maintained schools now have statutory duties to promote the well-being of children and young people (Children Act, 2004). The relationship between well-being, academic learning and mental health has been made clear. As Brooks (2013) reported, supporting physical and mental health, and promoting behaviour among pupils in school creates a 'virtuous circle' which strengthens pupils' attainment and achievement, and in turn enhances their well-being. Furthermore, the strong relationship between adolescents' well-being and satisfaction with life and their levels of academic success is something which persists into adulthood (Chanfreau et al., 2013). In contrast, those who participate in health-compromising behaviours tend to have limited academic engagement and low grades in school (e.g. Dryfoos, 1990) with a higher risk of further long-term negative outcomes. In sum, pupils' overall level of well-being impacts on their social behaviour and engagement in school and their ability to acquire academic competence and *vice versa*.

Most approaches to improving adolescents' well-being have focused on disease prevention or risk reduction. However, focusing on single risk factors has resulted in limited effectiveness (Catalano et al., 2002). Other researchers have proposed that more effective outcomes can be achieved by equipping children to cope with everyday stressors (e.g. Chaplain, 1994, 1996b, 1996c; Duncan et al., 2007). The importance of effective behaviour management in school on pupils' coping, well-being and resilience was made clear by the DfE (2016). The most significant factors that help adolescents to develop resilience include clear policies on behaviour, positive classroom management, a whole-school approach to mental health, and a sense of belonging. Pupils tend to be more resilient in schools where they enjoy the feeling of belonging (Osterman, 2000), and they are more likely to hold positive attitudes to learning, are more engaged with learning and feel safe.

Gutman and Feinstein (2008), in reporting that school ethos was associated with pupil mental health and prosocial behaviour, concluded that pupil-school fit may be more important for pupils' well-being than is attending a particular school. Establishing a positive pupil-school or indeed teacher-school fit is facilitated, in part, by the degree to which individuals have the opportunity to contribute to decision making which affects their well-being and daily experiences. Similarly, the negative effects of not including all pupils in decision making were highlighted by Jamal et al. (2013) in their analysis of 19 research studies. They found consistent evidence that limited involvement of pupils in decision making could result in them feeling they have no 'stake' in their school community, negatively affecting relationships with teachers and prosocial peers and encouraging antisocial behaviour, including increased involvement with risky behaviour. Adolescents who become disengaged from conventional groups (e.g. school, prosocial peers) are more likely to bond with disruptive peer groups in order to establish a social identity and sense of belonging (Fuligni and Eccles, 1993).

In the UK, 10% of pupils below the age of 16 suffer from a diagnosable mental health condition, with up to 20% experiencing cyberbullying on social media, which can lead to anxiety and depression. These concerns were highlighted by Prime Minister Theresa May (2017), who announced plans to offer every secondary school mental health training and to strengthen the links between schools and local NHS mental health staff. Furthermore, she announced a major review of adolescent mental health services across the country to identify what works and what does not. It is to be led by the Care Quality Commission, and will result in a green paper on young people's mental health setting out plans to transform services to schools.

In recent years, there has been increased interest in taking account of pupils' perspectives across a range of issues, including learning and school improvement as well as social and mental health (Bahou, 2011; Rudduck et al., 1996). Pupils' perspectives offer an essential dimension to the development of behaviour policies, and this is now formally recognised. The United Nations Convention of the Rights of the Child meant that pupils were entitled to have a voice in matters that affected them (Article 12 of the *United Nations Convention* on the *Rights* of the *Child,* 1989). As a result, all pupils must be allowed to help shape a school's behaviour policy. However, the government's response was somewhat pedestrian. Their official guidance stated that pupil involvement 'need not be laborious or burdensome for the governing body ... class teachers ... could simply talk to their class about the behaviour principles and gather any views' (DCSF, 2009).

Whilst the majority of adolescents emerge from the second decade of their lives without lasting difficulties (Graber et al., 1996), the many changes that occur during adolescence result in negative – and sometimes devastating – consequences for some; as, for example, those who do not experience positive peer and adult relationships, have limited coping skills, academic and behavioural difficulties (Feldman and Elliot, 1990; Lerner et al., 1996).

Pupils often report valuing support from teachers who showed a genuine interest in their learning and well-being (e.g. Chaplain, 1996b). However, social support has been shown to have differential effects. Schraml *et al.*, (2011) found lower levels of social support made a significant contribution to the variance explained in stress symptoms among adolescents. In contrast, whilst DuBois *et al.*, (1994) found an association between high levels of social support at school and positive pupil outcomes (better grades and lower risk-taking), it occurred *only* among pupils experiencing life (event) stressors, such as poverty or parents' divorcing, but did not find this among pupils who were not experiencing these stressors. The latter would include those who are coping with daily hassles.

There is a significant increase in the numbers of pupils reporting low levels of subjective well-being as they progress through secondary school compared to levels in the primary years. This dip may not attributable to age but to social context. Of note is the relationship between disruptive behaviour in class and low levels of subjective well-being. This effect was found to be the case 'both for the young people who were being disruptive, and for those who witness the disruption.' (Chanfreau *et al.*, 2013: 13). Therefore, establishing effective strategies for managing disruptive behaviour to minimise stress and promote well-being becomes as important for pupils as it is for teachers.

## Annotated further reading

Chaplain, R.P. (2008). Stress and psychological distress among trainee secondary teachers in England. *Educational Psychology*, 28(2), 195–209.

This article reports the findings of a study into the relationship between stress and psychological distress among a cohort of trainee secondary school teachers in England. Using a teacher stress questionnaire, three factors were identified as stressors: behaviour management, workload, and lack of support. A shortened version of a measure of well-being (General Health Questionnaire) was used to measure psychological distress at the end of the trainees' placements. Differences were identified between men and women in respect of both sources of stress and levels of psychological distress. Pupils' disruptive behaviour was found to be a significant predictor of psychological distress. The findings are discussed in relation to how well trainees are prepared for the challenges they are likely to experience as teachers and how they might be better prepared to manage pupil behaviour.

## Further reading to support M level study

Parker, P.D., Martin, A.J., Colmar, S., and Liem, G.A. (2012). Teachers' workplace well-being: Exploring a process model of goal orientation, coping behaviour, engagement, and burnout. *Teaching and Teacher Education*, 28(4), 503–513.

This study of 430 teachers used a transactional model of stress and coping and integrated self-worth and goal theory elements to test a structural equation model in which:

a   teachers' goal orientation (as indicated by mastery and failure avoidance) was hypothesized to predict their teaching coping strategies (as indicated by problem- and emotion-focused coping), and
b   teaching coping was hypothesized to predict occupational well-being (as indicated by engagement and burnout).

Their findings suggested that: teachers' goal orientations were strong and consistent predictors of their coping strategies; emotion-focused coping was a consistent and strong predictor of teachers' burnout and engagement; problem-focused coping was a relatively weak and inconsistent predictor of teachers' well-being; and some evidence was present that indicated recursive paths between teachers' well-being and goal orientation and coping. Implications for theory and practice were also considered.

# Chapter 3

# Teacher thinking and pupil behaviour

Much of what is written about classroom control focuses on observable behaviour – less is said about the cognitive, socio-emotional and neural processes that regulate that behaviour. Many such processes take place beyond your conscious awareness. Although you may be largely unaware of those processes and the nonverbal behaviour that they control, often your pupils are not. These behaviours can convey unintended messages that result in negative outcomes for teacher and pupils.

A popular belief, widely supported by regular references in government and school policy documents, is that having high expectations of pupils will result in better behaviour and performance in school. However, high expectations alone are not a solution for underachievement, but coupled with effective teaching methods, they can address educational inequality (Jussim *et al.*, 2009).

But what does having 'high expectations' mean in practical terms? Does it imply that a teacher should have the *same* high level of expectation for every pupil? That would certainly be high, but unrealistic. A more practical definition of high-expectancy teachers is those who have positive and realistic expectations (behavioural and academic) and translate them into challenging and engaging learning goals, appropriate to the developmental level of their pupils. Behaviour is included as well as academic expectations since research has shown that teachers who have high (realistic and challenging) expectations of their pupils tend to use more positive methods to manage their pupils and experience less disruption in their classes than do those with low expectations (Rubie-Davies, 2007). Teachers who have low tolerance to pupil behaviour tend to have lower expectations of disruptive pupils' academic potential (Woolfolk Hoy *et al.*, 2009).

The focus of this chapter is about the thinking processes that moderate teacher behaviour and the effects they have on psychological and behavioural outcomes for pupils.

## Teacher expectations: turning thoughts into action

Teacher expectancy processes link social perception to social behaviour. This phenomenon has been researched extensively for over 40 years, the central tenet being that by merely having false or inaccurate expectations of pupils, a teacher can unwittingly elicit behaviour that confirms the original (inaccurate) expectation to be true. As a result, some pupils can experience negative outcomes including becoming disaffected and/or disruptive.

Expectancy-confirmation effects can occur at two different levels:

1. *Cognitive confirmation effects* occur in the absence of any interaction between perceiver and perceived. For example, a pupil whom you have never met is due to join your class next term. Her older siblings, you have been told, previously attended the school and were all very challenging and disruptive. Her family are not supportive of school. Based solely on inferences drawn from this information, your existing knowledge and your experience of pupils – without even meeting her – you may generate a less-than-favourable expectation of how she is likely to behave. These expectations may influence how you prepare for and behave towards her when she arrives. In doing so, you will be depending on your existing models (implicit theories) of how pupils from different backgrounds are likely to behave. This type of expectancy formation exists in the mind of the teacher rather than in the behaviour of the pupil.
2. *Behavioural confirmation effect* or self-fulfilling prophecy (Merton, 1948), whereby early impressions of a pupil, often formed in brief first encounters, lead a teacher to generate an expectation (negative or positive) of how that pupil is likely to behave. The initial beliefs cause the teacher to channel the course of *interaction* with that pupil to elicit behaviours that confirm the teacher's original beliefs.

The origins of teacher expectancy research can be traced to the seminal work carried out by Rosenthal and Jacobson (1968). Rosenthal had demonstrated how, in experiments, researchers could unconsciously influence their subjects to behave in ways that confirmed the researcher's original hypotheses. So, he and Jacobson decided to test empirically whether a similar effect might occur in school. A school, with pupils from lower socio-economic backgrounds with low levels of achievement, was selected. Teachers in this school were told that a test that had been administered would identify 'late bloomers' i.e., pupils with latent ability who would 'bloom' later that year. In fact, the test did not identify latent ability, and the 'late bloomers' pupils had been picked at random. The false expectancy, however, had now been put into the minds of the teachers. The results confirmed that the 'late bloomers' generally showed greater improvement than the control group. Additionally, teachers considered the 'late bloomers' were 'better adjusted and more intellectually alive' than their peers. Although the results seemed clear and tantalising to many, there were criticisms of both the method and measure used in the experiment (e.g. Elashoff and Snow, 1971), criticisms later rebuked by Rosenthal and Jacobson (1992). Eventually, however, even their most determined critics did acknowledge how teacher expectations could affect the behaviour of pupils

(Snow, 1995). Rosenthal and Jacobson's experiment along with its criticisms provided the inertia for hundreds of subsequent studies using a range of different methods – some examining expectancy processes, others looking at outcomes (Harris and Rosenthal, 1986).

One particularly noteworthy, if disquieting, study was carried out by Rist (1970), who, using an ethnographic approach, observed the behaviour of a teacher with a class of 'ghetto' children over a two-year period. Almost immediately after their arrival and having only met the children briefly along with their parents, the teacher placed the children into three separate groups; 'cardinals', 'tigers' and 'clowns' (no prizes for guessing the status of the clowns!), putting each group on a separate table. As the teacher had no information about the academic performance of these children, they were classified on the basis of their socio-economic status (SES) and language skills. Rist argued that the teacher was comparing the children to her perception of the 'ideal' pupil, many features of which bore no relationship to academic ability. Children on the top table were considered cleaner, better dressed and better behaved than the middle group, who in turn were 'nicer' than the clowns. The most striking observation was that two years later these pupils were still in the same ability groups. Rist concluded that the expectations were formed on the basis of social class.

Rubie-Davies (2006) compared the effects of low- versus high-expectancy teachers on pupils' self-perceptions in reading and maths at the beginning and end of a school year. In her research, she differentiates high- and low-expectancy teachers by asking them to rate what level they expected the pupils to be achieving by the end of the year in relation to national average, using a scale between 1 (very much below average) to 7 (very much above average). High-expectancy teachers were those whose expectations were well above where pupils were actually performing. Conversely, low-expectancy teachers expected their pupils to achieve well below where they were actually performing. She found that, whilst the self-perceptions of pupils from both expectancy groups were not significantly different at the beginning of the year, they were at the end. By the end of the year, the self-perceptions of pupils with low-expectancy teachers had dropped dramatically in both reading and maths, whereas those with high-expectancy teachers has risen, and the differences were statistically significant in both cases. She added that:

> This change in self-perception came to match the teachers' expectations over the year. Perhaps more importantly, the students in the current study appeared to be aware of their teachers' expectations for the class since the students' perceptions of their teachers' opinions of their abilities also altered in line with the teachers' expectations.
>
> (2006: 548)

Some studies have found long-term negative outcomes associated with inaccurate expectations by teachers. Sorhagen (2013) for example, carried out a longitudinal study across ten school sites, tracking pupils through early years, primary and secondary schooling. She compared standardised tests, observations at home and schools, parent and teacher reports of behaviour gathered at age 5, 7, and 9, and finally at age 15. The results showed that teachers' inaccurate expectations of pupils at age 5 were found to be predictive of their maths, reading, vocabulary, and verbal reasoning standardised test scores at age 15 and that inaccurate expectations by teachers could have a lasting negative effect on pupil performance. She concludes:

> The fact that self-fulfilling prophecies in first-grade classrooms exerted an especially lasting impact on the achievement of disadvantaged pupils raises the possibility that teachers' underestimation of poor children's academic abilities may be one factor that contributes to the persistent and worrisome gap in achievement between children from different socioeconomic backgrounds.

But, on a more positive note …

> On the other hand, teachers' overestimation of abilities seemed to disproportionally help low-income students, suggesting that knowledge of self-fulfilling prophecies in the classroom could be relevant to policies aimed at ameliorating the achievement gap between low- and high-income students, especially considering the persistence of the achievement gap.
> (2013: 475–476)

The largest negative effect was on pupils from lower SES groups, a finding concomitant with that of Rist (1970) and others studying *at risk* groups; e.g. Hinnant *et al.* (2009). If pupils from low SES groups are expected to be less successful than other pupils, then any information the teacher takes in from interactions with this group will be filtered through this belief.

That teachers' expectations can result in unintended outcomes is well-documented in several meta-analyses. Stretching over several decades, significant reliable effects have been demonstrated (e.g. Harris and Rosenthal, 1986; Hattie, 2009; Jussim *et al.*, 2009), the largest negative effect being in respect of pupils from lower socio-economic backgrounds.

Good and Brophy (2008) highlighted the conditions under which expectations are likely to have most effect. They argued that, having formed expectations of their pupils based on existing knowledge, teachers naturally expect differences in performance and behaviour from different pupils. These expectations affect the decisions they make whilst teaching; for example, where pupils are seated, the type of work given to them, how often teachers speak to them and how long they wait for them to answer. In this way, pupils learn what they are expected to do and behave accordingly. Teachers notice the reciprocal behaviour (including negative), which confirms their original expectations and the cycle continues. But what if the pupils' behaviour does not confirm their original expectations, or the pupils attempt to change their behaviour? Does this result in changing a teacher's opinions? Not necessarily, according to the work of Schmuck and Schmuck (1992) or Rogers, who commented:

> ... the fact that the pupil's behaviour does not shift in the expected direction will not necessarily have the effect of weakening or changing the initial expectation. It will be the teacher's perceptions of events that count and these will not always be accurate.
> (1982: 59)

Unintended consequences occur most frequently when teaching large classes. Where teachers work with small groups or individuals they receive more immediate feedback and have the opportunity to gain greater knowledge of individual pupils. It provides them with more opportunity to observe behaviour changes and disconfirm inaccurate initial impressions. It is not unusual to hear stories of pupils who have been excluded from mainstream classes who 'become' well-behaved and communicative with their new teachers after having been placed in special units with smaller teaching ratios.

If the information received about a pupil is not diagnostically valid for determining likely behaviour (e.g. being told a pupil comes from a low socio-economic group should not in itself be diagnostically sound as an indicator of intellectual ability) a teacher is likely to avoid using it to draw conclusions about how that pupil is likely to perform. However, such information can be used to form hypotheses about likely qualities that they can test against behavioural evidence in order to make judgements. If the opportunity then arises to acquire behavioural information about someone, a 'confirming strategy' is used to find evidence supporting the original hypothesis by selective attention to particular behaviours whilst ignoring others. In other words, you *look* for evidence of the expected behaviour, weighting them in favour of those that confirm expectancy-beliefs. Inconsistent behaviour is explained in terms of the situation rather than the pupil; then reinterpreting inconsistent behaviour as being consistent with initial expectancy for example, a 'yob' behaving altruistically might be reappraised as disguising his/her *real* motivational intent (Darley and Fazio, 1980).

Expectancy research has generally supported the proposition that holding a particular expectation under certain circumstances can influence outcomes for others. These outcomes can be social and/or academic performance and either positive or negative. One set of questions for those involved with trying to bring about change in schools is as follows:

- How are expectancies formed?
- How are they mediated and under what conditions?
- Why do they persist if known to be inaccurate?

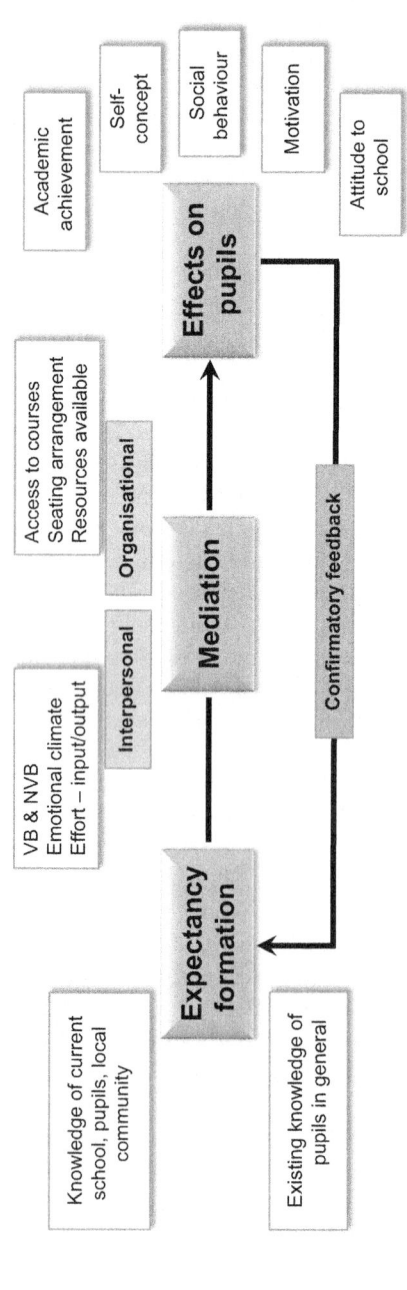

Figure 3.1 A simplified model of the teacher expectancy-confirmation process.

VB - verbal behaviour
NVB - nonverbal behaviour

- What are the likely outcomes?
- How can we guard against negative outcomes?

A number of researchers have offered models to explain the teacher expectancy-confirmation cycle (e.g. Rogers, 1982; Weinstein, 2002). Figure 3.1 offers a summary of the salient elements.

There are three stages in the expectancy cycle:

1  Forming expectations
2  Mediation to pupils
3  Potential outcomes.

I emphasise *potential*, since not all teachers' expectations are mediated to pupils or attended to by pupils and even where this happens, do not inevitably affect pupil outcomes. Nonetheless, a large number of studies have demonstrated that they can and do (Rubie-Davies, 2015). Where they result in the Pygmalion effect, i.e. where pupil performance improves, there is less cause for concern – however, where the opposite occurs, there is. The Golem effect (Babad *et al.*, 1982; Reynolds, 2007) is a negative effect of teacher expectancy. This happens when a teacher expects lower performance or problem behaviour from a pupil, which results in the pupil behaving in that way. There are difficulties in demonstrating this phenomenon since it is unethical to construct experiments that cause pupils to underachieve or to behave badly. Babad *et al.* (1989) demonstrated how subtle the process can be. They found that even when teachers consciously offered low-expectancy pupils extra learning support, they simultaneously transmitted negative messages nonverbally. These 'leakage' behaviours represent how the teachers really felt about the pupils and, being emotional, are harder to regulate. Babad (1998) found that where teachers did attempt to display emotional warmth in support of low-expectation pupils, the displays were not perceived as genuine by pupils because they were exaggerated.

## Understanding pupils' behaviour

In order to understand how teacher expectancy processes are instigated, attention is directed to social cognition, i.e. how we understand our social worlds and acquire social knowledge. Social cognition concerns how we think about people and how we *think* we *think* about people. It includes the processes people use in order to make sense of and guide their social behaviour (Abrams and Hogg, 1999). Social cognition has a particular relevance to classrooms and schools, as it provides a link between cognition and social behaviour; it is orientated towards processes and is concerned with real world issues. Social cognitive processes help explain interpersonal relationships in classrooms, including the expectancy process.

Our social behaviour arises from a combination of: how we believe we should act in social situations, how we expect others to behave, and our interpretation of the feedback we receive from others, all of which we use to regulate our own behaviour. However, we do not interact with the actualities of a situation but rather our perceptions of it (i.e. what we *believe* to be true). Furthermore, whether we like it or not, we all make assumptions about ourselves, other individuals, groups and the situations we find ourselves in. Many of these assumptions are functional, and we would not be able to go about our daily lives without using them. However, sometimes they can be dramatically inaccurate or overly rigid, thus resistant to change and result in unintended consequences, something which will be discussed later. We also rely on typical procedures or shortcuts to simplify complex behaviour.

Imagine going into a classroom full of pupils for the first time; you will perhaps think of how you might expect them to behave, irrespective of how much you know about the actual pupils. You may imagine a sequence something like: you enter the room expecting the pupils to stop talking or messing about; you scan the room, picking out specific individuals, gaining and maintaining eye contact, making a mental note of who does and does not respond to your presence; you move to a position in the classroom that gives you a good viewpoint; you say hello; pupils say hello back; you introduce yourself and let them know how you feel about their behaviour when you walked in (if necessary), and so on. This whole process is an example of what psychologists call an event schema or social script.

A social script is a generic mental structure (Taylor and Crocker, 1981) that contains organised prior knowledge of, for example, people, events, roles and self (NB there are many more possible types, and many overlap). They are cognitive representations of particular behavioural sequences in social interaction, which are connected, hierarchical and associated with emotions. We would have difficulty knowing how to function in our everyday lives without prior knowledge of people, social roles and events in our social world, and what to expect of them and ourselves in social encounters. Scripts are structures that allow people to simplify the storage of knowledge about their social worlds in an inclusive way, often discarding some data to give an overall impression – as opposed to sorting the data in an elemental way with every bit of knowledge being kept in a 'raw' form. Schema influence social information processing in three different ways: perception and encoding of new information; memory of old information and inferences about people where information is missing. A schema then, is a rough and ready but organised framework that allows the quick processing of information. For instance, the preceding event schema for entering a classroom is probably unremarkable and familiar and would be generally identifiable (with minor tweaks) in all schools. It is worth noting that the ritualised behaviour of such scripts can, in some conditions, undermine classroom relations. Where the script adopted for the first meeting with a class is negatively evaluated and the messages in both directions confirm expectations, this can result in a negative cycle, which continues if unchecked.

During the initial interactions with pupils or whole classes, you will automatically make rapid assessments of them. If teachers could not make assessments of their pupils, they would not be doing their jobs. In the preceding example of a script, you would probably note: who was first to respond to your arrival; who seemed to ignore you; who needed reminding about how they should behave; any possible troublemakers and the like. What you attend to will be influenced by a whole range of factors, including individual features of the pupils (e.g. sex, volume of speech or dress) and cultural (e.g. ethnicity or social class) as well as the situation and your own characteristics. Your assessments are based on a combination of what you know about schools and pupils that you have acquired over many years through experiences as a pupil and later as a teacher. Added to this data is what you know about the current situation from briefings by colleagues and senior staff, staffroom gossip, the reputation of the school and your class, and what you know of the local community and its residents. This information will influence your expectations and how you behave toward the group, regulating what you say and how you say it. If the school has a reputation for good behaviour and a class is noisy when you arrive, you may start with 'I don't expect to hear this sort of noise from a group of pupils in this school!' (i.e. emphasis on the behaviour being unacceptable to the social identity of the school or the group). If, on the other hand, the school/class has a reputation for disruptive behaviour, you may start with, 'This level of noise is not acceptable in my classroom!' (i.e. emphasis on a less abstract level – the behaviour being unacceptable to your personal standards or new standards being expected).

Social cognition operates at two levels – controlled and automatic or dual processing, a phenomenon common throughout social psychology (Chaiken and Trope, 1999). Controlled processes (e.g. preparing for an interview) are associated with being aware, intention, effort and maintaining focus (Wegner and Bargh, 1998). On the other hand, lower-order automatic processes operate outside this awareness and include subliminal priming, where our senses are primed but we have no awareness of it, or its effect on our responses. For example, angry faces elicit responses in the amygdala – an area of the brain implicated in detecting emotional stimuli – below the level of consciousness (Whalen et al., 1998). We are also more sensitive to negative than positive cues. So, hearing your headteacher is moving a very difficult pupil into your class is likely to have a bigger impact on your thoughts and emotions and expectations than being told you are receiving a well-behaved pupil. Detecting threat in this way activates other systems that help us prepare to cope (e.g. fight or flight). Higher-order automatic processes include the habitual coding of other people's traits e.g. assessing friendliness and trustworthiness. Professionals usually develop this automaticity through practice and regular exposure, e.g. experienced teachers judging (hopefully accurately) pupils' likely behaviour.

Social cognition includes a wide range of phenomena including: social perception (Zebrowski, 2007) and social categorisation (Hornsey, 2008), impression formation (Ambady and Skowronski, 2008), attribution theory (Graham and Folkes, 2014) and emotions (Fiske and Taylor, 2013).

Social perception concerns what we pay attention to, or consider relevant, in social encounters (e.g. sex, race, and age). Such features are related to how we then categorise others according to what is perceived as relevant. Allport (1954) argued that mere exposure to someone was sufficient to activate social categorisation and stereotyping.

The process of social categorisation is less a process of accurately matching an individual's attributes to a category than it is an inference process. A category may be generated when it is *sufficiently* related to a person rather than when it matches a person's attributes. As soon as you assign pupils to a particular category (e.g. disruptive) based on particular attributes (e.g. male, not wearing school uniform, continuing talking when you entered the room, and having their feet on the desk) you apply your existing generic knowledge structures of pupils in this category. Categories of social information and the perceived associations between them are activated automatically. As a result of these associations, judgements are made that go beyond the information available and can affect behaviour, whether accurate or not. You might conclude that your newly encountered pupil has a negative attitude towards authority and is likely to be disinterested in school. Alternatively, you might think you caught him off guard and give him the benefit of the doubt.

The sensitivity of schemata can be raised through priming. Priming relates to what information has preceded the event. If you were told beforehand to keep an eye out for certain boys who are disruptive, then your 'disruptive pupil schema' will be activated quickly and associated with the advice you have received about how to deal with disruptive pupils. This priming can result in you becoming overly sensitive to the likelihood that these pupils will be disruptive. Needless to say, this negative priming and hypersensitivity may influence how you behave towards them and subsequently how the pupils respond to you, with the potential of creating a negative cycle.

Whilst accurate objective determination of categories might be possible in biology, it is less so in the social domain. Here, people are categorised by their membership of 'fuzzy sets' (e.g. disruptive), which are without rigid boundaries (Fiske and Taylor, 2013). So, it is not always clear that someone belongs to a particular category (naughty or high-spirited), nor which attributes are being prioritised by the perceiver (positive or negative behaviour).

## Forming impressions of others

The processes involved in forming impressions about others are based on a combination of assigning them to a particular social category, our wider (distal) general knowledge of people in that category, alongside the knowledge we believe we have about the individual qualities in the immediate situation (proximal).

So how does this operate in practice? Here is how one pupil formed impressions of his new science teacher before and after getting to know him:

> Taylor and I were going upstairs to the lab for our first science lesson in Year 7. We heard someone shouting on the first floor. It was Mr 'Johnny' Sable who was doing his nut at a Year 10 pupil. He looked really angry. His face was as red as a beetroot! I said to Taylor that I didn't fancy going into his class, even though we knew we had to. He waved us into the room. We really weren't looking forward to his lesson. But, when he came in he smiled and said 'Hiya everybody welcome to your first science class. We've got some great things lined up for this term.' He was really funny and we did some great experiments. I even joined his science club and I did really well in the exams. People (including me) didn't mess about in his lessons though!
>
> (Kyle, aged 13)

So, how did Kyle form initial impressions and decide how to behave toward his new teacher? His initial data came from a rapid assessment, based on hearing Mr Sable shouting (priming a fear emotion), at which time he categorised this teacher negatively. Kyle had first categorised his future teacher in the 'strict and quite frightening' category. Having spent time with Mr Sable and initially treating him cautiously, he became aware of other qualities that he admired in teachers. Mr Sable was funny, helpful, supportive and an engaging teacher who was not prepared to put up with unacceptable behaviour in the science laboratories – a member of that pupils-preferred 'firm, fair with a sense of humour' teacher category.

There are two broad explanations of the impression formation process:

- theory-driven (inferential)—top-down processes; and
- data-driven (evaluative)—bottom-up processes.

Supporters of the theory-driven approach (e.g. Williams and Bargh, 2008) argue that we do not view unfamiliar people as a sum or average of their traits or 'ingredients', but rather as a complete psychological unit, fitting them into underlying implicit theories about people and their personalities. We combine the various components of a person's make up to produce an overall impression. In a famous series of experiments Asch (1946) showed how people could infer a whole range of traits about a non-existent person based on limited information about specific traits. In one experiment, he gave two groups of people two almost identical lists of seven words to describe an imaginary person (see Table 3.1a). The only difference between the two lists was that one contained the word 'warm' and the other the word 'cold'. He then gave each group a second, longer list of additional qualities and asked them to identify further traits to describe this imaginary person and found striking differences. Some of the results are shown in Table 3.1b. Those described by lists including the trait 'warm' were seen as generous and sociable; those described by lists including the trait 'cold' were seen as calculating and unsympathetic. Asch argued that the presence of the words 'warm' and 'cold' had disproportionate effects on the overall impression that the groups formed, since they were central traits. These central traits are linked to implicit personality theories, which are cognitive structures activated during social perception. Such structures hold groups of personality traits believed to be interrelated and are central to how we form impressions of other people – allowing someone to infer, based on a few traits, a whole range of additional implicated traits. It is important to remember that the two 'people' described by these seven words did not exist; however, despite this, the groups were readily able to differentiate between them and identify a whole range of contrasting personal characteristics. For example, the 'warm' person being considered much more happy, good natured and generous than the 'cold' person.

*Table 3.1* Implying personality from limited information

| a | Imaginary person | |
| --- | --- | --- |
| | A | B |
| Adjectives used to describe two imaginary people | Intelligent<br>Industrious<br>Skilful<br>Determined<br>Warm<br>Practical<br>Cautious | Intelligent<br>Industrious<br>Skilful<br>Determined<br>Cold<br>Practical<br>Cautious |

| b | Ratings of additional descriptors | |
| --- | --- | --- |
| | Person A 'Warm' (%) | Person B 'Cold' (%) |
| Generous | 91 | 8 |
| Wise | 65 | 25 |
| Happy | 90 | 34 |
| Good-natured | 94 | 17 |
| Humorous | 77 | 13 |
| Sociable | 91 | 38 |
| Popular | 84 | 28 |
| Humane | 86 | 31 |
| Altruistic | 69 | 31 |
| Imaginative | 51 | 19 |

Notes
Table 3.1a shows the initial information given to two separate groups of people. Each received seven adjectives that described an imaginary person, exactly the same, except for the words 'warm' and 'cold'.
Table 3.1b shows a sample of the ratings made by the two groups of additional characteristics, indicating the percentage who agreed each characteristic matched the two imaginary people. Results show clear differences, despite the fact that assessment by the two groups was based on minimal information.

More recently, Williams and Bargh (2008) repeated Asch's experiment, but instead of using the words 'warm' and 'cold', asked subjects to briefly hold either a warm or iced coffee on their way to the laboratory, before they made their judgements about the imaginary individuals. Their results were consistent with those of Asch – i.e. those holding the warm cup rated the stranger as having a warmer personality than those who held the cold cups – and concluded that physical warmth promoted interpersonal warmth. Whilst the main cues people use to assess and categorise people (Cuddy et al., 2008) are perceived competence and warmth – the most powerful dimension is warmth. This categorisation process occurs automatically and does not require any conscious intent (Williams and Bargh, 2008). In line with Bowlby's (1969) assertion of an infant's need for physical contact in the attachment process, an association between physical and psychological warmth develops. Williams and Bargh's finding is further supported by neuroscientific research that showed that tactile warmth is associated with psychological warmth and trust (Insel and Young, 2001) and located in the insula cortex – an area implicated in empathy, trust, guilt and embarrassment (Meyer-Lindenberg, 2008).

Supporters of the contrasting data-driven approach suggest perceivers attend in a more controlled way to specific characteristics of a person (intelligent, industrious, cold), evaluating these features individually in terms of their positive and negative qualities (Anderson, 1981). These individual characteristics are differentially weighted and averaged to form an impression. Thus, whilst being intelligent is positive, being cold is negative, which is more strongly weighted and results in a negative evaluation.

Various researchers have argued that singly, neither of two models offers a satisfactory explanation of how we form impressions. Dual-process models, in which theory or data-driven models operate under different conditions depending on the decision made by the perceiver, are proposed by Brewer (1988) and Fiske and Neuberg (1990). In these models, initial impressions are theory driven, or formed using pre-existing schema about categories of people. Person-based (data-driven) impressions are only activated if the target cannot be fitted to an existing category or if they are of interest or personal relevance to the perceiver. Whether you change that initial impression depends on whether you move on to using data-driven information (as Kyle did). However, as discussed earlier, Rogers (1982) reported that even when pupils' behaviour did not turn out as the teacher expected, teachers will not necessarily revise their initial expectations. In sum, research suggests impression formation is a dual process. The first is 'automatic' – quickly putting someone into a 'fuzzy' social category. If you then have no further involvement with them, you leave them there with all the inferred qualities – positive and/or negative – attached to that category. The second involves taking on board individuating information, which requires taking time to engage in learning about a person's individual characteristics and gaining understanding of why they behave the way they do.

## Causal explanations of behaviour

Explaining the causes of important events or attribution theory is a normal everyday activity carried out by everyone. Heider (1958), the reputed father of attribution theory, suggested people act like naïve scientists, forming hypotheses about what or who causes things to happen in their world, to help make life predictable. Attribution theory is concerned with the answer to three questions:

1   What are the perceived causes of an event?
2   What information influenced this causal inference?
3   What are the consequences of ascribing these causes?

An example will help to explain. Imagine you are walking through the school grounds and are hit on the back of the head with a conker. You are likely to want to find out who or what is responsible. You turn round and see a group of pupils who you had recently reprimanded for misbehaving in class, standing under a conker tree with handfuls of conkers and giggling. You might believe that the likely culprit to be one of this group, based on your interpretation of what you 'know about them' and their behaviour at the scene, despite them all denying it. The consequence might be that you further reprimand them. If, however, you turned round, saw no one, then heard a 'meow', looked up and saw a stranded cat in the conker tree above your head, struggling to balance and knocking leaves off in the process, you might infer a different cause and react differently. Neither example may be the real cause (in truth, a colleague had thrown it) – but it is the perceived causes of behaviour that really matters in understanding people's causal attributions.

According to attribution theorists, people seek to identify general causal principles, which they use to predict the future, control events and guide their own behaviour (Fosterling and Rudolph, 1988). People generate causal explanations for: their own behaviour (why they failed a test) known as intrapersonal attributions, and other people's behaviour (why a pupil misbehaves) known as interpersonal attributions, and groups generate causal explanations of other groups' behaviour (why colleagues in a different department do not follow the school behaviour policy) known as inter-group attributions.

There are a number of attribution theories that, although different, share a number of qualities. Deciding which one applies really depends on the conditions and the situation being analysed. As Fiske and Taylor put it:

> ... all of them have some validity, but under different circumstances and for different phenomena. The theories cannot be pitted against each other in the usual scientific manner. Rather, each outlines a series of processes that can be used to infer attributions if the appropriate circumstances are present.
>
> (1991: 40)

Two prominent contributions to our understanding of how people make inferences about other people's attributes and behaviour were firstly Jones and Davis's (1965) Correspondent Inference Model; and Kelley's (1967) Causal Schema, and the Covariation Model. The latter will be used to demonstrate the relevance of attribution theory to the teacher expectancy-confirmation cycle. Kelley argued that our knowledge of the social world is often limited and ambiguous. Whilst, under normal circumstances, we have sufficient information to enable us to cope, there are other times when we have difficulty doing so. For example, if our self-image is assaulted (professional or personal etc.) or where information is ambiguous, we are likely to engage in causal analysis i.e. search for an explanation for our predicament. If faced with a new class who are proving more difficult to manage than any previous classes, we are likely to look for a causal explanation. Am I up to the job? Are these pupils so challenging that no one could manage them? Is the school not providing sufficient support? The various potential explanations call for different responses. If I feel I am not up to the job, then I might consider attending a training course to develop my behaviour management skills or perhaps consider a career change. If I believe the pupils to be extremely challenging, I could request intervention by other professionals. If I consider the lack of resources unacceptable, I could ask for more support. This all sounds very logical and common sense – this is why Heider referred to it as common-sense psychology. However, it has been shown that we can be biased in our causal explanations or we make attributional errors.

The first error is a tendency – notably in western society – to overemphasise personality, as opposed to situational attributes, as causes of behaviour. In other words, if a pupil misbehaves, we are more likely to blame him or her than the situation. Secondly, in interpersonal situations there tends to be a difference between how the person in a situation infers causes, compared with how an observer infers them. This occurs more often in negative than positive situations, such as if a teacher was having difficulty managing pupils whilst being observed (Malle, 2006). Whilst the teacher is more likely to blame the situation or the pupils for what is happening, the observer is more likely to blame the teacher for not being in control. Thirdly, self-serving attributions is the tendency to attribute successes to ourselves and failures to others. Miller (1995) found that teachers were more likely to attribute causes of misbehaviour to parents/children, whilst attributing improvement to themselves. Furthermore, the areas of the brain implicated in self-serving bias are those associated with reward, suggesting such bias will likely make you feel good (Blackwood *et al.*, 2003). Attributing causality in these three ways serves to protect self-worth and maintain a positive self-image. Even though they may be incorrect, justifying our behaviour to ourselves and others by generating 'plausible' explanations or excuses is an important coping mechanism. The effects of doing so on others might not be so beneficial.

In his search to identify what information people use to arrive at causal explanations, Kelley developed two models: causal schema and covariation models. Causal schema are used when you have minimal information about someone, covariation the converse. Which one a perceiver uses to explain events depends on the amount of information available. As most teachers have access to information about pupils and usually see them more than once, the covariation model is the most appropriate.

In this model, the perceiver has access to information about the behaviour and intent of others from multiple events and can perceive how possible causes co-vary with what they are observing. Covariance refers to two events happening together and involves both social perception and self-perception. If your class only behaves unacceptably whenever a particular pupil is present, then there is a high covariance (i.e. you attribute the disruptive behaviour to his influence). If your class sometimes behaves badly when he is present and sometimes when he is not, there is low covariance as he may not be the sole reason for the disruption. If, on the other hand, the pupil was only problematic when you were teaching the class and this had occurred previously with you, but not with other teachers, you are likely to come to a different conclusion! Your perceptions will likely influence your subsequent behaviour. Kelley reasoned that to determine a causal explanation for someone's behaviour, people measure covariation across three dimensions:

- *Distinctiveness*—Does the behaviour only occur when this pupil is present but does not when he is absent?
- *Consistency*—Has this behaviour occurred when I have taught them in the past?
- *Consensus*—Do other teachers have the same problem when he is present?

Where high distinctiveness, high consistency and high consensus occur together, people are able to make attributions with confidence. Of the three dimensions, consistency or stability is the most preferred dimension for determining causality. Table 3.2 shows how three hypothetical causal explanations of disruptive behaviour differ, depending on which covariation pattern between the three variables is chosen.

Blame is thus directed at one of three targets – the pupil, the teacher or the environment/situation (e.g. problems at home/bullying). Different explanations result in different consequences. If Lee is seen as being the cause, then Mrs Black is likely to feel less inclined to want to teach him since she expects the same behaviour in the future. If she is seen as the problem, then a different set of responses are required, for example, attending a behaviour management course, mentoring or in-class support. If the situation is seen as the cause, Mrs Black may decide to talk to Lee and ask him if there is anything bothering him. The above description may imply that causal attribution is done in a rational, logical and just way when, in fact, that is not always the case.

Table 3.2 Explanations for Lee's misbehaviour

| Distinctiveness | Consistency | Consensus | Likely attribution |
|---|---|---|---|
| *Low* Lee is cheeky to most teachers. | *High* Lee is always cheeky to Mrs Black. | *Low* Other pupils are not cheeky to Mrs Black. | It is Lee's fault. |
| *High* Lee is not cheeky to teachers. | *High* Lee is always cheeky to Mrs Black. | *High* Other pupils are cheeky to Mrs Black. | It is Mrs Black's fault. |
| *High* Lee is not cheeky to teachers. | *Low* Lee has not been cheeky to Mrs Black before. | *Low* Other pupils are not cheeky to Mrs Black. | There is something different about the situation. |

Notes
The table shows three possible causal explanations in answer to the question – Why is Lee being cheeky to Mrs Black?
In Row 1 the problem appears to be with Lee, since he is *consistently* cheeky to most teachers, including Mrs Black, but other pupils are not.
In Row 2 the problem appears to be with Mrs Black, since Lee is not usually cheeky to other teachers but is to Mrs Black, as are most other pupils.
In Row 3 the problem appears to be something beyond the two individuals, since Lee is not usually cheeky to any teacher, including Mrs Black, and neither are any other pupils.

We attribute what we believe to be the cause. The self-serving bias and tendency to attribute causes to personality rather than situations discussed above means Mrs Black is *less* likely to attribute responsibility to herself. Observers are more likely to blame her, especially if they do not have problems managing Lee.

Attributing causality may involve deliberate and time-consuming logical analyses or may result from rapid cognitive processing to make a quick decision about what is happening and how you should react. If causality is regularly attributed in a particular direction, it can reach a point where it is done automatically or scripted, and hence difficult to break. Where the perceived cause has been attributed incorrectly, it may continue unchallenged, as shown in teacher expectancy research.

## Getting the message across: mediating expectations and effects on pupils

Forming an impression (positive or negative), categorising pupils as disruptive and attributing their behaviour to their dispositions does not mean you will necessarily communicate those thoughts to pupils, and, even if you do, that they will process them and fulfil your expectations. In order for this to happen, you need to mediate them, and the pupils need to recognise and accept the messages. Expectations are mediated in a variety of ways, including:

- verbal (supportive, encouraging comments versus non-supportive, discouraging comments)
- nonverbal (posture gesture, social distance, eye contact)
- organisational (ranging from being placed in ability groups which controls access to learning opportunities to where pupils are seated in relation to teacher and peers, or what resources they have access to).

Harris and Rosenthal (1986), in their meta-analysis of over 400 studies of teacher expectancy, identified four teacher factors that were central to, and most influential in, the mediation of expectancies and resultant pupil behaviour. These were:

- *Climate* (e.g. emotional support, warmth, nonverbal messages)
- *Input* (e.g. time spent with pupils)
- *Output* (e.g. opportunities to learn new materials), and
- *Feedback* (e.g. praise/criticism).

Climate is the most influential factor and feedback the least.

In a later meta-analysis, Rosenthal (1989) reduced the four-factor model to a two-factor model, namely: affect (emotional climate) and efforts (a teaching dimension that includes both input and output). Feedback was dropped because its effect size had become insignificant. According to Babad (2009), feedback had ceased to be significant in differentiating between high- and low-expectancy teachers because of the: 1) impact of expectancy literature that resulted in teachers consciously dispersing feedback more equitably, and 2) because low-achieving pupils had received increased amounts of learning support (at least quantitatively) during the 1980s. However, whilst learning support had increased for low-expectancy pupils, the same could not be said for emotional support. Whilst differentiating academic input to match ability is justifiable, the same should not occur with emotional support, but this was in fact the case. In earlier studies, Babad (1990, 1995) had already found that pupils reported teachers as giving more learning support to low-expectancy pupils but, in contrast, more emotional support (through being more attentive, warm and supportive) towards high-expectancy pupils. He adds that such behaviour undermines the positive intentions of providing more learning support to low-achievers.

Nonetheless, a word of caution in this respect was offered by Brophy and Evertson (1976), who, in their observational studies, found that 'affectionateness' was unrelated to pupils' learning gains. They found that ineffective teachers who held a romanticised notion of pupils as:

> ... warm wonderful, lovely, precious, etc., who were a great pleasure to be around ... were not more likely to be warm toward them ... in fact the more gushy teachers had more chaotic classrooms ... which occasionally became so out of control that the teacher exploded in anger and punitiveness in spite of herself.
>
> (1976: 43–44)

Whereas effective teachers liked their pupils, enjoyed positive relationships and took a professional view of them 'looking upon them as young learners with whom they interacted' (ibid.).

Nelson *et al.* (1998) examined emotions in respect of behaviour management, concluding that teachers who are able to address disciplinary issues objectively in an 'unemotional, limited and matter of fact' way are more effective classroom managers. In other words, not taking rule transgressions or challenging behaviour as a personal attack.

Babad found that pupils are highly sensitive to teachers' differential behaviour towards them and others and can describe the process almost as accurately as trained observers. From his extensive research, he concluded that pupils:

> ... are experts in deciphering and understanding the finest nuances of teacher behavior. Because of students' continuous dependence on their teachers, their sensitivity is highly adaptive and might contribute to their adjustment to school ... Many teachers are oblivious of their transparency to students, and unaware of the students' expertise in understanding them.
>
> (2009: 100)

A number of factors have been identified as being most likely to produce the expectancy-confirmation cycle (see Snyder [1992] for a review). These factors include those attributable to the perceiver (teacher), others to the target (pupil) and a third group related to situational variables (school). In summary:

- Teachers whose goals include getting along in a positive way with their pupils and who are motivated to develop an accurate, data-driven, flexible view of their pupils, are less likely to produce self-fulfilling prophecies than those who are motivated to arrive at a stable and predictable view of their pupils.
- Pupils who are uncertain of their self-worth, or who have unclear self-perceptions regarding their ability and their self-efficacy are more susceptible to social influences, including teachers' self-fulfilling prophecies. Where a pupil's self-perceptions are clear, they are more likely to convince others to view them as positively as they view themselves. Furthermore, if the motivational goals of the pupil can be facilitated by the teacher (e.g. help with a project, a good mark), then they are more likely to conform to the teacher's expectations.
- Pupils moving into new situations (such as moving to a new school or transitioning through school years) are more susceptible to the influences of teachers' expectations as they attempt to develop a social identity and to cope with their new surroundings and its demands, and so are likely to be less clear and confident in their self-perceptions. The timing of the mediation of expectancy effects is also an important factor. Experiments have shown that where a false expectancy has been introduced in the early stages of a teacher forming impressions about pupils, expectancy effects were more often found. When similar experiments were carried out after the teacher's impressions had crystallised, the effects were not found as regularly, reaffirming the early discussion about the impression-formation process.
- Effects seldom occur separately in social contexts (e.g. the classroom) since it is the cumulative effects, or their interactions with each other, that usually result in expectancy effects. Cumulative effects can include: cognitive (learning, self-efficacy), social (peer group relations), emotional (motivational style, joy, depression) and behavioural (disruptive versus prosocial behaviour) factors.

## Ways to avoid sending the unintended messages

There are a number of ways in which teachers can help to avoid negative expectancy effects:

- Objectively monitor your behaviour, including the type, amount and quality of interactions, to try and ensure equal treatment of pupils. Do not assume that you treat them all equally. A simple example is objectively

recording who you ask questions of or take answers from during your lessons. This is easily done using lollypop sticks with pupils' names on them and two pots. When you ask someone a question, move their stick to a second pot. At the end of the lesson, you will know all the pupils to whom you have asked a question, rather than believing you have asked questions of all of your pupils.
- Avoid using disruptive pupils as: messengers; monitors; sitting them at the back of the room; praising them for marginal or below average performance.
- Use the same sanctions for all pupils – whatever their ability.
- Contact parents of disruptive pupils for academic reasons, not just behavioural ones.
- Monitor and write down your explanations of the causes of disruption with different pupils and classes. Writing them down will make you engage more with your descriptions.
- Examine the *actual,* not perceived, behaviour of pupils, especially those who have been difficult in the past, to make sure your impressions are accurate.
- Focus on learning strategies, not just outcomes.
- Refrain from any grouping that conveys ability as the sole source of success.
- Determine pupils' perspectives on teaching, learning and behaviour (this does not mean your pupils have the answers).

Merely believing you have high expectations of your pupils is no guarantee that it will result in improved behaviour or academic performance. Processes outside volitional control influence teachers' behaviour, which can often unwittingly affect pupils' outcomes. Monitoring your behaviour towards all pupils is the best way to avoid this occurring. To take this a stage further, actively engaging in personal development of your knowledge and skills to match those observed in teachers whose expectations and behaviour foster better pupil behavioural and academic outcomes is necessary. Differences in the practices of high-expectancy and low-expectancy teachers (as defined earlier) have been shown to affect pupil outcomes and produce large effect sizes (e.g. Rubie-Davies, 2007, 2008; Rubie-Davies and Peterson, 2011).

Rubie-Davies and colleagues (Rubie-Davies *et al.*, 2015; Rubie-Davies and Rosenthal, 2016) developed intervention programmes designed to train teachers in the practices of high-expectancy teachers and how to utilise them in their teaching. The training focused on teaching strategies used by high-expectancy teachers in three areas: pupil grouping and learning; classroom climate and goal setting:

- *Grouping and learning*—Whilst high-expectancy teachers tend to use ability grouping for core subjects only and use more flexible groupings elsewhere to best match learning. low-expectancy teachers tend to keep their pupils in ability groups for all learning activities.
- *Classroom climate*—High-expectancy teachers use positive, preventive behaviour management strategies; create a warmer socioemotional

environment; are very positive towards students and promote student autonomy.
- *Goal setting*—High-expectancy teachers tend to set clear individual mastery learning goals, monitor progress carefully, provide feedback on progress, and teach pupils how to set their own goals.

The message is clear: critically examine your own thinking and practice and, if necessary, modify, adjust and expand those qualities that have been shown empirically to bring about the largest positive effects for your pupils.

## Annotated further reading

Consuegra, E., and Engels, N. (2016). Effects of professional development on teachers' gendered feedback patterns, students' misbehaviour and students' sense of equity: results from a one-year quasi-experimental study. *British Educational Research Journal*, 42(5), 802–825.

This quasi-experimental study used a repeated measures design to examine the effect of a professional development programme in which secondary teachers investigated their own teaching practice by means of collaborative appreciative inquiry. The aim of the study was to improve teacher feedback patterns, student behavioural responses and student perception of equitable treatment of boys and girls in the classroom. The results showed the positive and negative effects of the programme on levels of positive and negative teacher feedback and pupil misbehaviour and task engagement.

## Further reading to support M level study

Batzle, C.S., Weyandt, L.L., Janusis, G.M., and DeVietti, T.L. (2010). Potential impact of ADHD with stimulant medication label on teacher expectations. *Journal of Attention Disorders*, 24(2), 157–166.

This study investigated how teachers rated pupils' behaviour, IQ and personality based on the presence or absence of an attention deficit hyperactivity disorder (ADHD) label. Using vignettes and a seven-point Likert scale, the study tested the cognitive confirmation effect – that is, how teachers made decisions about the personal qualities of imaginary pupils based on a simple written description. Pupils with ADHD labels, whether receiving medication or not, were judged less favourably than those without the label, on all three dimensions; behaviour, IQ and personality.

Chapter 4

# Professional social skills

Behaviour management and pupil engagement with learning are dependent, to a large extent, on the quality of the social interaction between teacher and pupils. It is a complex and dynamic relationship, but it is one that can be observed, analysed and changed. This chapter presents an overview of some of the key elements in classroom social interaction and how they relate to establishing and maintaining teacher authority in an assertive way. This is done:

- at the macro level through a model of social competence; and
- at the micro level looking at nonverbal behaviours (which are the more difficult behaviours to control in social interaction).

When people use the expression 'she's a born teacher', what do they mean and what are the implications for those teachers who are not? No one is born with knowledge of the National Curriculum or with administration skills, and yet some people are extremely effective in communicating with and influencing others, in some cases from an early age. Such individuals are usually socially active and find it easy to make and keep friends, are confident, can communicate effectively, listen to others, manage their emotions, negotiate, help resolve conflicts, manipulate the behaviour of others and are able to read social situations quickly and accurately. Put simply, they are socially competent – but what are the characteristics of social competence, and are they inherited or learned? Whilst there are a number of competing and often conflicting explanations, most agree it is a combination of both.

## Social competence

Social competence (SC) is one component of an individual's overall personal competence. It concerns both self and social awareness – the way in which we understand ourselves and others – as well as social behaviour – so it is an important element of self-regulation. Whilst there are various models of SC, the framework for this chapter owes much to elements from a model proposed by Greenspan (1981). Here, SC is distinguished from conceptual competence (e.g. solving mathematical problems) and practical competence (e.g. wiring a plug) (see Figure 4.1). SC involves understanding and communicating with others (which includes interpreting their thoughts, intentions and feelings), to explain and predict their behaviour – a feature known by psychologists as Theory of Mind (ToM). Having a ToM enables an individual 'to reflect on the contents of one's own and other's minds' (Baron-Cohen, 2001: 174). ToM is a theory because we can never be sure what someone else is thinking. Saxe and Kanwisher (2003) suggest that ToM relies on distinct brain regions, sometimes referred to as the 'mentalising network'. Inevitably our perception and interpretation of what others are thinking and feeling is coloured by our own experiences, thoughts and feelings, which include biological and socio-cultural influences.

SC can be divided into four subcomponents:

- temperament
- character
- social awareness, and
- emotion regulation.

Differences in temperament identifiable in babies and are salient components of an individual's personality (Cloninger *et al.*, 2006). According to Kagan,

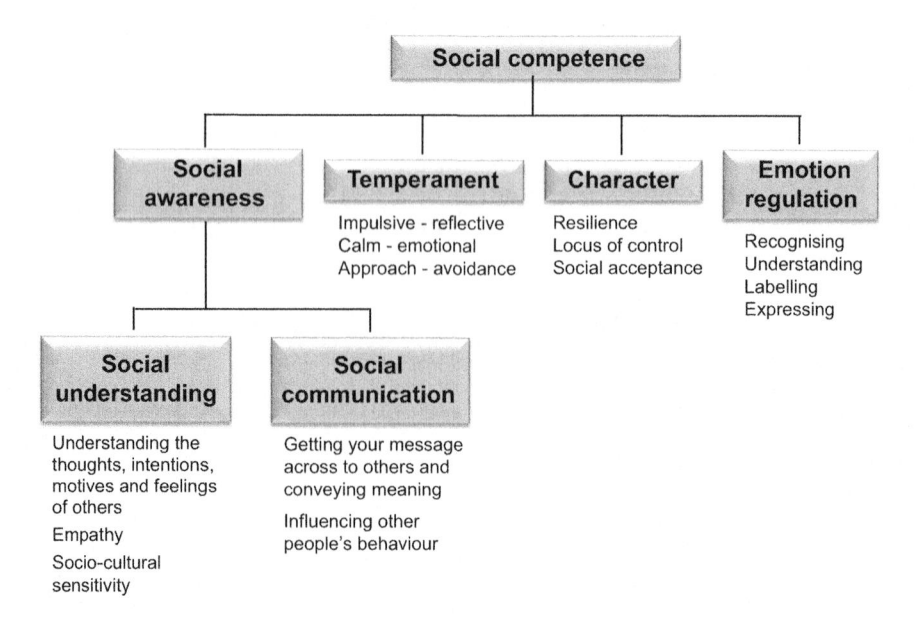

```
                          Social competence
        ┌───────────────┬──────────┬──────────────┬───────────────┐
       Social        Temperament   Character      Emotion
      awareness                                   regulation
                     Impulsive - reflective  Resilience
                     Calm - emotional        Locus of control   Recognising
                     Approach - avoidance    Social acceptance  Understanding
                                                                Labelling
                                                                Expressing
        ┌──────────────┬──────────────┐
      Social             Social
   understanding      communication

   Understanding the   Getting your message
   thoughts, intentions, across to others and
   motives and feelings conveying meaning
   of others
   Empathy             Influencing other
   Socio-cultural      people's behaviour
   sensitivity
```

*Figure 4.1* Elements of social competence.

temperament comprises of 'stable behavioural and emotional reactions that appear early and are influenced in part by genetic constitution' (1994: 40). It is the core from which the adult personality develops (alongside interaction with environment), is stable across time and situations, and influences adaptation to the internal and social environment. Clayson (1999) argued that effective teacher traits are linked with such stable features.

Although researchers differ on detail (Zentner and Bates, 2008), temperament includes approach-avoidance behaviours, anger proneness and impulsiveness. In contrast, character includes: resourcefulness, self-acceptance, locus of control, resilience, cooperativeness and social acceptance, each of which is on a continuum. These features are implicated in the general development of self-regulation of cognition, emotions and behaviour.

Social awareness includes: sensitivity to others' feelings; self-presentation and effective communication, each of which can be subdivided into verbal behaviour, nonverbal behaviour and the thought processes and emotions underlying them. Social awareness is more accessible, malleable and responsive to environmental influences than temperament and character, but its development is influenced by both. Shyness, for example, is a component of temperament, which can be measured at an early age (Kagan, 1994) but which can affect the quality of social interaction throughout the lifespan. However, the malleability of social awareness means that where people have difficulties with interpersonal communication, change is possible. For example, teachers can be taught effective strategies to improve their interpersonal skills (Richmond and McCroskey, 2004).

Given the importance of effective communication skills in teaching, one might expect significant parts of teachers' training to be spent developing them. In practice, however, few ITT courses provide any formal training in these important skills. This is unfortunate given that Richmond *et al.* (2006) showed how training teachers in nonverbal skills resulted in significant improvements in pupils' affinity towards their teachers, as well as gains in their academic learning compared with teachers who were teaching the same subjects but who were not trained in nonverbal skills. We are continually reminded of the problems that some teachers face on a daily basis managing pupils' behaviour – processes that require exceptional interpersonal skills, including negotiation, conflict resolution, questioning, emotion regulation and assertiveness. The fact that many teachers achieve this, despite receiving no specific training, is praiseworthy. At the same time, the stress and emotional damage reported by many teachers as a result of disruptive behaviour suggests it is achieved at some personal cost.

Being socially competent requires a large repertoire of social skills, including self-management, reading and interpreting social cues and being able to respond appropriately in different contexts. However, social interaction can be undermined by emotions, which in turn can affect self-presentation. An example will help to qualify this.

> **Case study**
>
> In week 4 of his first term, Mike, a newly qualified teacher, has been asked to teach personal, social, health and economic (PSHE) education to a year 9 class. His main subject is science, and he has had some good lessons so far, so he feels quite confident about teaching this year 9 group. However, PSHE is a subject about which he has little knowledge or experience teaching. He has done some preparation for his lesson: he has produced a detailed lesson plan, considered the classroom layout, school policies and having appropriate resources. He has thought about how and where to stand in the classroom to express authority and what to say. He arranges the room for groupwork – a discussion about drugs. However, when he asks for quiet so he can introduce the topic, the pupils seem slow to respond, then some start laughing. Just then, the Head of Year sticks her head around the door and asks if everything is OK, and Mike says 'Yes, thanks.' – the pupils laugh again. He smiles to the Head hoping to impress that he is not fazed by the laughter and to hide his anxiety. He raises his voice and tells the class that their behaviour is unacceptable, but some giggle, which annoys him further, so he puts two of the culprits in detention. The situation makes him feel increasingly uncomfortable. He feels hot, tense and his mouth feels dry. He has 'butterflies' in his stomach but is not sure why at this stage. Everything *ought* to be all right; after all, his science lessons have gone well with the other classes, and when he was on professional placement during training, he had coped extremely well. He went to a lot of trouble planning the lesson and producing resources. However, he is now feeling uncomfortable, anxious, uncertain, and unhappy that things are not going the way they should.

Mike's feelings – anxiety and probably embarrassment at the Year Head seeing him struggle – represent emotional reactions to his perceptions of: what he thinks 'should' or 'must' be happening in class for him to be considered a competent teacher, what he believes is actually happening, what he thinks are the causes and what he thinks the Year Head is thinking about him. Some cognitive behavioural theorists argue that negative feelings and beliefs are largely caused by faulty thinking patterns, notably in respect of self-presentation, such as second-guessing what others might be thinking about our behaviour. Being preoccupied with what 'ought' or 'must' be is irrational, unrealistic and can lead to all-or-nothing thinking and resultant negative self-evaluation (David *et al.*, 2010).

Feeling anxious is a preoccupation with the self and survival. What Mike is thinking and feeling will likely be communicated through his nonverbal behaviours, but he will probably be unaware of this, as many occur subconsciously. These behaviours include facial expression, eye contact, body posture, gesture, voice (pitch, speed and frequency), paralanguage, retreating to a defensible space, hanging on to something solid, increasing social distance, attempting to get out of the 'spotlight'. Facial expression is likely to signal fear by being more tense than normal, making it difficult to smile. The positioning of his eyebrows and mouth are also likely to signal to the pupils that he is frightened. Eye contact, so important in communication, becomes less likely. Body posture and gesture become protective and 'closed', rather than open and confident. Tension in the muscles and having a dry mouth may raise the pitch of the voice, making it sound 'squeaky'. He may retreat to a safer position, i.e. move away from the group to behind his desk – a physical barrier, again signalling fear. Finally, the need to 'get out of the spotlight' often results in a tendency to rush through explanations, to avoid taking the time to explain what is expected of the class/individual pupil, and instead to want them 'just to get on with it'. Unfortunately, the hurried instructions mean that some pupils do not know what is expected of them, so do nothing or become disruptive. Those that do try to participate may ask, 'What are we supposed to be doing?', which may be interpreted by the teacher as them not having paid attention. The pupils become increasingly aware that the signals seem wrong and will often respond negatively, exacerbating the teacher's anxiety and leading to further ineffective messages, perpetuating the cycle.

Self-presentation in social interaction is regulated by ongoing assessment, comparison, confirmation and impression management (Tedeschi, 2013). People use feedback loops to monitor whether the way they see themselves matches the way they perceive other people see them (Argyle, 1981). We behave in ways we hope will elicit the desired responses from others, that is, responses that confirm that others see us as the person we want them to think we are. We are attracted to people who confirm what we believe about ourselves and avoid, or are less receptive, to those who do not (Swann et al., 1989).

Effective communication is regulated through awareness of feedback, but we are not always consciously aware of all the messages we transmit. Adopting a more relaxed interactional style with pupils is, for many teachers, a valuable part of developing positive relationships with pupils. However, some pupils are more restricted in what they are allowed to say, determined by a teacher's perceptions of a pupil's ability to know where to draw the line. Pupils are aware of this, especially when a teacher's authority is not perceived to be fair and they feel picked on. As one pupil informed me during an interview:

> There are some (teachers) who like everyone else in class but they take it out on me. Well like, everyone will be talking in class but if I'm talking they take it out on me and no one else ... just one of those things. ... they get on to me and no one else.
>
> (Jordan, Year 9)

## Immediacy and social skills

Immediacy is an individual's perception of psychological and physical closeness of others and includes both verbal and nonverbal behaviours (Mehrabian, 1972). Whilst some verbal behaviours may also contribute to immediacy, the construct is primarily reserved for nonverbal behaviour. Richmond and McCroskey present nonverbal immediacy as physical proximity, body orientation, (appropriate) touch, eye contact, smiling, body movement, gestures and body posture. Teachers who engage in immediate behaviours are perceived more favourably than those who do not, since 'students are drawn to teachers they trust and perceive as competent and caring. Students avoid teachers that they do not trust or perceive as competent, caring and responsive' (2004: 65). McCroskey et al. (1996) demonstrated that vocal variability, eye contact and smiling were the immediacy behaviours most commonly related to effective learning. Immediate teachers also tend to use more positive than negative behavioural management methods. Richmond and McCroskey (2004) argued that teachers could manipulate their immediacy behaviours to present themselves as competent and caring thereby influencing the behaviour of their pupils.

Immediacy behaviours incorporate a range of social skills from simple microskills (e.g. eye contact) to the more complex (e.g. interview skills). They fall into two main categories:

- verbal behaviours (VB), and
- nonverbal behaviours (NVB).

VB include speaking clearly at the appropriate volume and using appropriate language and paralanguage (e.g. rhythm, pitch) – NVB includes everything else. Given the limitations of a single volume, it is impossible to cover both VB and NVB adequately. Since teachers usually plan what they want to say in a lesson, the focus here will be on the more subtle, less controlled NVB. This is not to suggest VB are not important – quite the contrary (see TTA, 2012). Language is a primary means of communicating, and teachers spend most of their working life speaking to children, hence voice awareness and healthcare are paramount. Voice problems have been identified as an issue resulting in absence from work and a contributory factor for some to leave the profession (Smith et al., 1998). Furthermore, teachers have been identified by the DfES as '... one of the occupational groups most likely to present with voice disorders' (2000).

They go on to suggest that education in voice projection, vocal care, and voice training could significantly reduce voice problems. To raise your voice awareness and learn how to manage and keep your voice healthy, see Rodenburg (2015).

Kostic and Chadee (2014) emphasise the significance of NVB in social relationships, because they express and reflect emotional states, primarily through facial expression (Ekman and Friesen, 1978). However, it is worth noting that facial expressions may sometimes be hard to interpret accurately because people may display affect blends, i.e. facial expressions in which one part of the face registers one emotion and another part registers a different emotion. Some nonverbal cues are universal, whereas others have specific cultural meaning. In general, spontaneous or unconsciously exhibited facial expressions are universal (Matsumoto, 2006), but rule-governed behaviours (e.g. standing up at assemblies) are socially constructed. Groups differ in their display rules, prescribing who can show which emotion to whom and under what circumstances. Failure to observe or to understand these rules draws (often unwanted) attention, since communication is hampered. Apart from obvious behaviours, such as eye contact, NVB also includes: touch, dress, appearance, choice of setting and so on. However, these visible features are just observable representations of cognitive processes (e.g. motivation, beliefs and personality traits).

Sometimes we say one thing but our bodies communicate, or are interpreted as communicating, something else – despite our efforts to avoid doing so. Pupils in your class may be paying attention, but cannot control a stray yawn, which you may interpret as their being bored. You may respond with 'Try and stay awake Holly', which in turn may be treated as a joke or be resented and stimulate a cycle of negative behaviour between you and the pupil.

Emotions can interfere with NVBs, especially when trying to conceal them, leading to conflicting messages. For example, a teacher who retreats from an argumentative or aggressive pupil to a position behind their desk and then points and shouts at the pupil from this position, is in danger of escalating the situation. 'Hiding' behind the desk and increasing the social distance suggests apprehension and may be paired with an emotional facial expression – such as fear. The finger-pointing is an aggressive gesture that may encourage an aggressive response from the pupil. Furthermore, the increased social distance effectively draws in other pupils, distracting the teacher and providing the pupil with an audience, who may find the whole thing highly amusing. Generally speaking, pupils view teachers who sit behind their desks as less immediate than those who teach among their pupils, who are viewed as more effective (Hesler, 1972).

Sometimes we can *sense* something is not quite right in a social interaction – a 'gut' feeling that something is amiss, but we cannot determine exactly what it is. This is usually because you are not consciously aware of all the NV cues that your brain is processing. For example, people trying to conceal emotions can be undermined by micro-expressions. These last for less than 0.5 seconds and do not match what is being said or gestured, revealing the true emotional state to the observer – unlike 'normal' emotional expressions, which last longer and match what is being said (Ekman, 2009). Porter and ten Brinke (2008) demonstrated that microexpressions occurred when individuals attempted to be deceitful about their emotional expressions.

## Monitoring nonverbal behaviour

The best way to determine what skills you need to develop is to audit your own NVBs, which can be done using a video recording device or an observer. Feedback from observers you feel comfortable with and whose opinion you respect is useful, but having them present in the classroom, specifically for that purpose, can promote different behaviour from you and your pupils than is normal. Asking other adults to interpret what you believed you were communicating is potentially problematic in itself. This is not to suggest that having a video recorder in class is necessarily an easy alternative, since initially it will distract both you and the pupils. Laptops with integral cameras placed on the teacher's desk can be used to capture a more natural record of your teaching behaviour when addressing the whole class. However, difficulties arise when you move around the classroom. The main advantage is that sequences can be played over and over again, allowing you to analyse your behaviour. When I use this technique to record teachers, they are often surprised to find that they had not said what they thought they had said, were standing awkwardly, or used 'novel' gestures and projected other unintended nonverbal messages. Their voices sounded unfamiliar with accents and pronunciation different to what they expected. Figure 4.2 gives examples of how information can be lost during transmission.

People seldom deliberately monitor or practice NVB, assuming they operate naturally and that they are OK – unless they become 'painfully' aware that they are not working, for example, having difficulty managing a situation. Even then, they tend to look for an explanation that is self-serving, such as blaming the situation. Social psychologists argue that in most social encounters, people rely on what is known as a 'script', which provides them with a typical sequence of events for familiar situations to aid understanding of a range of social phenomena (Lalljee et al., 1992). Our scripts help us to plan our behaviour, since they specify the behavioural steps that lead to effective interpersonal relationships, for example, the sequence of events in a lesson; see Table 4.1.

Table 4.1 A simplified script for a lesson

| Activity | Behaviour |
| --- | --- |
| Greeting | Saying hello. |
| Establishing relationships | Getting attention, assessing receptiveness of pupils, outlining objectives, giving instructions. |
| Completing the tasks | Pupils learning, monitoring their understanding and behaviour, controlling off-task behaviour. |
| Re-establishing relationships | Regaining class attention, pulling group together, summarising the lesson. |
| Parting | Saying goodbye. |

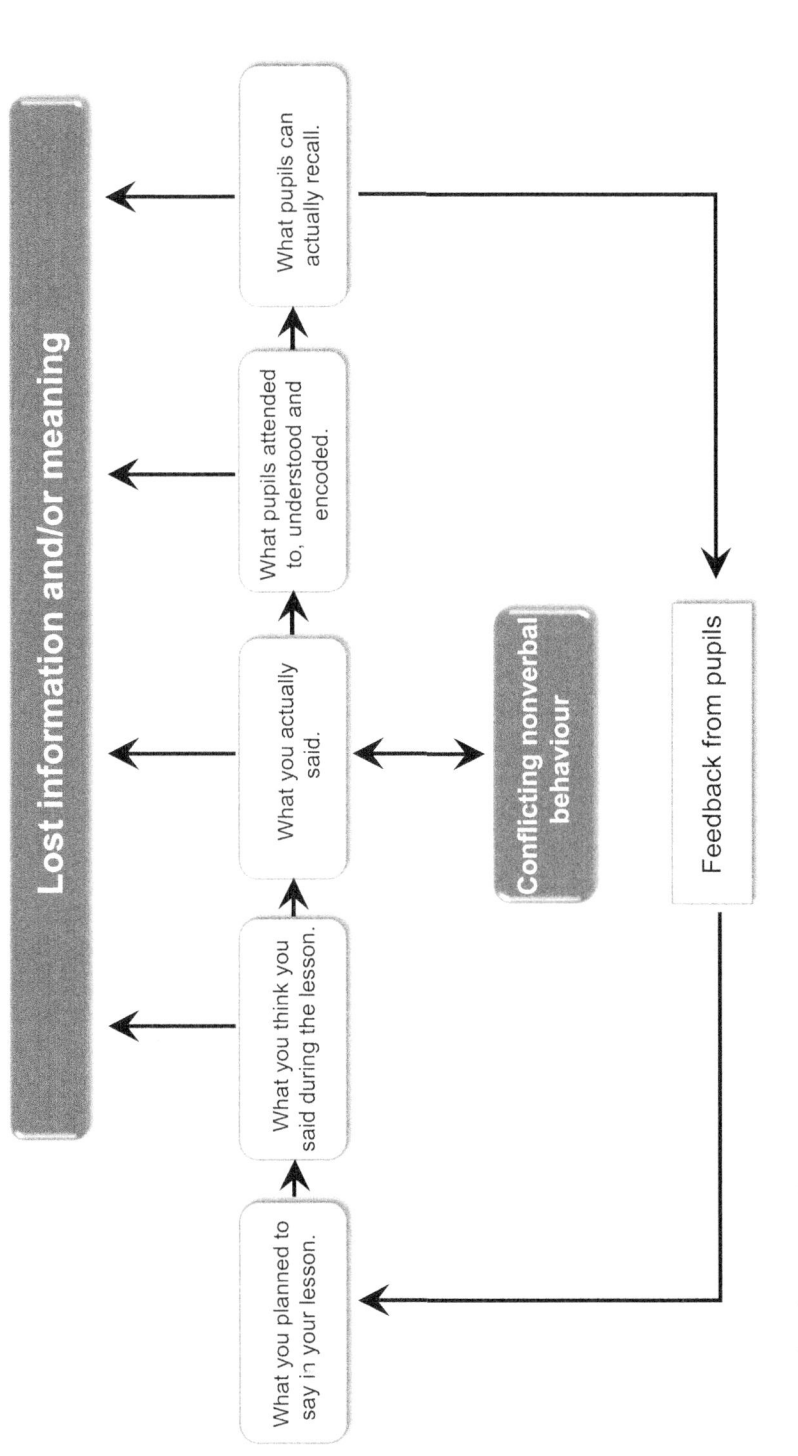

*Figure 4.2* Information loss in classroom communication.

Over time, these scripts become ritualised and assumptions are made about what is being said or done without conscious attention, and so, even when we are not being effective, the ritual continues. Ritualised behaviour can lead to us being insensitive to change within individuals, groups, relationships and contexts and can occur in any social institution. It is not uncommon for people in intimate relationships to speak of 'being taken for granted' or their 'partners not making an effort to notice how they have changed'. If this occurs with intimate relationships, it is hardly surprising that it happens in classrooms with pupils.

Social effectiveness can be explained in terms of input, process or outcomes. Teachers regularly use a wide range of professional social skills. Table 4.2 offers

*Table 4.2* Some examples of professional skills used by teachers

---

Listening skills

Assertiveness

Proposing ideas

Expressing dissatisfaction

Expressing emotion

Expressing authority

Supporting pupils having difficulty expressing themselves

Questioning

Disagreeing and criticising

Negotiating

Scaffolding pupils' ideas

Offering explanations, reasons and ways of coping with difficulties

Seeking clarification, explanation, information

Managing discussion

Encouraging the reluctant to speak

Tempering the over-enthusiastic

Interpreting pupils' ideas

Consolidating learning

Admitting difficulty

Managing aggression

Defending

Scanning the whole class whilst working with individuals

Deflecting challenges

---

a few examples, some of which will be discussed in detail. An effective teacher could be defined in terms of their social skills, or their ability to maintain the flow of the lesson (e.g. keep pupils focused, on task, not be distracted and maintain the interest of their audience), or their pupils' results. The three are not the same. Getting results indicates effectiveness, but if they are done in an aggressive way, they are less socially desirable. Pupils may behave appropriately despite the teacher. Alternatively, someone may possess the requisite social skills but have difficulty applying them in some contexts because they are anxious. Another may keep a lesson flowing, but pupils' results are below par, and so on.

## Understanding nonverbal behaviour

Professional social skills are arranged hierarchically in terms of their complexity (see Figure 4.3). The more complex behaviours ('withitness' – being aware of all behaviour taking place in your classroom and alert to subtle changes in pupils' behaviour which might indicate potential disruption or assertiveness) can be broken down into strategies (listening skills or questioning) or, further still, into basic skills (eye contact or posture). Whilst we do not usually communicate using single microskills, they are nonetheless triggers for behaviour in others (e.g. eye contact and/or facial expression alone can be powerful methods of communicating what you are thinking and feeling about someone).

In practice, we usually look for combinations of NV signals (macroskills) rather than individual microskills when communicating. Ekman (2004) identified five types of nonverbal communication. They are: emblems, illustrators, emotional expression, regulators and manipulators.

1 *Emblems* have a verbal equivalent, are easily recognised because they are frequently used in specific contexts and the recipient immediately understands what they mean. According to Ekman, 'Emblems are the only true "body language" in that the movements have a set of defined meanings ... are socially learned and thus like language, are culturally variable' (2004: 39). For example, extending the index and middle finger whilst clenching the remainder can mean: 'buzz off'; 'up yours'; 'victory'; 'peace'; the letter 'V' or '2' depending on whether the palm faces toward or away from the signer and the context in which it is used. Emblems usually involve the hands, but they may include shoulder and head movements. Teachers make daily use of familiar emblems (or invent their own) to manage behaviour e.g. folding arms to *say*, 'I'm waiting', or thumbs up or a wink to *say*, 'Well done', or clapping to *say*, 'Stop talking and look this way', and so on. Nevertheless, their impact is dependent upon the quality of the relationship between the teacher and the pupils. Once established, a NV signal to activate classroom routines is the most efficient way of managing such behaviours. However, an association must be established between a particular emblem and its meaning in terms of pupil behaviour – something which is best taught explicitly and

positively: 'When I raise my hand, it means I want you to look at me and stop talking so that I can give you the next instruction'.
2. *Illustrators* are intimately connected to speech and involve the hands, face and body to illustrate or clarify speech, e.g. using the hands to indicate size. They often operate subconsciously and throughout a conversation. They are meant to complement what is being said, but sometimes contradict it. For example, Ekman (2004) highlights the significance of eyebrow raising and lowering to convey emotions and positive or negative features respectively. Illustrators are also used to help speakers get through complex explanations when finding the correct words proves difficult. They also maintain self-presentation.
3. *Emotional expressions* are involuntary signals that convey basic emotions, and they evolved primarily to cope with life tasks, e.g. child care (Ekman, 1997). They are universal across cultures. Different emotions involve unique and distinctive movements of the facial muscles, which can be measured. Whilst some thoughts occur privately, basic emotions (e.g. anger, fear, surprise) are visible.
4. *Regulators* help control, adjust and regulate the flow of an interaction. They include head nodding, forward and backward lean, agreement smiles (plus eye contact, facial expression, etc.) and are important in maintaining flow between teachers and pupils. For example: a pupil lowering a brow might suggest a lack of understanding; a teacher extending her hand with palm down tells an enthusiastic pupil that she is not yet ready to receive the pupil's question; a hand to the ear signals that pupils should listen carefully; or a pupil dropping his head and rolling his eyes might suggest that a teacher should hurry up or be more interesting or perhaps indicate that the pupil is being cheeky!
5. *Manipulators* are behaviours that interfere with communication, where part of the face or body is manipulated by another body part or object. They are habitual and include scratching, self-touching, nail-biting, and hair twiddling, which suggests nervousness. Trainee teachers facing a new class whilst being observed are often anxious, resulting in increased use of manipulators, which in turn can trigger disruption. Manipulators tend to create negative impressions, e.g. they can be unsettling (teacher not appearing confident), irritating (pupils tapping pencils) or offensive (nose picking).

All of the preceding are macroskills. In the next section, I look more closely at microskills relevant to the classroom, focusing on:

- *The face*
- *Eye contact*
- *Posture*
- *Gesture*

Complex skills: Conveying authority, Assertiveness, Withitness

Strategies: Scanning, Negotiating, Questioning

Basic skills: Eye contact, Facial expression, Voice, posture, gesture

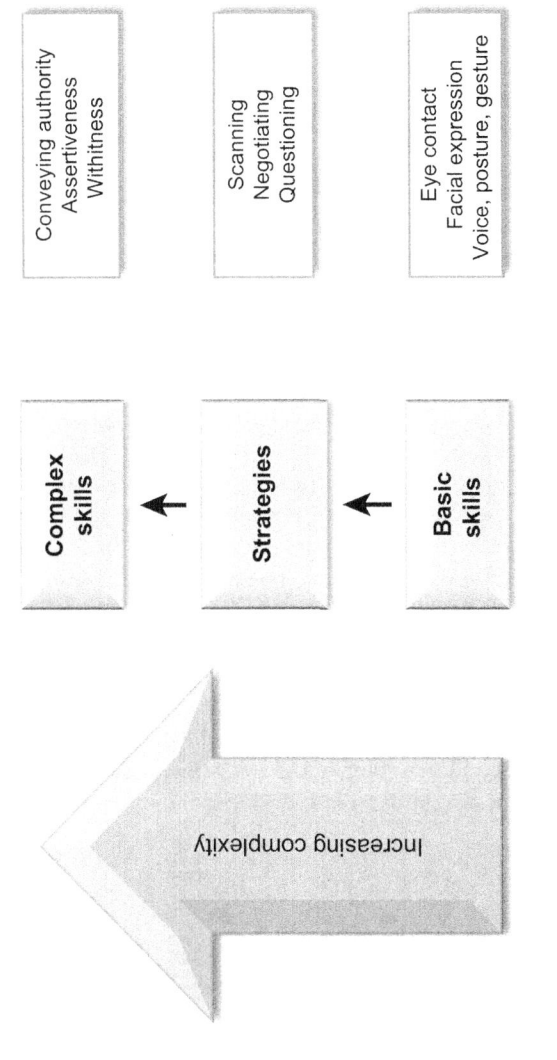

Increasing complexity

*Figure 4.3* A hierarchy of social skills used in teaching.

## The face

The face is probably our most powerful nonverbal communicator, and research has demonstrated that facial communication has deep evolutionary meanings (Harrison, 1976). It frames communication in developing infants (Vine, 1973) as well as in adults (Ekman and Friesen, 1975). Argyle suggested that the face conveys 'the main interpersonal relationships – dominant, submissive, threatening, sexual, parental, playful etc.' (1975: 212). Facial expression has also been linked to emotional feedback, not only in terms of the more familiar decoding of basic emotions in others by their expressions, but also how we interpret our own emotional state. That facial expression can influence emotions (proprioceptive feedback) has long been recognised (e.g. McIntosh, 1996) and Ekman *et al.* (1983) found that holding a particular facial expression intensified an emotional experience. For example, smiling is now used in behaviour therapy as an intervention for mood regulation (Botella *et al.*, 2012). However, whether it is the facial expression *per se* that influences the emotional experience or whether it is the associated muscle tension or respiratory changes is questionable – it appears to do so in some circumstances and not others (Buck, 1988). Feedback from facial expression has confirmatory role, appearing to contribute to emotional experience if, *and only if*, it complements an emotional state.

The importance of facial expression is established very early in human development. Young children prefer looking at faces more than other stimuli (Turati *et al.*, 2002), especially with eyes open and smiling, and to happy faces for longer than other expressions (Farroni *et al.*, 2007). Richmond (2002) found that teachers who smile and have positive facial affects are perceived as more immediate and likeable than those who do not.

Interest in facial expressions led researchers (particularly those working with children) to develop a facial code (Ekman and Friesen, 1978), a simplistic pictorial representation of the layout and dynamics of the face (see Figure 4.4), which are quickly recognised and interpreted, dependent on the direction of the eyebrows, mouth and diameter of the eyes. They are used to indicate the main influences in making judgements about socio-emotional states.

*Figure 4.4* Facial code – emotion signalled through facial expression.
Note
Simplified pictures to represent how basic emotion is signalled through facial expression and how it can be changed by manipulating one feature. Whilst A looks happy, B looks sad by merely inverting the 'mouth'. Whilst C looks angry, D looks worried by merely changing the direction of the 'eyebrows'.

## Eye contact

Ask people what they understand by the term 'nonverbal communication' and most will make reference to eye contact. This is hardly surprising, given that most sensory information passed to the brain comes from the eyes (Pease, 1997).

Gaze or looking intently at someone is another central component of interpersonal communication. Among NVB, gaze and mutual gaze are considered important cues for signalling social interest and a desire to communicate (Argyle and Cook, 1976). However, some pupils avoid eye contact and gaze when teachers ask questions, as doing so reduces cognitive load or avoids negative socio-emotional experiences (Doherty-Sneddon and Phelps, 2005). There are also cultural and age differences since, although young children and adults frequently engage in gaze, it is less common among adolescents who are more self-conscious, something of particular relevance to teachers (Argyle, 1975). Holding a steady gaze with an individual can be very difficult, since it intensifies communication and emotions and can thus prove uncomfortable and intimidating.

Motivating pupils to pay attention is an obvious prerequisite to learning. Pease (1997) highlights the importance of matching the content of what you say to what you are displaying visually. Imagine for example, a lesson in which you are using slides on an interactive whiteboard and pupils are required to observe whilst you are speaking. If the spoken content does not relate *directly* to the slide, then less than 10% of the information is likely to be absorbed by the pupils. In contrast, where the content of the slide is directly related to the speech, then between 25–30% is likely to be absorbed. Communication can be further enhanced by using a 'pointer' to gain and hold control of pupils' gaze whilst talking through what is being highlighted. When you need to move attention from the slide to speech alone, move your hand and hold it on an imaginary line between the pupils' eyes and your own. This has the effect of drawing the pupils' attention to what you are saying, re-establishing eye contact and achieving a more concentrated communication of your message (ibid.).

Eyes are used primarily to see rather than transmit messages, but, as Argyle (1981) points out, they transmit two types of information during social encounters. First, they indicate that you are prepared to receive information by signifying that the lines of communication are open. Second, they demonstrate your interest in the other person or persons. The amount of time you spend looking at someone is one indicator of the degree to which you are 'interested' in them or what they have to say. There is also interplay between conscious and non-conscious activity in respect of eye contact. For instance, some people might make a conscious effort and practice looking people in the eyes but find that when a particular encounter takes place they look away, despite making a determined effort to maintain eye contact. For example, if you were planning an encounter with someone you know to be aggressive, fear may override the conscious desire to make your point.

Eye contact can act as a measure of dominance or submissiveness as well as indicating sincerity. People often assume (inaccurately) that liars tend to look away when lying, that they are 'shifty eyed', hence the saying 'look me in the eyes and say that!' In reality, experienced liars are more likely to look you in the eye for longer periods than someone telling the truth. Furthermore, and perhaps surprisingly, people (including teachers) are generally not very accurate at detecting liars (Zuckerman *et al.*, 1981).

There are a number of references in everyday language to the power of eye contact in interpersonal relationships. For example, giving someone the 'evil eye', 'looking daggers', being 'gooey eyed'. Emotions such as excitement, anger or fear can be signalled through the size of an individual's pupils. When you are attracted to someone, your pupils dilate up to three times their normal size (Hess, 1972). In contrast, the pupils of someone who is angry or irritated will contract, hence the expression 'beady little eyes'. Detecting the size of someone's pupils is done without conscious awareness – you seldom walk around with a ruler measuring them. The subtle nature of reading people's thoughts and feelings through their eyes was demonstrated through experiments involving expert card players. Researchers found that experts won fewer games when their opponents wore sunglasses than when they could see their eyes or pupil signals. Whilst these signals are monitored subconsciously it is possible to influence the process consciously. Chinese traders were known to spend time studying the pupils of their buyers when negotiating prices, identifying their customers' level of interest in different products. Some military and law enforcement agencies use low-peaked hats, dark or reflective sunglasses to hide the eyes and prevent messages being transmitted by them.

There is evidence to demonstrate that we tend to look more often and for longer periods at people we find 'attractive'. If the recipient of our gaze registers this signal, they are likely to reciprocate positively, assuming they find us (or what we have to say) attractive also. In contrast, the anxious, timid or embarrassed individual is less likely to engage in mutual gaze and tend to blink more or look away when anxious (Argyle, 1975), so they are perceived as shifty and therefore not to be trusted. A simple technique to alleviate this when teaching is to look at your pupils' foreheads, which gives them the impression you are looking directly at them but without the intensity of direct eye contact.

Pease (1997) suggests consciously developing different gaze patterns to suit specific types of social interaction. He identifies three distinct gaze patterns:

- business,
- social, and
- intimate.

The first two are relevant for teacher-pupil interaction.

He recommends the business gaze (see Figure 4.5) for more serious encounters – i.e. letting people know that you mean business. Here, focus is maintained on an imaginary triangle, the base of which is a horizontal line joining the two pupils and the peak is the centre point between the eyebrows. Pease argues that, provided an individual's gaze does not drop below eye level, you can maintain control of the interaction, and so this would be particularly suitable when discussing a serious topic with a pupil.

The second type or 'social gaze' is used for more informal encounters. Here the focus of the gazer moves in a downward triangle, from the eyes to the mouth (see Figure 4.6).

The third type – the intimate gaze extends the downward gaze from the eyes to the chest and beyond, and is not suitable for encounters with pupils.

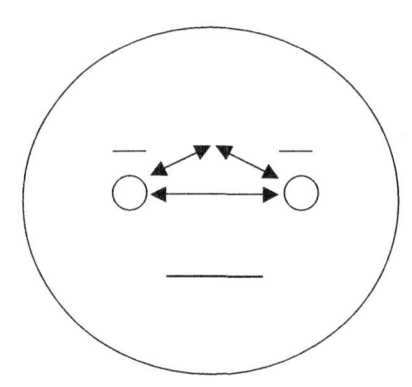

*Figure 4.5* The business gaze.

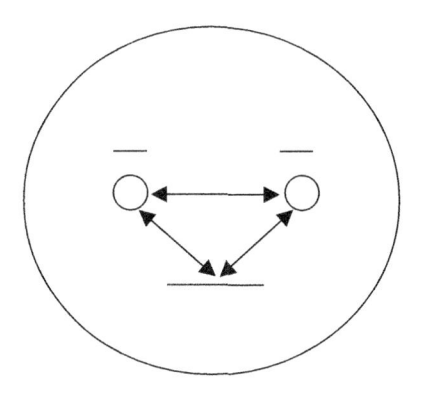

*Figure 4.6* The social gaze.

## Posture

Body posture transmits a whole range of messages – both intended and unintended – and is usually related to the type of activity being pursued. How you stand and your distance from your audience affect the way in which you are perceived. For example, a slight forward-leaning posture denotes a positive attitude towards another person (Mehrabian, 1972), and if you adopt this posture, the other person is more likely to pay attention to what you have to say.

According to Hargie (2011), there are four key human postures – standing, sitting, squatting, and lying. Within each category are a series of subcategories, each with its own combinations of arm and leg positions as well as body angles. These combinations can indicate authority, submissiveness or neutrality. In the classroom, a teacher is concerned with demonstrating confidence and authority, so awareness of stance and positioning of the arms and legs is important if you wish to avoid unwittingly undermining your authority.

Standing with your arms folded and legs crossed is generally seen as a defensive position, usually observed in first encounters when people are unsure of one another. In contrast, the open-handed (upward) gesture coupled with uncrossed legs suggests being relaxed. Standing with hands on hips and elbows bent can make us appear bigger and suggest assertiveness. When addressing the class, standing is the norm to communicate your authority to the whole class.

A teacher's awareness of the value of proxemics (personal space) can influence behaviour in the classroom. When working with pupils at their desks, standing and towering above them whilst trying to help can be off-putting to some pupils. Squatting or sitting to share the same head and eye level is a means of reassuring pupils that you are attending to what they have to say and this is less intimidating and more motivating (Van Werkhoven, 1990). Sitting or lying on tables or equipment whilst you teach may seem to be projecting a more relaxed persona, but can be problematic if pupils model the behaviour.

Knowing the effect of particular postures and gestures and deciding to apply them does not necessarily mean you will do so when under pressure, with emotions running high – i.e. when they are most needed. Practicing and overlearning them (in front of a mirror for instance) or in the classroom when pupils are not there is a means of being proactive in using body language to its best advantage.

## Gesture

Gestures are often used as social tools for expressing one's own feelings and thoughts, cooperating with others, and drawing others' attention to objects and events. People seldom keep their hands still when talking (try it), and there appear to be two distinct types of hand movement. The first, referred to as self-stimulation, includes body-focused movements, e.g. scratching, fiddling, rubbing the hands, nose and ears (Freedman and Hoffman, 1967). Observers often interpret such fumbling or 'preening' movements as indicators of stress or anxiety. In class, pupils are often quick to identify these signs:

> Mr Gerrard takes his glasses off and puts them on his desk, rubs his nose, then stares at you when he is annoyed.
>
> (Faye, Year 10)

> She just folds her arms and looks at her watch—that means if we don't shut up we will be staying in at breaktime.
>
> (Jack, Year 9)

The other type of hand gesture is related directly to speech. There are two theoretical explanations of these movements. The first is psychoanalytic and claims that hand gestures indicate a speaker's emotional state (Feldman, 1959). The second is that hand gestures represent a communication channel that either supplements speech, or replaces it (Baxter *et al.*, 1968) but reflect meaning in a distinct way from words. Gestures can also undermine communication. Overuse of arm gestures, moving your hands all the time and making large sweeping arm movements, can be off-putting to listeners. The major benefit of gestures is not always easy to demonstrate except, for instance, in communicating ideas about shape and size. However, it has been shown that changes occur in the quality of speech, notably content, fluency and size of vocabulary when people are not allowed to use gesture (Graham and Heywood, 1975).

Teachers often use hand gestures as a means of control. Pointing at someone or showing them the palm of your hand on an outstretched arm are ways of expressing authority but can have very different meanings. Pointing is perceived as signifying dominance but is more aggressive than using the palm of your hand. The palm acts more as a holding gesture, for example, signalling to an eager pupil to wait until instructed to add their contribution to a discussion, but, as with most gestures, there are different cultural interpretations of the same gesture.

## Listening skills and assertiveness

Listening skills are essential in teaching, particularly when trying to help pupils who are having difficulty with communicating their thoughts and feelings. Assertive behaviour is an effective way of expressing authority in the classroom whilst maintaining respect for pupils. The following sections examine these two important areas more closely.

### Listening skills

Effective listening is a complex skill often taken for granted in everyday teacher-learner situations. Listening is the first social skill we learn. It is the most used but least taught form of communication in schools (Steil, 1991). Whilst most people are capable of hearing what others say, it is not the same as listening. As a teacher, you invariably have to listen to people who are distressed, angry or confused and who may have difficulty expressing themselves. Effective listening requires attention to the motivational intent of the speaker and their nonverbal signals, as well as verbal components, and also being aware of the feedback you are giving to them. The effectiveness of NVB as a rapid means of assessing pupils' moods and how they are coping with learning, is something all teachers should be sensitive to. Angelo and Cross (1993) stated that, whilst other forms of classroom assessment may be more accurate, they are simply not as readily available as NVB. Expert and novice teachers differ in their ability to do this. Webb et al. concluded that:

> ... expert teachers are able to attend to myriad and complex information that they organise and interpret, and they appear to perceive and understand students' social information, and classroom events in a qualitatively different manner than less experienced teachers.
>
> (1997: 89)

The development of this ability can be left to time and chance (i.e. having the 'right' experience), or you can take control and actively develop your social awareness.

Pupils become irritated when teachers do not appear to be taking an interest in what they have to say, or worse, those who appear to be pretending to listen by making the right 'noises' by nodding and agreeing, but do not 'seem' interested. A teacher who is an effective listener is able to pick up on changes in the responses of the pupil(s) during a conversation by spotting a mismatch between what is being said and the accompanying body language, which may indicate a cause for concern. The effective listener will also be able to encourage and prompt an individual using illustrators and regulators (see above) to convey what they are thinking and feeling and moderate the interaction.

Not providing appropriate conditions for listening or the expected verbal and nonverbal feedback can result in a negative experience for both parties. The pupil will likely feel undervalued and the teacher will not get the required response. Sensitivity to physical presentation is important when interacting with pupils. Facing the whiteboard whilst teaching is not a good means of helping pupils to listen to what you have to say, nor for you to obtain feedback about their understanding and interest. Listening to individuals who have important (to them) things to say in a busy corridor, or offices with continual interruptions is not appropriate and does not suggest that you value what they are saying.

To create the conditions for effective listening and encourage pupils to talk you should:

- be accessible, have time for them, be genuinely concerned, enthusiastic, and take on board their concerns;
- provide an appropriate space – not busy corridors, classrooms or offices where staff wander in and out or are answering the telephone. Concentrate on the pupil even though there may be distractions that appear important;
- look relaxed and unhurried – this suggests you appear receptive to what is being said, making the encounter less threatening. Sitting bolt upright, standing with folded arms, slouching on a desk or appearing restless or impatient, fiddling with pens and paper can be stressful and make the pupil less willing to talk;
- show interest in what is being said through a slight forward lean and being aware of what you and the pupil consider appropriate social distance;
- match the mood and reflect the feelings of the pupil; and
- keep the conversation flowing by using appropriate supportive prompts – including verbal (such as, 'Go on …' 'Fancy that …' 'Yes …' 'I see …') and nonverbal regulators (such as gentle head nodding, smiling) to convey genuine involvement.

For a more comprehensive account of listening skills see Brownell, J. (2015). *Listening: Attitudes, principles, and skills*. Routledge.

## Asserting your authority

Assertive behaviour is that which satisfies an individual's goals whilst maintaining respect for the goals of others. This means tactfully and justly expressing preferences, needs, opinions and feelings. Assertiveness lies somewhere around the midpoint of a continuum that ranges from aggressive behaviour at one extreme and submissive behaviour at the other. The aggressive person is determined to get what they want, irrespective of the needs and feelings of others. In contrast, the submissive person puts the needs and feelings of others before their own. Being assertive in social situations fosters positive self-worth and is at the heart of effective social communication.

The non-assertive teacher i.e. either submissive or aggressive generates a negative culture. Indecisive, fearful and submissive teachers who cannot communicate what is required, or who do not carry out what they threaten, feel inadequate, frustrated and resentful of their pupils (Canter and Canter, 1976). Their pupils feel unsafe, irritated and resentful and likely to reciprocate in a negative way. The aggressive teacher uses harsh sanctions and maintains order at the expense of pupils, putting them down or humiliating them. Pupils are then fearful and may comply, but their confidence is likely to suffer. Romi et al. (2011) found that pupils' reactions to teachers who used aggressive management techniques included distraction, negativity toward teachers and perceptions that teachers' responses were unjustified. On the other hand, the assertive teacher is able to communicate their dissatisfaction when pupils do not adhere to the rules but are just as quick to express pleasure when pupils behave as expected.

Assertiveness is not just a matter of overcoming immediate problems; it represents a way of life and relates to self-respect, self-confidence, self-regulation, and meeting one's own needs and values, but not at the expense of someone else's. Being non-assertive can lead to feeling discomfort, tension, negative self-worth and self-anger and is marked by various behaviours such as feeling:

- you have to agree to something when you don't want to for fear of hurting someone else's feelings or incurring their anger;
- embarrassed about offering your opinion in case you appear incompetent or are criticised;
- unhappy or angry about being manipulated by others but feel incapable of stopping them;
- anxious about asking someone to do something, even though reasonable, in case they refuse; or
- you cannot say what you think and feel at the time it needs to be said but with hindsight, you wish you had.

Whilst standing up for yourself sounds reasonable, people are often reluctant to do so and make excuses because they worry about making the situation worse (Bower and Bower, 1976). Excuses for not being assertive may appear rational but are often just examples of submissive behaviour. For example, procrastination ('Perhaps I am overreacting – I'll give them another chance'), or hoping the problem will go away (it probably won't happen again), or fear of public shame (I don't want to make an embarrassing scene), or fear of the other party (he will get angry with me). The other party may well get angry with you, but the alternative is to get angry with yourself for not doing anything.

Other excuses suggest powerlessness, (everyone else seems to be prepared to tolerate this behaviour), or helplessness (I will not be able to make any difference whatsoever). Perceived helplessness is a major contributor to submissiveness and is self-deprecating. It externalises control of your life to unchangeable factors such as other people or systems which you cannot directly influence.

## Becoming more assertive

A person is seldom universally non-assertive. It tends to occur in specific situations. If you consider that you are not assertive in situations important to you – the classroom, the staffroom, staff meetings, or with managers, there are ways of improving your assertiveness. As with most topics in this book, there is no quick fix. You will not become more assertive overnight.

Schimmel (1976) identified a number of behaviours central to expressing assertiveness:

- Feeling able to say what you believe and comfortable asking for help from others.
- Insisting that you are respected as an equal who has rights; including the right to refuse to do things.
- Expressing negative and positive emotions and feeling comfortable declaring your feelings.
- Being happy giving and receiving compliments.
- Questioning and challenging routine and authority which affects control of your life to improve your situation.
- Feeling comfortable engaging, sustaining and concluding social interactions.
- Nipping problems in the bud before you become angry and resentful.

Assertive behaviour can be developed using a combination of methods including feedback from friends and colleagues, exploration of the problem and observing others dealing with similar situations (see Figure 4.7). Talking through problems and testing ways of coping is best done with a trained professional, however, positive results can also be achieved using informed colleagues and friends or through self-based methods (reading, mirrors, audio-visual aids). For more detailed information on how to develop these behaviours, see Paterson (2002).

## Problem clarification

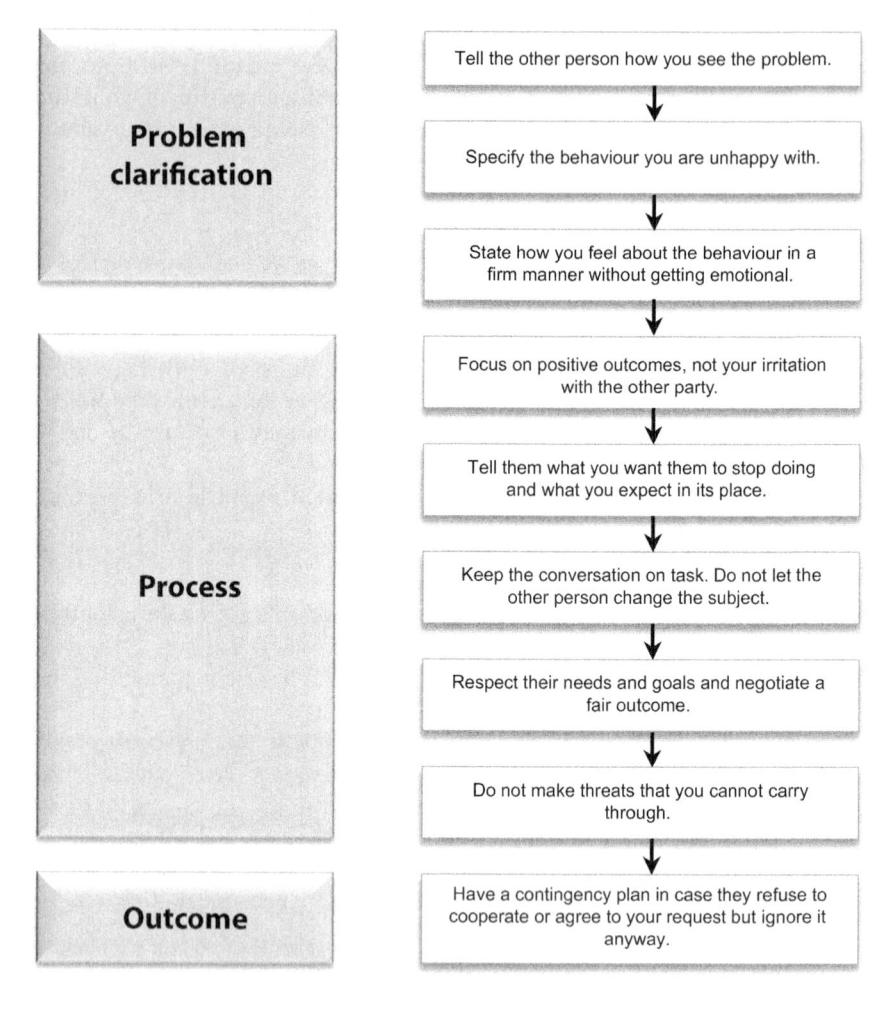

- Tell the other person how you see the problem.
- Specify the behaviour you are unhappy with.
- State how you feel about the behaviour in a firm manner without getting emotional.

## Process

- Focus on positive outcomes, not your irritation with the other party.
- Tell them what you want them to stop doing and what you expect in its place.
- Keep the conversation on task. Do not let the other person change the subject.
- Respect their needs and goals and negotiate a fair outcome.
- Do not make threats that you cannot carry through.

## Outcome

- Have a contingency plan in case they refuse to cooperate or agree to your request but ignore it anyway.

*Figure 4.7* A model for developing assertive behaviour.

The following examples compare assertive/non-assertive responses:

1. A colleague spends every breaktime complaining to you about problems with colleagues in their team.
    a. Assertive response: Every day this week we have spent all breaktime talking about the conflicts in your team. I enjoy talking with you, but I get fed up hearing about the pettiness, as I see it, of the people in your team. I miss talking about the news, my work, and going to play golf.
    b. Non-assertive response: the person would suppress his anger, pretend to be really interested or say nothing.
    c. Aggressive response: the person would blow his top and tell his colleague how boring and petty he is.

2   The deputy head repeatedly asks you to take assembly and then often cancels at the last minute:
    a   Assertive response: When you ask me to organise an assembly and then change your mind at the last minute – which you've done three out of the last four times – I feel irritated because I've wasted time preparing for a non-event. I also start to think that I am unappreciated and being used as a mug. In the future, if I am not required, could you give me more notice, at least the day before?
    b   Non-assertive response: the person might just let it go, fearing the manager will get angry.
    c   Aggressive response: the person might tell the manager how inconsiderate she is and how it is amazing that any staff are prepared to put themselves out for her at all.

For a more detailed account of developing assertiveness, see Hadfield, S., and Hasson, G. (2014) *How to be assertive in any situation*. UK: Pearson.

Verbal and nonverbal immediacy is central to effective teaching. If you cannot get the message across accurately, perceive, interpret and respond to feedback from pupils or influence the behaviour of others, then you are going to find teaching hard work. However, there is no reason why you cannot improve your professional social skills to make your life that much easier. It is important to remember the link between social skills and emotional control since the latter has the potential to undermine your social competence.

## Annotated further reading

Robertson, J. (1996). Expressing authority. In: *Effective classroom control*. London: Hodder and Staughton.

### Chapter 1: Expressing authority

This chapter examines nonverbal behaviour in teacher-pupil relationships. Topics covered include proxemics, posture, gesture and eye contact as well as the use of space and control of communication. Differences in the status of teachers and pupils affect the nonverbal behaviours each project. However, whilst teachers have ascribed power over students, in reality each teacher has to establish her own authority. Drawing on research into the social psychology of schooling and supported with case studies, illustrations and activities, the reader is shown which behaviours characterise authority and those which do not.

## Further reading to support M level study

Telli, S. (2016). Students' perceptions of teachers' interpersonal behaviour across four different school subjects: control is good but affiliation is better. *Teachers and Teaching*, 22(6), 729–744.

This study investigated the extent to which secondary school teachers' interpersonal behaviours are perceived differently by the pupils across different subjects. It further examined whether pupils' perceptions are related to their attitudes towards the subject whilst controlling for differences in pupils' achievement. A sample of 2305 adolescent male and female pupils from grades 9 to 11 and their teachers from one urban high school were surveyed. Using multilevel analysis, differences were found across subjects in respect of perceived control and perceived affiliation. Control was related to positive attitudes in science, literature and language only. In contrast, affiliation was related to positive attitudes across all subjects.

# Chapter 5
# Whole-school influences on behaviour management

## Behaviour policies and consistency in managing behaviour

Classroom management does not exist in a vacuum. The impact of whole-school approaches to behaviour management on how pupils behave in classrooms cannot be overstated. The behaviour policy is the formal representation of how behaviour will be managed throughout a school and should make explicit a school's values, expectations in respect of behaviour, inform practice and be an integral component of the school's organisational climate. The importance of behaviour policies in developing effective schools has been acknowledged for many decades (e.g. Department of Education and Science and the Welsh Office, 1989) and their necessity is firmly housed in recent legislation (Education Act [No2], 1986; Education Act, 1996; Education Act, 1997; School Standards and Framework Act, 1998; and Education and Inspections Act, 2006). The most recent guidance is not dissimilar to its predecessors in requiring 'Headteachers, proprietors and governing bodies must ensure they have a strong behaviour policy to support staff in managing behaviour, including the use of rewards and sanctions' (DfE, 2016: 3).

Taking account of their governing body's statements of behaviour principles, headteacher of maintained schools are required to produce behaviour policies that promote good behaviour, self-discipline and respect; prevent bullying; ensure pupils complete required work; regulate pupils' conduct and set out the disciplinary action that will be taken against pupils who are found to have made malicious accusations against school staff. Proprietors of academies and independent schools are required to ensure that a written policy to promote good behaviour among pupils is drawn up and effectively implemented. Whilst maintained schools must publish their behaviour policy on their website, academies and independent schools are not required to by law but are advised to do so (DfE, 2014a).

Other areas included in behaviour policies are measures introduced in the light of concerns about more challenging behaviour. The first relates to new powers given to teachers in respect of restraint. In the Education and Inspections Act 2006 under section 93, a member of staff may use such force as is reasonable in the circumstances for the purpose of preventing a pupil from:

a   Committing any offence;
b   Causing personal injury to, or damage to the property of, any person (including the pupil himself);
c   Prejudicing the maintenance of good order and discipline at the school or among any pupils receiving education at the school, during a teaching session or otherwise.

The second, introduced in the Education Act 2011, gave teachers the power to search pupils' clothing, bags or lockers for equipment such as mobile phones, iPods, iPads, MP3 players and other electronic gadgets, cigarettes and legal highs. Previously, they could only search for weapons, drugs, alcohol and stolen goods. The Act also provided for no notice detentions. The 2011 Education Act also changed the focus for the Ofsted inspection system, whereby state schools' effectiveness is measured against just four key benchmarks: pupil achievement, teaching quality, leadership and behaviour.

In contributing to a school's overall climate, the importance of getting behaviour policies right to maximise the use of whole-school strategies in collaboratively managing behaviour, cannot be over emphasised. This is not to suggest that activity at the organisational level is superior to or should replace a teacher's classroom control, but that they should be mutually supportive.

In advising on developing behaviour policies, the DfE (2016) states:

… the headteacher should reflect on the following …:
1   A consistent approach to behaviour management;
2   Strong school leadership;
3   Classroom management;
4   Rewards and sanctions;
5   Behaviour strategies and the teaching of good behaviour;
6   Staff development and support;
7   Pupil support systems;
8   Liaison with parents and other agencies;
9   Managing pupil transition; and
10  Organisation and facilities.

(DfE, 2016)

When a behaviour policy is well thought out, understood and generally accepted, proactive and applied consistently by all, it can eliminate or alleviate many minor disruptive behaviours almost 'automatically'. Universal schoolwide routines (for example, assemblies, timetable, movement, lining up, reporting, sanctions, rewards) serve to make visible the expectations and ethos of the school and what it values. The policy should provide the *structure* for behaviour management at the whole-school level, in the classroom and for the type of intervention strategies used for pupils with behaviour difficulties. To be effective, the policy must be supported by consistent application of what the school community (including teachers, support staff, senior leadership team [SLT], governors and pupils) have agreed are appropriate and expected levels of behaviour. Thus, whilst encouraging teachers to have their own style, including how they project themselves as individuals or interact at an interpersonal level, the agreed principles of the behaviour policy should be apparent in the classroom management techniques adopted to ensure consistency across all aspects of school life.

Schools that have significant discrepancies between the expectations of the behaviour policy, its application, how classrooms are managed, or how difficult pupils are supported, are less likely to function efficiently. Those that share a common negotiated agreement, regularly monitor what is happening and can respond quickly to changing demands are likely to function well. Monitoring includes evaluating both operational activity (what people do) and conceptual shift (movement from agreed principles). Policy development should be informed through evaluation of feedback from the 'chalkface' as well as changes imposed by external bodies.

## What is a behaviour policy?

A behaviour policy is a statement of aims, values and principles. It provides operational guidance on putting these aims into action. It should:

- have respect for persons, human rights and responsibilities, as its central tenet;
- facilitate effective learning;
- make the school community feel physically and psychologically safe, secure and predictable;
- specify behavioural expectations;
- encourage contributions from all members of the school community;
- make explicit the rewards for acceptable behaviour;
- make explicit the consequences of unacceptable behaviour;
- include feedback systems to monitor effectiveness and change.

To translate these requirements into a workable document first requires a number of issues to be addressed:

- *Shared meaning*—Ensuring that all parties are aware of what is meant by the content of the policy. In order to ensure a common understanding, where possible expectations should be stated objectively.
- *Ownership*—Behaviour policies should belong to the whole school including governors, professional and ancillary staff, pupils and parents,

all of whom should be encouraged to contribute, support and share ownership and responsibility.
- *Succinctness*—Long-winded and complicated policy statements are usually counterproductive, nebulous and can be the result of weak group decision making. Where possible, keep the content punchy and to the point to aid clarity.
- *Communication*—Unless communicated throughout the school community, the policy will not be worth the paper it is written on. Making the policy explicit through a range of media (e.g. in the school handbook, on the back of all official documents, publicly posted, and through assemblies) on an ongoing basis keeps it in the 'public' eye.
- *Positive*—The emphasis should be on what behaviour is valued and rewarded rather than focusing on negative behaviour.

Whilst all schools are required to have a behaviour policy, effectiveness depends on staff being committed to applying it consistently. Disagreements about its aims and expectations, if seen as ill-conceived or out-of-date, or there is uncertainty about its usefulness, does not make for an effective policy.

## School effectiveness, school improvement and pupil voice

School effectiveness and school improvement have taken centre stage in educational debates over the last 30 years. Much energy is being directed towards increasing school accountability and finding ways to enhance quality control and economic efficiency. Over the last decade, there has been a drive by Ofsted to identify underperforming schools and place them in Special Measures with a goal of raising their effectiveness. This desire for greater school accountability originates from several quarters, including government, parents and the schools themselves. This has also affected the way schools are created and governed with, for example, the introduction of Academies and Free Schools. A primary focus has been on identifying the characteristics of effective schools and developing strategies to improve ineffective ones. It is no surprise that schools differ in their ability to empower young people to succeed. Over three decades ago, Rutter *et al.* (1979) demonstrated that schools produced differential effects in terms of behaviour despite sharing similar catchment areas, staffing and funding. Criteria which distinguished the most effective schools included within school factors such as: good classroom management; the reward system; the school environment; opportunities for pupils to exercise responsibility; shared high expectations; pupil achievement, effective leadership and the importance of good behaviour i.e. maintaining an orderly or well-disciplined environment.

Although the primary emphasis of much school effectiveness research is on academic performance, a number have demonstrated significant differences in social behaviour (Mortimore et al., 1988; Sammons et al., 2007). In a study entitled 'Improving the Urban High School', Louis and Miles (1992) examined the long-term outcomes of the 'effective school' programme. The objectives of these programmes were a focus on strong leadership, a safe and orderly climate, an emphasis on acquiring basic academic skills, high teacher expectations and constant monitoring of pupils' performance. However, whilst almost half of the schools involved reported improved pupil attitudes and behaviour, less than 25% found similar levels of improvement in pupil achievement.

The strategy most commonly used to identify school effectiveness is to isolate internal characteristics (e.g. leadership style, pupil behaviour, climate, teaching styles, academic performance) and external characteristics (e.g. socio-economic status, funding) as the basis for comparison. The ability to identify those characteristics associated with effective schools and superimpose them onto less effective ones would be an attractive approach to school improvement. In practice, this is not as easy as it sounds since, as Gray and Wilcox argued, 'How an "ineffective" school improves may well differ from the ways in which more effective schools maintain their effectiveness' (1994: 2). The factors required to *change* systems are different from those required to *maintain* them.

School effectiveness and school improvement research, although often discussed together, have different methodological roots. In school effectiveness research, the most common approach is quantitative, where comparison is often made using sophisticated statistical analysis of value added to previous academic performance measured between different Key Stages (Goldstein, 1995).

School improvement studies tend to be more interpretative, utilising qualitative approaches. Emphasis here is on developing strategies for change which are grounded in the perspectives of the people involved. A common strategy to studying improvement is to utilise case studies where the emphasis is on detail and 'thick' description. Details of what is actually happening in a school are usually best understood in this way. There have been attempts to link school effectiveness and school improvement approaches (Townsend, 2007) and to working with schools to produce a more in-depth understanding of the research and its implications for practice (Stoll, 1996). However, this generates further difficulties in expanding the number of variations possible between schools, and they cannot be limited to simple responses. As Gray *et al.* (1996) point out, there is a need to obtain a better grasp of each institution's strengths and weaknesses as well as their starting position.

## Pupil voice, behaviour and well-being

Gaining a pupil perspective on school effectiveness and improvement has increasingly been recognised as a potentially valuable contribution. Gray

(1990) identified two simple indicators in addition to academic performance which require attention to pupils' perspectives:

- *Pupil satisfaction*—What proportion of pupils in the school are satisfied with the education they receive?
- *Pupil-teacher relationships*—What proportion of pupils in the school have a good or vital relationship with one or more teachers?

I would add a third: *Pupil well-being* – What proportion of pupils feel that the school helps them to cope emotionally and socially? – an area of considerable importance to the well-being of most pupils. My research into pupil stress highlighted the negative effects of some school structures and organisation on pupils' attitude to work, and well-being (Chaplain, 1996c, 2000a, 2000b), emphasising the nature of the interaction between pupils and their environment in supporting effective coping or generating stress and the same is the case for teachers. In their ongoing longitudinal study of school effects on children's well-being, Gutman and Feinstein (2008) reported that school ethos was associated with pupil mental health and prosocial behaviour. Furthermore, pupil-school organisation fit may be more important for pupils' well-being than is attending a particular school.

In *School Improvement: What can pupils tell us?* Rudduck et al. (1996) argued that too often pupil voice is absent from the literature on school improvement. Those pupils usually invited to contribute are the most academically or socially competent, whereas other groups who are seen as problematic or difficult, but who are equally entitled to offer suggestions are often marginalised. As the above authors (ibid.) point out:

> … if teachers have a view that pupils are adversaries, then it is unlikely that they can unravel the power relationship and convince pupils that they genuinely want to enter into dialogue with them about learning, to hear and take their views seriously …
>
> (1996: 2)

The negative effects of not including all pupils were highlighted by Jamal et al. (2013) in their analysis of 19 research studies. They found consistent evidence that limited involvement of pupils in decision making could result in them feeling they have no 'stake' in their school community, negatively affecting relationships with teachers and encouraging antisocial behaviour, including involvement with health-risk behaviour.

Pupils' perspectives offer an essential dimension to the development of behaviour policies, and this is now formally recognised. The United Nations Convention of the Rights of the Child meant pupils were entitled to have a voice in matters that affected them. As a result, all pupils must be allowed to help shape a school's behaviour policy; however, the government's response was somewhat pedestrian. Their official guidance stated that pupil involvement

> ... need not be laborious or burdensome for the governing body ... class teachers ... could simply talk to their class about the behaviour principles and gather any views.
>
> (DCSf, 2009)

In attempting to understand and utilise research on school improvement, it is imperative not to lose sight of the diversity and interrelatedness of factors involved. Concentrating on one or two initiatives may result in short-term gains but make little real overall or sustainable difference. Change requires attention to what Fullan called 'deeper organisational conditions' (1988: 29). Initiatives concerned with social behaviour, such as anger control for aggressive individuals, circle time to support withdrawn pupils or the use of pupil referral units may be effective for those immediately involved. However, unless social development is viewed as a priority for *all* pupils and it is owned, valued and committed to by the whole school, it remains a superordinate element of schooling – in effect reserved for individuals or groups with difficulties.

## Understanding your school: ethos, climate and culture

Research findings have consistently demonstrated a relationship between effective schools, positive climates and 'good' discipline (Sammons, 1999). In describing the qualities of a positive climate or ethos, Mortimore *et al.* (1988) concluded:

> ... an effective school has a positive ethos. Overall the atmosphere was more pleasant in the effective schools, for a variety of reasons.
>
> Both around the school and within the classroom, less emphasis on punishment and critical control, and a greater emphasis on praise and rewarding pupils had a positive impact. Where teachers actively encouraged self-control on the part of the pupils, rather than emphasising the negative aspects of their behaviour, progress and development increased. What appeared to be important was firm but fair classroom management.
>
> Outside the classroom evidence of a positive climate included: the organisation of lunchtime and afternoon clubs for pupils; teachers eating their lunch at the same tables as the pupils; organisation of trips and visits and the utilisation of the local environment as a learning resource ...
>
> The working conditions of teachers contributed to the creation of a positive school climate. Where teachers had non-teaching periods, the impact on pupil progress and development was positive. Thus, the climate

created by the teachers for the pupils and by the head for the teachers, was an important aspect of the school's effectiveness. This further appeared to be reflected in effective schools by happy, well-behaved pupils who were friendly towards each other and outsiders, and by the absence of graffiti around the school.

(1988: 122)

Mortimore's comments on the importance of generating a positive school climate by having an emphasis on rewarding desired behaviour as opposed to an emphasis on punishing undesirable reflected observations made earlier by Rutter et al. (1979). He and his team's seminal study of inner-city secondary schools followed 2,000 pupils from 12 schools over five years, recording the schools' effectiveness in terms of pupils' academic performance and behaviour. One particularly interesting finding was that, whilst schools differed in the types of punishment and reward used, on average punishment was used twice as often as reward. Furthermore, whilst punishment was unrelated to behaviour, reward was related to better behaviour.

Ethos, or school climate, is a popular term within the education community, and, whilst there are a number of definitions, most refer to the overall atmosphere of the school or how a school 'feels' (Mortimore, 1988) and contributes to school effectiveness (Bragg and Manchester, 2011) and 'good' behaviour (Gavienas and White, 2008). For Rutter et al. (1979) successful schools were pleasant working environments with an emphasis on learning and encouragement of personal responsibility in pupils. More recently, Cohen et al. suggested that a school's climate

> ... refers to the quality and character of school life. School climate is based on patterns of people's experiences of school life and reflects norms, goals, values, interpersonal relationships, teaching and learning practices, and organisational structures. This climate includes norms, values, and expectations that support people feeling socially, emotionally, and physically safe. People are engaged and respected.
>
> (2009: 182)

But beyond artefacts and interpersonal relationships, ethos also includes tacit assumptions about values and purpose – a school's climate can often be *sensed* upon entering the building.

Producing a 'good' climate in schools that deters antisocial behaviour (including violence) and promotes prosocial behaviour requires quality ongoing teacher education, peer support systems and enhanced personal and social education. It also requires attention to structural issues such as school security and communication systems (Smith, 2004).

A school's climate can help promote resilience in its pupils through the provision of a safe, clean, and orderly physical environment. However, a larger contribution is made through the interpersonal relationships between children (and their families) and teachers and in the pupils academic and social development (Esposito, 1999). Pupils are likely to be more resilient in schools where they experience belongingness, which, according to Osterman (2000), is a sense of relatedness, membership and community. Pupils who experience belongingness have more positive attitudes, are more engaged with learning, and participate in a wide range of school activities. Teacher-pupil relationships that are positive, and support pupils' adjustment to school, enhance their social skills, encourage academic mastery and nurture resiliency result in prosocial behaviour. In contrast, where relationships between teachers and pupils are negative (conflict and dependency) the opposite is the case, and this can have long-term negative outcomes. For instance, negative teacher-pupil relationships in kindergarten have been found to predictive of behaviour difficulties in secondary school, especially for boys (e.g. Hamre and Pianta, 2001; Rudasill *et al.*, 2010).

However, understanding why behaviour varies between schools – including numbers of pupils excluded for being disruptive – requires acknowledgement of wider issues which contribute to ethos. Examples include: regional socio-economic status (including social and educational disadvantage); the size and type of school; its governance and resources; pupil characteristics such as age, sex, ethnicity, social class, and family circumstances; and numbers of pupils with special educational needs.

Organisational climate differs from 'organisational culture' and is considered more analogous to morale or the quality of the internal environment of the organisation as experienced by its members, and which influences their behaviour (Taguiri, 1968). It is '… a relatively enduring quality of the school environment that is experienced by participants, affects their behaviour, and is based on their collective perceptions of behaviour in schools' (Hoy and Miskel, 1991: 212). Organisational culture on the other hand, has anthropological roots and concerns 'shared orientations that hold the unit together and give it a distinct identity' (ibid.).

One distinction between climate and culture is marked by the way they are measured. Typically, research on climate has used multivariate statistical analyses, whereas culture has been assessed using ethnographic approaches – methodological differences that have created a tension. Hoy (1990) argues that tension between the two approaches represents a healthy competition that should expand our knowledge of schools, something best achieved by allowing both traditions the opportunity to flourish. Much early work on organisational climate was carried out in educational institutions by Stern (1970), who went on to apply his findings to industrial contexts, looking at the relationship between personality and perceptions of the organisational climate. It is commonly accepted that an effective school needs a positive organisational climate, but measuring it is complex. Direct measures involve gathering data from pupils, staff and parents, typically through scales, questionnaires, interviews, or focus groups. Indirect measures include pupil attendance, behaviour (e.g. number of suspensions and exclusions) and staff turnover. They may also include physical condition of the building or displays of pupils' achievement or academic work.

Scales have been developed to measure organisational climate (Halpin and Croft, 1963; Brookover *et al.*, 1979) from which was developed the concept of loose- and tight-coupled school climates. Tight-coupled schools are highly centralised and formal (Hoy *et al.*, 1991), a tightly knit and closely related environment focused on organisational goals. In loose-coupled schools, there is more independence and less central control, with upper and lower phases and individual classrooms preserving their own identity (Weick, 1976). Murphy (1992) argued that effective schools are more tightly linked, operating as an organic whole with greater consistency than ineffective schools. Creemers and Reezigt (1996) endorsed this view by identifying four criteria present in effective schools (consistency, cohesion, constancy and control) – features associated with tight-coupled schools.

The Occupational Climate Description Questionnaire (OCDQ-RE) (Hoy *et al.*, 1991) distinguishes between open and closed climates by rating levels of supportive headteacher behaviour (helpful, concerned), directive headteacher behaviour (rigid and domineering), engaged teacher behaviour (proud of school, support each other), and disengaged teacher behaviour (overrun with routine and administration). In open climates, issues such as managing behaviour and teacher stress will be discussed, whereas in closed climates they are likely to be ignored. The questionnaire is designed for school self-assessment and for organisational development.

More recently Hoy *et al.* (2002) produced an Organisational Climate Index (OCI) – a short measure of organisational climate in schools. It contains 30 questions organised over four dimensions: leadership, teacher professionalism, pupil achievement, and school vulnerability to outside pressures (e.g. parents and other groups).

Open systems approaches (Open Systems Group, 1981) to organisational behaviour advocate a tight and focused environment committed to the overall purpose of the organisation. They provide a model for analysing the different subcomponents of an organisation that contribute to its overall structure. The organisation interacts with its environment, taking in information and resources as inputs and transforming them by various processes into outputs into the environment (Nadler and Tushman, 1980). In school, *inputs* include pupils, staff and the building; *processes* the teaching and learning and the *outputs* educated pupils (see Figure 5.1). Applying a systems approach to schools raises important questions regarding the purpose of schooling, achievement targets, and criteria which indicate success.

Table 5.1 shows in more detail the various types of data which can be collected and used to gain an understanding of strengths and weaknesses of a school generally and also in respect of social behaviour in particular.

Breaking down systems in this way enables identification of areas for development and an appreciation of the interrelatedness and interdependency

```
                    Feedback
        ┌─────────────────────────────────┐
        │                                 │
        ▼                                 │
    ┌───────┐       ┌─────────┐       ┌────────┐
    │ Input │  ──▶  │ Process │  ──▶  │ Output │
    └───────┘       └─────────┘       └────────┘
```

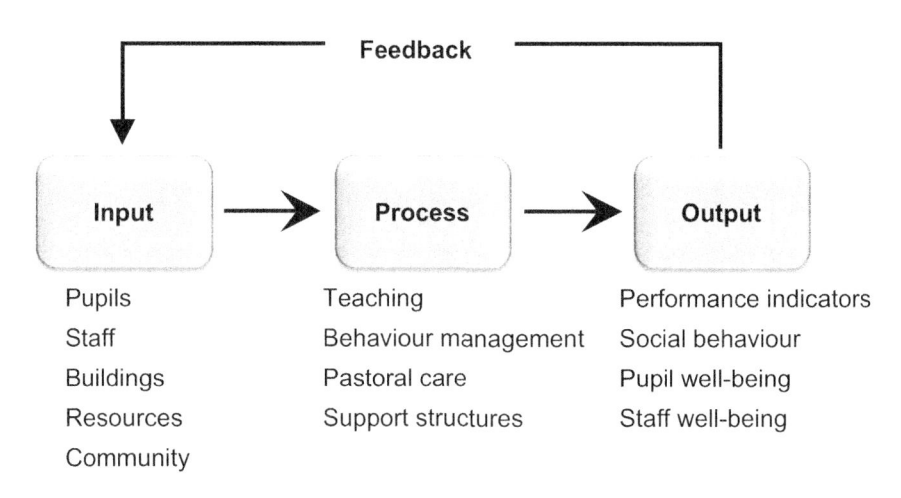

| Input | Process | Output |
|---|---|---|
| Pupils | Teaching | Performance indicators |
| Staff | Behaviour management | Social behaviour |
| Buildings | Pastoral care | Pupil well-being |
| Resources | Support structures | Staff well-being |
| Community | | |

*Figure 5.1* A simple systems model.

of the various component parts of the organisation, including phases. Whilst systems thinking presents schools as rational and predictable organisations, consistency, harmony and cohesion are not always evident between and within various different areas of the school or in classrooms. Furthermore, measuring some of the variables can be difficult, so individual schools need to decide how to quantify the quality of relationships or what constitutes acceptable behaviour. Stern (1970) suggested that climate could be measured by asking what proportion of the organisation agree or disagree with a particular description of a climate to justify describing it in that way, known as the aggregation issue. The more people that agree (or disagree) the more accurate the estimate of the climate is likely to be. He argued that 66% was an appropriate level of agreement; others have suggested it should be significantly more. Clearly, this approach personalises the measurement, grounding it in the population it serves. Irrespective of its critics, recording and analysing the data in this way forces discussion and critical thinking about what the school means to those who work there and, in that way, can be very positive.

A further issue in measuring climate arises from differences in perceptions at different levels of the hierarchy. Within schools there are likely to be different micro climates (e.g. subject departments, year groups), which may differ from the overall climate. For example, do teachers in the mathematics department share a similar view of the school climate to those of the drama department? Do non-teaching staff share the same view as teachers? Do parents and pupils and subgroups of both share similar views? Payne (1990) argued that subgroup agreement was only likely where a 'group' shared a common social identity and hence, where agreement was likely to help an individual to be supported by that group. Since subgroups are competing for

Table 5.1 A simple systems analysis of inputs, processes and outcomes

| Level of analysis | Focus | General example | Behaviour-related example |
|---|---|---|---|
| Inputs | Staff, pupils, building, curriculum. | Personal qualities of the staff and management (qualifications, personality, training, experience); levels of compatibility and person-environment fit; qualities of the pupils; quality and care of the buildings. | Pupils' backgrounds; community stability or change (e.g. large-scale redundancy; industrial/commercial growth; a major influx of socially excluded groups, SEN); staff specialist training (e.g. behaviour difficulties); staff cohesiveness; previous success of the school in managing behaviour; behaviour policy. |
| Processes | What happens in school. | Teaching methods; classroom organisation; sanctions; teacher and pupil support systems; extra-curricular activities. | Quality of interpersonal relationships between staff and pupils; level of parental support; discipline measures and rewards; in-school support systems; SEND provision, pastoral systems. |
| Outcomes | Short- and long-term effects on the behaviour and development of members of the school. | League tables; social behaviour; value added; inspection ratings; exam performance. | Numbers excluded; parental satisfaction; complaints from the local community; number of police visits; school appearance; pupils' satisfaction and motivation; staff turnover; job satisfaction and well-being. |

Notes
Column 3 shows general outcomes;
Column 4 shows those concerned with behaviour. However, many of the behaviour-related and general outcomes overlap, the above are merely offered as illustrative examples.

limited resources in school, there is always a potential for intergroup conflict that may undermine consistency in managing behaviour.

A positive climate is also represented through staff having a sense of community in which they feel supported and enjoy a diffuse role that brings them into contact with other adults in settings outside the classroom (Bryk and Driscoll, 1988). A shared commitment to organisational goals, staff well-being and recognition of personal goals and development can be supported through:

- making the work environment stimulating and engaging;
- opportunities for staff to make their own decisions and show initiative;
- encouraging new ideas and suggestions for improving the organisation;
- mutual trust;
- a dynamic but secure atmosphere;
- a sense of humour;
- encouraging different perspectives on behaviour;
- providing differentiated and appropriate social support;
- delegating responsibility and a preparedness to take risks;
- recognition of effort; and
- open and adequate communications between all levels of staff, pupils and their carers.

## Organisational climate and effective communication

The quality of communication in a school and its organisational climate have been described as mutually reinforcing. As Wilkinson and Cave proposed:

> The effectiveness of communication depends to a considerable extent on a favourable climate in the school. Conversely, the climate of the school depends largely on the quality of communication. Good morale, a feeling of confidence and a spirit of cooperation are unlikely to exist if there are continuing and frequent communication barriers and breakdowns. Thus, communication both creates and is influenced by the prevailing climate of the school.
>
> (1987: 139)

Too little or too much communication has been shown to be a source of conflict in organisations (Furnham, 2005). The method of communicating in a school is an indicator of the quality of interpersonal relationships. Death by a thousand memos usually suggests relationships are not good – people have stopped discussing issues, for whatever reason. We now live in a world where continual bombardment by a range of instant communication is the norm (social media, email, smartphones), all of which discourage talking and listening and seem to demand instant responses. It is probably true to say that, if anything, we receive too much information. Whilst we do not necessarily want to be distracted from whatever we are doing, some forms of communication suggest we should. Being interrupted when you are teaching by a note-wielding pupil when you have just managed to get your class settled is not relished since minimally it means valuable teaching time may be lost. Within a school, communication is multifaceted, and it is important to match the type of communication to the issue in focus. In most schools, information moves from top down and (usually less often) bottom up within the hierarchy, and sideways among colleagues as well as within and between phases.

Communication is a repeated concern in this book because of its role in:

- conveying expectations;
- persuasion, negotiation and conflict resolution;
- ensuring the smooth running of the system;
- learning; and
- managing behaviour.

With regard to behaviour management, there are three essential considerations in respect of communication:

- *Speed*—Some information needs to be communicated rapidly – a serious incident (e.g. physical assault), for instance. Others, such as calling a meeting to review the behaviour policy, is less urgent. However, in some schools, the levels of urgency seem undifferentiated. Being continually interrupted by pupils sent by colleagues or senior staff to announce a social event or changed agenda can unwittingly create unnecessary management problems for teachers, especially those establishing their authority.
- *Type*—Which means of communication to use should again be determined by the context. In the event of a serious incident, a verbal, face-to-face message (sending someone to get help) or some electronic form (bell or mobile) is probably the most appropriate.
- *Audience*—Who needs to know, when and how does the communication need to be recorded? In dealing with behaviour issues and not necessarily extreme behaviour, it is useful to think about ways of communicating potential problems or tense situations, as well as what to do when things have gone seriously wrong.

Some years ago, I was in a school for pupils with emotional and behavioural difficulties that had alarm buttons fitted in each classroom. No one seemed to know who had decided to have them fitted or was clear about when they should be used. New staff were merely told, 'This is the alarm button, which you can use if you have problems controlling the pupils'. Several staff were keen to tell me the story of a young teacher who, during his first week, was having problems with a group of pupils and had pressed the button. To his

Whole-school influences on behaviour management 119

horror, his actions triggered off a series of alarms, following which an army of teachers and a cook, complete with utensils, arrived at his classroom door. The humiliation of the poor unsuspecting teacher, who thought pressing the bell merely alerted a senior colleague, was complete when he had to explain the assembled rescue battalion that the emergency was little more than a group of Year 10 pupils being cheeky and refusing to work.

As a system of communication, it was quick and effective in getting attention, whether it was appropriate is more questionable, and the audience was certainly not who he had expected and somewhat larger than he anticipated! The main problem arose from an initial lack of information during induction where staff should have been made aware of under what circumstances it should be used, and how it would be responded to if activated. It later emerged that, far from being a planned response, staff had merely followed each other.

## Getting the message across: communication networks

Cole (1996) described different types of communication networks (Figure 5.2) that may exist in organisations, indicating which are likely to be most effective under different conditions. Which method of communication is used in a school often reflects management style and the size of the organisation.

In many schools, communication is hierarchical; for example, the chain arrangement that permits downward and, albeit less common, upward communication. The chain and wheel networks are evident in organisations

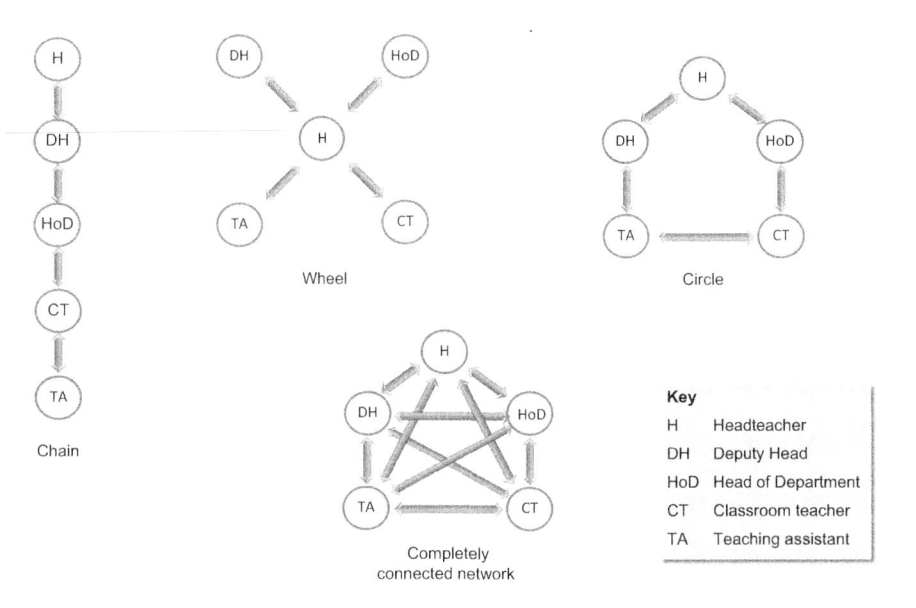

*Figure 5.2* Communication networks.

with mechanistic approaches (Cole, 1996). The wheel is the most structured and centralised pattern because each member can communicate with only one other person e.g. the headteacher in the centre. In a chain network only two people communicate with one another, and in turn each have only one person to whom they communicate, e.g. headteacher to deputy to coordinator to classroom teacher. Whilst chain and wheel have an ordered sequence and reduce time demands on senior managers, they are not the most effective way of communicating *all* information. For example, dealing with serious incidents requiring immediate responses. Under such circumstances, either a circle or completely connected network within designated areas of the school is likely to be most efficient, since both allow for multidirectional communication. The circle gives horizontal and decentralised communication with all staff having equal communication opportunities. The completely connected network is an extension of the circle network connecting everyone in the circle network.

Which type of communication network exists in a school will affect the speed of response, which is likely to have implications for a teacher's perceptions of how supported they are likely to feel when under pressure. A teacher who, when dealing with a difficult individual, knows they can quickly communicate a worsening situation to any one of a number of primed individuals, is likely to feel more confident and cope more effectively than someone who feels they have to communicate with a specific member of staff who may not be available at that time. Whilst a senior manager may have overall operational responsibility for behaviour management in a large school, supporting the interests of everybody simultaneously is not possible. Delegating responsibility (formally and informally) to individuals within teams who are available to support directly, but who meet as a group with the senior manager to provide feedback on concerns and needs, is one way of overcoming this problem. Some secondary schools now employ designated school behaviour coordinators and behaviour management support teams who circulate around classrooms to provide ongoing monitoring of behaviour and provide support throughout the school day.

## Communication under pressure: coping with difficult situations

When dealing with difficult pupils, it is easy to react too quickly, when emotions are running high, without due consideration of all the facts. Similarly, managers asking staff to deal with a challenging situation when already under pressure is unreasonable. The 'hot' emotional nature of such encounters tends to override 'cold' cognitive problem solving, sometimes with disastrous results as the situation spirals out of control. Organisations that rely on reacting to behaviour problems, forcing staff to make decisions whilst off guard, are not well managed and result in poor decision making and dissatisfied staff.

Much communication in schools is by word of mouth or informal notes. Although both are quick, they are prone to distortion and misinterpretation. I learnt early in my school managerial career that recording difficult situations in a written form during or immediately after an event and sending a copy to the person or people involved as verification of what we both understood to have happened was a useful safeguard against misinterpretation later. Similarly, incidents involving pupils and/or their families should always be recorded in writing at the time, or as near as possible afterwards, in case further problems arise.

When reporting problem encounters, keep the report objective, the language simple, non-judgmental and to the point. State the facts as you understand them and immediately record the names and observations of any witnesses. Where relevant, note any antecedents to the incident, the incident itself and what happened afterwards. It is likely you will want to share your observations with your manager, but, whatever you do, always keep a copy along with details of what you sent to others and when. Keeping such accurate records is time consuming and may sound a little dramatic, but it is an intelligent way of protecting yourself and your school should there be a problem at a later date.

Meetings with parents of difficult children can be quite harrowing. They are often (understandably) defensive if called into school to account for their child's misbehaviour. The defensive reaction may result from feeling embarrassed or angry. Parents in this position often feel like a naughty child themselves and may start acting like one: shouting, swearing, refusing to listen to the complaint, offering excuses and displacing responsibility for the problem elsewhere (other pupils or staff). Deflecting attention to other issues allows them to take control of their own situation. Only ever being invited to the school to be told how badly behaved your child is does not make school a community to which you seek to belong – certainly not in the same way as those parents whose children are behaving as required.

Dealing effectively with hostile, angry people requires exceptional social skills and emotional control. Many such encounters are one on one. The National Association of Head Teachers issued advice to schools on how to prepare for dealing effectively with angry parents and abusive visitors in school (www.naht.org.uk). You should make yourself aware of what your school's policy is in this respect. Angry parents should not have direct access to teaching areas and teachers. Stopping them doing so requires looking at procedures for receiving people into the school. Where staff are expecting a parent under difficult circumstances, advance arrangements can be made; however, some inevitably arrive unexpectedly. The sensible use of time delays can start diffusion of the aggression process, allowing people to calm down, but not forgetting that keeping people waiting too long can exacerbate the situation. Whilst a good well-briefed and prepared receptionist can usually achieve this, there should be a backup system which involves a designated member of the teaching/management staff who can be stealthily alerted that their help is required. For instance, if the receptionist feels that the waiting parent is getting more agitated, then calling the designated member of staff and saying, 'Mr Hawk called earlier, could you ring back' – *Hawk* being used as the trigger that their presence is needed at reception in a calm way. Having space in school for dealing with visitors away from pupils and other distractions helps avoid public embarrassment. Designing feedforward or anticipatory strategies, where a best estimate of what ought to be expected and how to respond when it does not occur, is the most effective way of dealing with difficult behaviour. However, reactive methods are inevitable where things are not going as they should. Being organised in advance for difficult events by developing and rehearsing procedures and strategies when not under pressure is the most effective way of being prepared.

## Balancing individual and organisational needs

Teachers having difficulties managing behaviour can often be judged as personally incompetent. However, to understand why an individual is having difficulties needs to be understood in relation to the context. Whilst teaching is not for everybody, having completed a training course and assuming they genuinely met the criteria to pass should be some indication that they are capable of teaching at some level. That being the case, a teacher struggling in one school where the leadership style and nature of collegiate support is not conducive to their personal style may well flourish in another school operated differently. This can be explained in part by understanding the construct person–organisation fit.

Person–organisation fit (Verquer *et al.*, 2003) concerns the degree to which an individual's dispositions, abilities, expectations and performance match the demands and expectations of the school. Each individual teacher has a set of dispositional characteristics, expectations, skills and experiences which she or he brings to a job. At the same time, the school (including governors, SLT, other teachers and support staff, pupils and their parents) will also have expectations and demands of that teacher. The degree to which there is synonymy between what a teacher provides to, and expects from, their school and what the school expects from, and provides to, the teacher, the higher the degree of person–organisation fit (see Figure 5.3). In situations where person–organisation fit has been identified as poor, a number of negative outcomes have been measured, including stress, job dissatisfaction and lower job performance. For instance, a teacher who feels the school's expectations regarding behaviour management are not compatible with their own values and beliefs is unlikely to function well. In contrast, where the person–organisation fit is good, the individual is likely to be more motivated and experience higher levels of job satisfaction. Moving to another school with a different *modus operandi* may significantly change how the teacher feels about themselves, their self-efficacy, their support and how they relate to others.

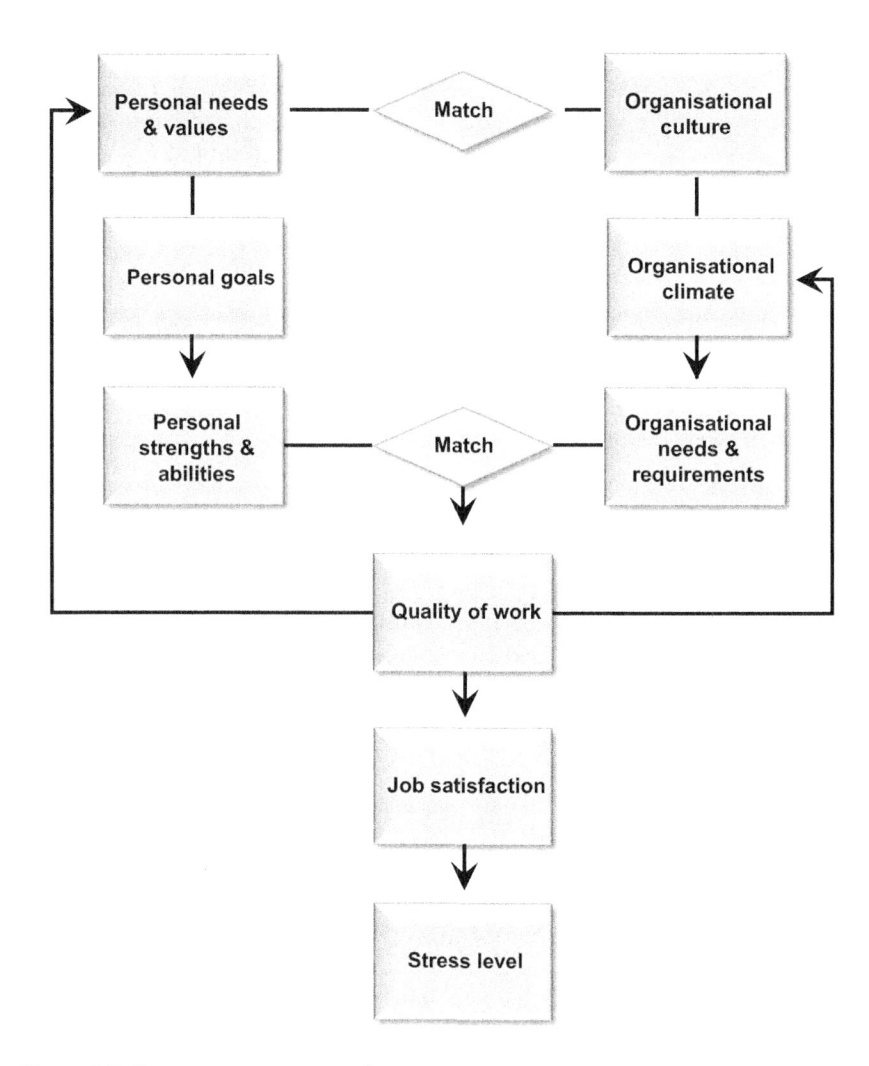

Figure 5.3 Person-environment fit.

Furthermore, whilst you may 'fit well' at one point in time, organisational changes to management (new head), structure (new legislative requirements), the pupil population (amalgamation of two schools) or you (marriage, divorce, training) can create imbalance at the individual, group or organisational level, creating disruption. A new head will inevitably differ from their predecessor, will have different expectations and different ways of working with staff, which may enhance or inhibit your performance. She or he may want to change the ethos of the school and may have been recruited specifically for that purpose.

Many advertisements for teachers ask for 'a good team player', but what constitutes being a good team player is not universal. Some teams require innovation and management of change, whilst others need to maintain or stabilise existing school climates, and each require different qualities. Furthermore, as schools develop, different qualities are required to cope with change from new initiatives and demands, which can threaten established group dynamics and expose weaknesses.

Taking time to understand the relationship between what a school values in respect of behaviour and how those values translate into practice is a worthwhile endeavour for anyone working in a school whatever their status. An effective school behaviour policy can have a positive impact on classroom management and support staff in their interactions with pupils. An ineffective policy can undermine classroom management and result in negative effects on teachers' well-being.

## Annotated further reading

Hallam, S., Rogers, L., Castle, F., Creech, A., Rhamie, J., and Kokatsaki, D. (2005). *Research and evaluation of the Behaviour Improvement Programme*. London: Department for Education and Skills (DfES).

This study reports the findings of an investigation into the effectiveness of the DfES funded Behaviour Improvement Plans (BIP). The scheme involved 34 local education authorities and was intended to support measures to improve overall standards of pupil behaviour and reduce unauthorised absence in secondary schools. Central to the approach was developing whole-school behaviour policies, raising staff skills and confidence in managing behaviour and introducing Behaviour and Education Support Teams (BESTs) – which drew together the full range of specialist support for vulnerable pupils and their families. The results indicated that the programme had a major impact on pupils' experiences in school, leading them to want to attend. There was also evidence of improved behaviour both in and out of classes and across schools.

## Further reading to support M level study

Deakin, J., and Kupchik, A. (2016). Tough choices: school behaviour management and institutional context. *Youth Justice*, 16(3), 280–298.

The policies adopted by schools with regard to punishment, exclusion and how challenging pupils are supported differ, which has a direct influence on the perceptions of staff working therein. This study focused on differences in staffs' perceptions of school discipline comparing those working in mainstream with those working in special contexts based in the United States and the United Kingdom. In both countries, there was considerable variation in how mainstream schools and alternative schools felt about punishment, the methods used to manage student behaviour and how pupils were supported. These variations are linked to organisational and structural differences, their objectives, resources and pressures they faced. Contemporary mainstream schools operate under pressure from market competition and performance monitoring. In contrast, alternative schooling is largely immune for such pressures apart from budgetary restrictions. The results raise a number of questions about the impact of different behaviour management approaches on children's experiences, particularly when pupils move between mainstream and alternative schools.

# Chapter 6
# Leadership and positive behaviour

According to Bush and Glover (2014), leadership is second only to classroom teaching in its potential to generate improvements in outcomes for pupils. The central role of the headteacher in the professional leadership of effective schools is well established (Sammons, 1999). As Gray makes clear, 'the importance of the headteacher's leadership is one of the clearest of the messages in school effectiveness research' (1990: 214). Leithwood *et al.* (2006) reported that no documented cases exist of schools being turned around successfully without talented leaders. However, given the size of most secondary schools, effective leadership is not exclusively the responsibility of the headteacher.

As MacBeath (1998) pointed out, in the UK most research energy focused on the importance of the head despite increased evidence stressing the advantages of a dispersed leadership. Silins and Mulford (2002) add further weight to this position, arguing that outcomes for pupils tend to be more significant where leadership decision making is distributed among the school community, including empowering teachers to make decisions in areas important to them.

The senior leadership team (SLT) is responsible for strategic planning, determining the future direction of the school and school improvement (leadership); staff related issues, financial control, health and safety, pupils' assessment, examinations and behaviour (management); administration and teaching. It suffices to say that all four elements make important contributions to creating and maintaining a well-behaved school.

Getting the balance right between the various elements in order to produce an effective school presents a challenge for leaders, as Dimmock pointed out:

> School leaders [experience] tensions between competing elements of leadership, management and administration. Irrespective of how these terms are defined, school leaders experience difficulty in deciding the balance between higher order tasks designed to improve staff, student and school performance (leadership), routine maintenance of present operations (management) and lower order duties (administration).
> (1999: 442)

Given the vast differences in the size, structure and governance of secondary schools, the proportions of these responsibilities and the numbers and designations of those responsible will vary considerably. It is beyond the scope of this single chapter to cover all variants.

Being proactive in the development of an effective behaviour policy and ensuring staff have appropriate professional development, support and resources to operate the policy at all levels, all form part of the leadership component. Monitoring and supporting the behaviour policy and classroom management, having a presence around the school (in teaching and recreational areas), being sensitive to the concerns and difficulties of staff, and being able to step up a gear when things are not going too well or at critical points in the school's development are all part of the management function.

A recent study by Ofsted found that teachers in a number of schools were concerned about the lack of support provided by some SLTs in respect of behaviour management. They commented that a number of teachers felt:

> … [that the] headteacher could do more to ensure that other staff applied policies consistently. This suggests that teachers are aware of internal variations in their own school and want senior leaders, who should be monitoring and taking more effective action, to take more responsibility for putting a stop to this.
>
> (Ofsted, 2014: 15)

Furthermore, headteachers who deliver school improvement have a no-compromise approach and 'will accept nothing less than good behaviour from all pupils' (Ofsted, 2012: 4). The SLT in such schools 'demonstrated how they wanted inappropriate behaviour dealt with, and raised expectations among pupils of how to behave' (ibid.: 6).

## Individual differences and management style

A belief persists that, in order to be effective, a headteacher must have particular dispositional qualities. However, the idea that a head, or indeed the SLT must share some common individual trait-like characteristics is overly simplistic.

Anyone who has experience of working with different headteachers will realise that, whilst individual characteristics are important, different contexts call for different leadership styles and personal qualities. No single style of leadership is universally appropriate for all schools (Bossert et al., 1982). Whilst some leaders may be powerfully charismatic or extrovert, not all are. Headteachers differ substantially at the personal and interpersonal level, as well as in terms of how they organise and lead their schools – idiosyncrasies that work well in one situation are not guaranteed to do likewise in another. Leadership behaviour welcomed at one stage of a school's development, would be extremely unpopular at a different stage of development. My own experiences, as a headteacher, and, in recent years, working with heads as consultant and as researcher, have reinforced these beliefs.

Sammons (1999) suggests three characteristics are frequently cited in the research literature: strength of purpose, involving other staff in decision making, and professional authority over teaching and learning. Identifying and developing these qualities is a *raison d'être* for organisational psychology and related disciplines, and there is substantial literature examining this area, some of which will be referred to later in this chapter.

## Blame it on the boss

When I ask groups of teachers what they expect of a headteacher (or head of department), I usually end up with long lists that include: senior teacher, leading professional, manager, leader, supervisor, accountant, trouble-shooter, chief executive, politician, ultimate behaviour sanction, facilitator. This diversity is not unlike the lengthy list one obtains when asking what is expected of a teacher – educator, social worker, counsellor, etc. – it seems that we expect a great deal from those working in education. In practice, any one or all of them could apply at any one time, depending on a range of variables including: the climate of the school, its values, stage of development, the perceptions and skills of the staff and the relationships between them – as well as external pressures.

As one head once said to me:

> They expect me to be all things, at all times, when it suits them! Like me to take the flack and lead the way when things aren't so good, but want me out of the way when they are—it's a bit like being a dad really.
> 
> (Jim, nine years' experience as a head)

Jim went on to say that he sometimes felt put out when, having dealt with something complex and often unpleasant, there seemed few words of praise for him and yet 'it seems staff expect to be told how well they are doing all the time'. It is not uncommon for employees in any organisation to question the role of and criticise their managers, and schools are no exception – staff, knowing more about the day-to-day running of their classroom, resent heads telling them how to do their job.

The process of claiming credit for all things good and externalising failure is known in social psychology as self-serving attributional bias (see Chapter 3). Blaming management when things go wrong can be an effective expedient coping strategy, whether true or not. Not being seen as personally responsible for failing to cope limits damage to your professional self – provided the explanation 'appears' credible. Whilst such a coping strategy may be ego protecting, it is likely to be short-lived. Furthermore, it does not help you to deal directly with the problem, since externalising responsibility puts the problem outside of your control (you probably cannot change this 'inefficient manager'). With managing pupil behaviour, it is highly improbable that blame can be ascribed to one individual – however convenient that may appear. The head, the pupil(s), other colleagues, parents will also be looking for an explanation that will probably include the teacher! Such misunderstandings and distorted perspectives can create negative cycles of blame that work against developing positive relationships and solving the difficulty.

## Low and high profile management: keeping everybody happy

A former headteacher colleague of mine, a man not renowned for sugar-coating his comments, once said:

> A good head should be part of the furniture when things are going well—almost invisible—just tweaking the knobs to keep things running smoothly. But when—as it's bound to at some point in this game—the shit hits the fan, they have to be capable of rising to the challenge and grasping the nettle'.
>
> (John, 20 years' experience as a head)

Bouncing between being 'almost invisible' and 'grasping the nettle' is not an unusual experience for many heads and is often expected by staff. Getting the balance right between the two ways of operating is difficult and, if not achieved, can be stressful for both the head and the staff.

Jones (1988) argued that historically the role of the head was perceived as 'simultaneously loved and hated, revered and ridiculed, powerful and naïve'; she went on to ask whether much had changed following the redefinition of the head as manager and chief executive. It has been long established by successive governments that leadership is a central component of school management and the group announced in the Green Paper on Leadership made this clear (DfEE, 1998). However, the degree to which a good manager also makes a good leader and vice versa is not always as clear.

In recent years, the move towards increased local management of schools and additional responsibilities for the controlled spending of large amounts of money have brought about changes to the general understanding of the head's role. On the one hand, more 'power' or responsibility has been given to schools; on the other, government directives have reduced autonomy by controlling key areas such as curriculum content and policies. Heads sometimes feel that staff do not appreciate the pressure put upon them, as the following quotes illustrate:

> The staff do not appreciate all the other demands on my time. Sure I would like to have more time for informal and professional talk, but

there are not enough hours in the day especially with the [new] building problems. They just don't appreciate what I am going through.

(Christine)

I can't understand why they [the staff] can't or won't accept my job is to manage and this can involve making unpleasant decisions. I can rise above it but I would rather have a more pleasant atmosphere.

(Jeffrey)
(Chaplain, 2001)

Differences in the size of schools invariably means wide discrepancies between them in terms of the nature of the relationship between SLT, teachers and other staff. It is not possible for a head to spend as much time with staff or pupils in a school with more than 1,500 pupils and its complement of staff compared to one with less than 500, and expectations on the part of head and staff should reflect this. In reality, this is not always the case (Chaplain, 1995). Heads often claim that the best part of their job is being with pupils, what Jones (1988) referred to as the 'wistful nostalgia ... about when they knew how to teach well, and make good relationships with pupils', but in practice they now have limited amounts of time to do so. The belief that the head should be a super teacher and demonstrate his or her classroom craft to other teachers seems somewhat strange, particularly in larger settings, given the number and diversity of other demands – (not forgetting the substantive teaching role of heads in some secondary schools). Nevertheless, heads recognise the popular belief that they must be viewed as experienced teachers. As Hustler *et al.* put it, 'governing bodies and especially parents on those bodies ... will want a head who has had a lot of experience as a teacher', (1995: 127) but there are limits to the amount of time they can spare, given 'headteachers have been increasingly taken out of the classroom' (ibid.: 139). With the best will in the world, the head of a large or medium sized school is going to be limited in the amount of time they can spend working directly with pupils. Invariably heads step in and fill the gap when there are shortages; however, whilst such activity offers a short-term solution for teachers, it is questionable whether it makes best use of a manager's time.

When things are running well in a school with pupils behaving appropriately, working on legitimate tasks and causing minimal disruption, low-profile monitoring is probably the most useful response. If the going gets tough, or the school is undergoing significant change, then a more visible presence and hands on approach is more usually needed. However, this is clearly an oversimplification for, if the head is spending more time at the 'chalkface', troubleshooting and making his or her presence felt, then it should not be at the expense of other vital leadership duties. Heads are often likened to the captain of a ship, but as Gray and Freeman (1988) pointed out, the captain of a ship does a very different job to the sailors – and furthermore, the ship would not get very far if the captain did not.

People differ quite markedly, and are often diametrically opposed in their perceptions of what constitutes an effective and supportive head and SLT. Nias (1986) offered multiple, and contrasting, accounts from similarly experienced teachers in different schools regarding their positive and negative perceptions of their heads. In many circumstances, these contrasts reflected either loose or tight-coupled organisational management. Some expressed dissatisfaction with 'passive' heads who seemed to respond too quickly to change. Three teachers described their feelings about such headteachers: 'He always seemed to be changing his ideas ... there was no sense or aim in the school, no philosophy'; 'The general attitude in the school is "you do what you think", and that's not very helpful when you have problems'; 'There was no ultimate purpose in what we did. ... As long as we didn't annoy the parents or let the kids get too noisy, the head didn't seem interested'.

In contrast, what was labelled the 'positive' head was often revered for 'setting the direction of the school and leading the way ... an old-fashioned patriarch ... who put them under quite strong pressure to conform in certain ways ... made the place full of certainties ... and a good place to start in', nevertheless there were drawbacks. For example, whilst many wanted the head to lead on formulating aims and policies: 'he should not take this entirely upon himself' nor 'deny staff a part in decision making'. Where this was not happening, it could lead to major job dissatisfaction and disaffection as one teacher said: 'all she (head) really wants from the staff and children is obedience. That's really why I'm giving up. I don't feel I have anything to contribute'. Another teacher spoke of 'smouldering in silence' at staff meetings and of the head 'not being interested in anything they had to say'. Many talked of 'mock democracy' and of staff meetings that were 'disguised dictatorships'.

A dilemma for heads, in deciding to extend power sharing and control with others, is the fear of letting go or delegating responsibility. As one head confided 'I need to become more comfortable about delegating tasks to other people. ... I am aware that I will burn myself out if I don't share out the burden' (Chaplain, 2001: 208). This can be especially true when a school has gone through a period of difficulty – managing a group of difficult pupils or major change for example. A head who has maintained a visible presence during a difficult period may find it hard to hand back the reigns if he or she perceives doing so might result in a return to the problem situation. The staff will often feel otherwise, wanting autonomy and to regain control of areas of the school they consider theirs. This ongoing conflict between sharing decision making and feeling in control is common to managers in any organisation.

The dynamics of relationships between the SLT and staff are multiple and varied. Interpersonal and inter-group relationships vary, contingent on both the individual identities (personal characteristics) of those involved on the one hand, and the social identities of the groups (e.g. SLT, department heads, or teachers) on the other. These variations can be in terms of the quality and/or the nature of relationships, irrespective of the size of a school. People categorise themselves as members of groups or as individuals depending on the context and what is seen as rewarding in the situation. For instance, a head may identify herself as part of the SLT with overall responsibility for pupil behaviour in one context, but as a competent art teacher in another, and other people should respect they are different roles with distinct meanings for the head.

## What makes a good leader?

Prior to 1945, theories about traits focused on identifying the exceptional qualities of leaders, based on the assumption that the people fell into one of two groups – leaders and followers, each having distinctly different qualities. For instance, it was believed that leaders had limitless energy, insight, foresight, persuasiveness and creativity. Unfortunately, these studies failed to identify any universal traits that would guarantee success as a leader. Other approaches attempted to identify particular skills of leadership. Katz (1955), for instance, identified three developable skills for effective management: conceptual skills (ability to see the organisation as a whole), technical skills (e.g. teaching), and human skills (ability to work as a team member).

More recently, changes to research methods have enabled researchers to identify relationships between effective leadership, leader behaviour and individual characteristics – most notably motivation and skills. However, whilst there is an impressive amount of empirical evidence to inform our understanding of the practice of effective leadership, there are still significant omissions. In their paper on educational leadership, Bush and Glover proposed there are many alternative, and competing, models of school leadership. They reviewed nine different theories and found that, whilst leadership models are subject to fashion, they often reflect and inform 'changes in school leadership practice' (2014: 553). They proposed a typology of leadership including managerial, transformational and instructional models. Furthermore, they go on to say that distributed leadership – a shift from solo, 'heroic' models to shared leadership – is 'the most significant contemporary example of the nature of theory in educational leadership' (ibid.: 561). Distributed leadership focuses on utilising expertise from anywhere within a school and relies on the interaction between those in formal and those in informal leadership roles (Harris and Spillane, 2008). However, Gronn (2010) warns that, whilst there is a shift from solo to distributed leadership, the latter does not mean the scope of the head's role has been diminished.

The dispositional qualities of a head will inevitably affect the style of leadership. Zaleznik (1977) suggested leaders determined major objectives and strategic courses, and brought about major change, whereas managers enforced rules and policies or implemented goals and changes initiated at a higher level. Historically, headteachers have enjoyed varying amounts of each role. Leaders engage in behaviours that inspire followers, generate high levels of motivation, beyond what might reasonably be expected, in order to accomplish a collective vision – even if that means foregoing self-interest. In other words, they are able to generate conditions in which individuals categorise themselves in terms of their social identity (the organisation) as opposed to their individual identity, and are committed to a common shared vision or aim. Managers, on the other hand, are in a position of formal authority and responsible for the coordination and implementation of strategies and policies and establishing administrative systems. Effective managers provide the rational-analytic content necessary for the smooth operation of the organisation. One essential difference between the two is that managers are in a position of formal authority, whereas a leader might not be, influencing change because of personal characteristics or skills rather than formal status.

A distributed perspective on leadership acknowledges the work of all individuals who contribute to leadership practice, whether or not they are formally designated or defined as leaders. It is an approach that utilises lateral, flatter decision making (Hargreaves, 2007) so includes teachers and all support staff in these processes. In respect of behaviour management, this means that a whole-school approach where all staff share a vision and apply an agreed policy consistently and individual skills are drawn upon to deal with the various behaviour challenges will be more effective than one that relies largely on referral of behavioural problems to the head or SLT. Sadly, I still come across the latter in schools, both in respect of response to pupils who behave as required as well as those who misbehave. In the case of the former, one school springs to mind that makes explicit that they 'never give any form of extrinsic reward to pupils' – a rule reiterated by staff and that (allegedly) applies to all staff. However, in reality, the head controls and issues various treats and privileges to pupils as she chooses.

The behaviour pattern of leadership, first described by Lewin *et al.* (1939), distinguished three styles: *autocratic*, *laissez-faire* and *democratic*. Since then, dozens of different models have been developed with the number of styles ranging from two to nine. However, there is something of a consensus in support of two styles of leadership – one is person-focused (or person-centred) and based on providing support and participating, whilst the other is task-focused and based on goal setting, direction, and appraisal (Burke *et al.*, 2006). These two factors were seen by some as independent of each other but could be present at different times and in different amounts, depending on need. Other writers suggested intermediate states or continua between the two extremes. Tannenbaum and Schmidt (1958) identified four subcategories between the managers concerned with results (task) at one end and relationships (person) at the other. Autocratic and democratic represent the two extreme positions, whilst paternalistic and consultative occupy the middle ground of the model. Later research demonstrated the need for both extremes to be present. Cox and Cooper (1988) in their study of managerial 'high-flyers', produced group profiles within which they identified key areas, including problem solving/decision-making ability, vision and people skills – which relate to both 'managerial types'.

Nevertheless, there is a popular if mistaken, belief that one style is invariably better in generating a positive organisational climate, which facilitates effective behaviour management. The general consensus among the many teachers I have worked with over the years has been that, if given the choice, most would prefer the 'person-focused' head because 'they would be more prepared to listen to what we have to say', 'they'd be more understanding, caring, take an interest in what their staff are doing and be generally supportive'. However, instrumental help with problem solving does not necessarily follow listening and being sympathetic. The preference for a person-centred manager reflects social motivation, people being attracted to those who are prepared to listen to them and, from this, often infer other positive qualities about them. The person-focused head, is viewed as being 'warm', whereas the business-like 'task-oriented' manager is seen as being 'cold'. The power of assumptions about people based on implicit beliefs about traits such as 'warm' or 'cold' is discussed elsewhere (see Chapter 3).

Whilst the person-centred head may offer some support, it is important to remember that social support is multifaceted and people require different types of support to cope with different pressures (Cutrona and Russell, 1990). Although the person-centred head might more readily be perceived as providing emotional support, they may be less effective in providing instrumental support or help with problem solving or emotional objectivity during crises. Different combinations, sequences and combinations of tailored support are likely to be needed as situations change and so are unlikely to all come from the same source, as, for example, if you have to deal with an unusual but extreme event – a pupil becoming physically violent, for instance. During and immediately after the event, you are likely to feel shocked and drained, and probably need someone to talk to and help you calm down (emotional support). Later, there are decisions to be made about what action to take with the pupil (instrumental support). Planning interventions to deal with future encounters with the pupil and other pupils who witnessed the event may well need additional training for staff as well as reassurance of teachers' capabilities (self-efficacy support). Each type of support is likely to come from different people and take different forms. Some will be administrative, some resource-focused and others emotional. The head is unlikely to provide all, irrespective of their leadership style.

Using the SLT inappropriately for support can be indicative of structural difficulties and negative routines in a school. As Ofsted pointed out in their report on exclusion:

> In high excluding schools (but not exclusively) year heads and heads of house worked hard but were often overwhelmed by numbers of pupils referred to them for indiscipline by classroom teachers. Frequently such

referrals short-circuited established systems and merely reflected the unwillingness of some staff to deal with problems at source. As a result, such problems escalated and, although pastoral heads spent much time with difficult pupils, often that time achieved little other than to register concern and pass sentence.

(1996: 19)

The behaviour policy is intended to represent what a school values and to specify hierarchically ordered procedures and sanctions. If these procedures are being short-circuited to pass on the problem to a manager, it suggests that they are ineffective, inappropriate or being ignored. Such behaviour could result from managers intervening too quickly or staff who are too eager to pass over control of the situation. Managers who intervene too quickly or who regularly get involved with minor behaviours are in danger of undermining both the teacher's status and self-efficacy as well as their own authority should future major problems occur. Empowering teachers by encouraging them to recognise that they have the power to control difficult behaviour and providing training in how to do so will encourage practices that result in positive outcomes.

## Supporting staff with behaviour management

It is very difficult to put oneself in another individual's role unless you have experienced it. As a classroom teacher dealing with the daily hassles of keeping pupils on task, managing low-level disruption, completing records, preparing lessons, administering and keeping track of developments in pedagogy, may make teachers feel that the SLT have an easy time – particularly in large schools where the head often has a minimal teaching role. There is a sense of reductionism in some schools – that everything is about teaching, when clearly that is not so. In order for a teacher to get on with the job of teaching, various systems require development. For example, if pupils are able to wander around a school unchecked or fail to turn up to lessons without some school-wide response, then classroom management will be affected negatively. Responding to such problems is difficult when you are trying to teach a class of 30 pupils. This is not to say the SLT should spend all day as 'sweepers', picking up all wanderers and strays – but a high profile pays dividends when done at strategic points in the day such as breaktime, lunchtime, lesson changeover etc. In a study of 95 schools, Ofsted highlighted the

> … importance of both senior leaders and individual teachers enforcing the school's expectations and codes of conduct in a way that is consistent for pupils. If the problem of low-level disruption persists in a school, it is plainly the responsibility of senior leaders to tackle this and also of governors to challenge them about it.
>
> (2014: 21)

The SLT are under pressure from multiple sources both internal and external. They have to cope with managing: themselves, the school, the curriculum, finance, and change. Interestingly, of all their roles, it is usually managing other people that creates the most job dissatisfaction for headteachers (Chaplain, 1995), as is the case in other organisations where managers are responsible for largely autonomous professionals.

What constitutes a "difficult to teach class" will inevitably vary – what is usually common is that pupils are not on task and that the teacher is not using appropriate coping strategies to deal with them. This can occur because the teacher:

- has not learned the appropriate strategies;
- finds difficulty applying them;
- lacks confidence or is anxious or both; or
- finds that the systems available to support her or him are ineffective.

To be effective, social support must be perceived by the recipient as appropriate; however, in some schools what is perceived to be supportive by those offering it is not received as such by those needing it. The following case study is one example of how a struggling teacher was offered inappropriate support by the SLT.

### Case study

Sarah joined a high school to teach English. This was her first teaching post, having previously worked for eight years in a human resources office. She came across as very confident at interview and had excellent reports from the schools in which she had trained. The head and the head of the English faculty had both been impressed and felt she would fit in well with the existing strong English department. Due to staff illnesses, induction had been limited to introductions to staff, details of timetables, policies, schemes of work, and health and safety rules being explained, but little else.

For the first few weeks everything seemed to be going well. She appeared relaxed with pupils around the school and quickly developed a rapport with her classes. The faculty head (her mentor) visited her occasionally in class and was generally pleased with how she was settling in. She soon settled into the staffroom, was friendly, chatty and humorous.

After about a month she began having difficulties with a group of boys in a Year 8 class who became increasingly disruptive, albeit low-level. Sarah responded to this by making them sit right in front of her desk, but this made no difference. Later she had one or two standing outside her classroom for part of the lesson, where they engaged in face pulling, dancing and other amusing (to pupils at least) activities. These distractions eventually had an effect on classrooms nearby, which resulted in other teachers having to speak to them. It seemed that nothing Sarah tried made any difference to the behaviour, including following the school's sanction hierarchy. Eventually, one of the other teachers informed the faculty head about what was happening. As it turned out, other pupils had already made him aware of the situation. The faculty head felt that what was happening reflected Sarah adjusting to the school and he did not want to undermine her authority by intervening. However, he agreed to have a word with her and so later spoke with Sarah and suggested she spend some time with the 'problem' pupils at lunch or after school to try and address the difficulties and build a positive relationship. He also suggested rearranging the seating, perhaps mixing girls and boys around the tables, rather than having all the boys together. He also added that if he had any further problems to let him know.

Sarah did have further problems. Following her lunchtime discussions with the boys, there was an initial improvement in their behaviour, but then others started being disruptive.

Sarah became visibly less happy and chatty around school and a less frequent visitor to the staffroom. The faculty head again spoke with Sarah (who was becoming more negative about the situation), advising her that 'things weren't that bad at least they didn't throw their books out of the window or run off' ... and that he had known teachers that had 'much more difficult first terms – things will settle down with experience', he suggested. He offered to come into class and help reorganise the children and work with Sarah to sort out the 'problem group'. Sarah felt more reassured. The following day the faculty head joined her for the first lesson. He spoke to the class, telling them that their behaviour was unacceptable and that if it continued they would not like the consequences. He quickly informed pupils where they were to sit before handing over to Sarah to start the lesson, as he had to rush off to meet with a parent. Shortly after he left, the difficulties began again. A further meeting with the faculty head resulted in him suggesting some of the pupils be exchanged with another Year 8 class. After negotiation with another teacher, this was agreed. The situation following the changes started quite positively, but soon deteriorated. Sarah left the school at the end of her first year.

Whilst we can never be certain of exactly what led to the problems described above, the following points highlight some potential contributory factors:

- Although the school had an induction programme, little attention was paid to teaching or familiarisation with the school and its pupils. It was generally assumed that a qualified teacher would cope.
- The faculty head, who was Sarah's 'mentor', was largely preoccupied with the many other difficulties around the school, trying to overcome lack of resources and staff absence, which meant there was less time to spend supporting Sarah. What was offered was little more than a token gesture.
- At no time was a planned, coordinated response worked out. It appeared that the faculty head relied upon whatever he thought up at the time. None of Sarah's attempts to follow the advice were evaluated in order to try and identify where the difficulties were occurring.
- Whilst a behaviour policy existed, it was not well thought out and was seen as 'unnecessary administration' by some teachers, notably those who had been there for some time. The existing staff were undoubtedly 'strong' individuals who were used to coping more or less independently.
- The school had not recruited a newly qualified teacher for many years, so were unused to supporting individuals at that stage of their professional development. Those who thought more should have been done to help tended to externalise blame to the SLT, ignoring how their potential contributions may have made a positive difference.
- Whilst the faculty head saw himself as a person-centred manager, many of the staff felt that, whilst this was what he said, it was not really so in practice. Other staff thought that, whilst he was an excellent administrator, he was not a particularly good teacher, so perhaps he should not have been the one supporting Sarah.
- Sarah felt uncomfortable asking for help, since she felt she should have been able to manage this group.

## Thanks, but no thanks: when is support not support?

Whilst all teachers want to feel secure and supported in their work, and all managers want to facilitate working environments that produce confident and competent teachers, resulting in well-behaved and successful pupils, what constitutes appropriate support is not always agreed. The following illustrates some manager behaviours that teachers do not appreciate – each accompanied with suggested alternative ways of dealing with the problem.

### Being told publicly theirs is the worst-behaved class in school

Talk to the member of staff in private and develop an action plan for that individual that may include specific management strategies, making structural changes to the class (e.g. routines) or sending him/her on a course as part of professional development. Make all staff formally responsible for the planned support of new colleagues.

## Managers walking into their classrooms, disciplining pupils and then walking out

The problem with this strategy is twofold. Firstly, *if* it is effective (i.e. the pupils make less noise) it usually only works whilst the manager is there, and shortly after they leave, the misbehaviour starts again. Secondly, it can make the teacher appear to be sharing identity with the group being disciplined, since control has clearly been taken away from him/her as they were seen as unable to control the group themselves.

Whilst a senior staff member walking into a noisy classroom may be a welcome intrusion, perhaps indicating that the management are being supportive, care should be taken to ensure the teacher is seen to remain in control as part of a shared responsibility for behaviour. Offering to look after the class and allowing the teacher to remove individuals or small groups to deal with the problem is one way of doing this. Alternatively, having spoken with the teacher first, acting as advocate at a later meeting between the teacher and the pupils concerned, thereby maintaining that the teacher is in control. These strategies clearly benefit from proactive planning, mutual understanding and consistent application.

## Offering simple or quick-fix solutions to complex problems

The case of Sarah (above) exemplified this. The faculty head, on that occasion, was aware that the situation was complicated and required attention to a number of structural, interpersonal and personal issues. Given other pressures, there was insufficient time available to deal with the situation properly, but he felt he had to offer Sarah something. Unfortunately, it was inadequate, inappropriate and resulted in further difficulties for both the school and the teachers involved.

## Letting struggling teachers get on with it

According to the head of Ofsted, lack of support for those entering the profession is a major contributor to the loss of young enthusiastic new teachers, he said:

> What used to upset me was talking to people who were bright-eyed and bushy tailed, hugely enthusiastic about coming into teaching and wanting to do well for disadvantaged youngsters, saying to me that they were put off teaching in the first few years because they weren't adequately helped and supported by leaders.
>
> (Wilshaw, 2015)

Sadly, lack of support and the 'throw them in at the deep end' philosophy is nothing new. As Wallace (1996) pointed out, 'there is still a tendency to leave teachers to "sink or swim" in the time-honoured professional fashion!' She goes on to identify the personal qualities of those who manage to 'swim to calmer waters', which were concerned with building effective relationships with pupils and having clear and consistent expectations. Being too busy or having other difficulties is a poor excuse for not supporting colleagues. It also has a payback, for the whole staff group. The degree to which staff pull together is an indicator of the school's organisational climate.

### Taking control of the class without first discussing it with the teacher

A colleague of mine was reminiscing about his first experiences as a deputy head, saying how, on reflection, his desire to provide support for staff in the early days was counterproductive. Whenever he heard what sounded like staff having difficulty with a pupil or group, he would intervene and 'support' the teacher, or so he thought, by engaging with difficult pupils, perhaps removing them from class or reprimanding them. Over time he became aware that staff relied on him for increasingly trivial issues, either sending pupils directly to him or sending a pupil to get him to come to the class to help. He eventually realised that, far from supporting the staff, he was generating a culture of dependency or learned helplessness, where staff used him as a first level response to discipline problems, he had unwittingly let them externalise control. Furthermore, involving himself at this level undermined any notion of hierarchical responses to disruptive behaviour. If pupils were seeing the deputy for minor issues, what happened if things got worse?

On the surface, the process appeared to be workable except, of course, if he was absent, something that occurred increasingly as his duties changed over time. Moreover, and ironically, whilst staff were happy to regularly refer pupils to him, they would often complain afterwards that his reprimands were not severe enough! He gradually withdrew from this approach, making staff take responsibility for coping with the behaviour themselves and supporting them in other ways including covering a class whilst a teacher dealt with an individual, being available to discuss difficulties, and setting up professional development sessions on behaviour management. This was done through a series of school-based problem-solving workshops, which were supported with inputs from outside trainers.

The job of managing schools is complex and often difficult. To be effective, it requires quite exceptional qualities and skills to keep abreast of a rapidly changing, often loosely coupled organisation. It can be equally difficult for others working in the organisation to realise this, given the pressures and demands on professionals who have to work largely autonomously. Making time to listen and take on board each other's perspective, being aware of limitations and responsibilities, and having reasonable expectations is a starting point for developing more effective ways of working.

## Annotated further reading

Day, C., Sammons, P., Hopkins, D., Harris, A., Leithwood, K., Gu, Q., Brown, E., Ahtaridou, E., and Kington, A. (2009). *The impact of school leadership on pupil outcomes*. Nottingham: The National College for School Leadership.

This paper reports the findings of a mixed methods study that examined the work of school leaders in a range of secondary schools recognised as having improved behavioural and academic outcomes for pupils over at least three consecutive years. Key features of success were the role of the head teachers' educational values and leadership strategies in shaping school and classroom practices alongside the establishment and maintenance of school-wide policies for behaviour.

## Further reading to support M level study

Burke, P.F., Aubusson, P.J., Schuck, S.R., Buchanan, J.D., and Prescott, A.E. (2015). How do early career teachers value different types of support? A scale-adjusted latent class choice model. *Teaching and Teacher Education*, 47, 241–253.

Early career teacher (ECT) retention has been identified as an international concern. One of the most significant predictors of ECT's intention to stay in the profession, and of their satisfaction in their new work environment is lack of support from principals and senior leaders of the school. This article reports the perceptions of 336 ECTs' in respect of their preferences for different types of support – including that from senior leaders – and how such preferences vary among ECTs. A model was developed to investigate perceived levels of each mode of support, giving rise to a discrete choice experiment (DCE). A DCE provides respondents with a series of alternatives and requires them to choose their preferences. Differences between 'stayers' and 'leavers' were identified, the latter experiencing less access to teaching resources, higher levels of isolation, and a lack of interaction with their assigned mentors. The authors highlighted the need for senior staff to establish organisational climates that are conducive to supporting ECTs, including helping beginning teachers feel they can positively fit into the school community.

# Chapter 7

# Classroom climate

## The physical and socio-psychological environment

Teachers expect pupils to make what Wehlage *et al.* called a 'psychological investment', measured by how pupils 'demonstrate attention to and involvement with their schoolwork' (1989: 177). This investment is facilitated by teachers producing a positive classroom climate through: making lessons interesting and challenging; providing a safe and stimulating environment and providing appropriate support for academic and social learning. Classrooms are represented in a number of ways, including social, psychological and physical dimensions. What constitutes an appropriate learning atmosphere will differ from teacher to teacher and subject to subject and be influenced by layout, seating, temperature and smell, as well as the quality of pupil-teacher interaction. According to Weinstein and David (1987), all classrooms should support pupils' development through nurturing personal identity and social interaction; facilitating growth and competence; providing security and promoting trust. Creating healthy, positive, motivational environments in which all pupils (including the vulnerable) can flourish academically and socially, establishes the conditions for nurturing positive interpersonal relationships (with staff and peers) and supporting the development of self-control and self-regulation. (Doll *et al.*, 2014)

Chapter 5 highlighted the role of school organisation in managing pupil behaviour. Here the emphasis moves to the classroom level. Whilst we are continually reminded of how the quality of interpersonal relationships between pupil and teacher is at the heart of managing behaviour, the physical environment can also exert significant influence on such behaviour. For example, the quality of teacher-pupil interaction is influenced by where pupils are seated in the classroom (Good and Brophy, 2008), with pupils sitting at the front of the room or down the centre 'action zone' receiving more attention from the teacher than those sitting elsewhere in the room. Hence the combined effect of the physical and psycho-social environment is one of the strongest forces in shaping the thoughts, feelings, motivation and behaviour of pupils (see Figure 7.1).

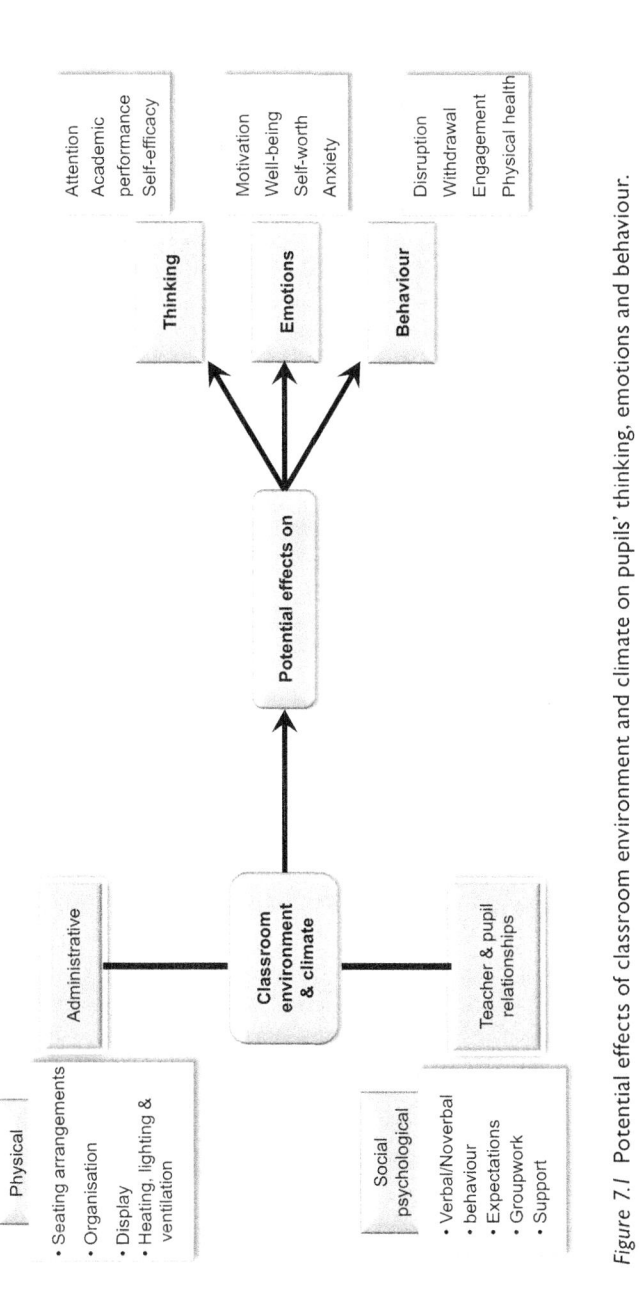

*Figure 7.1* Potential effects of classroom environment and climate on pupils' thinking, emotions and behaviour.

## The physical environment: organising the behavioural setting

Classrooms come in a wide range of shapes and sizes. Some are purpose built, whilst others are converted storerooms or outdoors – neither is a guarantee of quality teaching, positive behaviour or high levels of achievement. Physical characteristics such as heating, ventilation, noise, colours and lighting contribute to the quality of life for pupils and teachers. Efficient lighting is associated with improved academic performance and reduced disruptive behaviour (Schneider, 2002) and room colour is shown to influence the moods, judgements, and behaviour of pupils (Sleeman and Rockwell, 1981). A negative learning environment for pupils is created by poor classroom acoustics (Shield and Dockrell, 2003) and classroom temperature and ventilation significantly affected pupils' problem-solving abilities (Wargocki and Wyon, 2007).

Teachers should manipulate the physical environment to suit learning and behavioural needs. Paying attention to, and adjusting layout, decor and other physical factors can make teaching and learning more enjoyable, profitable and aesthetically pleasing. However, I have observed some badly managed lessons in purpose built, newly equipped rooms and some excellent ones in corridors and offices. It is the socio-psychological climate generated by the interaction between the setting and its occupants that matters most, and, in this respect, the teacher holds centre stage.

The room's function should be reflected in its décor and organisation, and should transmit what you expect to be going on in there and what is most valued. Posters or three-dimensional objects on display are useful and often necessary ways to present examples of what is expected. Piles of paper and junk do not suggest an organised and efficient workplace. Nonetheless, whilst decorating the walls of classrooms with lots of posters, brightly coloured borders and mounted pupils' work may be fashionable, it can also be distracting. This is particularly so when teaching in classrooms where much of the display may not be directly related to the topic of the lesson. Given that the development of self-regulatory attentional skills typically means distractibility decreases with age (Higgins and Turnure, 1984), one might conclude that classrooms for younger pupils or those with attention difficulties such as ADHD, should be decorated to reduce distractions. Where pupils are distracted from learning, there is increased likelihood of disruptive behaviour. Fisher et al. (2014) compared the on-task behaviour of pupils in highly and sparsely decorated classrooms and found that those in highly decorated classrooms were more distracted, spent more time off-task, and demonstrated smaller learning gains than when the decorations were removed.

Industry and commerce devote large amounts of time, energy and money to make sure equipment is designed to maximise efficiency and provide safe and comfortable working conditions. Schools should think likewise and be adaptive to the changing pedagogic, learning and physical needs of pupils.

A report into school furniture for the twenty-first century commissioned by the Furniture Industry Research Association (FIRA) reported that no account had been taken of the changing body shapes and sizes of pupils for over 30 years. Pupils have increased in size and height over this period with most growth in the arms and legs (Çaglar, 2001). As a result, they spend long periods on chairs that are the wrong size and lack ergonomic design, making them uncomfortable. This makes attention more difficult, creates disruption and, according to the Furniture Industry Research Association, is a significant cause of back pain in adolescence (FIRA, 2008).

However, a learning environment that is well-designed, whilst important, is no substitute for good teaching. Teachers vary in how they organise and operate their classrooms, including their levels of 'tidiness'. Whilst it is not necessary, nor desirable, for a classroom to be a showroom and look 'unlived in', there are obvious benefits to keeping a grip on classroom layout and location of equipment. Furthermore, Martella *et al.* (2003) found that well-organised classrooms are associated with more positive teacher–pupil interaction and reduced levels of disruption.

You may be a competent, inspired and highly motivated teacher, but perhaps untidy, so you need to develop systems to keep things in check. Having a layout map for the rooms you use and the different subjects and classes you teach, provides an *aide memoire*, helping overcome this problem. Without one, trying to remember how you previously organised seating arrangements and the location of resources is likely to create problems. Keeping a written record of equipment needs, and who sat where, takes a few minutes but is a valuable and accurate reminder of what you did previously and why. It helps avoid the problem of:

'Blane, sit where you were last time, over there', followed by,

'But I didn't sit here last time, Sir – I was over here next to Clive ... wasn't I Clive?'

'Yes, he was Sir', and so on.

Annotating the diagram, pointing out difficulties is also wise. Anyone who has attended a teacher training course will no doubt have been informed of the need to prepare well for their lessons, to be there in plenty of time, to have necessary and sufficient equipment ready and waiting for their pupils to maximise their time on task. Ensuring sufficient time to complete the lesson and put equipment away safely and correctly is similarly important. Timing in a lesson is everything, be it related to the speed at which you speak, when equipment is given out or when pupils are asked to start work on their own. Not knowing where equipment is in the classroom or not taking the time to make sure materials are there and working is not acceptable – assume nothing! Not having the right equipment, or having insufficient equipment available, is a potential recipe for management difficulties – waiting for a pupil to go and get the textbooks *you assumed* were still in your classroom creates a vacuum – 'Just read the notes again whilst Giani gets the textbooks from Mr Mellor' does not inspire confidence in your audience and means some will find alternative activities. Teachers expect pupils to turn up with the correct equipment, so they should do likewise.

### Seating arrangements to optimise learning and social behaviour

How seating is organised in classrooms directly influences the nature of social interaction (Good and Brophy, 2008) and should match your behavioural goals and your teaching style. Room layouts should enable frequent unhindered movement throughout the classroom and provide easy lines of sight to each pupil (Evertson *et al.*, 2003). However, having flexible seating layouts seems to present a problem for some teachers, despite evidence demonstrating that the nature of the learning task should dictate classroom seating arrangements rather than the other way round (Wannarka and Ruhl, 2008). I am always surprised how difficult many trainee teachers find asking their mentors if they can rearrange classroom furniture to suit their teaching style or lesson format. It is almost as if the desks are welded to the floor. Being a visitor to someone else's classroom, especially as a novice, can make asking to change things a little uncomfortable. However, I have found few mentors who objected to student teachers rearranging the furniture; in fact, most are just as surprised as I am.

The three key questions in deciding what type of seating arrangement to use are:

- How much interaction do you want pupils to have?
- How big is your audience?
- Can you monitor the behaviour of the whole class?

Let's assume, for the sake of illustration, that the room is big enough for the group, and furniture available is adequate. The usual arrangement for maximum interaction between pupils is to have groups around a table or open arrangement, whilst the more traditional row arrangement minimises group interaction but produces less disruption. Gump (1974) found pupils in open settings spent less time on task and were more often distracted than in traditional classrooms. Adding partitions to open classrooms improved on-task behaviour (Proshansky and Wolfe, 1974). However, these two options represent a continuum with various other arrangements between and within the two extremes. The following are some examples of variations on the two themes.

#### Organising classrooms in rows

*The Traditional classroom* facilitates interaction between audience and teacher but not between pupils. Figures 7.2a and 7.2b show single-desk and dyad

Classroom climate 147

(a)

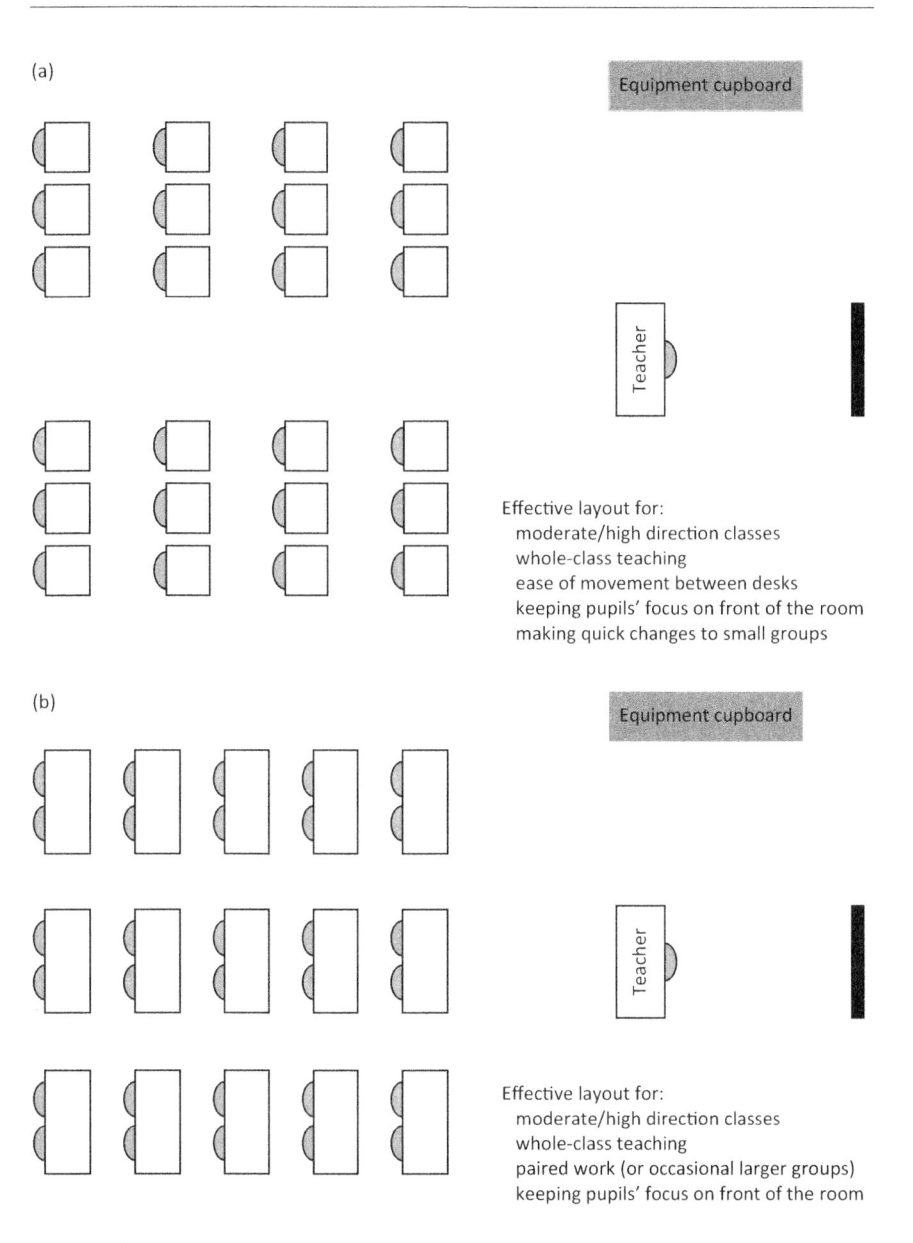

Equipment cupboard

Teacher

Effective layout for:
  moderate/high direction classes
  whole-class teaching
  ease of movement between desks
  keeping pupils' focus on front of the room
  making quick changes to small groups

(b)

Equipment cupboard

Teacher

Effective layout for:
  moderate/high direction classes
  whole-class teaching
  paired work (or occasional larger groups)
  keeping pupils' focus on front of the room

*Figure 7.2* Traditional classroom layout – (a) individual desks and (b) dyads.

arrangements. For presenting information, facts and rules to the whole class where pupils need to be facing the whiteboard, this arrangement is appropriate (Phillips, 1983).

Wheldall and Lam (1987) found that the level of academic work increases when pupils are arranged in rows, as opposed to groups. Wannarka and Ruhl

(2008) found that pupils in secondary schools behave more appropriately during individual tasks when they are seated in rows rather than groups, with disruptive pupils benefiting the most. Virtually all pupils' engagement with individual tasks is greater when they are sitting on their own or arranged in pairs, or where they are not facing another pupil, than when arranged in table groups, with mean gains in excess of 30% not uncommon and pupils with attention issues gaining most.

### Organising pupils in small groups

In recent years, it has been a popular assumption that groupwork inevitably enhances pupil learning. However, as with many other areas of education, whilst empirical evidence has shown that group-based activity, in *some* circumstances, is educationally sound (Rogers and Kutnick, 1992), it is not so in others. Kutnick *et al.* (2005) suggested that the rationale for organising pupils in groups has more to do with control issues than concerns about facilitating learning. Whilst theories of instruction and development (e.g. Vygotsky, 1978) highlight group-based factors in cognitive development (Light and Perret-Clermont, 1990), there is little evidence of this occurring in secondary classrooms (Blatchford *et al.*, 2001).

Doyle (1986) found teachers had a general feeling of ambiguity of purpose for groupwork. Some teachers feel less in control and experience increased disruption when pupils are arranged in small groups (Cohen and Intilli, 1981); others believe that it holds back more able pupils, as they are distracted from their own learning while helping others (Plummer and Dudley, 1993). As Hastings and Chantrey-Wood (2002a) point out, adults working on independent tasks would not usually seek the company of others to work on the same table, but this is how many pupils are expected to work. Merely placing pupils in small groups is no guarantee that 1) their performance will be any more enhanced than if they were to work alone, or 2) that all pupils are capable of working collaboratively in groups. Some pupils are arranged in groups by default rather than design. According to McNamara and Waugh, 'Group size often seems to be determined by furniture and its arrangement' rather than by 'educational or pedagogical considerations' (1993: 44). Physical limitations, room availability or making the best use of space or existing furniture, rather than sound educational or classroom management principles, may be the real reason for pupils being organised this way.

Awareness of how space can either promote or obstruct group dynamics, individual privacy, and feelings of crowdedness is an area seldom covered in teacher training (Lackney, 1994). Crowdedness is a psychological construct concerning the perception or feeling that there is insufficient personal space in a classroom as opposed to a measured physical space. Moore (1979) found that higher perceived crowdedness is associated with reduced attention, decreased task performance and increased behaviour problems, including aggression and withdrawn behaviour.

Sometimes groupwork is dictated by the numbers of books or equipment available, but this does not represent the optimum conditions for learning or collaboration. The standard practice of group seating is best suited to activities seldom used in classrooms and ill-suited to individual work – something conspicuously frequently used in those classrooms (Hastings and Chantrey-Wood, 2002a). Before you decide to use groupwork in your classroom, you should consider the evidence. For example, what are the optimum numbers of pupils to engage in particular activities – e.g. sharing a computer, solving a complex problem, carrying out an experiment, writing an essay or making a collage?

Decisions about group membership should be guided by objective information, not circumstance (Dean, 1992). Who you put with whom and why, for which topics, and for how long are important not just for making behaviour management easier but also for academic and social reasons. Making sure that pupils are *able* to collaborate with each other – to have the appropriate level of social competence, as well as academic competence – should be a fundamental consideration. Organising classes where all SEN pupils are in a single group may ease resource use, TA deployment and administration, but may also reduce the potentially positive effects of peer supported learning (Fuchs *et al.*, 1997). Unfortunately, low-attaining pupils, especially those with behaviour problems, are likely to be excluded from group working and made to work individually or with other low-attaining pupils, which is not conducive to the principle of scaffolding (Kutnick *et al.*, 2002).

Although there are many ways of organising groups in the classroom I will discuss four arrangements and highlight their suitability for different types of teaching and learning.

THE COFFEE BAR

Pupils are arranged in small groups around tables facing each other. This is a familiar sight in most secondary schools (see Figure 7.3). This arrangement maximises interaction and encourages talk, and spontaneity. It can facilitate group problem-solving activities or project work, and invites interpersonal communication. Such an arrangement also enables the teacher to circulate and interact with each group. Whilst this layout allows the teacher to lead the session, it is not the best way to make a presentation to the class, since not all pupils are able to see the teacher. Furthermore, whilst whole-class discussion is possible, it is not the best way of doing so, as some pupils will have their lines of communication obstructed.

150  Classroom climate

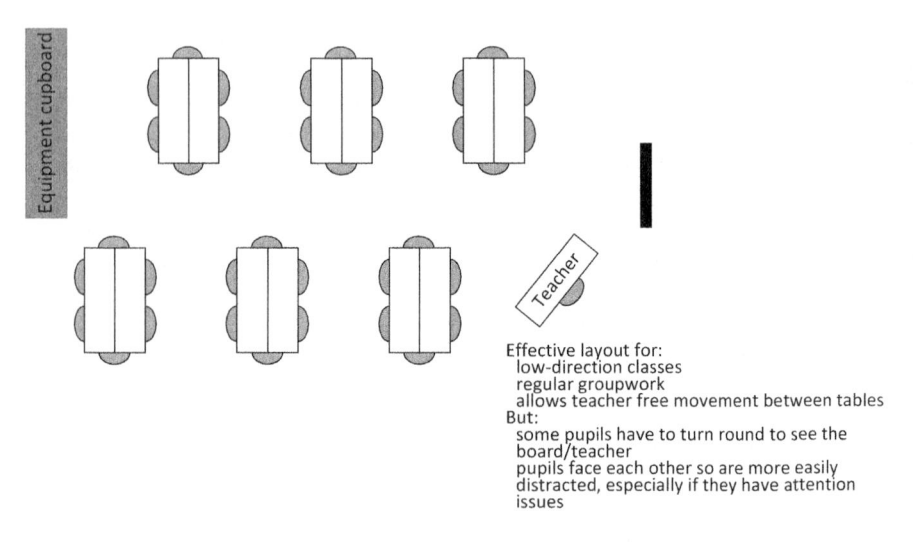

Effective layout for:
  low-direction classes
  regular groupwork
  allows teacher free movement between tables
But:
  some pupils have to turn round to see the board/teacher
  pupils face each other so are more easily distracted, especially if they have attention issues

*Figure 7.3* Coffee bar layout.

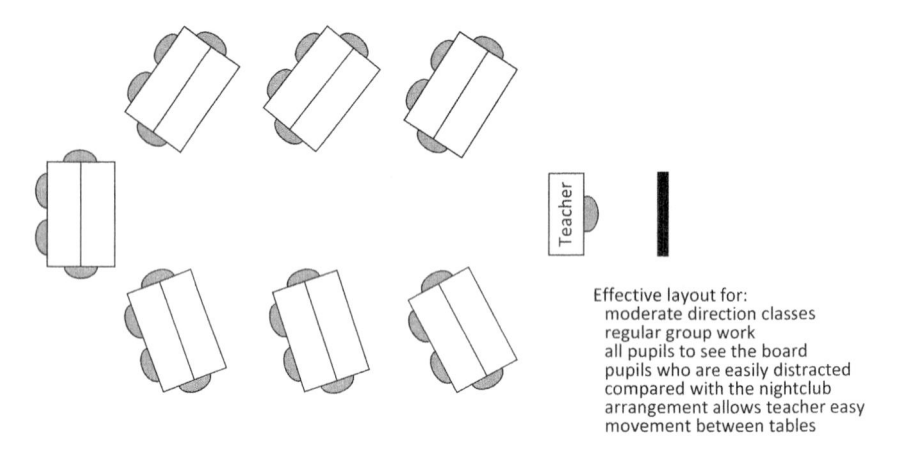

Effective layout for:
  moderate direction classes
  regular group work
  all pupils to see the board
  pupils who are easily distracted compared with the nightclub arrangement allows teacher easy movement between tables

*Figure 7.4* Nightclub layout.

THE NIGHTCLUB

The nightclub allows more multidirectional communication than some arrangements, but is also more 'untidy' than the above arrangements (see Figure 7.4). It represents a halfway house between the traditional classroom and group arrangement and enables more varied small-group interaction, but is more hectic because pupils are not facing each other. However, it also offers a better setting for teacher input to the whole class because none of the pupils have their back to the teacher. In this arrangement, tables tend to be bigger

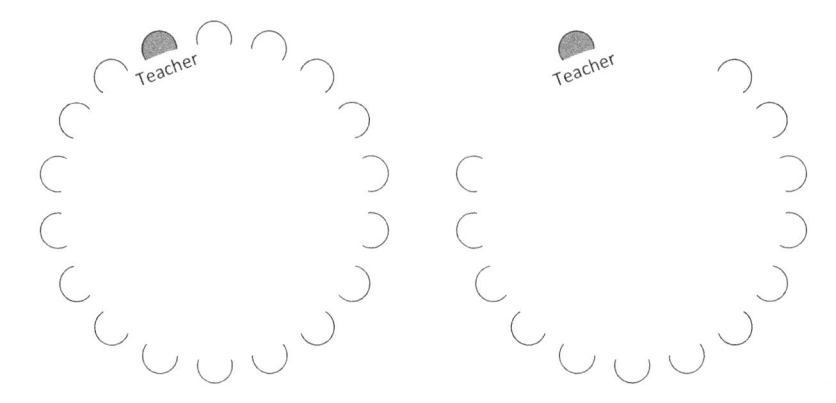

Effective layout for:
class discussion/circle time
ease of teacher-pupil and pupil-pupil direct interaction
smaller classes as is inefficient use of space
allows easy circulation
Horseshoe makes teacher monitoring of pupils easier than full circle

*Figure 7.5* Open circle and horseshoe layouts.

or put together to make a larger surface area than in the coffee bar setting, thus enabling pupils to move themselves and their work around more freely. It also makes adjustment of group sizes more easily during a lesson. However, changing group composition in this way requires caution to avoid creating behaviour-management problems and off-task activity. A variation on this theme is to organise the tables so that the overall pattern of the pupils is semi-circular, which helps the teacher present to the whole class.

THE OPEN CIRCLE (AND HORSESHOE)

This allows for most interactions between group members and the teacher usually forms part of the 'circle' as a group member (see Figure 7.5). It is a useful format for discussion, provided paperwork or writing is not required, as there are no tables or desks – it is the usual format for circle time and discussion activities. As group members do not have a table or barrier between them and other pupils, this arrangement can be very threatening to some pupils, since those involved are fully exposed and visible to each other. It can be helpful to note which pupils contribute and who is a wallflower and needs support – you can do this using sociogram or flow chart techniques (Hobart and Frankel, 1994).

## Classroom climate and pupil engagement

Significant relationships exist between classroom climate and pupil engagement, behaviour, self-efficacy, achievement, and social and emotional development (Freiberg, 1999). Classroom climate is influenced by the complex interaction of many factors that make objective measurement problematic, but several researchers have made attempts at doing so.

Moos (1979) adopted a socio-ecological approach based on the interaction between personal and environmental components. He proposed three dimensions for classifying social environments and used them to produce measures of classroom climate. The dimensions are:

- *Relationship*—The nature and intensity of personal relationships within the classroom—such as the degree to which people support each other and can express themselves.
- *Personal development*—The routes along which personal growth and self-enhancement usually occur.
- *System maintenance and change*—The degree to which the classroom is well-ordered, expectations made clear, control is maintained, and is receptive to change.

More recently, Haydn (2014) has produced a 10-point scale to measure classroom climate. It offers a series of descriptors that represent the extent to which a teacher appears to be in control of the classroom, and able to create and maintain a working atmosphere that optimises pupil learning. At level 10, a teacher is comfortable and relaxed teaching any type of lesson and behaviour management is not an issue. At the other extreme (level 1) the class is so out of control that it is difficult knowing where to begin making changes. In between the two (at level 5) some lessons are chaotic, but pupils can usually get on with their work, albeit in a noisy atmosphere. Inevitably, attempting to measure social interaction and engagement will be subjective, but Haydn provides a level of specificity absent in other assessments.

Social interaction is influenced by physical components of a classroom, which can be manipulated to make the process more positive. Key components of effective behaviour management skills (scanning, eye contact, social distance, posture and gesture) can also all be enhanced by attention to layout. Talking to the back of someone's head does little to aid communication. In large, spacious classrooms, with sufficient distance between desks allowing easy movement, teachers are probably *best placed* to spend equal, or similar, amounts of time with all of their pupils – and should monitor objectively that they are doing so. However, many classrooms are small and class sizes large. Even when this is the case, there are various options available to improve the learning environment: paying attention to where pupils are sitting; how they are grouped; their proximity to the teaching 'hub' or action zone; how often you interact with them; the nature of the interaction and your mobility. Permanently placing some pupils furthest from your desk, whiteboard or where you tend to stand most when teaching may be interpreted by them as not being valued members of your group. Reflecting on who you are sitting where, and the reason(s) for doing so, can provide the basis for thinking of how to develop positive relationships with pupils who are at risk of social exclusion.

At the beginning of this book, I stated that the aim of managing pupils' social behaviour was to maximise engagement with legitimate learning in school. Engagement in classroom activity means both academic engagement (e.g. time on task, attention) and social engagement (e.g. interacting with peers and teacher), both of which impact on achievement (Finn *et al.*, 2003). Classroom climate can have a direct impact on engagement and motivation since a positive climate is associated with a sense of connectedness and belongingness, enjoyment and enthusiasm. Pupils in classrooms who sense this tend to engage more in learning (Furrer and Skinner, 2003) and exhibit fewer problem behaviours (Crosnoe *et al.*, 2004). However, different pupils experience the same situation differently depending on how they interpret, appraise, and interact with their environment.

Where pupils are invited or told to sit, the type of work they are asked to undertake, the degree to which they feel secure asking questions, and the level of emotional warmth from the teacher are all potential influences on how pupils think and feel about themselves. These thoughts and feelings are associated with their academic and social motivation.

## Classroom climate and pupil motivation

Motivation is concerned with why people think and behave the way they do and what causes behaviour to start, be sustained or stop. It is linked to emotions, needs, desires, satisfaction, pride, happiness, fear of failure, etc. There are a number of different theories that seek to explain what motivates pupils to behave the way they do. Many contemporary explanations draw on social-cognitive theories, which are concerned with perceptions, beliefs and the strategies people adopt in order to cope (Schunk *et al.*, 2008).

Goal orientation, self-efficacy, self-determination and attribution theories (to name a few) all concern individuals' beliefs about themselves, their environment and their ability to influence important events in their lives but do so in different ways. Attribution theory concerns the explanations people (individuals and groups) hold or manufacture about the causes of their own and other people's behaviour. For example, pupils may seek to explain their successes and failures in important tests, which affects their subsequent behaviour. A number of factors can influence this process, one of which is the classroom climate. We seldom know for sure the real causes of human behaviour, so we base our decisions on what we *perceive* to be or *our theories* about the causes. The process is common to everybody, since it is how people make sense of their worlds and affects the way they behave and how they feel. People can be biased in their judgements, distorting reality to maintain consistency and predictability, make the evidence fit their beliefs and making fundamental errors in their explanations as discussed in Chapter 3. Making judgements and causal analyses can occur at two levels. The first is 'automatic', involves rapid cognitive processing and is influenced by experience. The second is deliberate and time-consuming, which one might expect would result in more accurate judgements, but bias means this is not always so. Weiner (1992) provided the impetus for the development of explanations as to why some pupils, when faced with new or difficult tasks, engage and persist, whilst others just give up at the first sign of difficulty. Weiner argued that thought processes and the resultant emotional reactions, were the principal agents in guiding behaviour. A central premise of the theory is that individual differences are qualitative and not quantitative, as suggested by some early theories. In other words, people don't have more or less motivation; their beliefs about the causes of their successes and failures affects their subsequent behaviour. Over time these beliefs produce different motivational styles; some are adaptive and functional, and others maladaptive, which leads to disengagement with learning. As Covington puts it:

> … teachers and students are linked cheek-by-jowl, by a common need to be appreciated for their interlocking roles. … the unattractive, often infuriating behaviors of some students, say, procrastination and indifferent effort, often go unappreciated by teachers for what they are, *fear of failure* driven strategies, not necessarily defiance or disrespectful challenging of authority. Yet it is all too easy for teachers to attribute such actions to a moral lapse of undeserving individuals. As a consequence, teachers often react with resentment, blaming students rather than searching for the true culprit in the relationship.
>
> (2009: 154)

How pupils think about themselves and their abilities, and what they think teachers think about their ability and motivation, influences whether they choose to engage or disengage with academic learning or become involved in disruptive activities. Messages likely to result in pupils disengaging from learning include when:

- Messages from significant others are interpreted as suggesting you are stupid.
- You find yourself spoken to by the teacher less frequently than others.
- The questions you are asked appear simpler than everybody else's.
- You get printed worksheets, and others have textbooks.
- You are seated right at the back, out of the way, or inches away from the teacher, so they can 'keep an eye on you'.
- The teacher visits your desk less frequently than others or does so to give you what you consider negative feedback.
- You receive inappropriate help with simple tasks, reaffirming your incompetence.

Over time these behaviours can become routine or ritualised and, as a result, some pupils:

- feel unable to succeed;
- fear failure;
- feel helpless;
- resent their treatment and respond negatively toward the teacher; or
- work to protect their self-worth often at the cost of academic learning.

Weiner (1992) proposed different consequences resulting from pupils attributing causes to their successes and failures in particular directions. He identified three dimensions – locus, stability and controllability. The first of these – locus of control – concerns whether you attribute your success/failure to factors within yourself (e.g. ability), or the situation, (e.g. good/bad teaching). A pupil failing on a test might conclude that he lacks ability (internal locus) or alternatively that he had a lousy teacher (external locus).

Whilst some causes are *internal* and others *external,* they also differ in terms of their permanence or stability. Ability and effort are both internal qualities, but the former is seen by some as a fixed or *stable* quality, whilst effort is changeable and hence *unstable*. Similar comparisons can be made for external factors with luck being *unstable* and level of task difficulty being *stable*.

Weiner then added a third dimension, controllability. He argued that, whilst a factor could have an internal or external locus of control, some could be controlled, whilst others could not. For example, physical appearance is largely *uncontrollable,* whereas dress is *controllable*. Table 7.1 gives example of some possible attributional explanations to success and failure in relation to the three dimensions. Behavioural outcomes differ dependent on which combination is selected.

Attributing failure to not having made enough effort (internal-unstable-controllable) will have different consequences than attributing failure to

*Table 7.1* Explaining the causes of success and failure

| | Locus of control | | | |
| --- | --- | --- | --- | --- |
| | Internal | | External | |
| Controllability | Stable | Unstable | Stable | Unstable |
| Controllable | Usual effort level | Temporary effort level | Teacher doesn't like me | Unusual help from others |
| Uncontrollable | Ability | Mood | Task difficulty | Luck |

Note
Examples of possible causal explanations a pupil might use to explain success or failure, based on three dimensions: controllability, locus and stability.

teacher bias (external-stable-controllable). Concluding your teacher has it in for you may well affect your expectations, as *you* have no control over him/her, so this is hardly the recipe for positive teacher-pupil relationships, nor an incentive to be well-behaved or make effort. Why would you want to respond positively to someone who you felt was treating you unjustly? Furthermore, the emotional consequences are also likely to be different, in the first example perhaps feeling guilty or ashamed, the second feeling hopeless or angry.

### *Adaptive and maladaptive motivational styles*

Attributing causes repeatedly in one direction or another leads, over time, to the development of motivational styles distinguished on the basis of whether an individual's goals are directed towards performance or mastery. Performance-oriented pupils are concerned with image, whereas mastery-oriented pupils are concerned with gaining knowledge and understanding. As Dweck argues, '... with performance goals, an individual aims to look smart, whereas with learning goals the individual aims at becoming smarter' (1985: 291).

Beliefs about ability are central to understanding differences between adaptive and maladaptive motivational styles. Pupils who attribute their successes to internal, stable factors (e.g. ability) and their failures to internal-unstable-controllable factors (e.g. lack of effort) are likely to develop an adaptive style referred to as mastery orientation (Dweck, 1990). In contrast, pupils who attribute their successes to luck and their failures to lack of ability are likely to develop maladaptive motivational styles. Beliefs about intelligence and ability discriminate between the two behaviour patterns based on implicit theories about the malleability of academic and social resilience. Some individuals, known as entity theorists, believe that ability is fixed and unchangeable (or fixed mindset); others, known as incremental theorists (or growth mindset), believe ability is malleable and can be changed by the amount of effort applied (Dweck, 1990, 2006). It is important to realise that a particular mindset is not necessarily universal. People have mixtures of fixed and growth mindsets that are linked to specific tasks. Hence, you may have a growth mindset in one aspect of learning or subject or skill but a fixed mindset in another. Teaching pupils how to think about intelligence in an incremental way can, along with appropriate study skills, testing new strategies and seeking information from others, improve performance and develop an adaptive motivational style (Blackwell *et al.*, 2007), thereby helping to develop their resilience and enhance their well-being

The fixed-mindset individual – who is performance-oriented – is influenced by the judgement of others. A performance goal-oriented pupil who thinks others are making positive judgements of his/her ability, is likely to persevere. If, on the other hand, they perceive that they are being judged negatively by others, it can lower their self-belief, and they disengage.

In contrast, a learning goal-oriented pupil (or growth mindset) considers ability to be changeable. Challenges can be overcome with extra effort. Failure is seen as a challenge or an incentive to solve a problem by searching for alternative approaches. A key difference between the two orientations is the degree to which each acknowledges the role of effort. If being smart or having ability is what really counts above all else, and a pupil believes they lack ability, a characteristic they consider to be unchangeable, what is the point of making an effort since they are likely to fail anyway? If, on the other hand, they believe that success is more to do with effort then they are more likely to engage and persevere with a task.

This is not to suggest that ability is unimportant, but even if you are not gifted, effort can make a big difference to outcomes. Although it is improbable that any teacher tells pupils that they are 'thick', a pupil may interpret their teacher's behaviour towards them as implying that is what they are thinking, based on how they read verbal, nonverbal and organisational messages from the teacher (see Chapter 3). If this behaviour also occurs outside the classroom, at home for instance, then the pupil is more likely to accept it as accurate.

People also make attributions about their social successes and failures. Imagine a pupil invites someone to go out with her on a date but is rejected; she may well seek a causal explanation. Again, the three above-mentioned dimensions come into effect. She may believe she was rejected perhaps because she thinks the person thinks she is ugly (internal-stable-uncontrollable) or because the person she asked had to attend a family function (external-unstable-uncontrollable). The two different explanations have the potential to influence what she thinks about herself and her emotional reaction in different ways – always remembering it is beliefs about causes not necessarily the real reasons that are important here.

The initial emotional reaction to both causal explanations will be similar; she is likely to feel sad (a basic emotion) at being rejected. However, if the goal was an important one (she really liked this person and thought they liked her), then she is likely to seek to further explain or think more about why she *believes* she was rejected and, as a result, feel either hopeless or hopeful about future outcomes. If she thinks she was rejected because she is ugly – something beyond her volitional control – she is likely to experience hopelessness, because the cause is down to her (internal locus), is unlikely to change over time (stable) and something she cannot control (uncontrollable). As a result, her self-worth is likely to be lowered (or reinforced if already low), may become depressed and affecting her future behaviour. In the second example, although initially sad, if she puts the cause of her rejection down to the other person being busy with a family function (external locus), which is not likely to happen continually (unstable), she will be more hopeful for success in the future.

*A closer look at maladaptive styles*

Those who repeatedly attribute their failures in both academic or social endeavours to internal-stable-uncontrollable factors (e.g. ability) and successes to external-unstable-uncontrollable factors (e.g. luck) develop maladaptive motivational styles.

Two types of maladaptive style have been identified – self-worth protection and learned helplessness. Whilst on the surface, the behaviour of pupils with maladaptive motivational styles may appear similar – both make minimal effort or give up prematurely, or cannot be bothered to complete work – the two styles are qualitatively different.

SELF-WORTH PROTECTION

Ability is a highly valued personal quality in the educational system. Perceiving you lack it affects various aspects of the self, including self-regulation, self-efficacy and self-worth. As Covington informs us:

> It is not surprising that the pupil's sense of esteem often becomes equated with ability – to be able is to be valued as a human being, but to do poorly is evidence of inability, and reason to despair of one's worth.
> (1992: 16)

Individuals who develop self-worth protecting styles are *unsure* of their own ability, believing they *may* have sufficient competence to be successful. However, they also recognise that ability is negatively correlated with effort (high ability = low effort). Consequently, making more effort to gain success must indicate low ability – a conclusion that presents them with a dilemma. Success with minimum effort is an indicator of *having* ability. Having to make more effort than your peers means you will be seen as lacking ability, and particularly so if the additional effort results in failure (Kun, 1977). The emotional consequences are feelings of shame and humiliation and lowered self-worth (Covington, 1998). Whilst being seen as competent is the best way to protect one's self-worth, the risks involved in trying to do so may be too great, making it better not to try than to try and fail. Fear-of-failure is a driving force for these individuals. Their self-worth is linked to performance goals, and hence determined by their achievements. In the same way, a teachers' sense of worth is linked to the effectiveness of their teaching (Covington, 2009). Nonetheless, suggesting these pupils are not motivated would be wrong – they are highly motivated – to avoid being seen as less able than their peers, thereby protecting their self-worth. They will risk all to avoid being seen as lacking ability, using various tactics, such as refusing to complete school work, procrastination and task avoidance, the lasting consequence of which is underachievement (Thompson, 1994). Whilst in the short term such strategies may be effective, their lifespan is usually short since other people eventually see through the veneer, making any doubt a pupil has about their competence a certainty.

This negative thinking can also pervade the emotional experiences of the pupil, changing hope to hopelessness. After all, what is the point of 'working hard' if failure is the inevitable outcome? Despairing of one's ability can lead to acquiescence or resentment towards those who are perceived to have contributed to the difficulty – teachers, for example.

In a study of engaged and disengaged pupils (Chaplain, 1996c), this feeling was made clear. Disengaged pupils were defined by teachers in terms of their personal qualities and disposition (e.g. antisocial), lacking ability and not making an effort, personality or developmental problems. The disengaged pupils admitted to behaving in ways not conducive with success in school, such as giving up easily with their school work, impulsiveness, difficulties understanding their work and feeling embarrassed if asked questions in public or singled out for special attention. Being seen to fail in public reinforces perceived lack of ability and lowers self-worth. Hence, the well-meaning teacher, who believes they are being supportive, is in fact perceived by the pupils as doing the opposite.

Teachers attempting to support pupils by offering uncalled-for help or unwarranted praise serve as cues to their low ability (Barker and Graham, 1987; Graham and Barker, 1990), contributing to the development of maladaptive motivational styles. Chaplain (1996c) found that disengaged pupils considered teachers unfair, especially to them; expressed negativity toward them both verbally and nonverbally; and considered them to be largely responsible for their failure at school. Unsurprisingly, disengaged pupils are also more likely to disrupt learning and more likely to drop out of school (Kaplan *et al.*, 1997). They often report being bored, anxious, or even angry about being in the classroom (Skinner and Belmont, 1993).

Determining who is responsible for the problem is far from straightforward and perhaps, in some ways, of little value since it detracts from thinking about how to provide an environment which is positive and provides motivational equity to all pupils regardless of ability. Sadly, pupils who float on the border of failure, disengagement and disaffection – those at risk – are perhaps the least well attended to in terms of resources in contrast to pupils who are receiving special measures or those considered able. The prognosis for the borderline group becomes increasingly poor when moving into and through secondary school, since access to credentialed qualifications becomes increasingly unlikely.

## LEARNED HELPLESSNESS

Learned helplessness (Smiley and Dweck, 1994) is characterised by a pupil who believes that they lack ability and without doubt will fail, no matter how hard they try. So, if faced with a difficult task, they give up rather than make extra effort because they believe changes to ability is beyond their control and do not recognise a link between effort and success. Pupils who develop learned helplessness feel a global lack of control over their lives and tend to externalise responsibility for important events to others, including their successes. As a result, their success is not rewarding, nor does it increase their pride and self-efficacy because they do not feel responsible. Help from teachers reinforces their beliefs in their own lack of competence. Once this motivational style is established, it is difficult to change. In some cases, beliefs about the inevitability of failure are so strong that attempting to convince them of the value of making more effort, of encouraging learned industriousness, is like telling someone who is clinically depressed to pull themselves together. Indeed, there is a relationship between learned helplessness apathy, despair and depression (Reivich et al., 2013)

## Intervening to support the development of adaptive motivational styles

Thinking about ways in which pupils' motivation differs is a useful starting point for developing ways of nurturing a positive psychological climate in the classroom. Classroom environments are teachers' territory, within which pupils' learning is on teachers' terms, placing teachers in probably the best position to positively influence pupils' beliefs about success and failure. Unfortunately, as Thompson points out, 'there is evidence that the potential is either largely unexploited or (more seriously) distorted in its application' (Thompson, 1994: 266).

Helping pupils to break maladaptive behaviour patterns requires getting them to rethink their reasons for failure and offering direction to bring about changes. Successes have been recorded with learned helplessness by helping pupils gain control of their outcomes through changing their attributions from external uncontrollable (luck) to internal controllable (effort) (Craske, 1988; Perry and Struthers, 1994; Toland and Boyle, 2008). Targeted praise for effort on specific tasks (not general praise) can produce positive results. However, just telling them that they are not making enough effort is, according to Nicholls (1989) almost as useless as doing nothing and particularly so with self-worth protecting pupils. The relationship between effort and ability is complex. Whilst teachers might praise and reward effort, the prediction of future success relies heavily on estimates of ability (Kaplan and Swant, 1973). According to Schunk (1987), awareness of both is important; encouraging pupils to attribute success to effort with new tasks, but later moving to attributing success to ability as they develop their skills, proved a successful approach. Differential age effects have been found, with younger pupils preferring ability feedback, whereas older pupils preferred effort feedback (e.g. Burnett and Mandel, 2010).

The focus throughout this book is on designing multilevel approaches to behaviour management, and this continues here. The behaviour management of pupils with maladaptive motivational styles, who disengage with learning and disrupt classes, can be helped to develop a more adaptive motivational style by incorporating different approaches at different levels, ranging from whole-school level to pupil level. Covington (1998) advocates a rethinking of schooling with a shift from obsession with ability to one orientated to pupils' future survival, developing a set of marketable skills, willingness to become engaged and preparation for the inevitability of change. Likewise, pupils can be empowered through the development of cooperative learning environments in which motivation, strategic thinking skills and how to learn from failure are developed and positively valued. The current pressures on improving performance in British schools are largely based on quantitative models of motivation. Government demands for more exams, more hours and more passes reflect a drive-theory approach to education that lacks imagination, particularly when laid alongside other concerns about pupil behaviour, school attendance and stress, predominantly for the failure-prone pupil.

At the classroom level, there are a number of interventions that have proven successful in changing pupils with self-defeating motivational styles. For example, Good *et al.* (2003) investigated the effects of using college students to mentor 138 adolescents, via weekly emails, to teach them different perspectives on school achievement. Specifically, they were taught one of three conditions. One group were told that intelligence is malleable (incremental theory). They also received some information about brain plasticity, about neurons and dendrites and about how the brain can form new neural connections throughout life. The second group were told that following transition to secondary school, pupils often experience a drop in performance but then bounce back after they adjust to the novelty of change, i.e. the attributional condition. The third group received combined incremental + attributional conditions. At the end of the twelve months, they found that the experimental groups (incremental, attribution and combined) had scored significantly higher in both maths and verbal achievement scores than the control group. The most marked improvement was amongst black girls in maths. Results for the experimental conditions were similar and perhaps unsurprising given Dweck's incremental-entity theory has its roots in attribution theory.

Creating a positive classroom climate requires attention to both physical and socio-emotional processes. Many common classroom management practices have been shown to *not* be the most effective way to manage behaviour and encourage engagement, but teachers persist in using them nevertheless. Interventions aimed at the individual and whole-class level to change pupils' self-defeating beliefs about their ability to control outcomes alongside teaching them about the plasticity of the brain have been successful in both academic and social domains (Good *et al.*, 2003). Taking the time to consult the evidence and basing your approach on interventions that have been shown to be most effective is the message here.

## Annotated further reading

Virtanen, T.E., *et al.* (2015). The relationship between classroom quality and students' engagement in secondary school. *Educational Psychology*, 35(8), 963–983.

This study examined the relationship between classroom quality and the level of behavioural engagement among 181 pupils in secondary school classrooms. Three dimensions of classroom quality (emotional, organisational and support) and pupil engagement were observed using the Classroom Assessment Scoring System. The results highlighted specific associations between the domains of classroom quality and pupil behavioural engagement in secondary school classrooms.

## Further reading to support M level study

Gregory, A., and Korth, J. (2016). Teacher-student relationships and behavioral engagement in the classroom. In: K. Wentzel and G. Ramani (eds.), *Handbook of social influences on social-emotional, motivation, and cognitive outcomes in school contexts* (pp. 178–191). New York: Taylor and Francis.

A large amount of research has supported the belief that high-quality teacher–pupil relationships create the conditions for eliciting pupil behavioural engagement in the classroom. This chapter provides a review of the literature, bringing together theory and research on the features of teacher–pupil relationships that best bring about such behaviour. The authors examine the processes that link these relationships to positive pupil behaviour and their social development.

Chapter 8

# Classroom structures
## The role of rules, routines and rituals in behaviour management

All aspects of our lives require us to operate within rules or boundaries of some sort, whether self-imposed or determined by others. Some rules seem clear, rational and reasonable – others seem petty and irritating.

Rules can be interpreted literally or in spirit, so care has to be taken with wording to avoid unintended consequences. Readers will probably be aware of the minute attention to detail that adolescent pupils often have when it comes to the interpretation of school rules, such as arguing about what constitutes 'appropriate footwear' and 'jewellery', how 'long' a skirt really is and how an unwary teacher can be drawn into a protracted discussion of these details. Such discussions are excellent tactics for avoiding schoolwork, providing the class with light entertainment and stopping you from teaching.

### The functions of rules

In the classroom, it is the teacher who should be in control at all times. Disruptive behaviour, refusing to work, insults, backchat, aggression and other tactics are attempts by pupils to take control. Intelligently constructed rules can help establish and maintain teacher control and facilitate learning, provided that: their meaning is clear; they are relevant; they are taught explicitly; supported by appropriate rewards and sanctions that are enforceable and asserted by teacher behaviour. Clear rules, such as 'follow your teachers' instructions' reduce ambiguity, whereas vague rules such as 'be in the right place at the right time' are ineffective (Doyle, 1989). Whilst a teacher is always responsible for the overall control of the classroom, classroom management is a balance between levels of teacher control and developing pupils' self-control and self-regulation. Achieving the optimal balance between the two can be difficult. Much depends on how a teacher perceives the level of maturity of the group as a whole, of subgroups and individuals and the interaction between them, something I discuss further in Chapter 10.

The main function of classroom rules is to provide structure and consistency, enabling teachers to focus on teaching (Anderson and Spauding, 2007) and setting limits to pupils' behaviour to make them aware of the conditions required for success (Charles, 1999). This does not mean pupils are not treated warmly or that humour, developing relationships and mutual respect are also not important. Indeed, a principal objective of having rules is to create a safe and warm classroom climate through making clear what the teacher values as important to ensure pupils' success and to develop positive working relationships. A forerunner of such relationships is setting behavioural boundaries within which teachers and pupils can develop and practice mutual respect and supportive interactions (Dirling, 1999). Rules and routines should operate in a preventative, proactive or feedforward way to establish and maintain order and momentum – rather than focusing on punishing non-compliance. They should be taught explicitly, reinforced and be concerned primarily with maximising pupils' engagement with learning. Expecting pupils to 'know' how different teachers want them to behave without telling them is a common mistake and leads to a case law, corrective or reactive approach. Emmer et al. (1980) found that teachers who begin the year teaching and reinforcing rules and routines increase the numbers of pupils who then engage in learning activities for the rest of the year (see also Marzano, 2003).

One common mistake when making rules is to focus on telling pupils what they should not do, rather than telling them what they should do. Telling pupils where they are *not* allowed to go creates more difficulties than telling them where they *are* allowed to go, since the former arouses curiosity – why can't we go there? What are they trying to hide? A cupboard or storeroom designated 'staff use only' can fire pupils' imaginations. Perhaps it contains some dark secret, something tasty or embarrassing: holiday snaps; love letters from the head; exam papers; chocolate … when, in reality, it contains photocopy paper and worn trainers!

Classroom rules can promote appropriate behaviour in four different ways by: helping individuals (teachers and pupils) to cope; framing interpersonal relationships; supporting whole-school behaviour policies; and helping create the conditions for engagement with learning. Thus, effective rules, linked to specific and appropriate consequences establish the boundaries of behaviour and provide a safe environment in which teachers and pupils can get on with their work.

Rules operate at both the classroom level and whole-school level, the latter representing the core behavioural expectations for the school, which should provide consistency and predictability for both staff and pupils. The primary function of school rules is to develop harmonious relationships among the school community, whereas the primary purpose of classroom rules is to maximise engagement with learning (Savage, 1991). Classroom rules, whilst guided by the school rules, will differ and reflect the personal values, aims, concerns and expectations of the teacher in charge of the class and the subject being taught. What one teacher considers 'quiet' will be considered 'noisy' by another, and what constitutes 'acceptable levels' of pupil movement during a lesson are not universally accepted. Provided classroom variations are not in conflict with the core school rules, they personalise the context, offering a slightly different angle on things and, in this way, are healthy. The object of having, and publicising, school rules is not to produce robots, but to make overall shared expectations and values clear, providing consistency, predictability and a solid framework on which the school can achieve its aims. Inconsistency in the enforcement of rules sends a message to the pupils that they have a good chance of 'getting away' with misbehaviour that can be a 'fun' challenge for some! Synchronising whole-school and classroom-based rules provides the school community with both consistency and distinctiveness. Where the behaviour of a teacher, or group of teachers, differs significantly from the overall agreed policy, it leads to ambiguity for both pupils and colleagues.

When discussing school placements with trainee teachers, I always direct them to first obtain copies of the school's behaviour policy and suggest that they read it in detail before they commence their practice. I also suggest that, on their initial visits, they try and match what they have read with what they observe, to determine how the rules are being interpreted and applied, and how sanctions and rewards are used. It is not uncommon for trainees to return and say that a teacher seems to do their own thing, something that the trainees, who are being assessed on their behaviour management abilities, can find difficult to cope with. This discrepancy is further compounded as, despite many schools publishing 'positive behaviour policies', there are often far more references to punishment of misbehaviour than rewards for behaving as required.

In schools experiencing difficulty, perhaps as a result of change, or those in which colleagues do not work together, there can be a tendency for individual teachers to rely solely on their own strengths. If the school behaviour policy is not agreed by all, or is perceived as being weak and ineffectual, teachers may feel the need to defend their own domain more than usual. After all, even if there are problems around the school, provided you can hold your class together things will be OK – won't they? The answer is, highly unlikely. If there are problems around the school, an individual teacher will eventually feel the effects, no matter how competent she or he is.

Rules are hierarchical and have different levels of permanency. At the 'highest' level there is government legislation, which usually takes time to change. At the opposite extreme, are the rules a supply teacher might use if covering a class they do not know for a single lesson. In the latter case, the teacher will try to establish order quickly, in a context with which he or she is not familiar. How an individual achieves this will vary somewhat and should be guided by three basic principles: that they are legally, professionally and morally acceptable.

Classroom rules have various functions. In practice, they should focus on keeping pupils on legitimate tasks, being prepared, and ready to learn (having the correct equipment); promoting appropriate social behaviour; and making a classroom safe. One obvious reason for having rules relates to physical safety. Rules to avoid the dangers of: running in class; messing about with science, craft or gym equipment; not warming up before vigorous exercise; road safety when out on school outings are clearly necessary. Physical safety also includes interpersonal issues such as reducing the likelihood of physical violence such as fighting or bullying.

In addition to physical safety, effective classroom rules can contribute to psychological safety and support emotional well-being. If pupils and teachers do not feel safe and secure in school or classroom, they will be less able to think about learning or teaching. Psychological safety is a tacit belief about the degree to which individuals feel confident taking risks in interpersonal settings. For example, pupils feeling safe to express themselves physically, cognitively, and emotionally are likely to be more engaged academically and socially in class. In contrast, feeling unsafe increases the likelihood of pupils being disengaged from learning and avoiding or withdrawing from interpersonal activity to defend their personal selves. This raises stress levels and impacts negatively on socio-emotional well-being.

Feeling psychologically safe is not limited to pupils. Employees (e.g. teachers) who feel psychologically safe function more effectively and collaborate more to achieve shared outcomes (Edmondson and Zhike, 2014) such as a whole-school behaviour policy. They also feel more confident publicly voicing their suggestions for organisational development (Liang *et al.*, 2012) and perform more effectively as a team (Schaubroeck *et al.*, 2011). Just as a teacher in a classroom is responsible for creating the conditions for psychological safety, the same is true for managers supporting their staff.

Disruptive behaviour in class undermines tacit feelings of safety and interferes with the learning process in various ways. Cognitive activity is affected because concentration, attention and memory are disturbed (Dalgleish, 1995); emotion regulation, by worry and anxiety (Ellis and Ashbrook, 1989) leads to further disturbance of cognitive processing (Eysenck *et al.*, 2007). Learning is impaired when excessive demands result in limited cognitive resources being redirected to control emotions (Ellis *et al.*, 1995). Classrooms, with unruly pupils who other pupils *perceive* their teacher cannot control, provide ideal conditions for generating anxiety among other pupils who, in turn, are likely to use whatever behaviour they feel necessary in order to cope; some acting out, some joining the chaos and others withdrawing.

Ever-growing digital technology, whilst expanding learning opportunities, has also added a new dimension to disruption in schools, including difficult to detect serious hazards for pupils. The inappropriate use of mobile smart devices has added to behaviour management issues through distractions in classrooms, cheating in examinations, and facilitated 24-hour cyberbullying. Access to the internet has created other dangers e.g. pupils transmitting personal data/images, viewing harmful material and becoming victims of sexual abuse and exploitation. Encouraging pupils to engage in online research, whilst ensuring they are safe requires new practices. One of these requires pupils and their primary carers to sign an Internet contract that makes explicit what is safe and acceptable online behaviour and what is not and outlines sanctions if the rules are contravened. (DfE, 2016)

## Rules and psychological safety

Maslow (1987) developed a hierarchical model that provides a useful basis for understanding the relationship between pupils' safety and learning. He argued that human beings are basically good and striving to achieve all that they wish to be (self-actualisation). There are seven levels to his hierarchy of needs, beginning with physiological or survival needs, and progressing through safety, belongingness, esteem, cognitive, and aesthetic needs with self-actualisation at the pinnacle. Upward movement is dependent upon the necessity of first satisfying lower level needs, *at least in part*. As one level is satisfied, the next highest level need then becomes the target of our energies. One implication of this is that before an individual can engage with their learning (cognitive needs, level 5) they must feel part of the class (satisfy their belongingness needs, level 4) and value themselves (satisfy their esteem needs, level 3), neither of which can be addressed before their physiological (level 1) and safety needs (level 2) have been met. Physiological, safety, belongingness and esteem needs are what Maslow described as deficiency needs. A deficiency is the difference between what *should be* and *what is*. Moreover, the greater the perceived deficiency, the greater the need.

The most basic needs are physiological and necessary for survival: they include eating, drinking, keeping warm and resting. Although considered basic, not all pupils arrive at school having eaten or sufficiently rested, so it is hardly surprising that they find it difficult to move on to a higher motivational target. The 'recent' practice of providing breakfast in some schools stands as testament to the concerns of some teachers in this respect.

Immediately above physiological needs are safety needs, and this is where rules and routines have a particular significance. It is worth noting here that feeling safe and secure is an individual perception. Telling and demonstrating to someone that they are safe and have nothing to worry about counts for nothing if the individual does not perceive the situation is safe. Anyone who has taught mountain climbing will know that informing someone that an abseiling rope meets safety standards and could support the weight of a large elephant, does not necessarily convince the anxious participant that it will not snap when they are on it. Whilst it may be scientifically proven and statistically improbable that the worst might happen, some individuals remain unconvinced. Safety and security is not just about physical factors, for pupils in a classroom it can come from:

- knowing what behaviour is expected of them and other pupils, coupled with what will happen if they *do* or *do not* meet those expectations;

- believing that their teachers have their best interests at heart and will do their utmost to ensure they succeed;
- feeling confident expressing their thoughts and that they can make mistakes without being ridiculed or put down;
- believing that they can trust their teachers and other staff to protect them from harm (physical or psychological) and if necessary will do so.

Trust is a key component of an effective classroom. Yet this tacit and common belief between pupils and teacher cannot be demanded nor will it inevitably emerge as a consequence of sharing a classroom.

I reiterate the point, that it is the pupil's *perception* that matters, not necessarily the actuality. The law might insist that a teacher has a duty of care to provide a safe environment, but that means nothing to pupils if they suspect their teacher might not be capable of doing so, especially if the teacher seems to struggle to control a class or individuals within it. When this uncertainty is sensed, pupils are likely to move away from attending to their learning needs and turning their energies towards satisfying their safety needs. For example, if they observe other pupils refusing to conform to behavioural expectations and teachers seem reluctant, or unable, to stop them, then a lack of belongingness and insecurity become apparent. For many pupils, observing others failing or refusing to conform, challenging authority and getting away with it, can make them question the teacher's ability to do their job, making them feel uncomfortable and anxious as the following quote illustrates:

> Well, we were having this lesson in Q12 and Mrs C was teaching us, yeah … and then these three Year 10's walked in and one hit Danny … then they walked out laughing and she never did anything. She just said 'Get on with your work. Just ignore them.' but that was when they had gone! It wasn't the first time, they are always wandering about and she's scared of them yeah—so are most people—but it shouldn't be allowed.
> (Jesse, Year 8)

Pupils also feel unfairly treated and angry when they are subjected to block punishments because teachers cannot control individuals who are misbehaving:

> He (teacher) said someone was playing with matches at the back of the class and said we would all have to stay back if someone did not own up no one did, so he said we will have a class detention. I said I wouldn't go 'cause I was sitting at the front next to him and it was at the back so it couldn't be me. He knows who it was but he daren't say. So, he sent me to Mrs H head of year but I'm not going to detention and that's it!
> (Gavin, Year 9)

Seeing others getting away with unacceptable behaviour can damage a developing or established class social identity or belongingness. Sharing a social identity with the group perceived as 'weak' (i.e. those behaving as required) can be less appealing than being a member of the 'stronger' (disruptive) group who appear to be in control by their refusal to conform to expectations. Hence, there may be a strong temptation to join the latter – not because they dislike the teacher as such, but because the alternative provides either a more effective coping strategy at the time – are swept along with the group or because it appears to be fun:

> She's (teacher) quite nice really but too soft. When the boys at the back start burping and that, she just looks at them in disgust—then everybody starts laughing and then you laugh as well—it's hard not to when everyone else is—but we like her really. Then she looks like she's going to cry and usually goes and gets Mr W who sorts them out.
>
> (Ellie, Year 9)

Based on Maslow's formulation, it is only when pupils feel safe and secure that they will move to satisfying their need for belongingness or social affiliation. Forming a cohesive settled class is central to teaching but unlikely to happen if pupils feel unsafe and insecure. When pupils feel their physiological, safety and belongingness needs are addressed – at least partially, then they can focus on their esteem needs, that is, liking themselves and feeling they are liked and respected by others. Maslow's hierarchy offers a different slant on trying to understand why some pupils may have low self-esteem and underperform. If part of satisfying esteem needs first requires taking care of lower level needs such as feeling safe, secure and being part of a group (class) that cares about them, and pupils perceive this is not happening, then it may affect how they feel about themselves, which may contribute to underachievement. Clearly, this is an oversimplification, not least in terms of causal direction. The commonly viewed link between self-esteem and academic achievement and social behaviour has been challenged by a number of researchers. As Baumeister *et al.* put it:

> Boosting people's sense of self-worth has become a national preoccupation. Yet surprisingly, research shows that such efforts are of little value in fostering academic progress or preventing undesirable behaviour.
>
> (2005: 84)

There are a range of other reasons why an individual may have difficulty liking themselves or feeling that others like them, or why they fail, but paying attention to these subordinate needs may be one way of eliminating some of the possibilities.

Maslow's hierarchy of needs theory has been criticised by a number of researchers (e.g. Wahba and Bridwell, 1976). One criticism relates to the

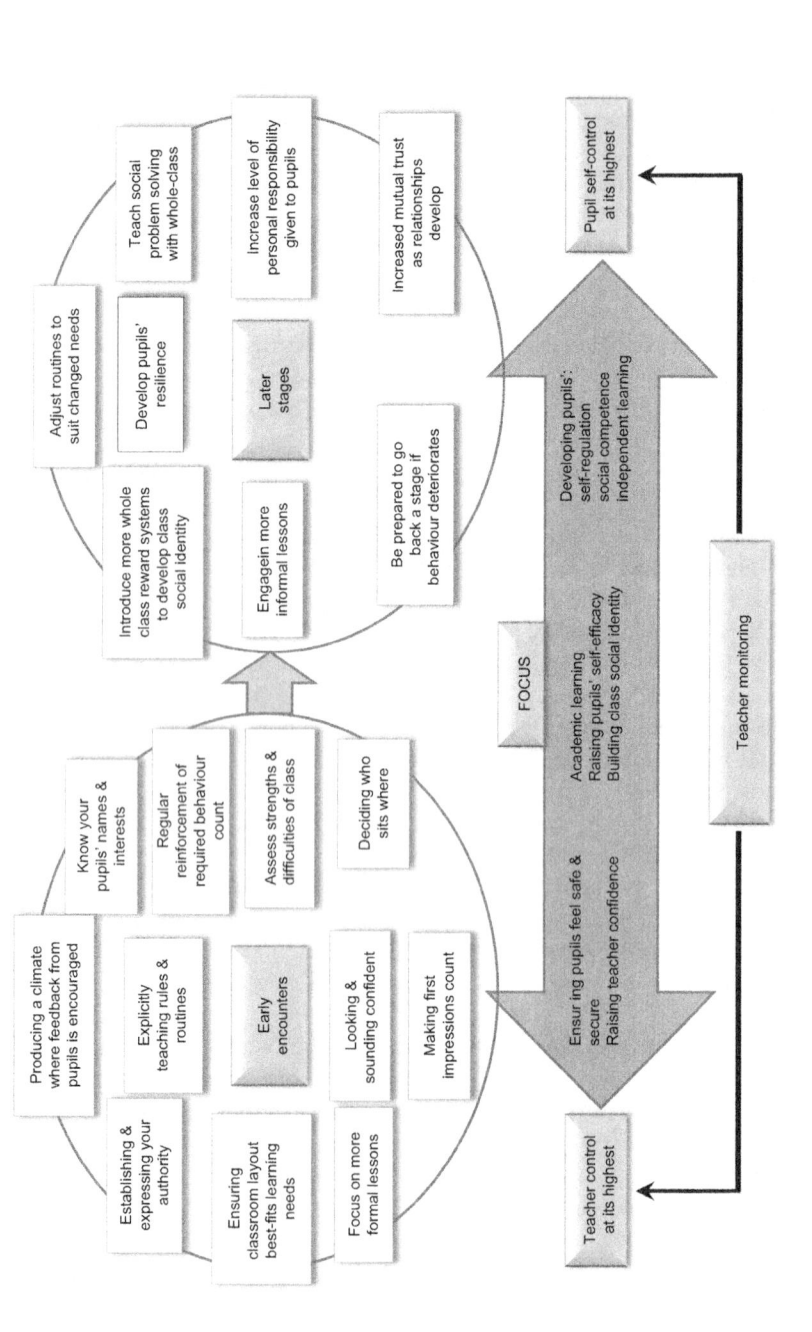

*Figure 8.1* A developmental perspective on classroom management comparing early and later encounters with a class.

fact that some people appear to focus on higher level needs, ignoring lower order needs. For instance, sacrificing personal safety to protect a loved one or doing without food and rest to complete a painting or book. Nevertheless, the model provides a general impression of how most people operate in everyday conditions. From a behaviour management perspective, it offers a sequential framework on which to build a discipline strategy, suggests what to concentrate on and in what order, and encourages teachers to monitor that all basic elements have been addressed, at least in part, before moving to higher-level aims.

Figure 8.1 shows how a teacher might support pupils' needs moving from early encounters to later in the school year. Early stages focus on defining expectations and boundaries and high levels of direction, whereas in later stages pupils are given differentiated levels of responsibility and diversity in learning, informed by performance feedback. Thus, in addition to signalling the rights and responsibilities of pupils, rules and routines are an essential component of the conditions for learning (Rudduck, Chaplain and Wallace, 1996) and also precursors to the development of behavioural self-control. Doll *et al.* (2014).

## Establishing classroom rules

So far, I have discussed the role and function of rules, without saying much about the rules themselves. There are a number of questions to consider in this respect, including: How many rules should there be? How should they be worded? How do you go about setting rules? Who should be involved in deciding which rules to have?

There are some obvious 'core rules' usually found in any school behaviour policy (e.g. treating others with respect, acting responsibly) that provide the baseline for classroom rules.

Merely writing down rules does not mean they will be communicated to those for whom they are intended, so attention needs to be paid to how the community is explicitly made aware of expectations. To do this requires answers to questions, such as: Who needs to be told? (e.g. pupils, teaching and ancillary staff, parents, governors, visitors.). How often do they need reminding? Should core rules be publicly displayed and if so, where and in what form? How do you monitor their effectiveness and relevance?

There are a number of ways of setting rules. Which approach you decide to adopt depends, to a large extent, on your beliefs about human behaviour. For instance, do you believe that your pupils:

- Should be treated with respect and hence rules should be negotiated with them from the start?
- Know how to behave, so they should not need rules spelling out?

- Are strongly influenced by context and group dynamics, so it is important to let them find boundaries which are acceptable to you and the school and then respond if they cross those boundaries?
- Will always try and push the boundaries, so they need them spelled out clearly at the beginning and reminding along the way?

Which approach (if any) you favour will reflect a combination of your previous experience, personality, confidence, what you know about the individuals or classes you work with, what you consider acceptable behaviour, along with what the school expects. There is no single correct approach, because none fit all individuals and contexts.

It would be unwise to opt for negotiating rules with a new class if you were not sure of your ability to negotiate with that particular group at that stage – however much you subscribe to democratic principles. New teachers dealing with new classes are unlikely to know the dynamics of the group or individual personalities. If the pupils are not used to dealing with that level of responsibility, have limited social competence and given they do not know you, negotiation at that stage may be problematic.

Stipek *et al.* (1992) argue that, whilst young people are often aware of standards and rules, assuming they 'know' how to behave in your class can be unwise, since each teacher has his or her personal expectations.

Getting on with teaching and waiting for pupils to do something wrong before correcting them is similarly inadvisable. Case law approaches rely on reacting to negative behaviour rather than teaching positive behaviour.

This leaves us with the final 'limit-setting' approach, i.e. the teacher spelling out boundaries in advance. This approach has several advantages, particularly when establishing authority with a new group, assuming that the rules have been well thought out, are appropriate and achievable by the group. A limit-setting approach is an effective method because it:

- provides pupils and teachers with a predictable and safe environment;
- unlike case law or negotiated approaches, limit-setting gives a relatively fixed point of reference for the teacher, since the rules will have been considered and rehearsed in advance rather than having to think on your feet;
- quickly projects the teacher's control of the situation;
- enables the teacher to consider the content and likely consequences of making specific rules before going into action, thereby being proactive.

However, this does not mean that inevitably pupils will not be involved in updating or renegotiating rules, as classroom relationships develop. The objective in setting limits in the early stages is to establish teacher control and provide a usable and predictable structure reflecting the safety and security needs identified by Maslow. Over time, as interpersonal relationships develop, the teacher can engage in negotiating new rules, should existing ones become redundant and he or she feels the pupils are sufficiently responsible and able to do so.

Early in their careers, or often when starting a new job, a teacher's primary concerns are likely to be self-oriented and focused on survival and adjustment to the school, so planning and prescribing rules at this stage is more likely to minimise threats to self and satisfy these concerns. As time progresses, a teacher's self-efficacy, relationships with pupils, knowledge of the group, its dynamics and individual pupils develop. Thus, concerns shift from survival towards wider developmental issues. Attention moves to increasing pupil autonomy and preparing them for transition to the next stage of their development and producing the conditions under which negotiation about expectations is more appropriate.

## Making rules work for you

Relying solely on word of mouth to communicate behavioural expectations is likely to be problematic and lead to unwanted modifications (we are all familiar with the game Chinese whispers). Likewise, merely recording them on a document that is given out at your first lesson, read briefly, then put away, is also not a good idea. The most efficient way of establishing rules is to have them posted in your classroom, but this does not mean they have to resemble fire regulations or be lacklustre. I have seen a wide range of different approaches to publicising rules, with younger pupils for example, some of the best being illustrated or in the form of cartoons. A light-hearted and nicely presented list of classroom (or school) rules grabs pupils' attention, makes learning them more fun and hence easier to recall.

To have a set of rules to cover all possible situations would result in a rather long unmemorable and unmanageable list, so the number of rules should be kept to a minimum. I recommend a maximum of five simply worded and easy-to-remember rules. Hargreaves *et al.* (1975) recommend five types of rules that relate to: movement; talking; time; teacher-pupil relationships and pupil-pupil relationships. However, there are clear overlaps between them. Canter and Canter (1992) suggest four generally applicable rules: follow directions; keep hands, feet and objects to yourself; no teasing or name-calling; no swearing.

When designing rules, consideration must be given to consequences for pupils who behave appropriately or inappropriately. Reinforcement (e.g. rewards) of those pupils behaving as required, alongside punishments (e.g. sanctions) for those who misbehave, needs careful consideration and must be made explicit, be organised hierarchically and be fair. (NB see Chapter 1 for explanation of the terms reinforcement and punishment.) Rules (and routines) established and maintained using reinforcement (e.g. rewards) and punishment (e.g. sanctions) and that demonstrate a clear cause-and-effect relationship removes ambiguity for staff and pupils. When deciding on which rewards and sanctions to use, it pays to carry out a consequence analysis to help clarify the likely value of rewards and sanctions to pupils. This allows you to consider the possible unintended consequences, for instance, selecting a punishment you would not be able to enforce.

Reinforcement for completing tasks might range from the abstract (praise/verbal support, smiles, nods) to the tangible (stickers, food, computer time).

Punishments should be predictable and hierarchical. Those broadcasted with an accompanying note of uncertainty and those that are threatened and not carried through, are a waste of time. Being clear about which sanctions are available in school and which are appropriate for particular types of misdemeanour, how they are organised and who has the authority to issue and carry them through helps to remove ambiguity and allows teacher and class to focus on the task in hand – that is, teaching and learning. Examples of hierarchical rewards and punishments are provided in Chapter 10.

The higher the level of sanction, the more likely it is to undermine relationships, so consideration has to be given to how relationships can be repaired afterwards.

Since punishment is used when teachers feel they are losing control, I strongly advise you to write the hierarchy down so you have a reference point when under pressure. Do not rush into punishments, especially with challenging pupils, as this can lead to a negative cycle. Offer the pupil alternatives, i.e. 'Get on with ... or ... it's your choice' and then walk away, perhaps passing a positive comment to someone else nearby who is doing what is required. Then return if they are still refusing to comply and rise to the next level: 'OK you are already staying on for two minutes. Either get on with ... or ... it's your choice.' Walk away. Keep your comments as emotionally bland and as matter of fact as possible, as showing you are getting irritated or angry can feed a confrontational pupil's learned negative aggressive script.

In classrooms where rules are applied inconsistently, behaviour is generally poor (Gottfredson, 1990) since pupils become unclear about expectations and that they apply to them (Evertson et al., 2003). If your rules are necessary to ensure the smooth running of your classroom, then not enforcing them is usually unwise. However, breaking the flow of the lesson to respond to a not serious breach of the rules, is not always the best strategy. Depending on how well you know the class or the individual involved, or whether you are dealing with other more serious behaviour at the time, you may choose not to respond immediately, preferring to use reorientation strategies. There are several reorientation techniques that can be used to deal with such problems (see Chapter 10). You might choose to defer your response until later, deliberately ignoring it, reinforcing those nearby who are behaving as required or defusing the situation with humour.

## Rules about rules

Whilst people differ in their beliefs about how to introduce and sustain rules, there are four basic principles that I advise people to consider when deciding how to develop rules, these are:

- *Keep 'em positive.* The wording of a rule can make or break it. Rules should reflect what you value and want to encourage in your classroom. Negative rules encourage a negative climate for both pupils and teacher. Negative rules (e.g. 'don't talk' or 'don't shout out'), although sometimes successful in terminating behaviour, do not teach the required positive behaviours. Becker *et al.* (1975) argued that such rules might be successful in the short term; they are likely to increase the frequency of the misbehaviour over time.
- *Keep 'em brief.* Rules should only include key concerns. Make sure they are kept brief and snappy. This makes them easier to remember.
- *Keep 'em realistic.* Set rules that reflect expectations that are appropriate. Only set rules that are enforceable and appropriate for your class.
- *Keep 'em focused.* The overall objective for having rules is to develop self-regulation, which is enabled through helping pupils to internalise those qualities necessary to facilitate their development. Rules should therefore concentrate on key issues, including: being aware of personal safety and the safety of others; considerate; cooperative; honest; friendly; as well as attending to legitimate classroom activity including appropriate noise levels for different contexts.
- *Keep 'em.* If the rule is worth having in the first place, then it needs to be regularly reinforced. Evertson (1985) found that behaviour and attitudes were unfavourably affected when teachers ignored infringements of classroom rules.

If you find a rule is not working or has lost its relevance, then either modify it or drop it. Do not make rules ineffective by applying them one minute and letting them slide the next. If they are necessary, they need to be applied consistently. If you cannot make your rules work for you, ask why? Are you unable to enforce them? Are they inappropriate or unreasonable?

## Routines and rituals: adding meat to the bone

Probably the most important activity in early encounters with any class is establishing daily routines, that is, how you want to operate your classroom and explicitly teaching them should begin in the first week (Backes and Ellis, 2003). Whilst rules specify general expectations, routines focus on specific behaviours (Evertson *et al.*, 2003).

The most competent and effective teachers spend considerable time teaching specific routines and continue doing so until their pupils can carry them out efficiently (Canter, 2009). As a result, their pupils become socialised and settled in more quickly (Evertson and Poole, 2008). Furthermore, starting with lessons that have lower content demands and a higher emphasis on routines, leads to effective classrooms, which then facilitates improved pupil learning over the year (Emmer et al., 1980).

Routines are procedural supports that are pivotal in managing everyday social and academic behaviour around school and in classrooms. They are often organised around a particular time (start of a lesson), a place (hall) or context (groupwork). Their object is to add meaning to rules; translate their spirit into action; maximise learning time; and make classroom life predictable, efficient, and safe. If established correctly and applied consistently, they become *automatic* and are usually triggered by a nonverbal signal (e.g. clapping).

If being polite is an important rule, then the routines established for greeting pupils and staff when they arrive in school or class, how equipment is shared, turn-taking in discussion, and empowering pupils to have their thoughts and feelings heard should reflect this. If not disturbing other pupils while working is a rule, then routines for checking or marking pupils' work, distributing materials, maintaining appropriate noise levels, and movement around the classroom should ensure that disruption to pupils is minimalised. Where considered, planned and communicated, routines facilitate the smooth running of lessons, keeping pupils on task and maintaining the efficient and ordered operation of your classroom – enabling you to teach.

Some routines operate at the school level (lunchtime, assemblies), others at the classroom level (getting work out, changing activities). Many routines are roughly similar in all schools, whilst others vary significantly between, or within, schools to reflect different organisational climates and school contexts, as well as the values and beliefs of those responsible for running it.

Different teachers and subjects require different routines. There are some common examples, including:

- entering the classroom;
- getting the attention of the class;
- dealing with latecomers;
- managing noise levels;
- emergency drills;
- getting out materials;
- marking work;
- changing activities – transitions;
- getting changed for physical activities;
- movement inside class;
- movement around school;
- movement outside school;

- going to the toilet;
- dealing with interruptions;
- keeping pupils on task;
- finishing the lesson;
- exiting the classroom.

Routines that are inefficient can take up substantial amounts of teaching and learning time – up to 50% of some lessons (Jones and Jones, 1990) and generate substantial disruption. In contrast, well-planned and well-executed routines can streamline these activities, increasing the time available for teaching and learning and make the classroom a calmer, safer, more predictable place. Having a calm classroom helps pupils concentrate but calmness does not mean lifeless. However, some of the techniques used by teachers to get the attention of the class raise noise levels and can create an atmosphere of chaos. When for example, pupils are discussing in small groups resorting to shouting, whistles, and similar loud devices to get their attention can be counterproductive. Using such methods usually indicates that pupils' noise levels are very high, so they have to be outdone. A calmer approach is to be mobile in your room and prompt groups at timed intervals before a transition is required. In doing so, taking the opportunity to warn pupils that you will be waiting to talk to them in three/two/one minutes whilst commenting on their work. This enables you to begin lowering the noise levels in advance of the transition. Making sure you inform pupils of the signal you will use to get their attention is also important.

Routines and rituals are a very powerful form of demonstrating authority to all members of the school community. They give shape to, and facilitate the smooth running of the school day. A ritual, such as assembly, requires participants to behave in a formalised way and includes particular actions, words and movements, and a series of routines occurring in a particular sequence. It operates as a social script (Abelson, 1981) with props (e.g. whiteboard), roles (speaker) and sequence rules (e.g. entry-exit sequence). How pupils enter assembly often reflects how they are expected to enter other formal areas, such as classrooms, but may be modified to give the assembly more status, such as playing music when people enter. The rules about who is expected or permitted to speak and in what order, is usually fairly easily understood. These routines and procedures are usually learnt, firstly by instruction, modelling and prompting, and later by internalising the various elements. The formality of the occasion encourages conformity, and those who fail to conform are often masked in large gatherings by the contributions of others. Singing 'alternative' words to songs and sniggering is usually localised. The 'power' of such rituals can be so great that, even when people feel unwell, they are reluctant to leave, even if the result is suffering the embarrassment and teasing from being sick where they sit. Rituals reinforce the status of the members of the community, often represented by who sits on the comfy chairs (and who does not), who stands up for who as a mark of respect and so on.

However, they also provide a sense of community and social identity, incorporating feelings of belonging and security, which can be emotionally uplifting, enhancing well-being, within which personal development can take place. In doing so, they help satisfy what Maslow identified as second- and third-level needs. These thoughts and feelings are experienced by both staff and pupils, since such rituals publicly reinforce their position in the organisation and helps them to psychologically accept that position. Assemblies are events that promote the social identity of the school and are used as a vehicle for reminding pupils of what is valued for example, giving prizes for positive behaviour or publicly admonishing unacceptable behaviour. Similar processes operate in the classroom but with less formality.

In the classroom, routine teacher behaviours include: standing or sitting in particular places; clapping; 'give me fives' or just raising their hands in order to elicit particular behaviour such as gaining pupils' attention. Other signals may communicate deviation from the required routine behaviour:

> When Mr H thinks people are talking too loud ... he starts tapping on his desk with a piece of wood ... he says he's the judge, it means silence in court!
>
> (James, Year 8)

Not all signals are effective, and some teachers are unaware of their ineffective behaviour. One example of this is using the terms '*ssh*' and '*erm*'. These two sounds are commonly associated with expecting people to be quiet (ssh) and indicating disapproval (erm) and are not uncommon generally (e.g. library and cinema). If they act as a trigger or reminder of a behaviour (e.g. you are expected to complete written work without talking) and bring about the desired behaviour, that is fine. Unfortunately, I have witnessed many teachers over the years using these two sounds repeatedly but having no effect. They have become automatic responses or employee strategies (see Chapter 2) but are ineffective. Whilst the teacher is busy '*sshing*' and '*erming*' the noise level remains unchanged and worse, he or she is seldom aware of either doing it or that it is ineffective – it has become habitual and beyond their conscious awareness. I have video recorded lessons, and it is only when these teachers see the replay that they realise what is happening. However, acknowledging the ineffectiveness of the behaviour is the easy part. Breaking the habit is usually harder, since it has become so automatic. Changing to a new strategy requires deliberate conscious effort and practice over a sustained period. Unfortunately, because the behaviour is so automatic, when under pressure we are more likely to revert to using it than the new, improved version. Overlearning a replacement strategy is an efficient way of retraining old habits.

Learning ineffective behaviours often begins when new or trainee teachers attempt to replicate the behaviour of a teacher they are observing. A teacher who perhaps by merely coughing or folding her arms, tapping a pencil or similar behavioural cue, might well trigger instant silence, gain the attention of the class or bring a halt to a squabble over who has the next turn on a computer. Unfortunately, as seductive as copying the behaviour might be, a new teacher is in no way guaranteed the same response if she or he does so. Merely copying one seemingly simple stimulus-response chain fails to acknowledge the sequence of events that led to the 'signal' and the response becoming associated. The individual's social competence, personal idiosyncratic features and belief systems, combined with other factors such as control of space, objects and setting, power and leadership and school policies, determine the power and effectiveness of behaviours.

## How effective are your rules and routines?

To determine the effectiveness of your rules and routines requires monitoring and evaluation. There are two issues here, namely competence (the routine is completed correctly) and speed (it is done quickly and safely), both of which can be recorded and evaluated (see Chapter 10). Measurement of time taken requires you to consider, for example, how quickly pupils in this group should be able to arrive at class and be ready to work, then test if it is possible to improve. Remember, every minute saved on administrative and logistic routines means more time for teaching and learning. Evaluation in this way will give you some insight as to whether or not particular routines are working as required, can be improved or need replacing. If they are working efficiently and effectively, that's fine. As the old saying goes, 'if it ain't broke don't fix it!' Nevertheless, it is worth remembering my earlier comments regarding the difficulties of self-evaluation and how they can be overcome with the assistance of a trusted colleague or use of audiovisual equipment. Feedback from these sources can be used to identify any automatic behaviours of which you may not be consciously aware, but which may be undermining the effectiveness of your routines.

## Evaluate your routines

Table 8.1 provides an example of the routines that might be used to introduce a lesson. Alongside each is a grid for evaluation of their effectiveness in achieving the required objective along with time taken. This can be used to highlight problems, determine what is working well, and identify priorities for change. Don't forget to focus on both time *and* competence.

Rules and routines are not an alternative to good teaching, but they help create the conditions for teaching and engagement with learning. To be successful, they need to be planned and taught, explicitly reinforced through practice, and revisited during the term until established. Teaching should be routine by routine and practiced until automatic. Monitoring allows you to determine if they continue to work as required or need modification.

Table 8.1 Evaluating classroom routines at the start of a lesson

| Routine | Behaviour | Works Well | Usually works | Not working | Action |
|---|---|---|---|---|---|
| Exchange greetings | I meet pupils at the classroom door. | x | | | |
| | I say hello and they respond | x | | | |
| Getting the class ready for work | Pupils walk quietly into the room | | x | | Will try changing reinforcers |
| | They go to their tables | x | | | |
| | I check pupils are all sitting where I want them to be | | | x | Will produce a new seating plan and direct pupils on arrival at class |
| | They have a quiz waiting to get them focussed | x | | | |
| | I get their attention | | x | | |
| | I ask them to get out the appropriate equipment | x | | | |
| Commencing the lesson | I introduce the topic | x | | | |
| | They are invited to ask questions | | x | | Need to work on encouraging boys to ask more questions; girls tending to do most of the asking |
| | I reinforce what they have to do | x | | | |

Along with other factors discussed in this book, they do have the potential to provide a framework for developing a smooth-running classroom and are a key component of a teacher's classroom management plan. Effective rules and routines are money in the bank for a teacher in managing pupil behaviour.

## Annotated further reading

Murray, C., and Pianta, R.C. (2007). The importance of teacher-student relationships for adolescents with high incidence disabilities. *Theory Into Practice*, 46(2), 105–112.

Common among the masses of literature is the importance of teacher-pupil relationships for adolescent mental health and social-emotional functioning but often with limited advice as to how this operates into practice. This articles reviews strategies that are effective in promoting and developing such relationships at the school and classroom level – including the often-neglected organisational and structural issues (e.g. rules and routines), which, if organised correctly, support the development of positive social interaction. Whilst each is considered separately to aid clarity, it is essential to recognise their interdependence and the need for them to be informed by a coordinated whole-school approach. The article is directed towards pupils with mental health issues, so it is timely given the substantive numbers of adolescents in the general population reportedly in need of support with these issues.

## Further reading to support M level study

Roache, J. (2011). Teachers' views on the impact of classroom management on student responsibility. *Australian Journal of Education*, 55(2), 132–146.

This study examined teachers' views of their classroom management style and compared it with pupils' views. Results indicated that coercive styles, i.e. those that combine punishment with aggressive and hostile behaviour, exacerbated misbehaviour and increased student distraction. In contrast, a combination of rewards and punishments encouraged student responsibility and reduced misbehaviour. When students misbehaved, their teachers increased the use of coercive management styles and simultaneously decreased their use of rewards.

# Chapter 9
# Managing difficult behaviour

Of all pupils in school, those with emotional and behavioural difficulties (EBD) are probably responsible for the highest levels of stress among teachers (Travers and Cooper, 1996). EBD are wide ranging. Teachers 'know' what they mean by the term, but their pupil with behavioural difficulties may be very different when with other teachers; it is seldom the case that pupils exhibit behaviour difficulties with all teachers or in all activities. Defining EBD and associated terms (e.g. maladjustment, disturbed, disturbing, disordered, difficult, challenging, antisocial) has a long history.

In the 1944 Education Act, the category 'maladjusted' was introduced and described as 'emotional instability' or 'psychological disturbance', neither of which was defined in the Act, which left meaning open to interpretation. Maladjustment was later considered 'medicalised', so the Special Educational Needs (SEN) Act (1981) shifted the emphasis to more educational language. Hence, 'maladjustment' was changed to 'emotional and behavioural difficulties' (EBD). As a result, 'the official abandonment of the medical model in the field of special education led to the official sanctioning of the ascendency of the educational psychologist' (Cooper, 1999: 25).

In 2008, a new category 'behavioural, emotional and social difficulties' (BESD) was introduced and defined as 'a wide range of SEN ... *including* ... emotional disorders, conduct disorders and hyperkinetic disorders (ADD/ADHD) ... *or* ... those with anxiety, who self-harm, have school phobia or depression, and those whose behaviour or emotional well-being are seen to be deteriorating' (DCSF, 2008), heralding a return to medical terminology, e.g. 'disorder'.

In 2014, it was changed to 'Social, Emotional and Mental Health' (SEMH) difficulties, which removed explicit reference to 'behaviour' from the title but not from the content, as the following quote illustrates:

> These may include becoming withdrawn or isolated, as well as displaying challenging, disruptive or disturbing behaviour. These behaviours may reflect underlying mental health difficulties such as anxiety or depression, self-harming, substance misuse, eating disorders or physical symptoms that

are medically unexplained. ... may have disorders such as attention deficit disorder, attention deficit hyperactive disorder or attachment disorder.

(DfE, 2014b: 98)

No doubt, in the life of this book, the semantic duelling will continue as government policy results in different agencies becoming more or less prominent in deciding how to respond to EBD. However, the behaviours it refers to will remain unchanged.

One of the arguments for removing the word 'behaviour' from the category and replacing it with 'mental health' was, according to Norwich and Eaton

> ... a policy of reducing the number of pupils identified as having SEN ... *but* ... the new category of SEMH is no different from the previous BESD ... *and lacks* ... a clear process for specifying the thresholds for identifying such difficulties.
>
> (2015)

The mental health of children (and adults) has been identified as a priority for the present Conservative government, which resulted in the appointment (in 2015) of the first DfE mental health champion for schools, who is tasked with helping to raise awareness and reduce the stigma around young people's mental health. One feature of the 'new' approach was *another call* for joined-up thinking between the many varied agencies with whom many pupils with EBD find themselves involved. The desire for multiagency working to support children and young people is nothing new, nor are the problems putting it into practice because of a lack of inter-professional understanding (e.g. Chaplain and Freeman, 1994; Davidson, 2008). For example, the recently abandoned category BESD, whilst a recognised category to some working in education (although referred to as SEBD by others in the same profession), was not a recognised term in the team who produced the guidelines for anti-social behaviour and conduct disorder (NICE, 2013a).

Whilst the terms 'challenging' or 'difficult behaviour' are widely used and commonly accepted as understood, they are socially constructed – one person's (or group's) beliefs about what behaviour is challenging and what is not – so they will differ from one another. Challenging or difficult behaviour results from the interaction of both environmental and personal factors, and the relationship between them and so any assessment or intervention should take this into account.

This chapter uses the term 'emotional and behavioural difficulties', which lies at the heart of whichever definition is flavour of the month – medical or educational. It is also the internationally recognised descriptor of this group (Cole *et al.*, 2013).

The category EBD includes both those pupils who internalise their difficulties (e.g. pupils who are withdrawn, shy, depressed or self-harming) and those who externalise their difficulties (e.g. being aggressive towards others). The latter group tend to receive the most attention in schools as they are hard to ignore and present a challenge to teachers' authority. EBD can occur alongside other issues such as underachievement, lack of persistence on academic tasks or social skills deficits and, because they are some of the most challenging pupils for schools to teach, they are the group most likely to be excluded from school.

Pupils with EBD can stir strong emotions among school staff, destabilising relationships and negatively affecting the expectations and well-being of those involved. Other concerns include the rising numbers of pupils in this category as the Association for Teachers and Lecturers (ATL) pointed out:

> The majority of education staff say there has been a rise in the number of children with emotional, behavioural or mental health problems over the past five years coupled with worsening student behaviour in schools.
> (2013: 1)

Since the closing of many special schools, the majority of pupils with EBD are now 'included' within mainstream schools where they receive varying and often haphazard levels of support, are recipients of ill-informed interventions and the staff responsible for them receive inadequate training. Again the ATL points out:

> Schools need to give their staff good and regular training so that they know how to work with students with behavioural or mental health problems and have confidence in handling pupils with challenging behaviour. Behaviour training also needs to be an integral part of teacher training.
> (ibid.: 3)

The challenges that EBD present in schools include:

- challenges to teachers' authority and competence;
- problems with emotional regulation, making prosocial relationships difficult;
- underachievement, frustrating teachers who are convinced that the pupil has ability;
- unpredictable behaviour that raises safety issues, especially with violent individuals;
- involvement with various human service agencies, e.g. social services and medical professions. There is no guarantee that schools will be kept informed of what other professionals are doing because of regulations governing data protection (Chaplain and Freeman, 1998).
- EBD in young children (e.g. early onset conduct disorder (CD)) can predict that bigger problems (e.g. criminality) are likely to follow

(Tremblay et al., 2004). This observation creates a dilemma about when to intervene. Whilst children are at their most aggressive around 3 years of age (ibid.), identifying atypical aggression in preschoolers remains problematic. Practitioners fear pathologising normal, age-appropriate behaviours when, for example, that aggressive behaviour in young children is often a precursor to developing assertiveness (Chazan et al., 2014). However, when dealing with very aggressive pupils in secondary schools, it is important to make yourself aware of the age at which these behaviours were first observed.

- the negative affect on other pupils' learning and social behaviour, something the DfE drew attention to in their guidance – on what action mainstream schools should take to identify and support all children with special educational needs (SEN) whether or not they have an Education, Health and Care (EHC) plan. This involves having clear policies on how such needs will be met including 'how they will manage the effect of any disruptive behaviour so it does not adversely affect other pupils' (DfE, 2014b: 98).

## Socio-emotional development in adolescence: typical and atypical development

Before going into detail about specific behaviour disorders, it is worth taking a little time to consider socio-emotional development during adolescence and how typical and atypical developmental trajectories differ. This will better help to understand differences between pupils who have social, emotional and behavioural difficulties and disorders and those whose behaviour represents typical adolescent development.

According to Santrock (2009), adolescence in western societies is largely accepted to fall between ages 10 and 22 years – but precise ages are not defined. It is viewed as a transitional period between childhood and adulthood. Early adolescence is between 10 and 13 years, middle adolescence between 14 and 17 years and late adolescence between 18 and 24 years (Ozer and Irwin, 2009). It is viewed by many researchers as a period of comparatively high neural plasticity, notably in those brain regions concerned with executive function and social cognition and hence of relevance to understanding social behaviour.

Adolescence is often referred to as a time of 'storm and stress' – a proposal not without its critics (Casey et al., 2010). Nonetheless, it is recognised as a period in which adolescents frequently experience intense negative affect, which has been linked to mood swings, risky behaviour and emotional volatility. The rate at which these changes take place can surpass the socio-emotional coping capacity of many young people and the resultant phenomenon of adolescent stress is widely acknowledged (Byrne et al., 2007). Exposure to stressors including social stress, (e.g. social isolation, peer group pressure) during adolescence may result in more protracted and qualitatively different effects than exposure to stressors at other ages, due to interaction between developing brain structures and specific hormones (McCormick et al., 2010).

Compas and Reeslund (2009) argued that the healthy development of adolescents can be put at risk through exposure to stressful events, both in and out of school, but they also acknowledged that there are individual differences. These differences result from the interplay of individual and environmental susceptibilities and resources, and the individual's range of coping strategies (see Chapter 2).

The importance of effective behaviour management on pupils' coping, well-being and resilience was made clear by the DfE (2015). The most significant school factors that protect adolescents and help them to develop resilience include: clear policies on behaviour; positive classroom management; a whole-school approach to mental health and support mechanisms. Pupils also tend to be more resilient in schools where they experience feelings of belongingness (Osterman, 2000) as they are more likely to hold positive attitudes to learning and social behaviour, are more engaged with learning and feel safe.

During adolescence, an individual will undergo changes to personal characteristics (physical, cognitive and emotional) as well as to social relationships with family, school and peer groups. These changes, both individually and collectively can have profound effects on behaviour, motivation and learning. The impact of puberty on their brains makes adolescents particularly sensitive to their social environments (Crone and Dahl, 2012). Changes in the brain's socio-emotional system result in increased reward-seeking and risk-taking behaviour especially when in the company of peers. Understanding the role of the brain in adolescent social development may have important messages for matching teaching practice to developmental levels to take advantage of periods of neural plasticity in order to maximise engagement with learning.

Although risk-taking usually declines in late adolescence as self-regulation develops, engaging in risky and emotionally charged behaviour is heightened during mid-adolescence. Reducing adolescent risk-taking relies primarily on school-based programmes such as PSHE. However, although these programmes increase pupils' knowledge and awareness, they seldom alter behaviour, not least because of the immaturity of the self-regulatory system, which is often not addressed through the programmes.

There is increased vulnerability to psychiatric conditions during adolescence, which are believed to be related to a combination of genetically controlled neural development alongside coping with novel stresses and challenges that emerge from the socio-cultural environment (Andersen and Teicher, 2008). Many of the changes adolescents undergo result from a significant remodelling of the brain's dopaminergic system. Dopamine is involved in a number of physiological and behavioural processes, including cognition, locomotion, mood, motivation and reward. Abnormalities in the central dopaminergic systems contribute to several neuropsychiatric disorders, including, attention deficit hyperactivity disorder (ADHD) and conduct disorders.

Typically, adolescence is a time when neurological tendencies and personal characteristics can predispose them towards behaving in ways that show a lack of consideration for others (Ashton and Lee, 2016). This includes being rude, ill-mannered and disrespectful to others, including teachers, as they focus on pursuing their own goals. Pupils behaving this way disrupt classroom relationships, reduce engagement with learning, and can undermine achievement (Hirschy and Braxton, 2004). Ignoring such behaviour, in the hope it will disappear as pupils mature, reinforces the message that such behaviour is acceptable, which can result in it being repeated and exacerbated (Feldmann, 2001). It is therefore important to intervene early to avert more serious antisocial behaviour and attitudes developing (Marini, 2007).

Rude and disrespectful behaviour is associated with particular temperamental traits including limited effortful control (the ability to inhibit an automatic response), low affiliation, and frustration (Spadafora et al., 2016), as well as antisocial beliefs and conduct problems (Farrell et al., 2015). In their study of 222 adolescents, Spadafora et al. (2016) found differences between unintentional and intentional rudeness or incivility.

Unintentional variants were associated with carelessness, lack of concern for others thoughtlessness, poor emotion regulation and lower effortful control and negatively correlated with frustration. In contrast, intentional incivility is purposefully engaging in behaviours to harm others (Marini et al., 2010). A high score on intentional incivility reflects adolescents who have little desire to build positive relationships with others and care less about how their behaviour affects others. However, it is important to be aware that aggressive behaviour can be an element of normal development or indicate a serious, ongoing mental health disorder that poses a safety concern. It follows that being able to differentiate between the two, in order to provide the most appropriate level and type of intervention, is essential to avoid over-or under-reaction.

Whilst most adolescents emerge from the second decade of their lives without lasting difficulties (Graber et al., 1996), the numerous changes that occur during adolescence can result in negative and sometimes overwhelming consequences for the young person themselves and for those around them. For example, those who do not experience positive peer and adult relationships, develop limited coping skills and/or academic, social and/or behavioural difficulties (Lerner et al., 2015).

To decide whether or not a behaviour is typical, atypical, or a significant problem, a number of factors need to be considered: the frequency and severity of unacceptable behaviour (compared with peers of the same age and sex); the nature of unacceptable behaviour and the context in which the behaviour takes place; the duration; and the impact on the child and others.

## A closer look at specific EBD

Given the limitations of a single chapter and the wide range of EBD, the discussion will focus on the three most prevalent mental disorders, namely, attention deficit hyperactivity disorder (ADHD), oppositional defiant disorder (ODD), and conduct disorder (CD). These labels represent clusters of behaviours, so as such are of little use in determining a classroom intervention. However, the clusters are composed of familiar behaviours (see Table 9.1) including low/moderate-level disruption (e.g. fidgets, argues with adults), which can be changed. It is only when moving to CD that more extreme behaviours are listed (e.g. physical violence). Nonetheless, even in CD not all symptoms are so extreme. Whilst ADHD, ODD and CD are listed separately, they can occur simultaneously. For example, up to 70% of children with ADHD also meet the criteria for ODD (Biederman, 2005), and 33% have both ADHD and CD symptoms (Faraone et al., 1991). The following sections discuss the individual and common features of each disorder.

### Attention Deficit Hyperactivity Disorder (ADHD)

ADHD is probably the most researched mental disorder in children and adolescents. Those affected tend to be impulsive, inattentive and overactive, so have difficulty waiting or sitting still for long periods of time and are easily distracted from learning tasks in school. ADHD is usually diagnosed between the ages of 3 and 7 years. Estimates suggest that up to 9% of UK children suffer from this disorder (NICE, 2013b) and that it is more common in boys than girls (ratios up to 9:1).

The Diagnostic and Statistical Manual of Mental Disorders – DSM-5 (American Psychiatric Association, 2013) – lists three types of ADHD presentation: inattentive, hyperactive-impulsive, and the most common, combined inattentive, hyperactive-impulsive (see Table 9.1). Impulsivity, and notably problems delaying gratification, are particularly high in ADHD. However, not being a unitary construct, levels of different elements of impulsivity are found in different types of ADHD (Sonuga-Barke, 2002). Impulsivity is a component of temperament, characterised by the tendency to behave before thinking. Impulsivity is a 'normal' characteristic of young children that typically decreases with age as they learn to regulate their impulses through effortful or deliberate cognitive control (Kauffman, 1989). However, it tends to be persistent with several behaviour disorders and has long-term effects on psychological adjustment. Mischel et al. (1972) devised a test to differentiate between impulsive and reflective children. Children were given one marshmallow and told that if they did not eat it they could have two when the researcher returned 20 minutes later. Some children managed to wait; others did not. The children were tracked into adolescence (and beyond), and those who had been able to delay gratification were found to be

Table 7.1 DSM-V Diagnostic criteria for ADHD, ODD and CD

| ADHD | ODD | CD |
|---|---|---|
| Must display 6 or more of the following symptoms.<br><br>**Inattentive:**<br>Fails to give close attention to details or makes careless mistakes.<br>Has difficulty sustaining attention.<br>Does not appear to listen.<br>Struggles to follow through on instructions.<br>Has difficulty with organisation.<br>Avoids or dislikes tasks requiring a lot of thinking.<br>Loses things.<br>Is easily distracted.<br>Is forgetful in daily activities.<br><br>**Hyperactive-impulsive:**<br>Fidgets with hands or feet or squirms in chair.<br>Has difficulty remaining seated.<br>Runs about or climbs excessively.<br>Difficulty engaging in activities quietly.<br>Acts as if driven by a motor.<br>Talks excessively.<br>Blurts out answers before questions have been completed.<br>Difficulty waiting or taking turns.<br>Interrupts or intrudes upon others.<br><br>**Combined inattentive & hyperactive-impulsive:**<br>Has symptoms from both of the above presentations | Must display 4 or more of the following symptoms. For children < 5 years old, the behaviour should occur on most days for a period of at least 6 months. Older than 5 years, the behaviour should occur at least once per week for at least 6 months.<br><br>**Angry/irritable mood:**<br>Often loses temper.<br>Often touchy or easily annoyed.<br>Often angry and resentful.<br><br>**Argumentative/defiant behaviour:**<br>Argues with authority figures or adults.<br>Actively defies or refuses to comply with requests from adults.<br>Deliberately annoys others.<br>Often blames others for his/her mistakes or misbehaviour.<br><br>**Vindictiveness:**<br>Spiteful or vindictive at least twice within the past six months. | Must display at least 3 of the following criteria in the previous 12 months, with at least one criterion present in the past 6 months.<br><br>**Aggression to people or animals**<br>Often bullies, threatens, or intimidates others.<br>Often initiates physical fights.<br>Has used a weapon (e.g. knife).<br>Physically cruel to people.<br>Physically cruel to animals.<br>Has stolen while confronting a victim (e.g. extortion).<br>Has forced someone into sexual activity.<br><br>**Destruction of property**<br>Deliberately set fires intending to causing serious damage.<br>Deliberately destroyed others' property (not by fire setting).<br><br>**Deceitfulness or theft**<br>Has broken into someone's property. Often lies to obtain goods, favours or avoid obligations.<br>Has stolen nontrivial items without confronting a victim (e.g. shoplifting).<br><br>**Serious violations of rules**<br>Often stays out at night despite parental prohibitions, beginning before age 13 years.<br>Has run away from home overnight at least twice while living in the parental or carer's home, or once without returning for a lengthy period.<br>Often truants from school, beginning before age 13 years. |

psychologically well-adjusted, more dependable and scored higher grades in school than their impulsive peers.

Although considered a brain-based disorder, the search for the precise cause of ADHD remains elusive. Nevertheless, some problems have been identified in the underlying neurochemistry (Dalley et al., 2008). For example, individuals with ADHD have at least one defective gene, which makes it difficult for neurons to respond to dopamine (Blum et al., 2008). Other research evidence points to hereditary influence, up to 60% of children with ADHD having at least one parent with ADHD (Barkley et al., 2008). Furthermore, children (mainly boys) of mothers who smoke, or who are stressed during pregnancy, are more likely to have ADHD (Rodriguez and Bohlin, 2005). Neuroscientists and medical researchers continue to search for an explanation of the likely causes of ADHD and provide us with interesting data, which may, in time, provide a solution to the problem. Currently, it tells us less about how to manage pupils with ADHD in the classroom. To date, there is no cure for ADHD, but there are ways to help manage the behaviours that disrupt the lives of pupils with ADHD and of those around them.

Treatment often includes a combination of medication (Methylphenidate e.g. Ritalin), manipulating the learning environment, changing teaching approaches and cognitive-behavioural interventions. Methylphenidate increases extracellular dopamine in the striatum (Volkow et al., 2007) and acts as a mechanism for improving attention by enhancement of task-related neuronal cell firing. Since dopamine also controls reward salience and motivation, it can augment engagement with a task by increasing interest, which results in improved attention and performance (Berridge and Robinson, 1997). The medication is intended to improve attention and motivation and hence engagement with learning.

However, whilst pupils with ADHD have difficulty sustaining engagement with school lessons, they will often concentrate for inordinate amounts of time if presented with a computer game that they like. Many computer games provide instant reinforcement that meets the needs of those who have difficulty delaying gratification. This is not to suggest that pupils should spend their lessons playing computer games, but highlights how changing the environment can change behaviour, including those behaviours associated with ADHD.

Manipulating the physical environment can improve persistence on tasks with ADHD (Abramowitz and O'Leary, 1991). Classrooms that have clear and predictable routines, which are 'enclosed' by four walls and a door, as opposed to 'open' (hence providing fewer distractions), and where attention is paid to using appropriate (to task and social relationships) seating arrangements, pay dividends when working with pupils who have ADHD. Other features of pupils with ADHD (and others with behaviour difficulties) are being easily distracted, disorganised, having short attention spans, procrastination, problems with self-control and self-regulation – the latter being the subject of the next section.

## ADHD and Executive Functioning

Many of the difficulties faced by those with ADHD have been linked to problems with executive functioning (Barkley, 2012), which includes the ability to control, inhibit, and monitor one's own physical and mental activities (Russell, 1996). Executive functions (EF) are the mental processes that empower individuals to focus attention, remember instructions, and manage multiple tasks. As Dawson and Guare put it: 'Executive skills allow us to organise our behavior over time and override immediate demands in favor of longer-term goals' (2010: 1). EF is involved in complex cognitions that include forming goals and devising ways to attain them, problem solving, adjusting behaviour in response to new information, generating strategies or coordinating complex actions (Anderson, 2002).

Individuals with ADHD have been found to have a deficit in respect of EF, notably working memory, planning and inhibition (Willcutt *et al.*, 2005), which affects social and academic learning behaviour. Barkley (2012) identified areas of EF deficit associated with ADHD, including working memory, emotion regulation, inner speech and planning and problem solving.

Working memory is responsible for the storage and manipulation of short-term information that is crucial for learning, decision making, and maintaining goal-directed behaviour (e.g., Baddeley, 2007). It includes the ability to hold events in mind, have an accurate sense of time and be able to follow rule governed behaviour and multiple instructions, which pupils with ADHD can find difficult. Take Ben, for example.

> ### Case study
>
> Ben (Year 7) and his classmates are asked by his teacher to put completed worksheets on the teacher's desk, return textbooks to the bookshelves, put the equipment they were using away in the store cupboard, and then sit down at their desks. Ben puts his worksheet on the desk then wanders around until he sees the other pupils sitting down at their desks and eventually follows suit.

Ben's condition (ADHD) makes it difficult for him to retain the required sequence of events. In this situation, he clearly does not retain anything beyond the first instruction, relying on cues from his classmates to sit down, but he fails to put his textbook and equipment away. This case study highlights the importance of making sure that instructions can be followed by all pupils, checking for understanding and providing appropriate prompts.

A second EF deficit relates to emotion regulation (ER), which includes understanding and differentiating more complex emotions. ER is important in learning to adapt to the social environment or to accomplish goals. ER development begins with self-awareness and understanding personal needs, wants and desires; moving to perspective-taking and empathy towards others; and finally, the development of moral judgement or making decisions based on sets of rules or standards (Brock *et al.*, 2009).

Evidence from neuroscience has indicated that the development of emotion regulation is influenced by several executive functions, including attention control, decision making and inhibition of inappropriate behaviours, among other higher-order cognitive processes that occur in emotionally demanding environments (Tottenham *et al.*, 2011). In practice, the ability to regulate one's emotions, in particular negative emotions, is one indicator of social competence. Ranting publicly in response to minor frustration is not considered socially acceptable in most cultures. It is well established that pupils with ADHD have problems regulating their emotions (Shaw *et al.*, 2014). Furthermore, boys with ADHD show less empathy and exhibit more behavioural expressions of negative emotions than those without ADHD (Braaten and Rosen, 2000).

Inner speech, or talking to yourself in silence, is believed to be a mechanism for self-regulation e.g. controlling impulsive behaviour. The ability to stand back or reflect provides an individual with the opportunity to marshal evidence and adapt existing coping resources when faced with novel situations. It follows that where this element of EF is deficient, individuals will have difficulty controlling impulsive behaviour or reactive emotions, as is the case with ADHD.

Planning and problem solving requires individuals to analyse and synthesise information held in their minds. Pupils with ADHD tend to have difficulty analysing and synthesising verbal and nonverbal responses, which limits their ability to engage in problem solving or planning (Oosterlaan *et al.*, 2005). Given the comorbidity of ADHD with other EBD many of the above EF deficits are evident in ODD and CD.

In school, these deficits manifest themselves through behaviours such as being disorganised, having trouble completing work, remembering instructions, equipment and information, tardiness, emotional reactivity, completing long-term projects and planning. That they find these activities difficult is no excuse for not putting mechanisms in place to help them to better cope with these difficulties. For example, providing visual prompts, shorter term targets for work, a clock as a time reference, an area with few distractions to complete individual work (see Chapter 10).

### *Oppositional defiant disorder (ODD)*

ODD is defined in the DSM-V as a repetitive pattern of defiance and disobedience and a negative and hostile attitude to authority figures lasting at least six months. According to Scott *et al.* (2001) around 15% of children suffer from ODD in the first five years of life. Among young children (ages three to seven years) it is more common in boys than girls. However, among teenagers the numbers for both sexes are more equal. Eight symptomatic behaviours are grouped under three headings: *angry/irritable mood* (loses temper), *argumentative/ defiant behaviour* (e.g. argues with adults) and *vindictiveness* (see Table 9.1). To qualify as ODD, four or more of these behaviours must have been present for more than six months. The behaviours must occur frequently and lead to impaired social and academic functioning to make the diagnosis. There is evidence to suggest that ODD precedes the development of CD in children (Burke *et al.*, 2010), which has led some researchers to suggest that ODD and CD are age-related representations of the same syndrome (Loeber *et al.*, 2009).

## Conduct disorder (CD)

> Conduct disorder (CD) is an overarching term used in psychiatric classification that refers to a persistent pattern of antisocial behaviour in which the individual repeatedly breaks social rules and carries out aggressive acts that upset other people.
>
> (NICE, 2013a: 15)

Conduct disorder is a heterogeneous category of antisocial disruptive behaviours. It is a mental disorder characterised by destructive and aggressive behaviour carried out at home and in school. It is widespread in the UK, with 8% of boys and 5% of girls aged 11 to 16 years having conduct disorders (NICE, 2013a). However, it is important to remember that defiant behaviour is part of normal adolescent development and social survival, but it tends to reduce with age. Adolescents who are too compliant and timid often cause concern to parents and others responsible for them.

The dominant feature of CD is a repetitive and persistent pattern of behaviours that violate social norms and the rights of others. CD is one of the most difficult and intractable mental health problems in children and adolescents. It involves a number of problematic behaviours, including oppositional and defiant behaviours and antisocial activities such as, lying, stealing, running away, and physical violence (see Table 9.1).

There are two 'types' of CD: child onset is observed before 10 years of age and adolescent onset between 10 and 16 years of age. The prognosis for the former is poor. For example, Piquero *et al.* (2010) found that 90% of severe, recurrent adolescent offenders showed marked antisocial behaviour in early childhood. As adults, this group are likely to be involved in criminality, experience chronic unemployment and develop antisocial personality disorders (NICE, 2013a).

Kimonis *et al.* (2014) identified two subtypes of child onset CD – 1) impulsive and 2) callous-unemotional. The impulsive subtype do not think before they act nor fully evaluate the consequences of their behaviour. This impulsivity is concomitant with strong *negative* emotions linked to biased social information processing, which results in them misinterpreting social cues and reacting negatively. One example of this process is 'hostile attributional bias' (HAB) (Steinberg and Dodge, 1983), where individuals have difficulty recognising certain emotions and social cues, so perceive hostile intent on the part of others even when it is not the case in reality. As Dodge reported:

> A basic task of social interaction is to learn to identify cues that signal that the actor has acted benignly rather than malevolently; such an attribution mitigates the tendency to retaliate with angry aggression.
>
> (2006: 2)

CD pupils also tend to blame others for their negative outcomes as opposed to themselves. CD is not, however, related to self-esteem, which can be low or high (ibid.). One important goal of intervention is to help pupils accurately interpret and appraise social behaviour and develop emotion regulation and control impulsive behaviour.

Individuals of the second subtype, callous-unemotional (CU), show low levels of emotional reactivity, a lack of empathy, guilt and compassion towards others. Between 12% and 46% of pupils with CD show CU traits, mostly among boys. Whilst both sexes display similar aggressive behaviours, girls show higher levels of relational aggression, i.e. using social skills to hurt someone by damaging his or her relationships with others (Crick and Grotpeter, 1995). Children with CU traits tend to display persistent violent patterns of behaviour (Frick and Viding, 2009). When this has been observed in pupils when at primary school, it is of particular concern, as they are less responsive to typical socialisation processes than other forms of CD (Oxford *et al.*, 2003).

Adolescent onset, as opposed to childhood onset, CD is influenced to a greater extent by socio-cultural factors – such as being a member of a negative peer group. Furthermore, much of their antisocial behaviour takes place in group contexts and the ratio of male to females with the condition is lower. The adolescent onset group tends not to have severe neuropsychiatric, learning or developmental difficulties nor do they exhibit as much aggressive behaviour, as do the childhood onset group.

The development of behaviour disorders results from a transaction between biological, psychosocial and educational factors. As Figure 9.1 shows, the processes are temporal, beginning with biological factors that can affect brain processing, resulting in cognitive deficits. These deficits manifest themselves in the core behaviours such as inattention, hyperactivity and difficulties regulating emotions. Finally, it illustrates how these behaviours can affect relationships with parents, carers and teachers. At each stage of the process environmental factors influence the development of the difficulties to varying degrees and, as a result, difficulties can be exacerbated or reduced by context. Factors such as, mothers' behaviour during pregnancy (e.g. smoking, stress, drugs) and the quality of care during preschool years (e.g. attachment, day care) and overall quality of schooling (e.g. staff expertise, interventions).

**Biological differences**
e.g. genetic.

*can lead to*

**Brain differences**
e.g. frontal lobe structure, neurotransmitter system.

*can lead to*

**Cognitive differences**
e.g. problems with - executive functioning, emotion control, temperament.

*can lead to*

**Core problems**
e.g. impulsiveness; emotion regulation, attention; hyperactivity.

*can lead to*

**Extended home/educational/social problems**
e.g. relationship problems with carers, teachers.

Environmental influences

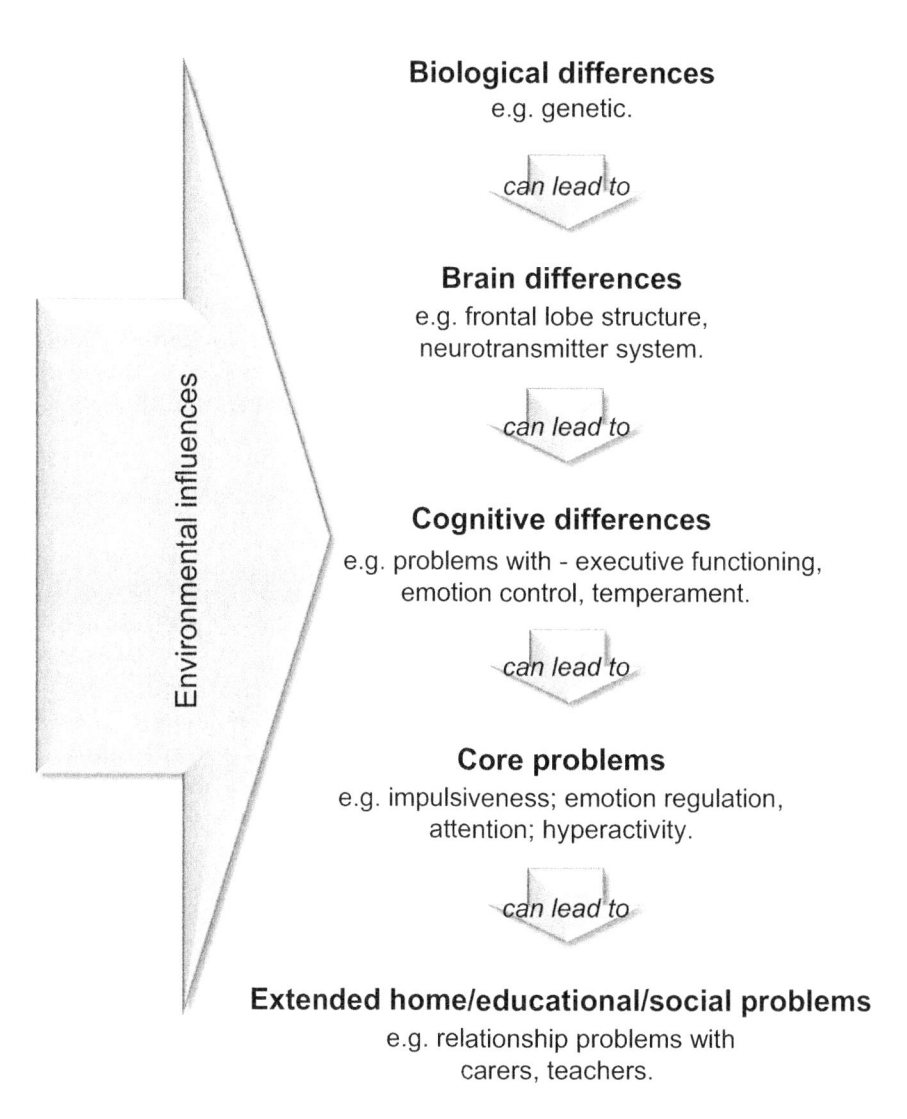

*Figure 9.1* Generalised temporal sequence for the development of behaviour disorders.

## Supporting pupils with EBD

In deciding how to intervene, ask yourself 'What do I expect from pupils with EBD that is in any way different to what I would expect from pupils without EBD?' The answer, I hope, is 'nothing', since I assume you want both to come to class, engage with their learning and behave in a socially responsible way. All adolescent pupils, however well motivated, are more than capable of disengaging from what they are required to learn at some point. Similarly, they are more than capable of acting in a socially unacceptable or socially incompetent way. What differentiates pupils with EBD from the rest is: 1) the frequency of low-level disruption (e.g. shouting out), and/or 2) challenging behaviour (e.g. physical aggression). The latter is a concern for everyone given that few people enjoy getting hurt or the possibly of being hurt. Remove physical aggression, and we are left with behaviours not uncommon among most pupils.

Many interventions are targeted at individual pupils, which can create problems for teachers who are simultaneously responsible for 20+ additional pupils. Individual-focused programmes can also backfire through modelling undesirable behaviour. If pupils who do not have EBD observe peers with EBD avoiding less favoured subjects or getting more attention than them, they may decide to behave likewise to achieve the same 'goal'.

### Case study

Winston's outbursts in school had caused concern among staff for some time. His mother and her boyfriend were not supportive of school and had been verbally abusive with staff when approached about Winston's aggressive behaviour towards his peers and the damage he caused to property. Initially his outbursts, whilst upsetting some of the other pupils did not result in copycat behaviour. The head decided that Winston was to be allowed to withdraw from situations if he was feeling angry and he was given permission to leave the classroom to go to a quiet area to calm down. However, Winston also left the classroom when he did not want to complete a task he did not like. His outbursts did not subside, rather, they became more frequent. Eventually two other boys began displaying similar outbursts – as 'modelled' by Winston – and insisted they also should be allowed space to calm down, which they were eventually granted.

This is an example of social learning theory in action. The problem with this approach was that, whilst it provided respite for the teacher and the rest of the class, it did nothing to help Winston expand his coping template.

In order to develop prosocial behaviour in a social environment, rather than moving to individual programmes, begin with an intervention designed to teach appropriate behaviour to the whole class, including those with EBD. You could, for example, introduce a new reward system targeted solely at specific required behaviours that operates alongside existing systems (see Chapter 10) in conjunction with developing social problem-solving skills.

## Assessing EBD

Objective information is required to determine the most appropriate intervention to use with pupils with EBD. There are a number of ways to do this including using published checklists and scales designed to measure social behaviour, as well as self-generated observation strategies.

Before launching into deciding which measure to use, the following questions should be addressed:

1. Why are we assessing this pupil?
2. What behaviour do we need to assess?
3. How should we assess this behaviour?

### Why are we assessing this pupil?

Asking why a pupil needs additional assessment is an important first stage and should be considered together with who is seeking the data and for what purpose. Another issue is whether the assessment is to explore the pupil's difficulties in more depth or to confirm what is already known. The two questions can mean very different things – the former appearing more diagnostic – a search for the causes of a difficulty or to perhaps obtain baseline data, on which to measure change. The second is often used to seek 'formal' evidence to support existing knowledge, insight or intuitive beliefs about an individual. Test results are often perceived as more official and scientific than data collected by other means, even if they are not. However, it is salient to ask where there are gaps in existing records and also what, if any additional or useful knowledge can be acquired through engaging in further data collection. Do not get drawn into the process of collecting data just because it can be collected. Consider why it is needed.

### What behaviour do we need to assess?

Having identified gaps and inconsistencies in existing information, the next stage is to decide what additional information is required. There are a number of possibilities; some relate to the pupil, others to the situation, including:

- the behaviour causing concern (frequency and/or duration; location, time, date);
- the pupil's
  - personal qualities (disposition, learning or motivational style, social skills) and/or
  - interpersonal relationships (with peers and staff, in and out of class);
- information from outside the school (e.g. family, other agencies);
- organisational factors (e.g. effects of classroom environment and climate, teaching styles, curriculum focus, learning resources, staff support).

### How should we assess this behaviour?

Data gathering falls into two broad categories: closed and open methods. The two approaches differ principally in the type of data recorded. In the first example, lists, scales or questionnaires are often used to determine what behaviour is recorded, which may mean 'fitting' an observation to a predetermined category. In the second approach, data is recorded in a more open-ended manner, which has implications for how it is analysed. Checklists can usually be analysed quantitatively, producing scores that can be compared with typical scores for an age group, along with how general population scores are distributed. Open data is more qualitative and interpretation is down to the individual or group conducting the analysis.

*Scales and checklists* – There are a number of measures on the market, some requiring specialist training to administer, whilst others are generally available for use by teachers e.g. Strengths and Difficulties Questionnaire (SDQ), Goodman (1997).

The SDQ is an evidence-based behavioural screening tool that is freely available. Unlike some measures, it requires you to record positive aspects of the pupil's behaviour as well as their difficulties, providing a useful baseline for expanding prosocial behaviour. It is simple to administer and recommended by the DfE for use in identifying mental health issues (DfE, 2015). There are several versions to cover different ages. The standard version covers ages 4 to 17 years. Scoring details, accompanying notes, and norm references for different age groups are provided at www.sdqinfo.com. Each version includes 25 items concerned with psychological attributes, divided equally across five subscales. Four subscales measure difficulties (emotional symptoms, conduct problems, hyperactivity/inattention, peer relationship problems) and one measures strengths -(prosocial behaviour). Scores on each question are totalled, and cut-off points are provided to identify 'normal' (80%); 'borderline' (10%) and 'abnormal' scores (10%). An abnormal score suggests a pupil is suffering from significant psychological difficulty. Extended versions include an impact supplement that enquires more about chronicity, distress, social impairment and burden to others.

In order to assess the impact of any intervention, follow-up versions of the SDQ are provided. These include the 25 basic items plus two additional questions: Has the intervention reduced problems? Has the intervention helped in other ways, e.g. making the problems more bearable?

You could design your own measure, but be aware of reliability and validity issues as well as the time required to design and test (Kershner and Chaplain, 2001).

*Open recording* – Open recording ranges from recording everything that goes on to focusing on specific events (e.g. temper tantrums, refusal to work) perhaps using a coding system. Alternatively, a diary approach might be useful in recording behaviour from lesson to lesson and during breaktime, over a fixed period, to map changes in different situations. Open methods usually produce more data than closed, so they often require more time to analyse, but the data is usually more detailed.

There are a number of things to consider in deciding where to assess a pupil, such as ethical or safety concerns observing some behaviours. For example, recording the behaviour of a pupil who is physically aggressive, in a busy classroom, can put other pupils and adults at risk.

### Helping pupils overcome their EBD

There are many different approaches available to help pupils overcome EBD. Some are designed for use in special environments, whereas others can be used successfully in mainstream classrooms. Some sound like a good idea but have little or no empirical research to support their effectiveness, whereas others have an evidence-based efficacy. The approaches recommended in this chapter are evidence-based and can be used in mainstream classrooms with individuals, groups or whole classes.

A progressive framework for intervening with EBD is shown in Figure 9.2. The underlying principle of the model is to use the least restrictive alternative to achieve behaviour change. Start by reviewing your own thoughts about and knowledge of EBD, then change teaching and learning arrangements for the whole-class before moving to an individual programme (see Chapter 10).

The explanations offered are necessarily brief in this chapter, so you should consult the references cited for details. Whilst the approaches described differ in their understanding of human behaviour, they all share the same goal, to empower the pupil to control his or her own behaviour or self-regulation, but they differ in the ways they achieve this aim.

### Behavioural approaches (BA)

The central principle of behavioural approaches is that all behaviour is learned and so can be unlearned and replaced with alternative behaviour, by reinforcing desired behaviour. Reinforcement being anything that follows a behaviour and results in that behaviour being maintained. BA have a long evidence-based history of success treating EBD. For example, Fabiano *et al.* (2009) analysed 174 research studies and found strong and consistent evidence that BA are effective for treating EBD.

BA have two phases: behaviour analysis and behaviour change – both are essential components that need to be applied methodically. Many pupils with EBD have a number of behaviours giving concern, the problem is deciding in what order to tackle them (see Table 9.2). Decisions about which behaviours to focus on first should be influenced by the degree to which it proves a threat to the health and welfare of the pupil, his/her peers, staff or property. Highest priority should be given to behaviours that threaten the safety of pupils or

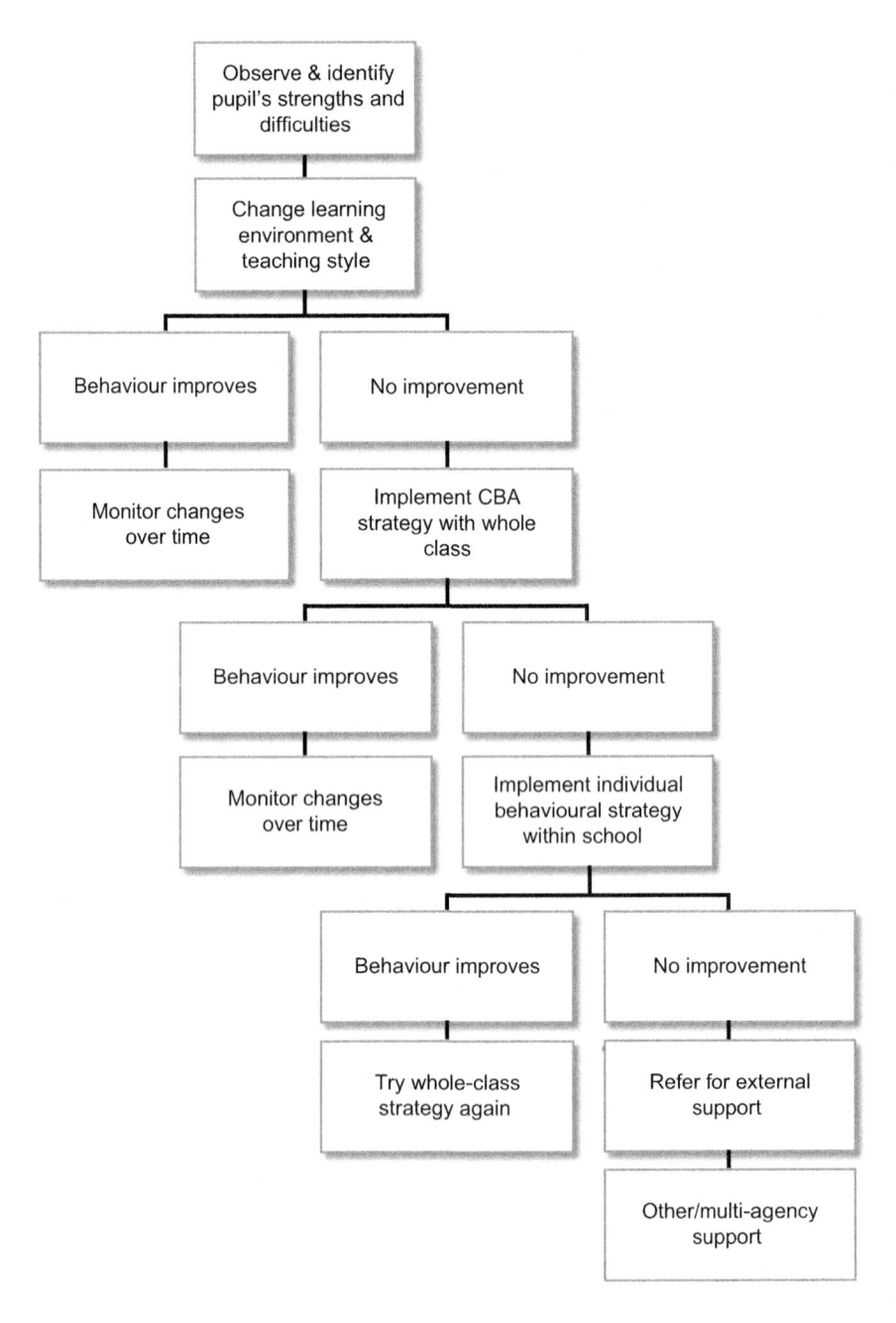

*Figure 9.2* An example of a progressive intervention for a pupil with EBD.

*Table 9.2* Relative seriousness of anti-social behaviours

| Priority | Example |
| --- | --- |
| High | Physical assault on pupils or staff; self-injurious behaviour; dangerous or reckless behaviour (setting fires, being irresponsible in high risk areas, e.g. gym or science laboratories). |
| Intermediate | Verbal abuse; refusal to attend class; disrupting other classrooms and refusing to leave; refusing to leave school premises when told to do so; damaging property; foul language. |
| Low | Refusing to work in class; out of seat without permission; continually failing to bring equipment or complete work; shouting out in class; refusing to obey class rules. |

staff (e.g. physical violence), lower priority being given to behaviours such as refusal to work.

Whilst physical violence is usually the top of many people's list of most extreme behaviour difficulties, it may never occur in your school. It could be that what is described here as 'intermediate priority' would be considered 'high priority' in your school. In responding to these behaviours, where pupils pose a danger to themselves or others, immediate action is required, which may necessitate restraint, removal from school and the involvement of outside agencies.

Dealing with complex and chronic behaviour, such as physical aggression, takes time. Do not expect quick results. Teaching an aggressive pupil how to cope in a more socially valued way, requires contingency arrangements to deal with outbursts, e.g. staff being available to restrain a pupil if necessary, or a time-out room (see Chapter 5). Such arrangements need to reflect procedures agreed by all staff and usually other pupils and be based on the principles contained in the school's behaviour policy, legislation, and official guidance.

Whilst high priority behaviour warrants a speedy response, it is perhaps not a good starting point for the inexperienced. I would suggest concentrating initially on low priority behaviours, until you feel sufficiently confident to move up a gear.

PHASE I: BEHAVIOUR ANALYSIS

Behaviour analysis is the systematic collection of measurable data, specifically, the behaviour causing concern, what precedes the behaviour (antecedent), and determining what keeps it going (consequence).

The first step in the process is to define the target behaviour (see Figure 9.3). The definition must be measurable and objective and pass the 'stranger test'. In other words, defined precisely enough that a stranger could come in and interpret the description accurately (Kaplan, 1995).

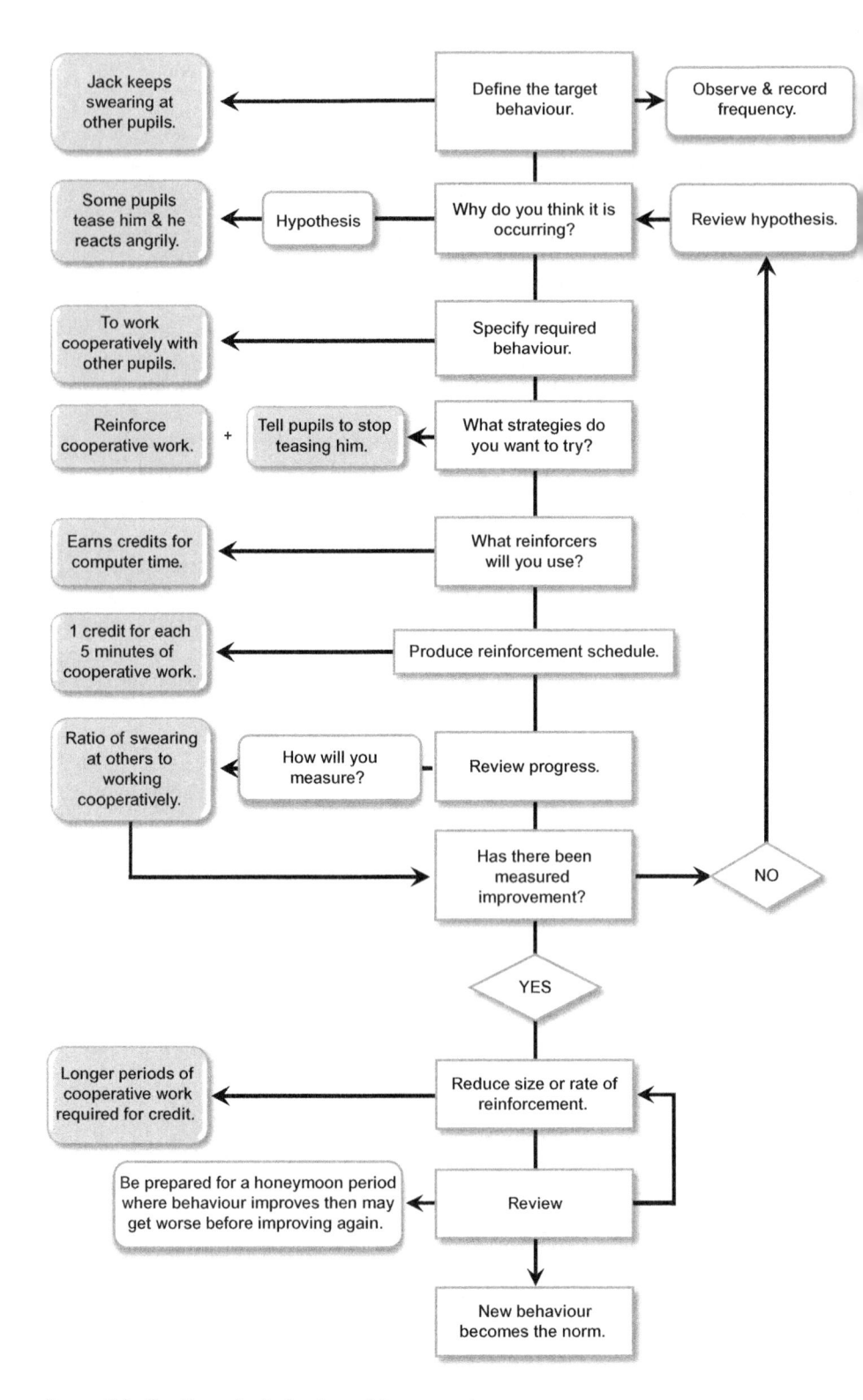

Figure 9.3 Outline of a behavioural intervention.

This is followed by observation over a period of time to establish: what is happening; who is involved; when it occurs and under what conditions. This information provides the *baseline* against which any changes in behaviour can be compared. Data regarding the frequency (number of times it occurs); rate (frequency within a fixed time period); or intensity (duration) of the behaviour is often summarised in the form of a graph (see Figure 9.4).

The second step, in behaviour analysis, is to identify the antecedent, which requires observation of what occurs before the unwanted behaviour and which you *believe* may be the trigger. This may be a particular activity; the presence of certain people; a time of day or lesson organisation etc. You are hypothesising (making an intelligent guess) about what might be the trigger – which you will later test with your intervention.

Step three is to identify the consequence, or what is reinforcing the undesirable behaviour. The reinforcer may be connected to the teacher (attention), other pupils (laughing) or factors outside the classroom (being sent to another staff member).

Fourthly, it is seldom possible to merely extinguish unwanted behaviour; it needs to be replaced with a more desirable alternative – known as a fair pair. You must decide precisely what replacement behaviour you want the pupil to be doing, the conditions under which they should be doing it and how much has to be completed successfully to be acceptable (Wolery *et al.*, 1988).

Finally, you should set a time frame against which you will measure the effectiveness of your intervention.

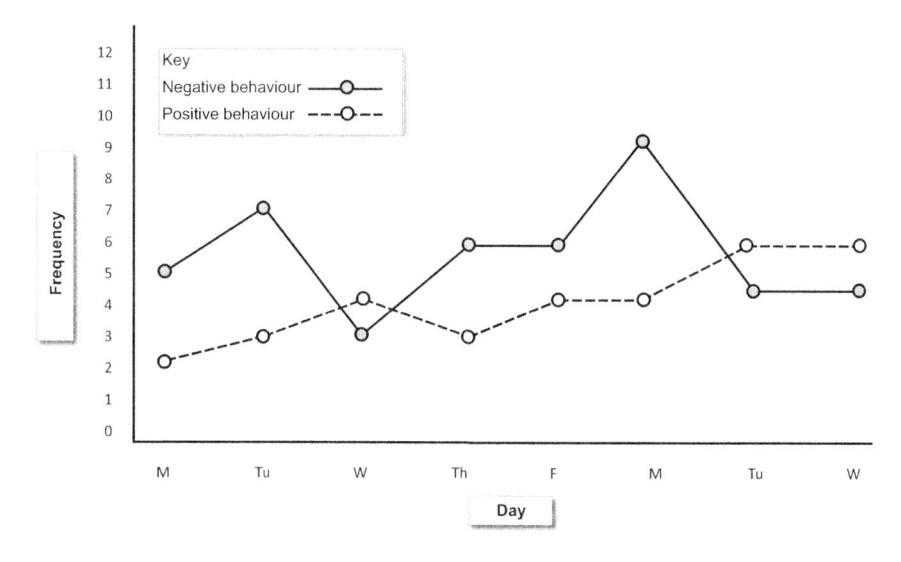

*Figure 9.4* Frequency graph showing number of occurrences of negative and positive behaviour recorded each day for eight days.

## PHASE 2: MODIFYING BEHAVIOUR

Having carried out the above analysis of the unwanted behaviour, its antecedents and consequences and what you wish to replace it with, you can move on to considering how to teach the replacement behaviour.

Behavioural approaches focus on manipulating the environment to change behaviour, beginning with changing the antecedent (seating arrangements, teaching style, lesson format, room layout, groupings, etc.). If these do not have the desired effect, then focus might shift to changing the consequences.

The desired behaviour can be taught through direct reinforcement or indirectly by vicarious reinforcement or modelling (social learning theory). In the case of the latter, the teacher, by reinforcing (e.g. with stickers) other pupils behaving as required (modelling), may lead to a pupil with EBD performing the same behaviour in anticipation of being likewise rewarded.

Reinforcing behaviour directly leads to its repetition, so choosing reinforcers needs careful thought – remember, not all school rewards are reinforcing to all pupils. Selecting the right reinforcer for particular pupils depends upon your knowledge of what interests them, what is appropriate for the situation, and school policy. The aim is to continue using external rewards to reinforce pupils exhibiting the required behaviour until they complete it for its own sake, i.e. self-reinforcement. With low-level disruptive behaviours (e.g. talking out of turn), behaviour change can be quick and lasting using this method. With more complex behaviour this is not the case and may require tangible reinforcement for long periods of time. Complex behaviours should be broken down into elements, which are addressed separately and sequentially. The pupil should only be reinforced when they demonstrate the required behaviour (in extreme cases you might initially reinforce behaviour that exceeds the baseline even if not quite as desired).

The intervention should be reviewed after having recorded the behaviour over a predetermined period of time (e.g. two weeks) and compare it with the baseline data (see Figure 9.4) to determine behaviour change. If the intervention has been successful (i.e. the behaviour has improved) you should next plan to reduce the size or frequency of reward given (e.g. shorter periods of time on the computer) or expect more for the same level of reinforcement (e.g. increasing the expected time spent on task or disturbing other pupils less frequently). Alternatively, you can reinforce behaviour intermittently. Remember, the object of the exercise is for the pupil to become self-reinforcing as soon as possible and not to be giving out concrete rewards (above what is given to all pupils) *ad infinitum*.

If you do not find measurable difference in behaviour, it is likely because: your hypothesis about the antecedent and/or consequence were incorrect or you chose the wrong reinforcer. You should revisit your original hypotheses about why the behaviour is occurring or what is keeping it going – and ask, what alternative stimuli or reinforcers are there? Are your contingent reinforcers the right ones? Are you sure what you are offering is seen as valuable by the pupil?

In short, behavioural approaches offer a practical and usable solution for use in the classroom. They do however, require you to follow the procedures carefully and pay attention to detail, systematically recording data and evaluation. (Alberto and Troutman, 2013, is the definitive guide to applying BA to classrooms.)

*Cognitive behavioural approaches (CBA)*

In purely behavioural approaches, cognition is not judged to be a salient explanatory variable for behaviour, so is not the focus of the intervention. In contrast, a key characteristic of cognitive approaches is the belief that behaviour disorders are cognitively mediated and that changing dysfunctional cognitions can bring about improved behaviour (Dobson and Dozois, 2001). So, pupils are encouraged to identify connections between their thoughts, emotions and behaviour in social situations. Whilst the focus here is on addressing individual behaviour difficulties, social problem solving interventions can be carried out with mixed groups and whole classes. Doing so facilitates the development of social competence of all pupils (Chaplain and Smith, 2006).

There is substantial evidence demonstrating the effectiveness of school-based CBA that help children with EBD overcome their difficulties. For example, with aggressive or disruptive behaviours: Wilson and Lipsey (2007); anger: Gansle (2005) and Ho *et al.*, (2010).

CBA are based on the premise that thinking, emotions and behaviour are interlinked and that our thoughts and feelings about events, even events that have not occurred, can have a profound influence upon our functioning, more so than the event itself. In order to be effective, CBA requires acceptance by the pupil that they have a problem, otherwise they see no reason to change. Introducing programmes such as social problem solving requires time, which subject teachers may consider they cannot afford. As a result, they are often reserved for pupils with difficulties away from the main group, which weakens their effectiveness in developing social competence. One way of overcoming this is to use them during tutorial periods or as a part of a PSHE programme. These intensive activities can be supported by encouraging subject teachers to supplement them within regular teaching sessions, such as during group discussion.

#### RATIONAL EMOTIVE THERAPY

A number of studies have demonstrated that using rational emotive therapy (RET) with children and adolescents is effective, and the largest effect change was with disruptive behaviour (Gonzalez et al., 2004). One approach developed by Ellis (1962), is based on a few simple principles:

- People are responsible for their own emotions and action.
- Harmful emotions and dysfunctional behaviours are the product of irrational thinking.
- People can learn more realistic views and, with practice, make them a part of their everyday behaviour.
- People will experience a deeper acceptance of themselves and greater satisfactions in life if they develop a reality-based perspective.

Ellis emphasised the relationship between the degree to which we are 'rational' or 'irrational' in our thinking about an event, and the resultant positive or negative emotional experience. Where the thinking is irrational, not only will it trigger unwanted negative emotion, but is often overly dramatic – what he referred to as catastrophising. This reaction may lead to pathological anxiety. Irrational thinking for Ellis concerns beliefs that things 'must', 'ought' or 'should' be so; otherwise, life will be awful. There are three categories of must statements: personal, interpersonal and situational, any or all of which can cause dysfunctional thinking (see Table 9.3).

A teacher thinking that all his/her pupils *must* behave impeccably at all times, or that all pupils *must* like her or him, is irrational. A rational thinker may *expect* or would *prefer* the class to always be well-behaved, and while preferring to be liked by all their pupils all the time, is more flexible and tolerant of the likelihood of this not always being the case. A teacher who

*Table 9.3* Categories of irrational teacher 'must' statements

| Level | Irrational thoughts | Effect on emotions and coping |
|---|---|---|
| Personal<br>Demands on self | 'I ought be able to control any class at any time. If I cannot, it is awful and means I am a worthless teacher'. | Feeling incompetent, anxious and depressed. |
| Interpersonal<br>Demands on others | 'I must be liked and respected by all of my pupils, and if they do not, they are horrible and do not deserve to be taught by me'. | Resentment, hostility, disaffection. |
| Situational<br>Demands on situations | 'I should be given all the necessary resources in order to teach properly, and if I am not, it is unfair and dreadful'. | Hopelessness, procrastination. |

thinks that *all* members of her class 'must' like her and 'must' always behave well because that is fair and just is likely to be disappointed.

The emphasis in RET is getting individuals to self-regulate by restructuring their thinking, moving from irrational to more rational alternatives. To do this, a helper challenges irrational thinking by asking:

- What evidence is there to support your (irrational) thoughts?
- What is another way of looking at the situation?
- So what if this terrible thing does happen?

There are various ways of responding to the answers to these questions, each tending to follow a sequence. When working with a pupil, the sequence might be:

1. information-gathering from existing sources;
2. identifying areas of difficulty (for example, getting angry and lashing out when provoked);
3. getting the pupil and others close to him or her, to list his strengths and weaknesses – emphasising her/his strengths and challenging self-deprecating thoughts such as, 'I have always been useless at school, so what's the point?';
4. making clear those areas of the pupil's life where he or she can take control;
5. guiding the pupil toward rational explanations for his thinking and emotions;
6. setting a baseline and agreeing on new specific targets and a time frame.

There are also several strategies that can be employed to help pupils identify, challenge and restructure the sources of their difficulties:

- challenging irrational beliefs by pinpointing their source and questioning established negative statements – 'I cannot control my anger';
- putting things into perspective by challenging attributions that result in self-blame for things over which they have no control – 'I only get things right when I am lucky';
- looking for evidence of negative self-talk and put downs – 'I can't do it' or 'I'll never be able to cope';
- getting the pupil to challenge the evidence and validity of their negative beliefs – 'Teachers never give me a chance to put things right'.

To make these strategies work requires a positive relationship between helper and pupil, made possible by having the 'core conditions' of warmth, genuineness and empathy but are also structured and strongly directive. In order to achieve success using this or other similarly structured and directive behavioural approaches, you would need to feel comfortable with these requirements.

## SOCIAL PROBLEM SOLVING (SPS)

The ability to manage one's emotions and social behaviour and develop meaningful peer relationships are important lifelong skills. Whilst this skill emerges naturally in typical development, there is a substantial body of research indicating that children with behaviour difficulties show social, cognitive, and behavioural deficits (e.g. Coie and Dodge, 1998). Children's socio-emotional competence can be enhanced directly by training them to manage their social, cognitive, and emotional skills using techniques such as friendly communication, anger management and social problem solving (ibid.).

Social problem solving (SPS) refers to having the necessary strategies to cope with everyday interpersonal problems in a socially acceptable way. In CBA there is a four step procedure for solving social problems:

1. Identify the problem.
2. Think about solutions.
3. Think about what will happen if I choose a particular solution and how the other pupils will feel if I do.
4. Try the solution.

The programme can be used with whole classes or focus groups and is adapted for use with all ages. Using whole classes mixes different levels of socio-emotional development, potentially enabling peer modelling and scaffolding.

If there is whole-school commitment to this approach, pupils can be supported further by reinforcing problem solving steps through role-playing (or modelling) different scenarios throughout the day. Achieving this requires effective communication between departments to coordinate the programme. Over time this will help all pupils to learn how to generalise their social competence, but it should be done in a planned way. Once a solution has been agreed upon, pupils can then role-play the solution. Posting problem solving steps at pupils' eye level (e.g. as artwork, posters, etc.) and referring to them frequently during interactions is a useful means of reinforcing SPS. The procedure can be used along with self-instruction training to help develop self-regulation. See Chaplain and Smith (2006) for details on how to apply this method.

How to merge pupils with EBD into mainstream classrooms is an ongoing concern for many teachers since it can negatively affect classroom climate. This effect can be eased by developing your knowledge of established evidence-based approaches, such as CBA, that have a track record in helping pupils overcome their difficulties.

## Annotated further reading

Chaplain, R., and Smith, S. (2006). *Challenging behaviour.* Cambridge: Pearson Publishing.

This text is designed for non-specialist teachers and other staff who do not necessarily have ready access to specialists outside mainstream school, to support their work with pupils who present difficult and challenging behaviours. Three different but complementary approaches are presented along with practical materials and examples of application to classrooms. The reader is informed of potential difficulties and how to develop techniques in a safe environment – for example, with colleagues – before using the approaches with pupils.

## Further reading to support M level study

Frick P.J., and Viding, E. (2009). Antisocial behavior from a developmental psychopathology perspective. *Development and Psychopathology*, 21, 1111–1131.

This paper reviews research on chronic patterns of antisocial behaviour and places this research into a developmental psychopathology framework. The authors highlight the developmental processes that increase the risk for children to act in an antisocial and aggressive manner and propose which interventions are best suited to meet the needs of those who have experienced different causal pathways. As I pointed out in the chapter it is important to distinguish between different types of conduct disorder as the age of onset has short- and long-term implications. Three developmental pathways through which adolescents and children can develop severe antisocial behaviours are identified in this paper. One pathway begins in adolescence, and two begin in childhood but differ dependent on the presence or absence of callous, unemotional traits. In outlining these distinct pathways to antisocial behaviour, the authors stress the importance of understanding the interface between normal and abnormal development, and the importance of using multiple levels of analyses to develop causal theories. They also show how this development model can be used to enhance existing interventions for antisocial individuals.

# Chapter 10

# Classroom management planning

This chapter describes how to custom build a classroom management plan and support professional development through a series of activities which illustrate the links between theory, research and classroom practice. The first activities encourage reflection on personal strengths and concerns and how they link to whole-school factors. The focus then moves to the classroom management strategies and techniques needed to establish and maintain authority, with an emphasis on preventing disruptive behaviour and promoting prosocial behaviour. Finally, the reader is shown ways to develop self-regulation and social competence in pupils, including those with emotional and behavioural difficulties.

## Introduction

Not having an effective classroom management plan (CMP) can result in the everyday smooth running of a classroom becoming problematic. As Charlie Taylor made clear, 'Managing a school or a class is a complex operation and because of this complexity it is easy to fail to get the simple, but essential, things right' (DfE, 2011: 2). The most effective classroom management planning takes account of all essential elements, including the complex (e.g. being assertive) as well as the simple (e.g. learning your pupils' names). Furthermore, your plan should be proactive (teaching pupils the required behaviour) rather than being focused on how to react to undesirable behaviour. Both are necessary – it is the emphasis that matters most.

Developing a CMP before you begin teaching your class will prepare you to cope with the behaviour, both positive and negative, of your pupils (Alberto and Troutman, 2013). There is no one-size-fits-all CMP, so you need to custom-build one that is evidence-based and best fits your expectations and personal characteristics, the developmental stage of your pupils and the expectations of the school.

The sequencing of this chapter broadly follows the order of the preceding chapters, beginning with your personal qualities and how they fit with whole-school factors, determining which classroom management techniques

## Classroom management planning 211

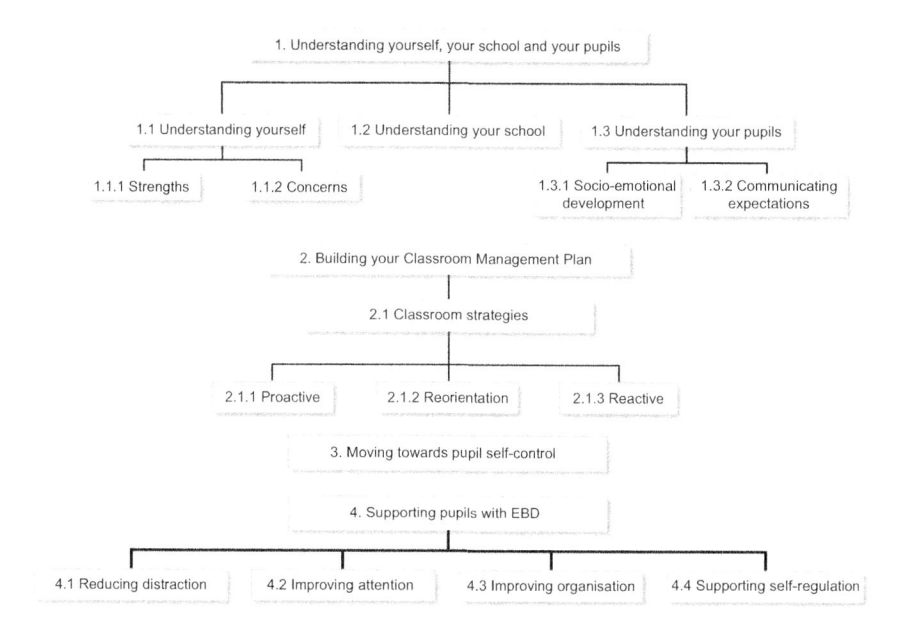

*Figure 10.1* Chapter 10 outline.

to use and, finally, how to manage pupils with EBD. As this book is aimed at both trainee and qualified teachers, with differing levels of knowledge, experience and skills, not all of the following sections will necessarily have equal relevance to all readers. For example, a teacher in post may be able to directly influence whole-school policy, whereas a trainee on short-term placement will likely not at that point but should nonetheless be aware of its role in behaviour management.

Your CMP should address the following factors:

- *Personal*—Ensuring you have the necessary knowledge and skills, teaching strategies and coping strategies for the groups you will be teaching.
- *Interpersonal*—Ensuring you have the social competence, professional social skills and social support required for you to develop professional relationships with your pupils and colleagues.
- *Organisational*—Planning how you will organise your classroom environment (layout, group dynamics, seating arrangements) and teach your expectations through rules and routines. Ensure that, whilst distinctive, your classroom environment is in sync with schoolwide policies and systems.

The chapter is arranged in four parts (see Figure 10.1). The first looks at the foundation for developing your plan: reflecting on your personal beliefs, strengths and personal concerns; your knowledge of your pupils and school; and the availability of interpersonal and organisational support. The second part focuses on the contents of the CMP, offering a sequential guide to establishing and maintaining your authority in the classroom through a combination of routines and specific interpersonal behaviours (e.g. withitness) designed to maximise pupil on-task time, as well as the manipulation of the classroom environment. A positive proactive approach is adopted to establish efficient routines and procedures by explicitly teaching, reinforcing and modelling prosocial behaviours. As the relationship with your class develops, you should adjust the balance between behavioural and cognitive strategies to further develop pupils' social competence, always being conscious of the differing social developmental levels of your pupils. This is the substance of the third part.

The fourth part concerns how, despite all of the preceding working successfully with the majority of your class, pupils with EBD require you to introduce additional support, including a combination of scaffolding and modelling through whole-class social problem-solving and individual behaviour plans.

# 1 Understanding yourself, your school and your pupils

## 1.1 Understanding yourself (Chapters 1, 2, 3 and 4)

Self-awareness is important for reflecting and identifying how your thoughts, feelings and behaviours interact with organisational and interpersonal factors and subsequently influence how you manage behaviour. Identify and reflect on your strengths and concerns by answering the following questions:

### 1.1.1 Strengths

PERSONAL STRENGTHS

- Which theory of behaviour management do you subscribe to?
    - Does the weight of empirical evidence suggest it is the best practice?
    - What does your chosen theory tell you about why pupils behave the way they do?
    - What are the practice implications of following your chosen theory/ knowledge base?
    - Does it guide your classroom management practice based on empirical evidence?
- Which of your existing personal qualities do you consider to be of most value to you in the classroom and which might you wish to develop?

- Which pupil behaviours most concern you?
  - What action have you taken to develop your knowledge about them and the skills required to deal with them?
- What experience do you already have of managing children's behaviour?
- How assertive are you?
  - Where do you feel most and least assertive?
  - Who makes you feel least assertive (managers, colleagues, pupils) and why?
  - What situations make you feel least assertive?

### How to become more assertive

Start by identifying the situations in which you feel change is needed and that you believe are within your rights. Learn and practice new assertive behaviours, such as social problem-solving skills and conflict resolution e.g. through role-play with a friend. Begin with real, but not too difficult, issues to experience success and build confidence, then move on to more challenging examples. Be prepared for setbacks along the way; not everyone will respond as you might hope to your new behaviours, as it will upset established routines. Not all difficulties can be dealt with directly, so think about possible consequences (intended and unintended) before taking any action.

- How capable do you feel managing different behaviours?

### How to assess your behaviour management efficacy

In response to the last question, use Table 10.1 as a guide to assess how capable you feel you will be managing the different behaviours on the list. Rate your efficacy on each element on a scale with a score between 1 and 5. A score of 5 means you feel very confident that you have the capability to manage the element. A score of 1 means you do not feel at all confident in your capability to manage the element. Intermediate scores (2–4) indicate levels of uncertainty. Try carrying out this assessment at the beginning and ending of placement or term – has your perceived efficacy level changed? Can you explain why?

#### INTERPERSONAL STRENGTHS

- Make a list of people in your social network – both your personal and professional life.
- Alongside each name, identify what support function you think they should fulfil and alongside the type of support they actually provide (emotional, practical, informational and esteem (use Table 10.2 as a guide).
- Is there a balance, or are there gaps?
- What additional social support do you feel you need in order to cope more effectively? How might you obtain this support?

*Table 10.1* Assess your behaviour management efficacy

| Behaviour management element | Not at all confidence ←→ | | | | Very confident |
|---|---|---|---|---|---|
| **How capable do you feel to manage:** | | | | | |
| low-level disruption (e.g. pupils talking out of turn) | 1 | 2 | 3 | 4 | 5 |
| moderate disruption (e.g. pupils refusing to work) | 1 | 2 | 3 | 4 | 5 |
| whole-class teaching | 1 | 2 | 3 | 4 | 5 |
| small-group work | 1 | 2 | 3 | 4 | 5 |
| pupils with autism | 1 | 2 | 3 | 4 | 5 |
| pupils with ADHD | 1 | 2 | 3 | 4 | 5 |
| aggressive pupils | 1 | 2 | 3 | 4 | 5 |
| distressed pupils | 1 | 2 | 3 | 4 | 5 |
| apathetic pupils | 1 | 2 | 3 | 4 | 5 |
| withdrawn pupils | 1 | 2 | 3 | 4 | 5 |
| outside school activities (e.g. school trips) | 1 | 2 | 3 | 4 | 5 |
| breaktime misbehaviour | 1 | 2 | 3 | 4 | 5 |
| bullying behaviour | 1 | 2 | 3 | 4 | 5 |
| managing other adults in your classroom | 1 | 2 | 3 | 4 | 5 |

*Table 10.2* Evaluating sources of social support

| Type of support | Fulfils a little | Fulfils moderately | Fulfils completely | How important is this to you as a teacher? |
|---|---|---|---|---|
| E.g. listening | Partner (Al) | Colleague (Sue) | Deputy head (Jo) | |
| Listening | | | | |
| Professional appreciation | | | | |
| Emotional | | | | |
| Sharing reality | | | | |
| Self-esteem | | | | |
| Instrumental (practical) | | | | |
| Distraction (fun) | | | | |
| Resources | | | | |

ORGANISATIONAL STRENGTHS

- To what extent do you feel the school behaviour policy is supportive of your approach to managing pupil behaviour in your school?
- To what extent do you feel the SLT is supportive of your approach to managing pupil behaviour in your school?

### 1.1.2 Concerns

- What personal skills and knowledge do you feel need improvement?
- What behaviour problems do you face (or think you might face):
  o around school?
  o in your classroom?
  o with individual pupils?
- Which disruptive behaviours are you most concerned about?
- Which behaviours have caused you difficulty in the past?

In analysing your concerns, note:

- Which are within your control (e.g. behaviour in your classroom) and so you can change?
- Which are not within your control (e.g. circumstances at home) and so you cannot change?

Determine what support you need to deal with issues outside your personal control. Taking time to consider the above questions and seeking answers away from the classroom helps prepare you to build your coping repertoire and to prepare for future potential stressors. Having a framework for analysing stressful events can help in this respect; for example, consider having to deal with a pupil who suddenly starts throwing chairs around. In responding, your appraisal might be something like the following:

- *Situational*—What's happening? Is this a threat to me? Is it a threat to my pupils? Do I understand what is going on?
- *Personal*—Am I coping? If not, why not? Do I feel capable of coping with this situation? Can I gain control of what is happening using my previous experience, assertiveness, or bluff? How am I feeling (anxious, angry)?
- *Interpersonal*—Who can help me? Are they available? What type of help do I need?
- *Organisational*—What does the school policy say about how to deal with this situation? What resources/training are available to support me?

You can use this framework after the event to reflect or plan alternative strategies. Your coping response will be affected by your ability to regulate your emotions, e.g. fear, which may be strong when dealing with aggressive behaviours; your previous experience (and level of successful coping) and/or your proactive management planning. Planning for future probabilities is central to this process. Ask yourself, what the likelihood of a pupil throwing a chair (or similar aggressive behaviour) is at some point. If you think it is likely, then planning how to respond is far more practical than *hoping* it never happens – hope, like luck, is unpredictable and uncontrollable. In recent years, I have had to help schools deal with increasing numbers of aggressive pupils of all ages having regular outbursts, and some of the strategies being used added to the problem. In some cases, the response was to remove the rest of the class from the room – not a good idea if someone continues to throw equipment, whilst adults try to escort 29 other children past flying missiles. In such cases, if all else has failed, restraint might be the only option, which has implications for training. Reviewing your concerns using this type of analysis when not in the situation is a starting point for developing your coping repertoire.

By carrying out the analysis of significant events, you can begin the planning process to determine how you could prevent it from occurring again, or how to respond more effectively if it does. However, it is insufficient to merely plan new coping strategies. They need to be rehearsed when you are not under pressure.

### 1.2 *Understanding your school (Chapters 5 and 6)*

- How would you describe the climate of your school?
  o Do you think teachers in different departments share a similar view of the school climate?
  o Do you think the non-teaching staff share the same view as teachers?
- Do pupils enjoy coming to your school?
- Do staff and pupils value being a member of the school?
- Do staff feel supported by the SLT in managing behaviour?
- Are teachers and pupils optimistic?
- Do teachers have positive and realistic expectations for all pupils?
- Does your school's behaviour policy encourage prosocial behaviour across the whole school?
- Do you think management of behaviour in your school generally reflects the aims of the behaviour policy?
- Is the policy applied consistently across the whole school?
- Are behaviour problems handled quickly and efficiently?
- Do you have established systems for raising issues concerned with behaviour management and for getting help quickly should you need it?
  o Do they work?
- Are the school's core rules made explicit?
  o Are they teachable and enforceable?
  o Are they taught and enforced by all staff?

- Are there school wide programmes to support *all* pupils' socio-emotional well-being?
- Are there proactive efforts to develop positive relationships with parents of all pupils?

## *1.3 Understanding your pupils (Chapters 3, 7, 8 and 9)*

Understanding your pupils at both the personal level and how they function as a group is central to how you decide to manage their behaviour.

Learn your pupils' names and what they are interested in as quickly as possible. This can be done quickly by using the 'All about me' questionnaire (Figure 10.2). It takes a few minutes to complete but gives you some useful insights into your pupils and can be read at your leisure. You may want to modify it to suit your context, perhaps change content or appearance. If working with pupils who have learning difficulties, have an adult help complete the form whilst working with individuals or small groups.

Any class of pupils will exhibit behaviour on a continuum that ranges from those who *never* seem to misbehave to those who seem to *always* be in trouble. In an 'average' classroom, in any year group, we might expect the distribution of this continuum to resemble a normal (bell-shaped) curve (see Figure 10.3). The high point of the graph is where most pupils are located and who might occasionally engage in disruptive behaviour. A few pupils who are 'always in trouble' are in the left-hand tail and a few who 'never misbehave' in the right-hand tail. However, some classes have a high proportion of pupils who 'usually misbehave', whilst others have a high proportion of pupils who are 'usually well-behaved', which skews or pushes the peak of the curve to the left or the right respectively. The point of these rather crude descriptors is that different classes require different levels of teacher direction. In a classroom where a large majority of pupils are: usually able to control their impulses to talk when they are not supposed to be talking; are not easily distracted; who respond quickly to the teachers' instructions and maintain engagement with required tasks, only minimal teacher direction (LTD) is required, enabling more informal teaching methods and small-group work. Where the majority of pupils regularly misbehave and have difficulties regulating their behaviour, a high level of teacher direction (HTD) is required. Here, a higher percentage of formal lessons and individual tasks that are easier to manage should be used but with a view to adjusting this balance over time. Between the two extremes are classes that require moderate teacher direction (MTD). It is also important to be aware of how a minor change can affect a group's behaviour, e.g. the addition of a pupil with a behaviour disorder can affect the group dynamic substantially, changing a low-direction to a high-direction group very quickly, again highlighting the need for forward planning. You should determine the level of direction needed for each of the classes you teach in planning your behaviour management strategies. Whilst for most pupils

**All about me**

Name:                                       Class:

What I like to do most at home is

My hobbies are

My favourite activities at school are

My favourite after-school activities are

My favourite TV shows are

My favourite books are

My favourite magazines are

My favourite comics are

My favourite computer games are

My favourite films are

My favourite sports are

My favourite foods are

If I had one wish I would want to

When I leave school I would like to

School would be better if

What my teachers did last year that I liked the most was

What my teachers did last year that I liked the least was

My best friends are

*Figure 10.2* All about me questionnaire.

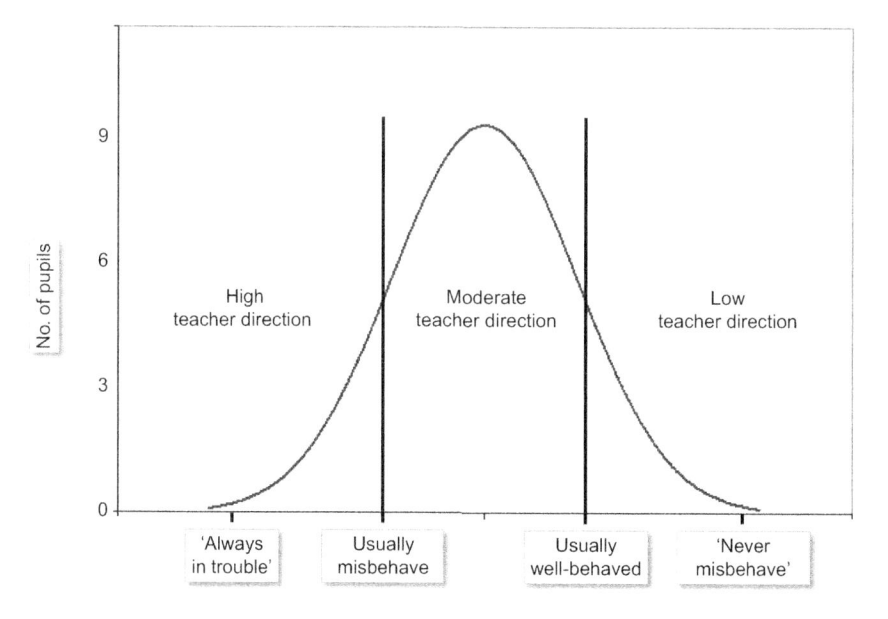

*Figure 10.3* Normal distribution of pupils.

self-control and self-regulation tend to increase with age, it is not the case for all. Added to which, whilst individual pupils may display self-control if on their own, when in certain social groups, they are more likely to engage in more risk-taking behaviours, e.g. disruptive behaviour (see Chapter 9).

### 1.3.1 Socio-emotional development

- What level of social and emotional development have pupils in your classes reached?
    o To what extent is your understanding of this development based on your own experience, popular opinion or advice of others?
    o What contemporary empirical evidence do you have to support your assumptions about adolescent social development?
- If the class is organised in small groups, how well do they relate to one another? (use a sociogram to measure this)
    o What level of variation exists among the groups you teach?
- What action are you taking to develop their socio-emotional skills in and out of class?
- Is their emotional development comparable to norms for their age group?
- What formal action are you planning/taking to help them develop/ enhance their emotion-regulation skills?

#### PUPIL WELL-BEING

NICE guidelines (2009) recommend that teachers and staff in secondary schools should have the knowledge, understanding and skills required to develop young people's socio-emotional well-being. This involves promoting positive behaviours and successful relationships to reduce disruptive behaviour and bullying and should be evident across all curriculum subjects. Focus should be on developing pupils' motivation, self-awareness, problem-solving, conflict management and resolution, collaborative working, understanding and management of feelings and managing relationships.

- What gaps are there in your knowledge, understanding and skills that are needed to develop young people's social and emotional wellbeing?
- To what extent does the current teaching of your subject *explicitly* and effectively address the preceding seven pupil skills?
- To what extent are these areas covered schoolwide?

#### 1.3.2 Communicating your expectations

Monitor what you actually do and say (as opposed to what you think you do and say), focusing on the leakage between the two. This can be done using a trusted colleague or by video recording yourself (NB ensure child safeguarding policies are followed when using recording equipment in the classroom). Areas to focus on include:

- which pupils you asked most questions of;
- who you allowed to ask you most questions and the quality of your responses to them (and others);
- what you said and how you said it;
- whether or not you smiled;
- what postures and gestures you used;
- your proximity in relation to different pupils or groups;
- the amount of 'banter' (humorous chat) you engaged in with different groups of pupils – was it balanced?
- who you selected for different tasks;
- your nonverbal behaviours – were they as you expected them to be? – did they convey confidence?
- whether your instructions were clear, audible and unhurried;
- which pupils you communicated most with and under what circumstances;
- Did you check for understanding?

## 2 Building your classroom management plan (CMP)

At this point, it is assumed you have read the preceding sections and reflected on your personal qualities, your school and the pupils you teach.

The CMP should be seen as an integral component of your schemes of work and lesson plans, since behaviour management extends over all aspects of your teaching. The school behaviour policy specifies general expectations in all contexts, whereas the CMP covers behaviours required to work together in a specific classroom.

The CMP specifies how you plan to:

1   Organise your classroom environment to facilitate pupils' engagement with learning and promote prosocial behaviour.
2   Plan what you expect other adults to be doing, whilst assisting you with your teaching, e.g. where you want them to be and which responsibilities you would like them to take on in respect of behaviour and learning. Not being clear in these respects can create role ambiguity, a phenomenon long established as a stressor (e.g. Kahn et al., 1964).
3   Plan and develop effective classroom management strategies, including proactive (teaching required behaviour), reorientation (redirecting misbehaviour early) and reactive strategies (correcting unacceptable behaviour) with the primary emphasis on explicitly teaching, modelling and reinforcing desired behaviour.
4   Over time, shift emphasis from teacher control to pupil self-control.
5   Develop individual programmes for challenging pupils who do not respond to whole-class interventions.

## 2.1 Classroom management strategies

The strategies are organised sequentially. Begin with proactive or preventative strategies, elements of which can be organised before you even meet your pupils (e.g. classroom layout) then focus on using interpersonal skills to establish your authority and elicit the desired behaviour. The intention being to create a positive climate that engages pupils with learning through teaching prosocial behaviours.

### 2.1.1 Proactive strategies

Throughout this book, I have emphasised the importance of planning and reflection to develop effective behaviour management skills. I have also emphasised the importance of adopting a positive approach in which pupils are taught explicitly the behaviours required to engage successfully in learning, and that make life in their classroom calm, pleasant and safe. In this section, the focus is on how to bring that about by taking control of and manipulating the classroom environment, developing effective routines and procedures, and building positive teacher-pupil and pupil-pupil relationships.

MANIPULATING THE PHYSICAL ENVIRONMENT

The physical layout of your room can be an easy-to-change resource or can create problems. For example, the familiar practice of leaving pupils organised in small groups for all activities has been challenged by a number of researchers. Hastings and Chantrey-Wood (2002b) found teachers tended not to change table group layouts to individual, paired, small or large group seating in order to ensure best fit for specific learning tasks, despite considerable evidence demonstrating the advantages to learning and behaviour of doing so.

That different seating layouts need to be matched to specific learning tasks, age and the level of social development of your pupils in order to be most effective in promoting learning is well established in the research literature. However, despite the empirical evidence in support, Kutnick *et al.* found that:

> Teachers seemed aware that effective grouping practices in classrooms required training and application of specific skills by children, but this was not included in their planned work.
>
> (2006: 6)

You should carefully consider why you are organising your pupils in a particular way, taking time to examine the evidence as to what layout (group, individual desks etc.) works best for the learning activities you are planning. Besides learning, there are other considerations – managing behaviour, supervision and administration. Effective teachers engineer a well-planned classroom layout in advance to facilitate engagement with learning (Gettinger and Ball, 2008), ensure they can quickly and easily scan the room (Pedota, 2007) and make sure people can move around unhindered (Jenson *et al.*, 2009). When deciding what you want your classroom to look like, keep in mind the importance of adopting approaches that have empirical evidence showing that they work. In classes organised around tables pushed together for groupwork, a little time spent on how they are oriented can make changing the classroom an orderly, rapid event, as opposed to being noisy and chaotic. Consider the evidence in respect of displays as promoters of curiosity versus source of distraction, again in conjunction with knowing your class in terms of age, learning needs and attention span, as well as whose work is displayed and how.

Having laid out your classroom(s), ask yourself:

- How does it look and feel?
- Is it an inviting and stimulating environment?
- What do you think of the décor, the materials on show, your desk, pupils' desks, and other furniture and fittings?
- Try sitting in all the chairs and see how easy it is (or not) to see the whiteboard or teacher's desk.
- Plan, map and practice movement around the room to identify (and change) bottlenecks.
- Do you think it is well laid out?
- Could it be improved?

Classroom management planning 223

- What is good about it?
- What is lacking?
- Is it fit for purpose? That is, does it match the type of teaching and learning you are planning to adopt, or is it how the last teacher left it?
- How adaptable is the room for making quick changes of layout?

Decide who is going to sit where and keep a simple seating plan in your records for each class – include a note of any concerns.

The beauty of classroom physical layout is that it can usually be manipulated in advance of your pupils arriving, i.e. when under less pressure.

### ESTABLISHING RULES AND ROUTINES

Establish your rules and routines using the following steps:

1. Be clear about your behavioural expectations.
2. From day one, begin teaching your expectations explicitly through your rules – four or five positively worded rules indicating behaviour that applies in all contexts, e.g. keep your feet and hands to yourself, bring the correct equipment; etc. Always check that your pupils have understood what you require of them; do not rush. This can be difficult in your first lessons, as you may be a little anxious, so write notes to yourself on your lesson plan to remind you about pace and pause (e.g. slow down).
3. From day one, begin teaching and reinforcing pivotal routines. They are pivotal because the focus here is in establishing your authority, keeping pupils focused on learning and the lesson flowing. Focus on:
    i entering the classroom
    ii getting the attention of the class
    iii managing noise levels
    iv getting out and putting away materials and equipment
    v changing activities – transitions
    vi dealing with interruptions
    vii keeping pupils on task
    viii tidying up and finishing the lesson
    ix exiting the classroom

These are not the only routines and procedures; others are also important, e.g. emergency drills (see Chapter 8 for more details). Do not try teaching all routines at the same time. Explicitly teach one routine at a time and reinforce until established and revisit as necessary. For example, upon entering the classroom:

- Decide how you want your pupils to enter and where you want them to be.
- Meet and greet pupils at the door.

- Tell them how you want them to enter the room and what you want them to do once inside – ideally an engaging individual activity and not forgetting rules for where personal equipment is to be placed, e.g. bags. In regular classrooms, this is usually on the floor, but in laboratories and workshops, they are best stored away from work areas. Decide what you want them to do with mobile phones, tablets, smart watches, etc. There may well be a whole-school or department/faculty policy covering these items.
- Make sure they have the correct personal equipment for the lesson.
- Reinforce the first three or four who respond as required, thereby acknowledging completion of the desired task and for doing it quickly. How to reinforce is discussed in detail below.

School policies differ in respect of how children enter classrooms, some being anti-lining-up, others insisting on it. So, you may need to tweak the method to suit the context. For example, where lining up is not accepted, movement into the room can be managed by standing in the doorway to control flow and by using the opportunity to interact positively with your class. Avoid standing by your desk fiddling with paper or equipment especially at the beginning of the day. Grab the opportunity to make a positive start by complimenting and engaging in some banter with your pupils.

There are many ways to get pupils' attention, some noisy, some quiet; whichever you decide on, make sure you teach pupils what your signal means.

*The noisy way*, e.g. tapping, clapping, timers, asking pupils to show hands, sit up straight, be quiet, and so on. Which you select is up to you (and perhaps school/department policy). Teach by saying something like, 'When I clap my hands I want you all to stop what you are doing put your pens down and face me'. The problem with making loud noises is that they can encourage a noisy atmosphere, and if used with noisy/excitable groups, getting attention becomes a shouting match.

*The quiet way* relies on nonverbal signals: raising hands, folding arms and other gestures. Nonverbal gestures can be very powerful tools, and the more you use them for managing behaviour, the better, as it makes for a calmer, more peaceful environment. Again, teach by saying at the start of the lesson something like, 'When I raise my hand I want you all to stop what you are doing, put your pens down and look at me', then try it and reinforce the first three or four that respond quickest.

In sum:

- Think about what routines are needed to manage key points of the day/lesson.
- Plan precisely what behaviour you want and in what order.
- Teach associated signals for required behaviour and be consistent in their use.
- Reinforce the pupils who respond as required and do so quickly.

- Teach, model, reinforce and practice required behaviour until automatic.
- Over time, evaluate the effectiveness of your routines. Do they achieve the required goal and do so quickly? If not, make changes. Use Table 10.3 as a template to evaluate your routines.

## REINFORCING BEHAVIOUR

As I pointed out elsewhere, in behavioural approaches, a distinction is made between rewards and reinforcers. Rewards are usually some form of gift, e.g. certificate or sticker, etc. Reinforcers, however, refer to anything that happens following a behaviour that results in or increases the likelihood of it being repeated. A reward may or may not achieve this. Reinforcers can be external (teacher control) or internal (self-reinforcement). The aim in this book is to work towards teaching pupils to self-reinforce, to develop their self-control and self-regulation, but also acknowledging that this will occur at different rates, depending on level of development, age and behaviour patterns of the pupils.

In the following example, I will assume you are teaching a 'moderate direction class' (based on the categories LTD, MTD, HTD in Figure 10.3), where you consider most of the class behave reasonably well most of the time with a few who prove challenging. We shall focus on developing one routine – getting the attention of the class.

*Table 10.3* Evaluating classroom routines

| Routine | Procedure | Works well | Usually works | Not working | Action |
|---|---|---|---|---|---|
| Entering the classroom | | | | | |
| Getting the attention of the class | | | | | |
| Managing noise levels | | | | | |
| Getting changed/ safety equipment | | | | | |
| Getting out materials | | | | | |
| Changing activities - transitions | | | | | |
| Keeping pupils on task | | | | | |
| Tidying up and finishing the lesson | | | | | |
| Exiting the classroom | | | | | |

Note
Use this template to make a list of the routines you use and associated procedures in order to identify areas for development.

Imagine you are a trainee or new teacher visiting a school. Prior to teaching there you are watching the teacher manage a Year 8 class that you will be teaching. She says to the class, 'I am waiting for silence, and we will not begin until everybody is silent and facing me.' You notice that, despite waiting, not all of the pupils stop chatting, and, whilst a number of the pupils face her, some do not (including those who carry on talking). She repeats her instruction; still not all respond. She then threatens to put the names of those still not responding on the board, and eventually, after around five minutes, all but two boys are doing as instructed, and she begins the lesson.

You do not think this is an effective routine, given that the instruction 'We will not begin until everybody is silent' is not carried through. You decide to try an alternative approach when you start at the school. On day one you say to your pupils, 'When I raise my hands, I want you all to stop what you are doing, put your pens down and face me'. You demonstrate this a couple of times, then carry on with the lesson. A short time later you raise your hands, and the first four or five pupils who stop what they are doing and face you receive a token, e.g. cloakroom ticket. As you give them out, you say clearly why they have received it, e.g. 'I am impressed to see how these people remembered to stop talking and face me when I raised my hands' so that they associate verbal support from you for the specific behaviour at the same time as they receive the ticket. You repeat this process regularly with each routine until it is established. Over time, you use more intermittent reinforcement as the verbal support increases in strength. However, you continue to monitor performance, and if the behaviour starts to slip, you will reintroduce more tangible alternatives to grab their attention or just use them to add a little variety (see Figure 10.4).

The cloakroom tickets, in themselves, are relatively meaningless, so they usually need to translate into some form of reward. However, several pupils recently told a teacher colleague that they had kept every cloakroom ticket they had received, even sticking them on pinboards at home. This highlights the importance of measuring the effect of a 'reward' rather than what adults assume is their value to pupils. A reward can be given out following a draw, which strengthens the association between the desired behaviour and something novel and fun (re-read Chapter 1 for details). Many items can act as reinforcers – everything from nonverbal behaviours (thumbs up, smiles), verbal support, time on special activities, food or school equipment. Which reinforcer you select should be determined by a combination of what is acceptable in your school and the effect of that reinforcer on behaviour.

Another advantage of this approach is its inclusiveness compared with the familiar points-collecting approaches (i.e. pupil with highest number of points wins), where pupils who are challenging have no chance whatsoever of winning (unless you fiddle the results), so it fails to act as an incentive to behave. The draw on the other hand can be accessed by gaining a single ticket,

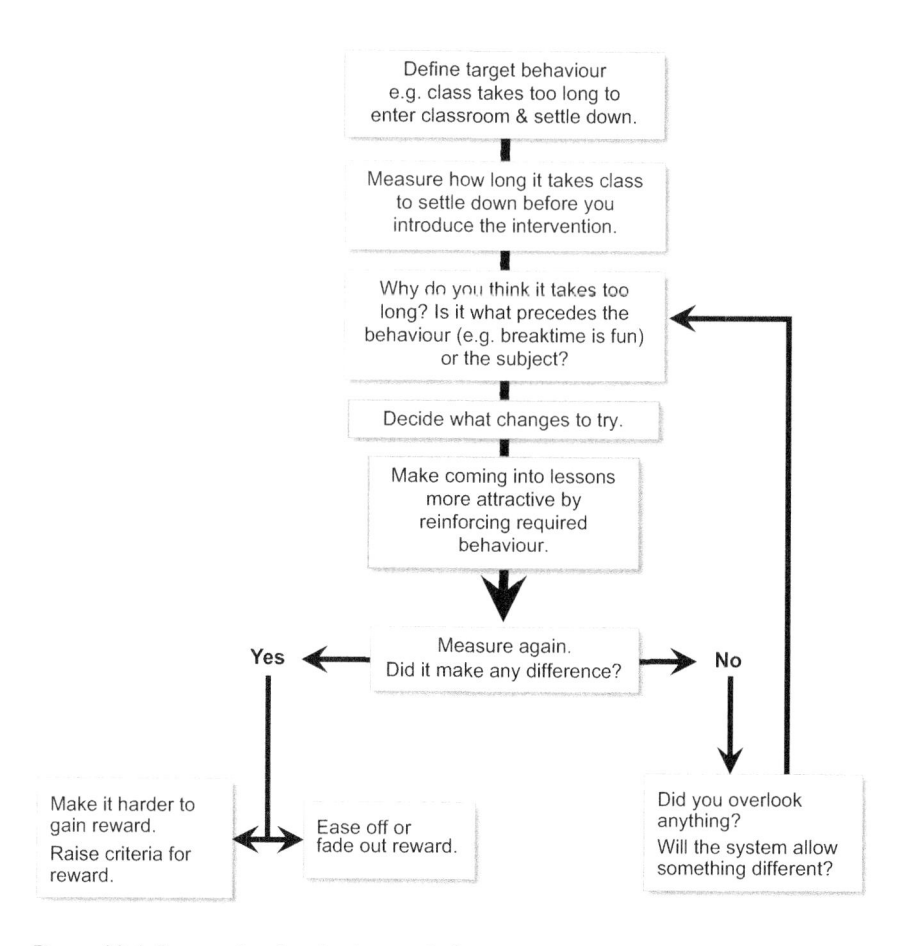

```
                    ┌─────────────────────────────┐
                    │  Define target behaviour    │
                    │  e.g. class takes too long  │
                    │  to enter classroom &       │
                    │  settle down.               │
                    └──────────────┬──────────────┘
                                   │
                    ┌──────────────▼──────────────┐
                    │  Measure how long it takes  │
                    │  class to settle down       │
                    │  before you introduce the   │
                    │  intervention.              │
                    └──────────────┬──────────────┘
                                   │
                    ┌──────────────▼──────────────┐
                    │  Why do you think it takes  │
                    │  too long? Is it what       │◄────┐
                    │  precedes the behaviour     │     │
                    │  (e.g. breaktime is fun)    │     │
                    │  or the subject?            │     │
                    └──────────────┬──────────────┘     │
                                   │                    │
                    ┌──────────────▼──────────────┐     │
                    │  Decide what changes to try.│     │
                    └──────────────┬──────────────┘     │
                                   │                    │
                    ┌──────────────▼──────────────┐     │
                    │  Make coming into lessons   │     │
                    │  more attractive by         │     │
                    │  reinforcing required       │     │
                    │  behaviour.                 │     │
                    └──────────────┬──────────────┘     │
                                   ▼                    │
                    ┌─────────────────────────────┐     │
          Yes ◄─────│  Measure again.             │───► No
                    │  Did it make any difference?│     │
                    └─────────────────────────────┘     │
                                                        │
                                                        ▼
┌──────────────┐   ┌──────────────┐         ┌──────────────────┐
│ Make it      │   │              │         │ Did you overlook │
│ harder to    │◄──│ Ease off or  │         │ anything?        │
│ gain reward. │   │ fade out     │         │ Will the system  │
│ Raise        │   │ reward.      │         │ allow something  │
│ criteria for │   │              │         │ different?       │
│ reward.      │   │              │         │                  │
└──────────────┘   └──────────────┘         └──────────────────┘
```

*Figure 10.4* Stages in developing a behavioural intervention to address an inefficient routine.

and gaining two increases your odds – giving you the opportunity to teach probability at the same time! After the first week or two, depending on the response, you might move from reinforcing regularly to a more intermittent schedule (see Figure 10.5). If the required behaviour is sustained, then you are in effect beginning the move from teacher control to pupil self-control. If behaviour deteriorates, increase the frequency of reinforcement. Adjust the frequency up or down based on objective data, e.g. how quickly pupils respond to an instruction. This approach allows you to move back and forth to produce the desired effect – to encourage engagement with learning and prosocial behaviour.

## Reinforcement schedule

**Extinction** — Reinforce no responses

If teacher attention is reinforcing a behaviour, then ignoring it could extinguish it.

**Continuous** — Reinforce every correct response

Grab the attention of the group or individual in the early stages by regularly reinforcing the desired behaviours. Then move to intermittent interval or ratio depending on the type of behaviour.

**Intermittent** — Reinforce some responses

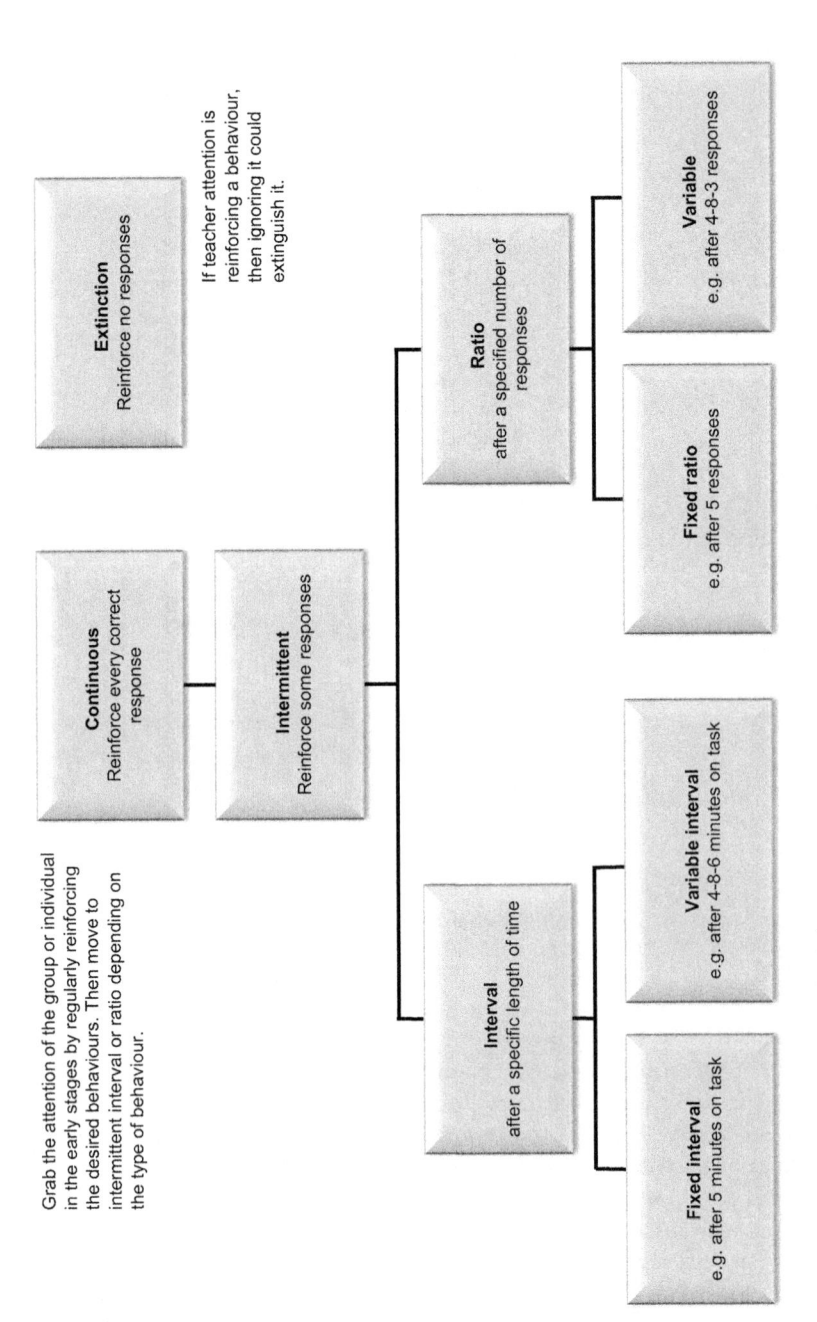

- **Ratio** — after a specified number of responses
  - **Fixed ratio** — e.g. after 5 responses
  - **Variable** — e.g. after 4-8-3 responses
- **Interval** — after a specific length of time
  - **Fixed interval** — e.g. after 5 minutes on task
  - **Variable interval** — e.g. after 4-8-6 minutes on task

*Figure 10.5* Reinforcement schedule.

The following guidelines offer advice on how to use reinforcers successfully:

- Reinforce *only* the desired behaviour, as soon as it is performed.
- Frequently reinforce a new behaviour.
- Make eye contact when giving a reinforcer – eye contact can be reinforcing in itself.
- Describe the behaviour being reinforced as you issue the reinforcer.
- Build anticipation for reinforcers – e.g. keep your tokens/prizes in an attractive container to help keep focus.
- Even highly desirable reinforcers lose their effectiveness over time, so be prepared to change.
- Use differential attention to encourage *on-* and *not* off-task behaviour, i.e. make sure the reinforcement of desired behaviour is done more enthusiastically than reprimands.
- If the learning environment is not engaging, then removal from it is a reward – behaviour management is no solution to lacklustre lessons.
- Gradually involve pupils in setting new goals.
- Over time make reinforcement more intermittent as pupils' self-reinforcement is more established.

The effectiveness of using reinforcement in reducing disruptive behaviour has been demonstrated in a number of studies. For example, Stage and Quiroz (1997) found that both reinforcement and punishment were effective in reducing disruption. However, using a combination of reinforcement and punishment had the largest effect on behaviour, followed by reinforcement alone and lastly, although still effective, punishment alone. Punishment is dealt with under Reactive Strategies.

## PROFESSIONAL SOCIAL SKILLS AND GROUP MANAGEMENT

Kounin (1970) developed a classroom management system that focused on teachers being aware of their environment and using specific techniques (e.g. withitness, overlapping) to keep pupils busy on learning tasks and minimise behaviours problems. Maintaining interest and challenge is achieved by varying content, teaching style, managing movement, pacing lessons, and managing transitions. He developed a number of terms to describe behaviours used by effective teachers; the following examples are worthy of particular note:

- *Withitness* is being aware of all behaviour taking place in your classroom and conveying that to your pupils. Being alert to subtle changes in your pupils' verbal and nonverbal behaviour, which might indicate potential disruption. An awareness informed by understanding their pupils, e.g. knowing their names, interests, goals, strengths and weaknesses and so on.

- *Scanning* is an important skill to practice and requires you to think about your location in the classroom and use peripheral vision to gauge what is going on around the room. Always ensure you can keep a check on the whole class from wherever you are (standing or seated) and whatever you are doing. For example, if you are working with a small group, position yourself so that you can, with minimal effort, see the rest of the class. Try walking around your classroom when it is empty to determine how easy it is (or not) to view all areas to determine if the layout is supportive of scanning – if not change it. Repeat the process, sitting down at different points around the room to determine the best places to sit when working with small groups, dyads, etc. Make a note on a room plan of where these points are.
- *Ripple effect*: reprimanding one individual can have a knock-on vicarious effect with other pupils. It can also be used positively, so if one pupil is off task on a table you can reinforce those on task – if the pupil values your acknowledgement or other reinforcer, he/she is likely to follow suit.
- *Overlapping* is where a teacher is able to carry out multiple tasks at the same time. For example, redirecting off-task pupils at the back of the class whilst working with a group at the front but maintaining flow.

### 2.1.2 Reorientation strategies

These are used to check individuals who are drifting off task or not paying attention, talking out of turn, etc., and are designed to do so whilst maintaining the flow of the lesson. They are used to keep the pupil(s) focused on learning rather than using punishment.

They include nonverbal behaviours, such as:

- Prolonged eye contact with a pupil, whilst continuing to teach – This lets him/her know you are aware of what is happening and that he/she should stop whatever they should not be doing.
- Gestures and posture – Gestures like an eyebrow raise or a raised first finger are often used to support or emphasise prolonged eye contact.
- Proxemics – Moving closer to a pupil increases perceived control and reminds them you are there and aware of what they are doing.

and verbal behaviours:

- Mentioning someone's name who is perhaps talking to a neighbour when they should be listening to you – again, whilst continuing to teach. We are all attuned to picking up on people mentioning our name. For example, 'So the Vikings came from Scandinavia, *John*, and landed ...' Dropping the name without looking at the pupil conveys that you are aware of what he is doing – a sign of withitness.

- Verbally supporting pupils who are behaving as required, near to someone who is not doing so, can be an effective way of combining direct reinforcement with modelling, provided the pupil values your verbal support.
- Restating a rule – remind pupils about what is expected publicly – 'OK, can anyone tell me what we do when we want to ask a question?'
- Use targeted encouragement to get a pupil(s) back on task – 'Scott, you have been working really well so far – keep it up …'
- Having a sense of humour is a quality often cited by pupils as characteristic of a good teacher. It can often be successful for relieving tension in a situation but should not be used to ridicule pupils.
- Being mobile whilst teaching helps monitor behaviour with all age groups and, whilst on the move, use nonverbal gestures to address individuals who are off task, whilst maintaining the flow of your teaching or conversations with other pupils. Do not let furniture dictate how you teach; you do not have to spend an entire lesson welded to the smartboard.
- Deliberately ignoring a minor misbehaviour to maintain the flow of the lesson and followed up later if you think necessary. For example, having a quiet word before they leave the classroom to let them know you were aware and, if it happens again, there will be negative consequences.

## 2.1.3 Reactive strategies

These strategies are the last resort, since they are used when the proactive and reorientation has not worked. I repeat my earlier comment that unacceptable behaviour is always unacceptable, whatever an individual's circumstances. Just because someone has anger control issues or unfortunate home circumstances, does not justify assaulting someone else or creating chaos that disturbs the learning of others. It should trigger additional efforts to help the pupil develop self-control, but it is no excuse for the misbehaviour.

It is important to remember the behavioural approach definition of punishment, which is adopted here:

> A punishment is *only* ever a punishment if it reduces or stops an undesirable behaviour.

Your school may have many sanctions/consequences, etc., but if they fail to reduce or stop the undesired behaviour, they are not punishments, and in some cases, they act as reinforcers.

When planning what reactive tactics to use, there are a number of things to consider:

- Punishment should be appropriate to a pupil's age group and level of development.

- The punishment should be directed to the behaviour, not the child – 'Blade, do not push other people ...' as opposed to 'Blade, you are a very unpleasant young man...'
- It should be something pupils do not like.
- Do not take unacceptable behaviours (e.g. insults) personally. Remember when angry, people (including adults) sometimes say things they later regret. Reactive anger occurs outside the brain's self-regulation or executive functioning systems. Again, the behaviour is still unacceptable, so work at being emotionally objective under such circumstances – keep your cool and issue an appropriate sanction – if it stops the behaviour, then it qualifies as a punishment.
- When addressing misbehaviour, keep the focus on its interference with planned work – 'Gemma, you do not have time to chat to Rosie about make-up when you have important work to finish' as opposed to 'Gemma, stop gossiping to Rosie – it is very irritating'.
- Use 'thank you' rather than 'please' when admonishing pupils since it communicates an assumption that they will stop the misbehaviour, rather than sounding like you are pleading with them. For example, 'Demarco, put the pens back in the box, thank you' as opposed to 'Demarco, please put those pens in the box'.
- Provide positive alternatives at each stage – 'Jo, you can either get on with the ... or you will have to stay in for three minutes at break ...' Then if she does not do as required, raise the level – 'Jo, you are already staying in for three minutes; get on with ... or you will be staying in for five minutes' – and so on. This allows more levels of negotiation than 'Jo, you can either get on with ... or you will be staying in at breaktime', since, if it does not have the desired effect, you have reduced your options.
- Punishments should be simple to operate and given as near to the event as possible. The longer the delay between the event and the punishment, the weaker the association between the two, meaning it will be less effective.
- Keep a note of actions taken.
- Do not choose a punishment because someone suggested it or because they worked for another teacher – make sure they fit your teaching style/personality and school policy, are enforceable and bring about the desired outcome.
- Having punished someone for unacceptable behaviour, be prepared to reinforce any subsequent positive behaviour.
- Do not link punishment and reward systems. Some schools have systems whereby points are often recorded on a chart so pupils can go up and down. Consequently, pupils who are challenging spend their time going up and down like yoyos. Having the systems separate keeps the incentive for positive behaviour clear.
- Start each new day with a clean slate and a positive note to avoid developing a negative cycle with the class – leave your 'baggage' outside the classroom.

- Write down your list of punishments as they are often used when you are under pressure or feeling you are losing control. Having them organised in a hierarchical list gives you a reference point to help clarify your thinking and makes jumping up the hierarchy too quickly less likely. Your school will have a list of punishments/sanctions in the behaviour policy, but remember that as your relationship with the class develops, your verbal and nonverbal behaviour will have a more immediate and effective impact than using abstract sanctions. Your reaction to disruption should focus on being disappointed or annoyed, as opposed to being angry that someone is misbehaving, since showing that a behaviour is 'getting to you' will be a source of entertainment to some individuals. So, try as much as possible not to show emotion when issuing punishment. Issue the sanction and walk away; don't get drawn into a discussion as to the rights and wrongs. If the behaviour persists, move up the punishment hierarchy.

The following is one example of a hierarchy of punishments:

1. nonverbal signal (e.g. flat of hand or index finger raised, prolonged eye contact);
2. verbal reprimand(s) and warnings;
3. in-class suspension – separate from partner or group in class (offer an incentive: 'If you can demonstrate to me that you can act responsibly, I will allow you to sit back with …');
4. keep back at breaktime (<2 mins + +)[*];
5. record name on personal behaviour chart;
6. teacher detention;
7. departmental/faculty detention;
8. temporary removal from classroom;
9. refer to SLT;
10. contact parents/carers;
11. on report;
12. behavioural contract with child, teacher and parents/carers;
13. longer term separation from group, working in isolation;
14. referral to on-site unit;
15. suspension;
16. fixed-term exclusion;
17. permanent exclusion.

---

[*] Adjust time to suit age of group. If you tell someone they are staying in for two minutes at break, you always have the option of increasing the time if they persist, and at each point, they have the option of behaving as required. Keeping someone in for two minutes may not sound like much, but it inconveniences them, especially if they want to rush off to football practice.

So, what should you do if the preceding strategies do not have the desired effects? It means you were either incorrect about what was causing the behaviour and what was keeping it going, or what you think is a punishment is not. You will need to revise your theory about what preceded the behaviour (antecedent, e.g. coming in from playtime), the behaviour itself (e.g. very hard to settle down after break) and what follows the behaviour and what you believe keeps it going (consequence e.g. being sent out of the lesson). Alternatively, the reward you selected for behaving as required (house point) was ineffective or not as strong as missing part of the lesson.

## 3 Moving towards self-control: combining behavioural and cognitive strategies

As you adjust the use of reinforcement and punishment, you can begin introducing social problem-solving activities (see Chapter 9) alongside the direct reinforcement.

> ### Case study
>
> In her NQT year, Melissa had been given a lively Year 7 class for maths, who were also her tutor group, which included a group of boys who were considered by her colleagues to have ADHD, based on their extremely short attention spans. She decided to introduce a whole-class, inclusive cognitive-behavioural intervention that utilised a combination of stickers with self-instruction in a group setting. The target behaviour was increasing time on task in her lessons. Two weeks of observation revealed that the mean time on task was just over three minutes before one or more of the boys was off task and disturbing each other and or the class. She made up a series of reward cards on to which they could attach simple stickers (emoticons), which were issued immediately after they met their target time on task, which was adjusted lesson by lesson. Each pupil in the class was also given a book with outlines of different popular cartoon characters, one of which they would receive whenever they gained five simple stickers. This provided a triple incentive: i) earn a simple sticker, ii) collect five and get a special sticker at registration and iii) collect all of the cartoon characters and fill the book. At tutorial session at the end of each day, pupils were encouraged to tell the rest of the group why they had received their sticker, reinforcing the behaviour and engaging in self-instruction. At the end of a two-week period they had all at least tripled the amount of time they spent on-task before requiring a prompt. Both Melissa and her TA said that the process was quick to administer and produced very good results, not only on terms of maths engagement, but also in terms of their general behaviour and classroom relationships.

## 4 Supporting pupils with EBD

The cognitive-behavioural interventions discussed above can be augmented by organising your classroom and adopting teaching strategies that help pupils with ADHD and other behaviour difficulties to be more attentive, organised and focused on learning. These proactive strategies can be used with the whole class, as they will not be detrimental to any other pupil's learning or behaviour since they represent good teaching practice. This is a starting point and not an exhaustive list.

### 4.1 Reducing distractions

- Limit the amount of display material; include only that which is directly related to the topic in hand.
- Maximise space between desks.
- Match seating to task and pupils rather than the other way around.
- Provide quiet space for individual work and testing.
- Stand near to easily distracted pupils when teaching and sit them away from doors and displays.

### 4.2 Improving attention

- Provide written instructions to support verbal.
- Break down work into small chunks.
- Provide worksheets that have limited information/questions.
- Use frequent short questions rather than long for measuring progress.
- Record length of time persisting with tasks to measure improvement.
- Give instructions one at a time; once completed issue next instruction.
- Play listening and attention games.
- Teach realistic goal setting.

### 4.3 Improving organisation

- Use folders and boxes to organise their learning materials.
- Colour code materials by subject and/or topic.
- Issue instructions with time limit and have a clock visible so they know how long they are required to stay on task.
- Check for understanding.
- Provide a written timetable for daily activities.
- Encourage them to make and use checklists, crossing items off as they are accomplished.

### 4.4 Support self-regulation

- Offer dichotomous choice (rather than multiple options).
- Summarise information using pictures and charts.

- Model and teach self-monitoring strategies, e.g. know your triggers, breathing, having realistic expectations of others, coping with failure, the role of appraisal and interpretation of events.
- Use questions rather than directions to encourage reflection.
- Provide a reference for noise levels for different activities.
- Make expectations explicit.
- Keep instruction short, clear and simple.
- Use a reinforcement schedule that is sensitive to changes in pupils' behaviour in order to maximise engagement with work, gradually moving to self-reinforcement and regulation.
- Teach pupils to self-instruct.
- Keep records of your observations, share with other staff and learn from them, e.g. use to anticipate potential problems, e.g. playing up just before PE to avoid the lesson.
- Measure change and adjust the level of teacher-pupil control to maximize engagement and development.

If inclusive whole-class strategies do not bring about behaviour change with pupils with EBD, you might adopt an individual programme to focus on a specific behaviour with a view to returning to the whole-class strategies, once the issue has been addressed, in order to take advantage of social group problem solving. For details on how to develop an individual intervention strategy see Chapter 9.

Having read this and previous chapters, you should have considered many aspects that relate directly to the smooth running of the classroom and should now be able to produce a classroom management plan. As stated earlier, there is no one-size-fits-all CMP. Every context is different and what works for one individual might not work for another what works with one group will not work with another so be flexible and be guided by the effects of your approach. Lastly, classroom dynamics are fluid, so to make your CMP effective, you need to evaluate its effectiveness in responding to a changing context.

# References

Abelson, R.P. (1981). Psychological status of the script concept. *American Psychologist*, 36, 715-729.
Abramowitz, A.J., and O'Leary, S.G. (1991). Behavioral interventions for the classroom: implications for students with ADHD. *School Psychology Review*. 20, 219–233.
Abrams, D. and Hogg, M.A. (1999) *Social Identity and Social Cognition*. Oxford: Blackwell.
Alberto, P. A., and Troutman, A. C. (2013). *Applied behavior analysis for teachers*. (9th ed.). Cambridge: Pearson.
Allen, S. J., and Blackston, A. R. (2003). Training preservice teachers in collaborative problem solving: An investigation of the impact on teacher and student behavior change in real-world settings. *School Psychology Quarterly*, 18(1), 22.
Allport, G.W. (1954). *The nature of prejudice*. Reading, MA: Addison-Wesley.
Ambady, N., and Skowronski, J.J. (eds.). (2008). *First impressions*. New York: Guilford Press.
American Psychiatric Association. (2013). *Diagnostic and statistical manual of mental disorders* (5th ed.). Washington, DC: American Psychiatric Association.
Anderson, C., Berkowitz, L., Donnerstein, E., Huesmann, L., Johnson, J., Linz, D., Malamuth, N., and Wartella, E. (2003). The influence of media violence on youth. *Psychological Science in the Public Interest*, 4(3), 81–110.
Anderson, C.M., and Spauding, S.A. (2007). Using positive behaviour support to design effective classrooms. *American Educational Research Journal*, 16, 27–31.
Anderson, N.H. (1981). *Foundations of information integration theory*. New York: Academic Press.
Anderson, P. (2002). Assessment and development of executive function (EF) during childhood. *Child Neuropsychology*, 8(2), 71–82.
Andersen, S.L., and Teicher, M.H. (2008). Stress, sensitive periods and maturational events in adolescent depression. *Trends Neuroscience*, 31, 183–191.
Angelo, T.A., and Cross, K.P. (1993). *Classroom assessment techniques: a handbook for college teachers* (2nd ed.). San Francisco, CA: Jossey Bass Publishers.
Argyle, M. (1975). *Bodily communication*. London: Methuen.
Argyle, M. (1981). *Social skills and health*. London: Methuen.
Argyle, M., and Cook, M. (1976). *Gaze and mutual gaze*. Cambridge: Cambridge University Press.
Asch, S.E. (1946). Forming impressions of personality. *Journal of Abnormal and Social Psychology*, 42, 1230–1240.
Ashton, M.C., and Lee, K. (2016). Age trends in HEXACO-PI-R self-reports. *Journal of Research in Personality*, 64, 102–111.

Ashton, P.T., and Webb, R.B. (1986). *Making a difference: teachers' sense of efficacy and student achievement.* New York: Longman.

Association of Teachers and Lecturers (ATL). (2013). Press release – Disruptive behaviour in schools and colleges rises alongside increase in children with behavioural and mental health problems. Association of Teachers and Lecturers survey.

Axelrod, S. (1996). What's wrong with behavior analysis? *Journal of Behavioral Education,* 6(3), 247–256.

Babad, E. (1990). Calling on students: how a teacher's behavior can acquire different meanings in students' minds. *Journal of Classroom Interaction,* 25, 1–4.

Babad, E. (1995). The 'teacher's pet' phenomenon: teachers' differential behavior, and students' morale. *Journal of Educational Psychology,* 87, 361–374.

Babad, E. (1998). Preferential affect: the crux of the teacher expectancy issue. *Advances in Research on Teaching,* 7, 183–214.

Babad, E. (2009). *The social psychology of the classroom.* New York: Routledge.

Babad, E., Bernieri, F., and Rosenthal, R. (1989). Nonverbal communication and leakage in the behavior of biased and unbiased teachers. *Journal of Personality and Social Psychology,* 56(1), 89.

Babad, E., Inbar, J., and Rosenthal, R. (1982). Pygmalion, Galatea and the Golem: investigations of biased and unbiased teachers. *Journal of Educational Psychology,* 74, 459–474.

Bacharach, S.B., Bauer, S.C., and Conley, S. (1986). Organizational analysis of stress: the case of elementary and secondary schools. *Work and Occupations,* 13(1), 7–32.

Backes, C., and Ellis, I. (2003). The secrets of classroom management techniques. *Connecting Education and Careers,* 78, 5.

Baddeley, A. (2007). *Working memory, thought, and action.* New York: Oxford University Press.

Bahou, L. (2011). Rethinking the challenges and possibilities of student voice and agency. *Educate,* 1(1), 2–14.

Bandura, A. (1981). Self-referent thought: a developmental analysis of self-efficacy. In: J. Flavell and L. Ross (eds.), *Social cognitive development: frontiers and possible futures.* Cambridge: Cambridge University Press.

Bandura, A. (1986). *Social foundations of thought and action: a social cognitive theory.* Englewood Cliffs, NJ: Prentice-Hall.

Bandura, A. (1995). *Self-efficacy in changing societies.* New York: Cambridge University Press.

Bandura, A. (1997). *Self-efficacy: the exercise of control.* New York: Freeman.

Bandura, A. (2001). Social cognitive theory: an agentic perspective. *Annual Review of Psychology,* 52(1), 1–26.

Bandura, A., and Locke, E.A. (2003). Negative self-efficacy and goal effects revisited. *Journal of Applied Psychology,* 88(1), 87–99.

Bandura, A., Ross, D., and Ross, S.A. (1961). Transmission of aggression through the imitation of aggressive models. *Journal of Abnormal and Social Psychology,* 63(3), 575–582.

Bandura, A., Ross, D., and Ross, S.A. (1963). Imitation of film-mediated aggressive models. *Journal of Abnormal and Social Psychology,* 66(1), 3–11.

Barfield, V., and Burlingame, M. (1974). The pupil control ideology of teachers in selected schools. *The Journal of Experimental Education,* 42(4), 6–11.

Barker, G.P., and Graham, S. (1987). Developmental study of praise and blame as attributional cues. *Journal of Educational Psychology,* 79(1), 62–66.

Barkley, R.A. (2012). *Executive functions: what they are, how they work and why they evolved.* New York: Guilford Press.
Barkley, R.A., Murphy, K.R., and Fischer, M. (2008). *ADHD in adults: what the science says.* New York: Guilford Press.
Baron-Cohen, S. (2001). Theory of mind and autism: a review. *Special Issue of the International Review of Mental Retardation,* 23, 169–204.
Baudson, T.G., and Preckel, F. (2013). Teachers' implicit personality theories about the gifted: an experimental approach. *School Psychology Quarterly,* 28(1), 37–46.
Baumeister, R.F., Bratslavsky, E., Finkenauer, C., and Vohs, K.D. (2001). Bad is stronger than good. *Review of General Psychology,* 5(4), 323–370.
Baumeister, R., Campbell, J., Krueger, J., and Vohs, K.D. (2005). Exploding the self-esteem myth. *Scientific American,* January.
Bavelas, A. (1950). Communication patterns in task-oriented groups. *Journal of the Acoustical Society of America,* 22, 723–730
Baxter, J.C., Winter, E.P., and Hammer, R.E. (1968). Gestural behavior during a brief interview as a function of cognitive variables. *Journal of Personality and Social Psychology,* 8, 303–307.
Beck, J.S. (1995). *Cognitive therapy: basics and beyond.* New York: Guilford Press.
Beck, R., and Fernandez, E. (1998). Cognitive-behavioral therapy in the treatment of anger: a meta-analysis. *Cognitive Therapy and Research,* 22(1), 63–74.
Becker, W.C., Englemann, S., and Thomas, D.R. (1975). *Classroom management.* Henley-on-Thames: Science Research Associates.
Berkowitz, L. (1993). *Aggression: its causes, consequences, and control.* Boston, MA: McGraw-Hill.
Berridge, K.C., and Kringelbach, M.L. (2011). Building a neuroscience of pleasure and well-being. *Psychology of Well-being,* 1(1), 1–26.
Berridge, K.C., and Robinson, T.E. (1997). What is the role of dopamine in reward: hedonic impact, reward learning, or incentive salience? *Brain Research Reviews,* 28(3), 309–369.
Bettinger, E., and Slonim, R. (2007). Patience among children. *Journal of Public Economics,* 91(1), 343–363.
Bibou-Nakou, I., Stogiannidou, A., and Kiosseoglou, G. (1999). The relation between teacher burnout and teachers' attributions and practices regarding school behaviour problems. *School Psychology International,* 20(2), 209–217.
Biederman, J. (2005). Attention-deficit/hyperactivity disorder: a selective overview. *Biological Psychiatry,* 57(11), 1215–1220.
Blackwell, L.S., Trzesniewski, K.H., and Dweck, C.S. (2007). Implicit theories of intelligence predict achievement across an adolescent transition: a longitudinal study and an intervention. *Child Development,* 78(1), 246–263.
Blackwood, N.J., Bentall, R.P., Simmons, A., Murray, R.M., and Howard, R.J. (2003). Self-responsibility and the self-serving bias: an fMRI investigation of causal attributions. *NeuroImage,* 20(2), 1076–1085.
Blatchford, P., Kutnick, P., Clark, H., MacIntyre, H., and Baines, E. (2001). *The nature and use of within class groupings in secondary schools.* Final Report. Economic and Social Research Council.
Blum, K., Chen, A.L.C., Braverman, E.R., Comings, D.E., Chen, T.J., Arcuri, V., and Oscar-Berman, M. (2008). Attention-deficit-hyperactivity disorder and reward deficiency syndrome. *Neuropsychiatric Disease and Treatment,* 4(5), 893.

Bossert, S., Dwyer, D., Rowan, B., and Lee, G. (1982). The instructional management role of the principal. *Educational Administration Quarterly*, 18, 34–63.

Botella, C., Mira, A., Garcia-Palacios, A., Quero, S., and Navarro, M.V., et al. (2012). Smiling is fun: a coping with stress and emotion regulation program. *Studies in Health Technology and Informatics*, 181, 123–127.

Bower, S.A., and Bower, G.H. (1976). *Asserting your self.* Reading: Addison-Wesley.

Bowlby, J. (1969). *Attachment and loss* (3 vols). London: Hogarth.

Braaten, E.B., and Rosen, L.A. (2000). Self-regulation of affect in attention deficit-hyperactivity disorder (ADHD) and non-ADHD boys: differences in empathic responding. *Journal of Consulting and Clinical Psychology*, 68(2), 313.

Bradshaw, C.P., Mitchell, M.M., and Leaf, P.J. (2010). Examining the effects of schoolwide positive behavioral interventions and supports on student outcomes: results from a randomized controlled effectiveness trial in elementary schools. *Journal of Positive Behavior Interventions*, 12(3), 133–148.

Bragg, S., and Manchester, H. (2011). *Creativity, school ethos and the creative partnerships programme*. London: Creative Partnerships.

Brewer, M.B. (1988). A dual process model of impression formation. In: T.K. Srull and R.S. Wyer, Jr (eds.), *Advances in Social Cognition*, vol. 1. Hillsdale, MI: Lawrence Erlbaum.

Brock, L.L., Rimm-Kaufman, S.E., Nathanson, L., and Grimm, K.J. (2009). The contributions of 'hot' and 'cool' executive function to children's academic achievement, learning-related behaviors, and engagement in kindergarten. *Early Childhood Research Quarterly*, 24(3), 337–349.

Brockner, J. (1988). *Self-esteem at work: research, theory and practice*. Lexington, KY: Lexington Books.

Bronfenbrenner, U. (1979). *The ecology of human development: experiments by nature and design*. Cambridge, MA: Harvard University Press.

Brookover, W.B., Beady, C., Flood, P., Schweitzer, J., and Wisenbaker, J. (1979). *Schools, social systems and student achievement: schools can make a difference*. New York: Praeger.

Brooks, F. (2013). Life stage: school years. In: C. Lemer (ed.), *Annual report of the child Medical officer 2012, our children deserve better: prevention pays*. London: The Stationery Office.

Brophy, J. (1981). Teacher praise: a functional analysis. *Review of Educational Research*, 51(1), 5–32.

Brophy, J.E., and Evertson, C.M. (1976). *Learning from teaching: a developmental perspective*. Boston, MA: Allyn and Bacon.

Bruan, L.M. (1989). Predicting adaptational outcomes from hassles and other measures. *Journal of Social Behavior and Personality*, 4(4), 363–376.

Bryk, A.S., and Driscoll, M.E. (1988). *An empirical investigation of the school as a community*. Chicago: University of Chicago School of Education.

Buck, R. (1988). *Human motivation and emotion* (2nd ed.). New York: Wiley.

Burchfield, S.R. (1985). *Stress: psychological and philosophical interactions*. London: Hemisphere.

Burgess, S., Metcalfe, R., and Sadoff. (2016). Understanding the response to financial and non-financial incentives in education: field experimental evidence using high-stakes assessment. Working Paper, University of Bristol, Centre for Market and Public Organisation.

Burke, C.S., Stagl, K.C., Klein, C., Goodwin, G.F., Salas, E., and Halpin, S.M. (2006). What type of leadership behaviors are functional in teams? A meta-analysis. *The Leadership Quarterly*, 17(3), 288–307.

Burke, J.D., Waldman, I., and Lahey, B.B. (2010). Predictive validity of childhood oppositional defiant disorder and conduct disorder: implications for the DSM-V. *Journal of Abnormal Psychology*, 119(4), 739.

Burn, K., Hagger, H., Mutton, T., and Everton, T. (2003). The complex development of student–teacher thinking. *Teachers and Teaching: Theory and Practice*, 9, 309–331.

Burnett, P.C. (2001). Elementary students' preferences for teacher praise. *Journal of Classroom Interaction*, 36(1), 16–23.

Burnett, P. (2002). Teacher praise and feedback and students' perception of the classroom environment. *Educational Psychology*, 22(1), 5–16.

Burnett, P.C., and Mandel, V. (2010). Praise and feedback in the primary classroom: teachers' and students' perspectives. *Australian Journal of Educational and Developmental Psychology*, 10, 145–154.

Bush, T., and Glover, D. (2014). School leadership models: what do we know? *School Leadership and Management*, 34, 5.

Bushman, B.J., and Huesmann, L.R. (2006). Short-term and long-term effects of violent media on aggression in children and adults. *Archives of Pediatrics and Adolescent Medicine*, 160(4), 348–352.

Byrne, D.G., Davenport, S.C., and Mazanov, J. (2007). Profiles of adolescent stress: the development of the adolescent stress questionnaire (ASQ). *Journal of Adolescence*, 30(3), 393–416.

Çaglar, L. (2001). *Anthropometric survey of school children*. FIRA.

Calder, B.J., and Gruder, C.L. (1988). *A network activation theory of attitudinal affect, unpublished manuscript*. Kellogg School of Business, Northwestern University.

Cameron, J., Pierce, W.D., Banko, K.M., and Gear, A. (2005). Achievement-based rewards and intrinsic motivation: a test of cognitive mediators. *Journal of Educational Psychology*, 97(4), 641–655.

Cameron, O. (2002). *Visceral sensory neuroscience: interoception*. New York: Oxford University Press.

Camp, B., Blom, G., Hebert, F., and Van Doorninck, W. (1977). 'Think aloud': a program for developing self-control in young aggressive boys. *Journal of Abnormal Child Psychology*, 5(2), 157–169.

Canter, L. (2009). *Assertive discipline: positive behavior management for today's classroom* (4th ed.). Bloomington, IN: Solution Tree Press.

Canter, L., and Canter, M. (1976). *Assertive discipline: a take charge approach for today's educator*. Los Angeles, CA: Lee Canter and Associates.

Canter, L., and Canter, M. (1992). *Assertive discipline: positive behaviour management for today's classroom*. Santa Monica, CA: Lee Canter and Associates.

Capel, S. (1997). Changes in students' anxieties and concerns after their first and second teaching practices. *Educational Research*, 39, 211–228.

Carlson, S.M., and Moses, L.J. (2001). Individual differences in inhibitory control and children's theory of mind. *Child Development*, 72, 1032–1053.

Carver, C.S., and Scheier, M.F. (1988). A control-process perspective on anxiety. *Anxiety Research*, 1(1), 17–22.

Case, R. (1996). Introduction: reconceptualizing the nature of children's conceptual structures and their devolvement in middle childhood. *Monographs of the Society for Research in Child Development*, 61(1–2), 1–26.

Casey, B.J., Jones, R.M., Levita, L., Libby, V., Pattwell, S.S., Ruberry, E.J., Soliman, F., and Somerville, L.H. (2010). The storm and stress of adolescence: insights from human imaging and mouse genetics. *Developmental Psychobiology*, 52(3), 225–235.
Cassidy, T. (1999). *Stress, cognition and health*. London: Routledge.
Castellanos, F.X., Sonuga-Barke, E., Milham, M., and Tannock, R. (2006). Characterizing cognition in ADHD: beyond executive dysfunction. *Trends in Cognitive Science*, 10(3), 117–123.
Catalano, R.F., Hawkins, J.D., Berglund, M.L., Pollard, J.A., and Arthur, M.W. (2002). Prevention science and positive youth development: competitive or cooperative frameworks? *Journal of Adolescent Health*, 31(6), 230–239.
Chaiken, S., and Trope, Y. (1999). *Dual-process models in social psychology*. New York: Guilford Press.
Chan, D.W. (2002). Stress, self-efficacy, social support and psychological distress among prospective Chinese teachers in Hong Kong. *Educational Psychology*, 22(5), 557–569.
Chance, P. (1993). Sticking up for rewards. *Phi Delta Kappan*, 787–790.
Chanfreau, J., Lloyd, C., Byron, C., Roberts, C., Craig, R., De Feo, D., and McManus, S. (2013). *Predicting well-being, research report*. London: National Center of Social Research.
Chaplain, R. (1995). Leading under pressure: Headteacher stress and coping. In: D. Hustler, T. Brighouse, and J. Rudduck (eds.), *Heeding heads: secondary heads and educational commentators in dialogue*. London: David Fulton.
Chaplain, R. (1996a). Stress and job satisfaction: a study of English primary school teachers. *Educational Psychology*, 15(4), 473–489.
Chaplain, R. (1996b). Pupils under pressure: coping with stress at school. In: J. Rudduck, R. Chaplain, and G. Wallace (eds.), *School improvement: what can pupils tell us?* London: David Fulton.
Chaplain, R. (1996c). Making a strategic withdrawal: disengagement and self-worth protection in male pupils. In: J. Rudduck, R. Chaplain, and G. Wallace (eds.), *School improvement: what can pupils tell us?* London: David Fulton.
Chaplain, R. (1996d). *Pupil behaviour*. Cambridge: Pearson.
Chaplain, R. (2000a). Helping children to persevere and be well motivated. In: D. Whitebread (ed.), *The psychology of teaching and learning in the primary school*. London: Routledge.
Chaplain, R. (2000b). Beyond exam results? Differences in the social and psychological perceptions of young males and females at school. *Educational Studies*, 26, 2.
Chaplain, R. (2001). Stress and job satisfaction among primary headteachers: a question of balance? *Educational Management and Administration*, 29(2), 197–215.
Chaplain, R. (2008). Stress and psychological distress among trainee secondary teachers in England. *Educational Psychology*, 28(2), pp. 195–209.
Chaplain, R., and Freeman, A. (1994). *Caring under pressure*. London: David Fulton Publishers.
Chaplain, R., and Freeman, A. (1996). *Stress and coping*. Cambridge: Pearson.
Chaplain, R., and Freeman, A. (1998). *Coping with difficult children: emotional and behavioural difficulties*. Cambridge: Pearson.
Chaplain, R., and Smith, S. (2006). *Challenging behaviour*. Cambridge: Pearson.
Charles, C.M. (1999). *Building classroom discipline: from models to practice* (6th ed.). New York: Longman.

Chazan, M., Laing, A.F., and Davies, D. (2014). *Emotional and behavioural difficulties in middle childhood: identification, assessment and intervention in school.* London: Routledge.
Children Act: Elizabeth II. Chapter 31. (2004) London: The Stationery Office.
Choe, D.E., Shaw, D.S., and Forbes, E.E. (2015). Maladaptive social information processing in childhood predicts young men's atypical amygdala reactivity to threat. *Journal of Child Psychology and Psychiatry*, 56(5), 549–557.
Christner, R.W., and Mennuti, R.B. (2008). *School-based mental health: a practitioner's guide to comparative practices.* London: Routledge.
Cicchetti, D., and Toth, S.L. (2005). Child maltreatment. *Annual Review of Clinical Psychology*, 1, 409–438.
Cinelli, L.A., and Zeigler, J. (1990). Cognitive appraisal of daily hassles in college students showing type A or type B behaviour patterns. *Psychological Reports*, 67, 83–88.
Clayson, D.E. (1999). Student's evaluation of teaching effectiveness: some implications of stability. *Journal of Marketing Education*, 21(1), 68–75.
Cloninger, C.R., Svrakic, D.M., and Przybeck, T.R. (2006). Can personality assessment predict future depression? A twelve-month follow-up of 631 subjects. *Journal of Affective Disorders*, 92(1), 35–44.
Coates, T.J., and Thoresen, C.E. (1976). Teacher anxiety: a review and recommendations. *Review of Educational Research*, 46(2), 159–184.
Cobb, S. (1976). Social support as a moderator of life stress. *Psychosomatic Medicine*, 38(5), 300–314.
Cohen, E.G., and Intilli, J.K. (1981). Interdependence and management in bilingual classrooms. Final Report No. NIE-G-80-0217. Stanford University, School of Education.
Cohen, J., McCabe, L., Michelli, N., and Pickeral, T. (2009). School climate: research, policy, practice, and teacher education. *Teachers College Record*, 111(1), 180–213.
Cohen, S., and Wills, T. (1985). Stress, social support and the buffering hypothesis. *Psychological Bulletin*, 98, 310–357.
Coie, J.D., and Dodge, K.A. (1998). Aggression and antisocial behaviour. In: W. Damon and N. Eisenberg (eds.), *Handbook of child psychology* (5th ed.), vol. 3: *Social, emotional, and personality development.* New York: Wiley.
Cole, G.A. (1996). *Management theory and practice.* London: Letts.
Cole, T., Daniels, H., and Visser, J. (eds.). (2013). *The Routledge international companion to emotional and behavioural difficulties.* Abingdon: Routledge.
Colvin, G. (2004). *Managing the cycle of serious acting-out behavior.* Eugene, OR: Behavior Associates.
Compas, B.E., and Reeslund, K.L. (2009). Processes of risk and resilience during adolescence. In: R.M. Lerner and L. Steinberg (eds.), *Handbook of adolescent psychology* (3rd ed., pp. 561–588). Hoboken, NJ: John Wiley and Sons, Inc.
Condon, C. (2002). The entertainment industry markets violent media to children. In: J. Torr (ed.), *Is media violence a problem?* San Diego, CA: Greenhaven Press.
Cooper, J., Heron, T., and Heward, W. (2007). *Applied behaviour analysis.* Hoboken, NJ: Pearson.
Cooper, P. (1999). *Understanding and supporting children with emotional and behavioural difficulties.* London: Kingsley.

Corey, G. (1986). *Theory and practice of group counselling and psychotherapy* (3rd ed.). Monterey, CA: Brooks/Cole.
Covington, M.V. (1992). *Making the grade: a self-worth perspective on motivation and school reform*. New York: Cambridge University Press.
Covington, M.V. (1998). *The will to learn: a guide for motivating young people*. New York: Cambridge University Press.
Covington, M.V. (2009). Self-worth theory: retrospection and prospects. In: K.R. Wentzel and A. Wigfield (eds.), *Handbook of motivation at school*. New York: Routledge.
Covington, M.V., and Müeller, K.J. (2001). Intrinsic versus extrinsic motivation: an approach/avoidance reformulation. *Educational Psychology Review*, 13(2), 157–176.
Cox, C., and Cooper, L. (1988). *High flyers: an anatomy of managerial success*. Oxford: Blackwell.
Craske, M.L. (1988). Learned helplessness, self-worth motivation and attribution retraining for primary school children. *British Journal of Educational Psychology*, 58, 152–164.
Creemers, B.P.M., and Reezigt, G.J. (1996). School level conditions affecting the effectiveness of instruction. *School Effectiveness and School Improvement*, 7(3), 197–228.
Crick, N.R., and Grotpeter, J.K. (1995). Relational aggression, gender, and social-psychological adjustment. *Child Development*, 66(3), 710–722.
Crone, E.A., and Dahl, R.E. (2012). Understanding adolescence as a period of social-affective engagement and goal flexibility. *National Review of Neuroscience*, 13, 636–650.
Crone, E.A., Bunge, S.A., Latenstein, H., and van der Molen, M.W. (2005). Characterization of children's decision making: sensitivity to punishment frequency, not task complexity. *Child Neuropsychology*, 11(3), 245–263.
Crone, E.A., Will, G.-J., Overgaauw, S., and Güroğlu, B. (2014). Social decision-making in childhood and adolescence. In: P.A.M. van Lange, B. Rockenbach, and T. Yamagishi (eds.), *Reward and punishment in social dilemmas*. New York: Oxford University Press.
Crosnoe, R., Johnson, M.K., and Elder, G.H. (2004). Intergenerational bonding in school: the behavioral and contextual correlates of student–teacher relationships. *Sociology of Education*, 77(1), 60–81.
Cuddy, A.J., Fiske, S.T., and Glick, P. (2008). Warmth and competence as universal dimensions of social perception: the stereotype content model and the BIAS map. *Advances in Experimental Social Psychology*, 40, 61–149.
Cutrona, C.E., and Russell, D.W. (1990). Types of social support and specific stress: toward a theory of optimal matching. In: B.R. Sarason, I.G. Sarason, and G.R. Pierce (eds.), *Social support: an interactional view*. New York: Wiley.
Dalgleish, T. (1995). Performance of the emotional Stroop task in groups of anxious expert, and control participants: a comparison of computer and card presentation formats. *Cognition and Emotion*, 9, 326–340.
Dalley, J.W., Mar, A.C., Economidou, D., and Robbins, T.W. (2008). Neurobehavioral mechanisms of impulsivity: fronto-striatal systems and functional neurochemistry. *Pharmacology, Biochemistry and Behavior*, 90, 250–260.
Darley, J.M., and Fazio, R.H. (1980). Expectancy confirmation process arising in the social interaction sequence. *American Psychologist*, 35, 867–881.
David, D., Lynn, S.J., and Ellis, A. (eds.). (2010). *Rational and irrational beliefs in human functioning and disturbances; Implication for research, theory, and practice*. New York: Oxford University Press.

Davidson, J. (2008). *Children and young people in mind: the final report of the National CAMHS Review.* London: DCSF/DoH.

Dawson, P., and Guare, R. (2010). *Executive skills in children and adolescents: a practical guide to assessment and intervention* (2nd ed.). New York: Guilford Press.

Dean, J. (1992). *Organising learning in the primary school.* London: Routledge.

Deci, E., Koestner, R., and Ryan, R. (1999). A meta-analytic review of experiments examining the effects of extrinsic rewards on intrinsic motivation. *Psychological Bulletin,* 125, 627–688.

Department for Children, Schools and Families (DCSF). (2008). *The education of children and young people with behavioural, emotional and social difficulties as a special educational need.* London: DCSF.

Department for Children, Schools and Families (DCSF). (2009). *School discipline and pupil behaviour policies: guidance for schools.* London: DCSF.

Department for Education (DfE). (2011). *Getting the simple things right: Charlie Taylor's behaviour checklists.* London: DfE.

Department for Education (DfE). (2012). *Improving teacher training for behaviour.* Crown Copyright. London: DfE.

Department for Education (DfE). (2014a). *Behaviour and discipline in schools: advice for headteachers and school staff.* Crown Copyright. London: DfE.

Department for Education (DfE). (2014b). *Special educational needs and disability code of practice: 0 To 25 Years.* Crown.

Department for Education (DfE). (2015). *Mental health and behaviour in schools.* London: DfE.

Department for Education (DfE). (2016). *Keeping children safe in education. Statutory guidance for schools and colleges.* September.

Department for Education and Employment (DfEE). (1998). *Green paper, teachers: meeting the challenge of change.* London: The Stationery Office.

Department for Education and Skills (DfES). (2000). *Fitness to teach: occupational health guidance for the training and employment of teachers.* London: DfES.

Department of Education and Science and the Welsh Office. (1989). *Discipline in schools: report of the committee of inquiry chaired by Lord Elton.* London: Her Majesty's Stationery Office (HMSO).

Dimmock, C. (1999). Principals and school restructuring: conceptualising challenges as dilemmas, *Journal of Educational Administration,* 37 (5), 441–462.

Dirling, J. (1999). Inclusion: enhancing resilience. *Preventing School Failure: Alternative Education for Children and Youth,* 43(3), 125–128.

Dobson, K., and Dozois, D. (2001). Historical and philosophical basis of cognitive-behavioral therapy. In: K. Dobson (ed.) *Handbook of cognitive-behavioral therapies.* New York: Guilford Press.

Dodge, K. (2006). Translational science in action: hostile attributional style and the development of aggressive behavior problems. *Developmental Psychopathology,* 18, 3.

Doherty-Sneddon, G., and Phelps, F.G. (2005). Gaze aversion: a response to cognitive or social difficulty? *Memory and Cognition,* 33(4), 727–733.

Doll, B., Brehm, K., and Zucker, S. (2014). *Resilient classrooms: creating healthy environments for learning* (2nd ed.). New York: Guilford Publications.

Donahoe, J., and Dorsel, V. (eds.). (1999). *Neural network models of cognition: biobehavioral foundations.* Amsterdam: Elsevier.

Doyle, W. (1986). Classroom organization and management. In: M.C. Wittrock (ed.), *Handbook of research on teaching* (3rd ed.). New York: Macmillan.

Doyle, W. (1989). Classroom management techniques. In: O.C. Moles (ed.), *Strategies to reduce student misbehavior*. Washington, DC: Office of Educational Research and Improvement.

Dryfoos, J.G. (1990). *Adolescents at risk: prevalence and prevention*. Oxford: Oxford University Press.

DuBois, D.L., Felner, R.D., Meares, H., and Krier, M. (1994). Prospective investigation of the effects of socioeconomic disadvantage, life stress, and social support on early adolescent adjustment. *Journal of Abnormal Psychology*, 103(3), 511.

Duncan, P.M., Garcia, A.C., Frankowski, B.L., Carey, P.A., Kallock, E.A., Dixon, R.D., and Shaw, J.S. (2007). Inspiring healthy adolescent choices: a rationale for and guide to strength promotion in primary care. *Journal of Adolescent Health*, 41(6), 525–535.

Dunham, J. (1989). Stress management – relaxation and exercise for pupils in secondary schools. *Pastoral Care in Education*, 7(2), 16–20.

Dweck, C. (1985). Intrinsic motivation, perceived control and self-evaluation maintenance: an achievement goal analysis. In: C. Ames and R. Ames (eds.), *Research in motivation in education, vol 2: the classroom milieu*. London: Academic Press.

Dweck, C. (1990). Self-theories and goals: their role in motivation, personality and development. In: R. Dienstbier (ed.), *Nebraska symposium on motivation*. Lincoln: University of Nebraska Press.

Dweck, C.S. (2006). *Mindset*. New York: Random House.

Edmondson, A.C., and Zhike, L. (2014). Psychological safety: the history, renaissance, and future of an interpersonal construct. *Annual Review of Organizational Psychology and Organizational Behavior*, 1, 23–43.

Edwards, S.L., Rapee, R.M., and Kennedy, S. (2010). Prediction of anxiety symptoms in preschool-aged children: examination of maternal and paternal perspectives. *Journal of Child Psychology and Psychiatry*, 51(3), 313–321.

Eisenberger, N.I. (2012). The pain of social disconnection: examining the shared neural underpinnings of physical and social pain. *Nature Reviews Neuroscience*, 13(6), 421–434.

Ekman, P. (1997). Expression or communication about emotion. In: N. Segal, G.E. Weisfeld, and C.C. Weisfeld (eds.), *Genetic, ethological and evolutionary perspectives on human development: essays in honor of Dr Daniel G. Freedman*. Washington, DC: American Psychological Association.

Ekman, P. (2004). Emotional and conversational nonverbal signals. In: J. Larrazabal and L. Perez-Miranda (eds.), *Language, knowledge, and representation*. Amsterdam: Klower.

Ekman, P. (2009). Lie catching and micro expressions. In: C. Martin (ed.), *The philosophy of deception*. New York: Oxford University Press.

Ekman, P., and Friesen, W.V. (1975). *Unmasking the face*. Englewood Cliffs, NJ: Prentice-Hall.

Ekman, P., and Friesen, W.V. (1978). *Facial action coding system: a technique for the measurement of facial movement*. Palo Alto, CA: Consulting Psychologists Press.

Ekman, P., Levenson, R.W., and Friesen, W.V. (1983). Autonomic nervous system activity distinguishes among emotions. *Science*, 221, 1208–1210.

Elashoff, J.D., and Snow, R.E. (eds.). (1971). *Pygmalion reconsidered*. Worthington, OH: Charles A. Jones.
Ellis, A. (1962). *Reason and emotion in psychotherapy*. Secaucus, NJ: Lyle Stuart.
Ellis, A., and Dryden, W. (1987). *The practice of rational-emotive therapy*. New York: Springer.
Ellis, H.C., and Ashbrook, P.K. (1989). The "state" mood and memory research: a selective view. In: D. Kuiken (ed.), Mood and memory: theory, research and applications. Special issue of *Journal of Social Behaviour and Personality*, 4, 1–21.
Ellis, H.C., Seibert, P.S., and Varner, L.J. (1995). Emotion and memory: effects of mood states on immediate and unexpected delayed recall. *Journal of Social Behaviour and Personality*, 10, 349–362.
Emmer, E.T., and Aussiker, A. (1990). School and classroom discipline programs: how well do they work? In: O.C. Moles (ed.), *Student discipline strategies: research and practice*. New York: State University of New York Press.
Emmer, E.T., Evertson, C.M., and Anderson, L.M. (1980). Effective classroom management at the beginning of the school year. *The Elementary School Journal*, 80(5), 219–231.
Eron, L., Huesmann, L., Lefkowitz, M., and Walder, L. (1972). Does television violence cause aggression? *American Psychologist*, 27(4), 253–263.
Esposito, C. (1999). Learning in urban blight: school climate and its effect on the school performance of urban, minority, low-income children. *School Psychology Review*, 28(3).
Evans, J. (2008). Dual-processing accounts of reasoning, judgment, and social cognition. *Annual Review of Psychology*, 59, 255–278.
Evertson, C.M. (1985). Training teachers in classroom management: an experimental study in secondary school classrooms. *The Journal of Educational Research*, 79(1), 51–58.
Evertson, C.M., Emmer, E.T., and Worsham, M.E. (2003). *Classroom management for elementary teachers* (6th ed.). Boston, MA: Allyn and Bacon.
Evertson, C.M., and Poole, I.R. (2008). Proactive classroom management. In: T. Good (ed.), *21st century education: a reference handbook*. London: Sage.
Eysenck, M., Derakshan, N., Santos, R., and Calvo, M. (2007). Anxiety and cognitive performance: attentional control theory. *Emotion*, 7(2), 336.
Fabiano, G.A., Pelham, W.E., Coles, E.K., Gnagy, E.M., Chronis-Tuscano, A., and O'Connor, B.C. (2009). A meta-analysis of behavioral treatments for attention-deficit/hyperactivity disorder. *Clinical Psychology Review*, 29(2), 129–140.
Faraone, S.V., Biederman, J., Keenan, K., and Tsuang, M.T. (1991). Separation of DSM-III attention deficit disorder and conduct disorder: evidence from a family-genetic study of American child psychiatric patients. *Psychological Medicine*, 21(1), 109–121.
Farrell, A.H., Provenzano, D.A., Spadafora, N., Marini, Z.A., and Volk, A.A. (2015). Measuring adolescent attitudes toward classroom incivility exploring differences between intentional and unintentional incivility. *Journal of Psychoeducational Assessment*, 34, 577–588.
Farroni, T., Menon, E., Rigato, S., and Johnson, M.H. (2007). The perception of facial expressions in newborns. *European Journal of Developmental Psychology*, 4(1), 2–13.

Feindler, E., Ecton, R., Dubey, D., and Kingsley, D. (1986). Group anger control training for institutionalised psychiatric male adolescents. *Behaviour Therapy*, 17, 109–123.

Feldman, S.S. (1959). *Mannerisms of speech and gestures in everyday life.* New York: International University Press.

Feldman, S.S., and Elliott, G.R. (1990). *At the threshold: the developing adolescent.* Cambridge, MA: Harvard University Press.

Feldmann, L.J. (2001). Classroom civility is another of our instructor responsibilities. *College Teaching*, 49(4), 137–140.

Finn, J.D., Pannozzo, G.M., and Achilles, C.M. (2003). The "why's" of class size: student behavior in small classes. *Review of Educational Research*, 73(3), 321–368.

Fisher, A., Godwin, H., and Seltman, H. (2014). Visual environment, attention allocation, and learning in young children: when too much of a good thing may be bad. *Psychological Science*, 25, 7.

Fiske, S.T., and Neuberg, S.L. (1990). A continuum of impression formation, from category-based to individuating processes: influences of information and motivation on attention and interpretation. In: M.P. Zanna (ed.), *Advances in experimental social psychology.* New York: Academic Press.

Fiske, S.T., and Taylor, S.E. (1991). *Social cognition.* New York: McGraw Hill.

Fiske, S.T., and Taylor, S.E. (2013). *Social cognition: from brains to culture.* London: Sage.

Folkman, S. (2013). *Stress: appraisal and coping* (pp. 1913–1915). New York: Springer.

Fosterling, F., and Rudolph, U. (1988). Situations, attributions and the evaluation of reactions. *Journal of Personality and Social Psychology*, 54, 225–232.

Freedman, N., and Hoffman, S.P. (1967). Kinetic behavior in altered clinical states: approach to objective analysis of motor behavior during clinical interviews. *Perceptual and Motor Skills*, 24, 527–539.

Freeman, A. (1988). Stress and coping: the idea of threshold. *Educational and Child Psychology*, 5(1), 37–40.

Freiberg, H. (ed.). (1999). *School climate: measuring, improving, and sustaining healthy learning environments.* London: Falmer Press.

Frese, M. (1999). Social support as a moderator of the relationship between work stressors and psychological dysfunctioning: a longitudinal study with objective measures. *Journal of Occupational Health Psychology*, 4(3), 179–192.

Frick, P., and Viding, E. (2009). Antisocial behavior from a developmental psychopathology perspective. *Developmental Psychopathology*, 21(4), 1111–1131.

Friedberg, R.D., and McClure, J.M. (2002). *Clinical practice of cognitive behavioral therapy with children and adolescents: the nuts and bolts.* New York: Guilford Press.

Fuchs, D., Fuchs, L., Mathes, P., and Simmons, D. (1997). Peer-assisted learning strategies: making classrooms more responsive to diversity. *American Educational Research Journal*, 34(1), 174–206.

Fuligni, A.J., and Eccles, J.S. (1993). Perceived parent-child relationships and early adolescents' orientation toward peers. *Developmental psychology*, 29(4), 622.

Fullan, M. (1988). *Change processes in secondary schools: towards a more fundamental agenda (mimeo).* Toronto: University of Toronto.

Fuller, F.F. (1969). Concerns of teachers: a developmental conceptualisation. *American Educational Research Journal*, 6, 207–226.

Funk, S.C. (1992). Hardiness: a review of theory and research. *Health Psychology*, 11(5): 335–345.

Furnham, A. (2005). *The psychology of behaviour at work: the individual in the organisation.* Hove: Psychology Press.

Furniture Industry Research Association (FIRA). (2003). *Safe seats of learning: how good school furniture can make a difference.* Stevenage: Furniture Industry Research Association (FIRA).

Furrer, C., and Skinner, E. (2003). Sense of relatedness as a factor in children's academic engagement and performance. *Journal of Educational Psychology*, 95(1), 148–162.

Gable, R.A., Hester, P.H., Rock, M.L., and Hughes, K.G. (2009). Back to basics rules, praise, ignoring, and reprimands revisited. *Intervention in School and Clinic*, 44(4), 195–205.

Gale, C.R., Batty, G.D., and Deary, I.J. (2008). Locus of control at age 10 years and health outcomes and behaviors at age 30 years: the 1970 British Cohort Study. *Psychosomatic Medicine*, 70(4), 397–403.

Galloway, D., Boswell, K., Panckhurst, F., Boswell, C., and Green, K. (1985). Sources of satisfaction and dissatisfaction for New Zealand primary school teachers. *Educational Research*, 27, 44–51.

Galván, A. (2013). The teenage brain sensitivity to rewards. *Current Directions in Psychological Science*, 22(2), 88–93.

Galván, A., Hare, T.A., Parra, C.E., Penn, J., Voss, H., Glover, G., and Casey, B.J. (2006). Earlier development of the accumbens relative to orbitofrontal cortex might underlie risk-taking behavior in adolescents. *The Journal of Neuroscience*, 26(25), 6885–6892.

Gansle, K.A. (2005). The effectiveness of school-based anger interventions and programs: a meta-analysis. *Journal of School Psychology*, 43(4), 321–341.

Gavienas, E., and White, G. (2008). Ethos, management and discipline in the primary school. In: T.G.K. Bryce and W.M. Humes (eds.), *Scottish education*. Edinburgh, TX: Edinburgh University Press.

Gavish, B., and Friedman, I.A. (2010). Novice teachers' experience of teaching: a dynamic aspect of burnout. *Social Psychology of Education*, 13(2), 141–167.

Geeraert, N., and Yzerbyt, V.Y. (2007). Cultural differences in the correction of social inferences: does the dispositional rebound occur in an interdependent culture? *British Journal of Social Psychology*, 46(2), 423–435.

Gettinger, M., and Ball, C. (2008). Best practices in increasing academic engaged time. *Best Practices in School Psychology V*, 4, 1043–1057.

Gibson, S., and Dembo, M.H. (1984). Teacher efficacy: a construct validation. *Journal of Educational Psychology*, 76, 569–582.

Goddard, R.D., Hoy, W.K., and Hoy, A.W. (2000). Collective teacher efficacy: its meaning, measure, and impact on student achievement. *American Educational Research Journal*, 37(2), 479–507.

Goldstein, H. (1995). *Multilevel statistical models* (2nd ed.). London: Edward Arnold / New York: Halsted Press.

Gonzalez, J.E., Nelson, J.R., Gutkin, T.B., Saunders, A., Galloway, A., and Shwery, C.S. (2004). Rational emotive therapy with children and adolescents: a meta-analysis. *Journal of Emotional and Behavioral Disorders*, 12(4), 222–235.

Good, C., Aronson, J., and Inzlicht, M. (2003). Improving adolescents' standardized test performance: an intervention to reduce the effects of stereotype threat. *Journal of Applied Developmental Psychology*, 24, 645–662.

Good, T.L., and Brophy, J.E. (2008). *Looking in classrooms* (10th ed.). New York: Pearson Education, Inc.

Goodman, R. (1997). The strengths and difficulties questionnaire: a research note. *Journal of Child Psychology and Psychiatry*, 38, 581–586.

Gottfredson, D.C. (1990). Developing effective organizations to reduce school disorder. *Student Discipline Strategies: Research and Practice*, 47–62.

Graber, J.A., Brooks-Gunn, J.E., and Petersen, A.C. (1996). *Transitions through adolescence: interpersonal domains and context*. Mahwah, NJ: Lawrence Erlbaum Associates, Inc.

Graham, J.A., and Heywood, S. (1975). The effects of elimination of hand gestures and of verbal codability on speech performance. *European Journal of Social Psychology*, 5, 189–195.

Graham, S., and Barker, G.P. (1990). The down side of help: and attributional developmental analysis of helping behaviour as a low-ability cue. *Journal of Educational Psychology*, 82(1), 7–14.

Graham, S., and Folkes, V.S. (2014). *Attribution theory: applications to achievement, mental health, and interpersonal conflict*. Hove: Psychology Press.

Gray, H., and Freeman, A. (1988). *Teaching without stress*. London: Paul Chapman Press.

Gray, J. (1990). The quality of schooling: frameworks for judgement. *British Journal of Educational Studies*, 38(3), 204–223.

Gray, J., Jesson, D., and Reynolds, D. (1996). The challenges of school improvement: preparing for the long haul. In: J. Gray, D. Reynolds, C. Fitzgibbons, and D. Jesson (eds.), *Merging traditions: the future of research on school effectiveness and school improvement*. London: Cassell.

Gray, J., and Wilcox, B. (1994). *The challenge of turning round ineffective schools*. Paper presented to the ESRC Seminar Series on school Effectiveness and School Improvement, Newcastle University, October.

Greenspan, S. (1981). Defining childhood social competence: a proposed working model. In: B. Keogh (ed.), *Advances in special education* (vol. 3). Bingley: JAI Press.

Gronn, P. (2010). Where to next for educational leadership? In: T. Bush, L. Bell, and D. Middlewood (eds.), *The principles of educational leadership and management*. London: Sage.

Gruber, S.A., and Yurgelun-Todd, D.A. (2005). Neurobiology and the law: a role in juvenile justice. *Ohio State Journal of Criminal Law*, 3:321, 321–340.

Gump, P. (1974). Operating environments in schools with open and traditional design. *School Review*, 82(4), 575–593.

Gutman, L., and Feinstein, L. (2008). *Children's well-being in primary school: pupil and school effects [Wider Benefits of Learning Research Report No. 25]*. Centre for Research on the Wider Benefits of Learning, Institute of Education, University of London.

Halpin, A.W., and Croft, D.B. (1963). *The organizational climate of schools*. Chicago, IL: Midwest Administration Center, University of Chicago.

Hampson, P.J., and Morris, P.E. (1989). Imagery, consciousness and cognitive control: the BOSS model reviewed. In: P.J. Hampson, D.F. Marks, and J.T.E. Richardson (eds.), *Imagery: current developments*. London: Routledge.

Hamre, B.K., and Pianta, R.C. (2001). Early teacher-child relationships and the trajectory of children's school outcomes through eighth grade. *Child Development*, 72, 625–638.

Hargie, O. (2011). *Skilled interpersonal communication: research, theory and practice* (5th ed.). London: Routledge.
Hargreaves, D. (2007). *System re-design—1: the road to transformation.* London: SSAT.
Hargreaves, D.H., Hestor, S., and Mellor, F. (1975). *Deviance in classrooms.* London: Routledge and Kegan Paul.
Harris, A., and Spillane, J. (2008). Distributed leadership through the looking glass. *Management in Education,* 22(1), 31–34.
Harris, M.J., and Rosenthal, R. (1986). Four factors in the mediation of teacher expectancy effects. In: R.S. Feldman (ed.), *The social psychology of education: current research and theory.* New York: Cambridge University Press.
Harrison, R.P. (1976). The face in face-to-face interaction. In: G.R. Miller (ed.), *Explorations in interpersonal communication.* London: Sage.
Hart, N.L. (1987). Student teachers' anxieties: four measured factors and their relationships to pupil disruption in class. *Educational Research,* 29, 12–18.
Hastings, N., and Chantrey-Wood, K. (2002a). *Group seating in primary schools: an indefensible strategy?* The Annual Conference of the British Educational Research Association: University of Exeter, England, 12–14 September.
Hastings, N., and Chantrey-Wood, K. (2002b). *Reorganising primary classroom learning.* Buckingham: Open University Press.
Hattie, J.A.C. (2009). *Visible learning: a synthesis of 800+ meta-analyses on achievement.* Abingdon: Routledge.
Haydn, T. (2014). To what extent is behaviour a problem in English schools? Exploring the scale and prevalence of deficits in classroom climate. *Review of Education,* 2(1), 31–64.
Hazlett-Stevens, H. (2001, August). *Cognitive flexibility deficits in generalized anxiety disorder.* Paper presented at the Annual Convention of the American Psychological Association, San Francisco, CA.
Head, J., Hill, F., and McGuire, M. (1996). Stress and the postgraduate secondary school trainee teacher: a British case study. *Journal of Education for Teaching,* 22, 71–84.
Health and Safety Executive (HSE). (2000). *The scale of occupational stress: a further analysis of the impact of demographic factors and the type of job.* CRR 311.
Health and Safety Executive (HSE). (2001). *Tackling work-related stress: a manager's guide to improving and maintaining employee health and well-being.* London: HSE Books.
Heider, F. (1958). *The psychology of interpersonal relations.* New York: Wiley.
Hesler, M.W. (1972). An investigation of instructor use of space. *Dissertation Abstracts International,* 33, 3044A (University Microfilms No. 72–30, 905).
Hess, E.H. (1972). Pupilometrics. In: N.S. Greenfield and R.A. Sternback (eds.), *Handbook of psychophysiology.* New York: Holt, Reinhart and Winston.
Hewstone, M. (1989). *Causal attribution: from cognitive processes to collective beliefs.* Oxford: Blackwell.
Hiebert, B., and Farber, I. (1984). Teacher stress: a literature review with a few surprises. *Canadian Journal of Education,* 9 (winter), 14–27.
Higgins, A.T., and Turnure, J.E. (1984). Distractibility and concentration of attention in children's development. *Child Development,* 1799–1810.
Hills, H., and Norvell, N. (1991). An examination of hardiness and neuroticism as potential moderators of stress outcomes. *Behavioural Medicine,* 17(1), 31–38.
Hinnant, J.B., O'Brien, M., and Ghazarian, S.R. (2009). The longitudinal relations of teacher expectations to achievement in the early school years. *Journal of Educational Psychology,* 101(3), 662.

Hirschy, A., and Braxton, J. (2004). Effects of student classroom incivilities on students. *New Directions for Teaching and Learning*, 99, 67–76.
Ho, B.P.V., Carter, M., and Stephenson, J. (2010). Anger management using a cognitive-behavioural approach for children with special education needs: a literature review and meta-analysis. *International Journal of Disability, Development and Education*, 57, 245–265.
Hobart, C., and Frankel, J. (1994). *A practical guide to child observation*. Cheltenham: Stanley Thornes.
Hongwanishkul, D., Happaney, K.R., Lee, W.S.C., and Zelazo, P.D. (2005). Assessment of hot and cool executive function in young children: age-related changes and individual differences. *Developmental Neuropsychology*, 28(2), 617–644.
Hornsey, M.J. (2008). Social identity theory and self-categorization theory: a historical review. *Social and Personality Psychology Compass*, 2(1), 204–222.
Hoy, W.K. (1990). Organizational climate and culture: a conceptual analysis of the school workplace. *Journal of Educational and Psychological Consultation*, 1(2), 149–168.
Hoy, W.K., and Miskel, C.G. (1991). *Educational administration: theory, research and practice* (4th ed.). New York: McGraw Hill.
Hoy, W.K., Smith, P.A., and Sweetland, S.R. (2002). The development of the organizational climate index for high schools: its measure and relationship to faculty trust. *The High School Journal*, 86(2), 38–49.
Hoy, W. K., Tarter, C.S., and Kottkamp, R.P. (1991). *Open schools: healthy schools*. London: Sage.
Hurley, S., and Chatter, N. (2004). *Perspectives on imitation: from cognitive neuroscience to social science*. Cambridge: MIT Press.
Hustler, D., Brighouse, T., and Rudduck, J. (eds.). (1995). *Heeding heads: secondary heads and educational commentators in dialogue*. London: David Fulton.
Hyland, K., and Hyland, F. (2006). Feedback on second language students' writing. *Language Teaching*, 39(2), 83–101.
Insel, T.R., and Young, L.J. (2001). The neurobiology of attachment. *Nature Reviews Neuroscience*, 2(2), 129–136.
International Labour Organisation (ILO). (1982). *Employment and conditions of work of teachers*. Geneva: ILO.
Jamal, F., Fletcher, A., Harden, A., Wells, H., Thomas, J., and Bonell, C. (2013). The school environment and student health: a systematic review and meta-ethnography of qualitative research. *BMC Public Health*, 13(1), 798.
Jarvis, M. (2002). Teacher stress: a critical review of recent findings and suggestions for future research directions. *Stress News*, 14(1), 12–16.
Jenson, W.R., Rhode, G., and Reavis, K.H. (2009). *The tough kid toolbox*. Eugene, OR: Pacific Northwest Publishing.
Jerusalem, M. (1993). Personal resources, environmental constraints, and adaptational processes: the predictive power of a theoretical stress mode. *Personality and Individual Differences*, 14, 15–24.
Johnson, B., Down, B., Le Cornu, R., Peters, J., Sullian, A., Pearce, J. and Hunter, J. (2010). *Conditions that support early career teacher resilience*, refereed paper presented at the Australian Teacher Education Association Conference, Townsville, 4–7th July.
Jones, A. (1988). *Leadership for tomorrow's schools*. Oxford: Blackwell.
Jones, E.E., and Davis, K.E. (1965). From acts to dispositions: the attribution process in person perception. *Advances in Experimental Social Psychology*, 2, 219–266.

Jones, V.F., and Jones, L.S. (1990). *Comprehensive classroom management* (3rd ed.). Boston, MA: Allyn and Bacon.

Jordan, A., and Stanovich, P. (2003). Teachers' personal epistemological beliefs about students with disabilities as indicators of effective teaching practices. *Journal of Research in Special Education*, 3(1), 1–14.

Jussim, L., Robustelli, S., and Cain, T.R. (2009). Teacher expectations and self-fulfilling prophecies. *Handbook of Motivation at School*, 349–380.

Kagan, J. (1994). *Galen's prophecy: temperament in human nature*. New York: Basic Books.

Kahn, R., and Antonucci, T. (1980). Convoys over the life course: attachments, roles and social support. In: P. Baltes and O. Brim (eds.), *Lifespan development and behaviour* (vol. 3). New York: Academic Press.

Kahn, R., Wolfe, M., Quinn, R., Snoek, D., and Rosenthal, R. (1964). *Organizational stress: studies in role conflict and ambiguity*. Oxford: Wiley.

Kalker, P. (1984). Teacher stress and burnout: causes and coping strategies. *Contemporary Education*, 56(1), 16–19.

Kaplan, J. (1995). *Beyond behavior modification: a cognitive-behavioral approach to behavior management in schools* (3rd ed.). Austin: Pro-Ed.

Kaplan, D.S., Peck, B.M., and Kaplan, H.B. (1997). Decomposing the academic failure–dropout relationship: a longitudinal analysis. *The Journal of Educational Research*, 90(6), 331–343.

Kaplan, R.M., and Swant, S.G. (1973). Reward characteristics in appraisal of achievement behaviour. *Research in Social Psychology*, 4, 11–17.

Katz, R.L. (1955). Skills of an effective administrator. *Harvard Business Review*, January–February, 33–42.

Kauffman, J.M. (1989). *Characteristics of behavior disorders of children and youth* (4th ed.). Columbus: Merrill.

Kauffman, J.M. (2008). Would we recognize progress if we saw it? A commentary. *Journal of Behavioral Education*, 17, 128–143.

Kazadin, A. (1977). *The token economy*. New York: Plenum.

Kelley, H.H. (1967). Attribution theory in social psychology. In: D. Levine (ed.), *Nebraska symposium on motivation* (vol. 15). Lincoln: University of Nebraska Press.

Kendall, P. (1982). Individual versus group cognitive-behavioral self-control training: 1-year follow-up. *Behavior Therapy*, 13, 241–247.

Kendall, P. (ed.). (2000). *Child and adolescent therapy: cognitive-behavioral procedures* (2nd ed.). New York: Guilford Press.

Kendall, P.C., and MacDonald, J.P. (1993). *Cognition in the psychopathology of youth and implications for treatment*. San Diego: Academic Press.

Kendall, P.C., and Zupan, B. (1981). Individual versus group application of cognitive-behavioral self-control procedures with children. *Behavior Therapy*, 12, 344–359.

Kershner, R. and Chaplain, R. (2001) '*Understanding Special Educational Needs: A teacher's guide to effective school-based research*', London: Fulton.

Kershner, R., and Pointon, P. (2000). Children's views of the primary classroom as an environment for working and learning. *Research in Education*, 14, 64–77.

Kessels, U., Warner, L., Holle, J., and Hannover, B. (2008). Threat to identity through positive feedback about academic performance. *Zeitschrift für Entwicklungspsychologie und Pädagogische Psychologie*, 40(1), 22–31.

Kihlstrom, J.F. (1999). Conscious and unconscious cognition. In: R.J. Sternberg (ed.), *The nature of cognition*. Cambridge: MIT Press.

Kimonis, E., Ogg, J., and Fefer, S. (2014). The relevance of callous-unemotional traits to working with youth with conduct problems. *Communiqué: The Newspaper of the National Association of School Psychologists*, 42(5), 16–18.

Klassen, R. (2010). Teacher stress: the mediating role of collective efficacy beliefs. *The Journal of Educational Research*, 103(5), 342–350.

Klassen, R., Perry, N., and Frenzel, A. (2012). Teachers' relatedness with students: an underemphasized component of teachers' basic psychological needs. *Journal of Educational Psychology*, 104, 150–165.

Kostic, A., and Chadee, D. (eds.). (2014). *The social psychology of nonverbal communication.* Basingstoke: Palgrave MacMillan.

Kounin, J.S. (1970). *Discipline and group management in classrooms.* New York: Holt, Rinehart and Winston.

Kun, A. (1977). Development of the magnitude-covariation and compensation schemata in ability and effort attributions of performance. *Child Development*, 48, 862–873.

Kutnick, P., Blatchford, P., and Baines, E. (2002). Pupil groupings in primary school classrooms: sites for learning and social pedagogy? *British Educational Research Journal*, 28(2), 187–206.

Kutnick, P., Hodgkinson, S., Sebba, J., Humphreys, S., Galton, M., Steward, S., Blatchford, P., and Baines, E. (2006). *Pupil grouping strategies and practices at Key Stage 2 and 3: case studies of 24 schools in England.* Research Brief No: RB796.

Kutnick, P., Sebba, J., Blatchford, P., Galton, M., and Thorp, J. (2005). *The effects of pupil grouping: literature review.* London: DfES.

Kyriacou, C. (1997). *Effective teaching in schools* (2nd ed.). Cheltenham: Stanley Thorne.

Kyriacou, C. (2001). Teacher stress: directions for future research. *Educational Review*, 53(1), 27–35.

Kyriacou, C., and Butcher, B. (1993). Stress in Year 11 school children. *Pastoral Care in Education*, 11(3), 19–21.

Kyriacou, C., and Kunc, R. (2007). Beginning teachers' expectations of teaching. *Teachers and Teaching*, 23(8), 1246–1257.

Lackney, J. (1994). *Educational facilities: the impact and role of the physical environment of the school on teaching architecture and urban planning.* Milwaukee: Wisconsin University.

Lalljee, M., Lamb, R., and Abelson, R.P. (1992). The role of event prototypes in categorization and explanation. *European Review of Social Psychology*, 3(1), 153–182.

Lambert, R.G., McCarthy, C.J., O' Donnell, M., and Wang, C. (2009). Measuring elementary teacher stress and coping in the classroom: validity evidence for the classroom appraisal of resources and demands. *Psychology in the Schools*, 46, 973–988.

Lannie, A.L., and McCurdy, B.L. (2007). Preventing disruptive behavior in the urban classroom: effects of the good behavior game on student and teacher behavior. *Education and Treatment of Children*, 30(1), 85–98.

Larson, J., and Lochman, J.E. (2003). *Helping schoolchildren cope with anger.* New York: Guilford Press.

Laughlin, A. (1984). Teacher stress in an Australian setting: the role of biographical mediators. *Educational Studies*, 10(1), 7–22.

Lazarus, R.S. (1966). *Psychological stress and the coping process.* New York: McGraw-Hill.

Lazarus, R.S., and Folkman, S. (1984). *Stress, appraisal, and coping.* New York: Springer.

Leinhardt, G., Weidman, C., and Hammond, K.M. (1987). Introduction and integration of classroom routines by expert teachers. *Curriculum Inquiry*, 17(2), 135–176.

Leithwood, K., Day, C., Sammons, P., Harris, A., and Hopkins, D. (2006). *Successful school leadership: what it is and how it influences pupil learning*. Nottingham: National College for School Leadership and Department for Education and Skills.

Lerner, R.M., Lerner, J.V., von Eye, A., Ostrom, C.W., Nitz, K., Talwar-Soni, R., and Norwich, B., and Eaton, A. (2015). The new special educational needs (SEN) legislation in England and implications for services for children and young people with social, emotional and behavioural difficulties. *Emotional and Behavioural Difficulties*, 20, 2.

Lerner, R.M., Lerner, J.V., von Eye, A., Ostrom, C.W., Nitz, K., Talwar-Soni, R., and Tubman, J.G. (1996). Conditions of continuity and discontinuity across the transition of early adolescence: a developmental contextual perspective. In: J.A. Graber, J. Brooks-Gunn, and A.C. Petersen (eds.), *Transitions through adolescence: interpersonal domains and context* (pp. 3–22). Mahwah, NJ: Lawrence Erlbaum Associates, Inc.

Lewin, K., Lippitt, R., and White, R.K. (1939). Patterns of aggressive behaviour in experimentally created social climates. *Journal of Social Psychology*, 10, 271–279.

Liang, J., Farh, C., and Farh, J. (2012). Psychological antecedents of promotive and prohibitive voice: a two-wave examination. *Journal of Academic Management*, 55, 71–92.

Light, P., and Perret-Clermont, A.-N. (1990). Social context effects in learning and testing. In: P. Light, S. Sheldon and M. Woodhead (eds.), *Learning to think*. London: Routledge.

Lochman, J.E. (1992). Cognitive-behavioral intervention with aggressive boys: three-year follow-up and preventive effects. *Journal of Consulting and Clinical Psychology*, 60(3), 426.

Loeber, R., Burke, J., and Pardini, D.A. (2009). Perspectives on oppositional defiant disorder, conduct disorder, and psychopathic features. *Journal of Child Psychology and Psychiatry*, 50, 133–142.

Louis, K., and Miles, M. (1992). *Improving the urban high school: what works and why*. London: Cassell.

Loveless, T. (1996). Teacher praise. In: H. Reavis, M. Sweeten, W. Jenson, D.P. Morgan, D.J. Andrews, and S. Fister (eds.), *Best practices: behavioral and educational strategies for teachers*. Longmont: West Educational Services.

Luria, A.R. (1961). *The role of speech in regulation of normal and abnormal behavior*. Oxford: Pergamon Press.

Luria, A.R. (1971). Memory disturbances in local brain lesions. *Neuropsychologia*, 9, 367–375.

Luria, A.R. (1973). *The working brain: an introduction to neuropsychology* (trans. by B. Haigh). New York: Basic Books.

Luria, A.R. (1981). *Language and cognition*. New York: Wiley.

Lyubomirsky, S., and Nolen-Hoeksema, S. (1993). Self-perpetuating properties of dysphoric rumination. *Journal of Personality and Social Psychology*, 65, 339–349.

Maag, J. (2001). Rewarded by punishment: reflections on the disuse of positive reinforcement in schools. *The Council for Exceptional Children*, 67, 173–186.

MacBeath, J. (ed.). (1998). *Effective school leadership: responding to change*. London: Sage.

Maier, S.F., Laudenslager, M.L., and Ryan, S.M. (1985). Stressor controllability, immune function, and endogenous opiates. In: F.R. Brush and J.B. Overmier (eds.), *Affect, conditioning, and cognition: essays on the determinants of behaviour*. Hillsdale, MI: Erlbaum.

Malle, B.F. (2006). The actor-observer asymmetry in attribution: a (surprising) meta-analysis. *Psychological Bulletin*, 132(6), 895.

Manning, B. (1991). *Cognitive self-instruction for classroom processes*. Albany: University of New York Press.

Marini, Z.A. (2007). *The Academic In/Civility Questionnaire (AI/CQ-V.1): assessing intentional and unintentional in/civility*. Unpublished manuscript, Department of Child and Youth Studies, Brock University, St. Catharines, ON, Canada.

Marini, Z., Polihronis, C., and Blackwell, W. (2010). Academic in/civility: co-constructing the foundation for a civil learning community. *Collected Essays on Learning and Teaching*, 3, 89–93.

Martella, R., Nelson, J., and Marchand-Martella, N. (2003). *Managing disruptive behaviors in the schools: a schoolwide, classroom, and individualized social learning approach*. Boston, MA: Allyn and Bacon.

Martella, R., Nelson, J., Marchand-Martella, N., and O'Reilly, M. (2012). *Comprehensive behavior management* (2nd ed.). Thousand Oaks, CA: Sage.

Martin, R.A., and Dobbin, J.P. (1988). Sense of humor, hassles and immunoglobulin A: evidence for a stress-moderating effect of humor. *International Journal of Psychiatry in Medicine*, 18(2), 9–105.

Marzano, R.J. (2003). *What works in schools*. Alexandria: ASCD.

Maslow, A.H. (1987). *Motivation and personality* (3rd ed.). Boston, MA: Addison Wesley.

Matsumoto, D. (2006). Culture and nonverbal behavior. In: V.L. Manusov and M.L. Patterson (eds.), *The SAGE handbook of nonverbal communication* (pp. 219–236). Thousand Oaks, CA: Sage Publications.

May, T. (2017). *Five Year Forward View for Mental Health: government's response. January 2017*. London: HM Government (Department of Health / Public Health England / NHS England), January 9th 2017.

McAteer-Early, T. (1992). *The impact of career self-efficacy on the relationship between career development and health-related complaints*. Paper presented at the Academy of Management Meeting, Las Vegas.

McCormick, C.M., Mathews, I.Z., Thomas, C., and Waters, P. (2010). Investigations of HPA function and the enduring consequences of stressors in adolescence in animal models. *Brain and cognition*, 72(1), 73–85.

McCroskey, J.C., Sallinen, A., Fayer, J.M., Richmond, V.P., and Barraclough, R.A. (1996). Nonverbal immediacy and cognitive learning: a cross-cultural investigation. *Communication Education*, 45, 200–211.

McIntosh, D.N. (1996). Facial feedback hypotheses: evidence, implications, and directions. *Motivation and Emotion*, 20(2), 121–147.

McNamara, D., and Waugh, D. (1993). Classroom organisation. *School Organisation*, 13(1), 41–50.

Mehrabian, A. (1972). *Nonverbal communication*. Chicago, IL: Aldine-Atherton.

Meichenbaum, D. (1977). *Cognitive-behavior modification*. New York: Plenum.

Mennuti, R.B., Freeman, A., and Christner, R.W. (2012). *Cognitive-behavioral interventions in educational settings: a handbook for practice*. New York: Routledge.

Merrett, F., and Wheldall, K. (1992). Teachers' use of praise and reprimands to boys and girls. *Educational Review*, 44(1), 73–79.
Merton, R.K. (1948). The self-fulfilling prophecy. *The Antioch Review*, 193–210.
Meyer-Lindenberg, A. (2008). Impact of prosocial neuropeptides on human brain function. *Progress in Brain Research*, 170, 463–470.
Millar, K.U., Tesser, A., and Millar, M.G. (1988). The effects of a threatening life event on behavior sequences and intrusive though: a self-disruption explanation. *Cognitive Therapy Research*, 12, 441–458.
Miller, A. (1995). Teachers' attributions of causality, control and responsibility in respect of difficult pupil behaviour and its successful management. *Educational Psychology*, 15(4), 457–471.
Miller, A. (2003). *Teachers, parents and classroom behaviour: a psychosocial approach.* Maidenhead: Open University Press.
Mischel, W., Ebbesen, E.B., and Raskoff-Zeiss, A. (1972). Cognitive and attentional mechanisms in delay of gratification. *Journal of Personality and Social Psychology*, 21(2), 204.
Moore, G. (1979). Environment-behaviour studies. In: J. Snyder and A. Catanese (eds.), *Introduction to architecture.* New York: McGraw-Hill.
Moos, R.H. (1979). *Evaluating educational environments.* San Francisco, CA: Jossey-Bass.
Morris, J.A., and Feldman, D.C. (1996). The dimensions, antecedents, and consequences of emotional labor. *Academy of Management Review*, 21, 986–1010.
Mortimore, P., Sammons, P., Stoll, L., Lewis, D., and Ecob, R. (1988). *School matters: the junior years.* Somerset: Open Books.
Moyles, J. (1992). *Organising for learning in the primary classroom.* Buckingham: Open University Press.
Murphy, J. (1992). School effectiveness and school restructuring: contributions to educational improvement. *School Effectiveness and School Improvement*, 3(2), 90–109.
Murray-Harvey, R.T., Slee, P., Lawson, M.J., Silins, H., Banfield, G., and Russell, A. (2000). Under stress: the concerns and coping strategies of teacher education students. *European Journal of Teacher Education*, 23(1), 19–35.
Nadler, D., and Tushman, M. (1980). A model for diagnosing organisational behaviour. *Organisational Dynamics*, 9, 35–51.
National Institute for Health and Clinical Excellence (NICE). (2009). *Social and emotional wellbeing in secondary education: NICE public health guidance 20.* National Institute for Health and Clinical Excellence.
National Institute for Health and Clinical Excellence (NICE). (2013a). *Antisocial behaviour and conduct disorders in children and young people: recognition, intervention and management.* NICE guidelines [CG158].
National Institute for Health and Clinical Excellence (NICE). (2013b). *Attention deficit hyperactivity disorder.* NICE Quality standard 39, issued July 2013.
Nelson, J.R., Martella, R., and Galand, B. (1998). The effects of teaching school expectations and establishing a consistent consequence on formal office disciplinary actions. *Journal of Emotional and Behavioral Disorders*, 6(3), 153–161.
Nias, J. (1986). Leadership styles and job-satisfaction in primary schools. In: T. Bush, R. Glatter, J. Goodey, and C. Riches (eds.), *Approaches to school management.* London: Harper Row.

Nicholls, J.G. (1989). *The competitive ethos and democratic education.* London: Harvard University Press.
Norwich, B., and Eaton, A. (2015). The new special educational needs (SEN) legislation in England and implications for services for children and young people with social, emotional and behavioural difficulties. *Emotional and Behavioural Difficulties,* 20(2), 117–132.
NUT. (2000). *National Union of Teachers Conference 2000: Resolution of teachers' stress and workplace bullying.* Harrogate, UK (October).
Ofsted. (1996). *Exclusions from secondary schools 1995/6.* London: Ofsted Publications.
Ofsted (2008). *University of Cambridge Secondary Initial Teacher Training Short Inspection Report 2007/08.* (70133) London: Ofsted Publications.
Ofsted (2011). *University of Cambridge Initial Teacher Education Inspection Report.* (70133) London: Ofsted Publications.
Ofsted. (2012). *Getting to good: how headteachers achieve success.* London: Ofsted Publications.
Ofsted. (2014). *Below the radar: low-level disruption in the country's classrooms.* London: Ofsted Publications.
Oosterlaan, J., Scheres, A., and Sergeant, J.A. (2005). Which executive functioning deficits are associated with AD/HD, ODD/CD and comorbid AD/HD + ODD/CD? *Journal of Abnormal Child Psychology,* 33(1), 69–85.
Open Systems Group (ed.). (1981). *Systems behaviour.* London: Harper and Row.
Osterman, K.F. (2000). Students' need for belonging in the school community. *Review of educational research,* 70(3), 323–367.
Owen-Yeates, A. (2005). Stress in year 11 students. *Pastoral Care in Education,* 23(4), 42–51.
Oxford, M., Cavell, T.A., and Hughes, J.N. (2003). Callous/unemotional traits moderate the relation between ineffective parenting and child externalizing problems: a partial replication and extension. *Journal of Clinical Child and Adolescent Psychology,* 4, 577–585.
Ozer, E.M., and Irwin, C.E. (2009). Adolescents and young adult health. *Handbook of Adolescent Psychology.* New York: Croom Helm.
Pajares, F., and Urban, T. (2006). *Self-efficacy beliefs of adolescents.* Greenwich: Information Age Publishing.
Paterson, R. (2002). *The assertiveness workbook: how to express your ideas and stand up for yourself at work and in relationships.* Oakland, CA: Harbinger.
Patterson, D., DeBarryshe, B., and Ramsey, E. (1990). A developmental perspective on antisocial behavior. *American Psychologist,* 44, 329–335.
Payne, R.L. (1990). Method in our madness: a reply to Jackofsky and Slocum. *Journal of Organizational Behaviour,* 11, 77–80.
Pease, A. (1997). *Body language: how to read others' thoughts by their gestures.* London: Sheldon Press.
Pedota, P. (2007). Strategies for effective classroom management in the secondary setting. *The Clearing House,* 80(4), 153–166.
Perry, R.P., and Struthers, C.W. (1994). Attributional retraining in the college classroom: some causes for optimism. American Educational Research Association annual meeting, New Orleans, LA, April.
Phillips, S. (1983). *The invisible culture: communication in classroom and community on the warm springs Indian reservation.* New York: Longman.

Pickehain, L. (1999). The importance of IP Pavlov for the development of neuroscience. *Integrative Physiological and Behavioral Science*, 34(2), 85–89.

Pierce, W.D., Cameron, J., Banko, K.M., and So, S. (2003). Positive effects of rewards and performance standards on intrinsic motivation. *Psychological Record*, 53, 561–579.

Piquero, A.R., Farrington, D.P., Nagin, D.S., and Moffitt, T.E. (2010). Trajectories of offending and their relation to life failure in late middle age: findings from the Cambridge study in delinquent development. *Journal of Research in Crime and Delinquency*, 47(2), 151–173.

Plummer, G., and Dudley, P. (1993). *Assessing children learning collaboratively: classroom action research studies, and ideas by Essex teachers focusing on issues of assessment*. Essex: National Curriculum and Collaborative Learning, Essex Development Advisory Service, Education Department.

Porter, L. (2006). *Behaviour in schools: theory and practice for teachers* (2nd ed.). Maidenhead: Open University Press.

Porter, S., and ten Brinke, L. (2008). Reading between the lies: identifying concealed and falsified emotions in universal facial expressions. *Psychological Science*, 19(5), 508–514.

Power, M.J., and Brewin, C.R. (1991). From Freud to cognitive science: a contemporary account of the unconscious. *British Journal of Clinical Psychology*, 30, 289–310.

Power, M., and Dalgleish, T. (2007). *Cognition and emotion: from order to disorder*. Hove: Psychology Press.

Proshansky, E., and Wolfe, M. (1974). The physical setting and open education. *School Review*, 82(4), 556–574.

Reivich, K., Gillham, J.E., Chaplin, T.M., and Seligman, M.E. (2013). From helplessness to optimism: the role of resilience in treating and preventing depression in youth. In: S. Goldstein and R.B. Brooks (eds.), *Handbook of resilience in children* (pp. 201–214). New York: Springer US.

Reyna, V.F., and Farley, F. (2006). Risk and rationality in adolescent decision making implications for theory, practice, and public policy. *Psychological Science in the Public Interest*, 7(1), 1–44.

Reynolds, D. (2007). Restraining Golem and harnessing Pygmalion in the classroom: a laboratory study of managerial expectations and task design. *Academy of Management Learning and Education*, 6(4), 475–483.

Rhode, G., Jensen, W., and Reavis, H.K. (1996). *The tough kid book: practical classroom management strategies*. Longmont, CO: Sopris West.

Richmond, V. (2002). Teachers non verbal immediacy uses and outcomes. In: J. Chesebro and J. McCroskey (eds.), *Communication for teachers*. Boston, MA: Allyn and Bacon.

Richmond, V.P., Lane, D.R., and McCroskey, J.C. (2006). Teacher immediacy and the teacher-student relationship. In: T.P. Mottet, V.P. Richmond, and J.C. MeCroskey (eds.), *Handbook of Instructional Communication: Rhetorical and Relational Perspectives* (pp. 167–193). London: Routledge.

Richmond, V., and McCroskey, J. (2004). *Nonverbal behaviors in interpersonal relations* (5th ed.). Boston, MA: Allyn and Bacon.

Rist, R.G. (1970). Student social class and teacher expectation: the self-fulfilling prophecy in Ghetto Education. *Harvard Educational Review*, 40, 441–451.

Rizzolatti, G., Fadiga, L., Gallese, V., and Fogassi, L. (1996). Premotor cortex and the recognition of motor actions. *Cognitive Brain Research*, 3(2), 131–141.

Robertson, J. (1996). *Effective classroom control* (3rd ed.). London: Hodder and Stoughton.

Rodenburg, P. (2015). *The right to speak: working with the voice* (2nd ed.). London: Bloomsbury.

Rodriguez, A., and Bohlin, G. (2005). Are maternal smoking and stress during pregnancy related to ADHD symptoms in children? *Journal of Child Psychology and Psychiatry*, 46(3), 246–254.

Rogers, C.G. (1982). *A social psychology of schooling: the expectancy process.* London: Routledge.

Rogers, C., and Kutnick, P. (eds.). (1992). *The social psychology of the primary school.* London: Routledge.

Romi, S., Lewis, R., Roache, J., and Riley, P. (2011). The impact of teachers' aggressive management techniques on students' attitudes to schoolwork. *The Journal of Educational Research*, 104, 4.

Rosenthal, R. (1989). *Experimenter expectancy, covert communication, and meta-analytic methods.* Paper presented at the Donald T. Campbell Address at the Annual Meeting of the American Psychological Association, New Orleans.

Rosenthal, R., and Jacobson, L. (1968). *Pygmalion in the classroom: teacher expectation and pupils' intellectual development.* New York: Holt, Rinehart and Winston.

Rosenthal, R., and Jacobson, L. (1992). *Pygmalion in the classroom.* New York: Irvington.

Rosenthal, T.L., and Rosenthal, R.H. (1985). Clinical stress management. In: D. Barlow (ed.), *Clinical handbook of psychological disorders.* New York: Guildford.

Rubie-Davies, C.M. (2006). Teacher expectations and student self-perceptions: exploring relationships. *Psychology in the Schools*, 43(5), 537–552.

Rubie-Davies, C.M. (2007). Classroom interactions: exploring the practices of high- and low-expectation teachers. *British Journal of Educational Psychology*, 77(2), 289–306.

Rubie-Davies, C.M. (2008). Teacher expectations. In: T. Good (ed.), *21st century education: a reference handbook* (pp. 254–262). Thousand Oaks, CA: Sage Publications.

Rubie-Davies, C.M. (2015). *Becoming a high expectation teacher.* Abingdon: Routledge.

Rubie-Davies, C.M., and Peterson, E.R. (2011). Teacher expectations and beliefs: influences on the socioemotional climate. In: C.M. Rubie-Davies (ed.), *Educational psychology: concepts, research and challenges* (pp. 134–149). London: Routledge.

Rubie-Davies, C.M., Peterson, E.R., Sibley, C.G., and Rosenthal, R. (2015). A teacher expectation intervention: modelling the practices of high expectation teachers. *Contemporary Educational Psychology*, 40, 72–85.

Rubie-Davies, C.M., and Rosenthal, R. (2016). Intervening in teachers' expectations: a random effects meta-analytic approach to examining the effectiveness of an intervention. *Learning and Individual Differences*, 50, 83–92.

Rudasill, K.M., Reio, T.G., Stipanovic, N., and Taylor, J.E. (2010). A longitudinal study of student-teacher relationship quality, difficult temperament, and risky behavior from childhood to early adolescence. *Journal of School Psychology*, 48(5), 389–412.

Rudduck, J., Chaplain, R., and Wallace, G. (1996). *School improvement: what can pupils tell us?* London: David Fulton.

Russell, J. (1996). *Agency: its role in mental development.* Hove: Lawrence Erlbaum.

Rutter, M., Maughan, B., Mortimore, P., Ouston, J., and Smith, A. (1979). *Fifteen thousand hours: secondary schools and their effects on children.* Somerset: Open Books.

Sammons, P. (1999). *School effectiveness: coming of age in the twenty-first century.* Lisse: Swets and Zeitlinger.
Sammons, P., Sylva, K., Melhuish, E.C., Siraj-Blatchford, I., Taggart, B., and Grabbe, Y. (2007). *Influences on children's development and progress in Key Stage 2 Social/ behavioural outcomes in Year 5. Research Report RR007.* London: Institute of Education, University of London.
Sandberg, S., and Rutter, M. (2008). Acute life stresses. In: M. Rutter, D. Bishop, D. Pine, S. Scott, J. Stevenson, E. Taylor, and A. Thapar (eds.), *Rutter's child and adolescent psychiatry.* (pp. 394–408). Oxford: Blackwell Publishing.
Santrock, J.W. (2009). *A topical approach to life-span development* (5th ed.). Boston, MA: McGrawHill.
Sarason, B.R., Sarason, I.G., and Pierce, G.R. (1990). *Social support: an interactional view.* New York: Wiley.
Savage, T. (1991). *Discipline for self-control.* Englewood Cliffs, NJ: Prentice-Hall.
Sawka, K.D., McCurdy, B.L., and Mannella, M.C. (2002). Strengthening emotional support services: an empirically based model for training teachers of students with behavior disorders. *Journal of Emotional and Behavioral Disorders,* 10(4), 223–232.
Saxe, R., and Kanwisher, N. (2003). People thinking about thinking people: the role of the temporo-parietal junction in 'theory of mind'. *Neuroimage,* 19(4), 1835–1842.
Schaubroeck, J., and Ganster, D.C. (1991). Associations among stress-related individual differences. In: C.L. Cooper and R. Payne (eds.), *Personality and stress: individual differences in the stress process.* Chichester: Wiley.
Schaubroeck, J., Lam, S.S., and Peng, A.C. (2011). Cognition-based and affect-based trust as mediators of leader behavior influences on team performance. *Journal of Applied Psychology,* 96(4), 863.
Schimmel, D. (1976). Assertive behavior scales: global or subscale measures. Unpublished paper.
Schmuck, R.A., and Schmuck, P.A. (1992). *Group processes in the classroom.* Dubuque, IA: William C Brown.
Schneider, M. (2002). Do school facilities affect academic outcomes? National clearinghouse for educational facilities. *Environmental Education,* 1(3), 167–173.
Schraml, K., Perski, A., Grossi, G., and Simonsson-Sarnecki, M. (2011). Stress symptoms among adolescents: the role of subjective psychosocial conditions, lifestyle, and self-esteem. *Journal of Adolescence,* 34(5), 987–996.
Schunk, D.H. (1987). Self-efficacy and motivated learning. In: N.J. Hastings and J.J. Schwieso (eds.), *New directions in educational psychology 2: behaviour and motivation in the classroom.* London: Falmer Press.
Schunk, D.H., Pintrich, P.R., and Meece, J.L., (2008). *Motivation in education: theory, research, and applications.* Upper Saddle River, NJ: Pearson/Merrill Prentice Hall.
Schwartzer, R. (1992). Self-efficacy in the adoption and maintenance of health behaviours: theoretical approaches and a new model. In: R. Schwartzer (ed.), *Self-efficacy: thought control of action.* Washington, DC: Hemisphere.
Scott, S., Webster-Stratton, C., Spender, Q., Doolan, M., Jacobs, B., and Aspland, H. (2001). Multicentre controlled trial of parenting groups for childhood antisocial behaviour in clinical practice. Commentary: nipping conduct problems in the bud. *British Medical Journal,* 323, 194.

Séguin, J.R., Nagin, D., Assaad, J.M., and Tremblay, R.E. (2004). Cognitive-neuropsychological function in chronic physical aggression and hyperactivity. *Journal of Abnormal Psychology*, 113(4), 603.

Séguin, J., Parent, S., Tremblay, R., and Zelazo, P. (2009). Different neurocognitive functions regulating physical aggression and hyperactivity in early childhood. *Journal of Child Psychology and Psychiatry*, 50(6), 679–687.

Shaw, J.A. (2003). Children exposed to war/terrorism. *Clinical Child and Family Psychology Review*, 6(4), 237–246.

Shaw, P., Stringaris, A., Nigg, J., and Leibenluft, E. (2014). Emotion dysregulation in ADHD. *American Journal of Psychiatry*, 171(3), 276–293.

Shield, B., and Dockrell, J. (2003). The effects of noise on children at school: a review. *Building Acoustics*, 10(2), 97–116.

Shonkoff, J., and Phillips, D. (2000). *From neurons to neighborhoods: the science of early childhood development*. Washington, DC: National Academy Press.

Sibrava, N.J., and Borkovec, T.D. (2006). The cognitive avoidance theory of worry. In: G.C.L. Davey and A. Wells (eds.), *Worry and its psychological disorders: Theory, assessment and treatment* (pp. 217–237). West Sussex, UK: John Wiley & Sons.

Silins, H., and Mulford, B. (2002). *Leadership and school results second international handbook of educational leadership and administration*. Alphen aan den Rijn: Kluwer Press.

Skinner, B.F. (1961). Why we need teaching machines. *Harvard Educational Review*, 31, 377–398.

Skinner, B.F. (1974). *About behavior*. London: Cape.

Skinner, E., and Belmont, M. (1993). Motivation in the classroom: reciprocal effects of teacher behavior and student engagement across the school year. *Journal of Educational Psychology*, 85(4), 571.

Sleeman, P., and Rockwell, D. (1981). *Designing learning environments*. New York: Abe Books.

Smilansky, J. (1984). External and internal correlates of teachers' satisfaction and willingness to report stress. *British Journal of Educational Psychology*, 54(1), 84–92.

Smiley, P.A., and Dweck, C.S. (1994). Individual differences in achievement goals among young children. *Child Development*, 65, 1723–1743.

Smith, E., Lemke, J., Taylor, M., Kirchner, H.L., and Hoffman, H. (1998). Frequency of voice problems among teachers and other occupations. *Journal of Voice*, 12(4), 480–488.

Smith, P.K., ed. (2004). *Violence in schools: the response in Europe*. London: Routledge/Falmer.

Smithers, A., and Robinson, P. (2000). *Attracting teachers: past patterns, present policies, future prospects*. Liverpool: Centre for Education and Employment Research, University of Liverpool.

Snow, R.E. (1995). Pygmalion and intelligence? *Current Directions in Psychological Science*, 4, 169–171.

Snyder, M. (1992). Motivational foundations of behavioral confirmation. *Advances in Experimental Social Psychology*, 25, 67–114.

Sonuga-Barke, E.J. (2002). Psychological heterogeneity in AD/HD – a dual pathway model of behaviour and cognition. *Behavioural Brain Research*, 130(1), 29–36.

Sonuga-Barke, E.J. (2005). Causal models of attention-deficit/hyperactivity disorder: from common simple deficits to multiple developmental pathways. *Biological Psychiatry*, 57(11), 1231–1238.

Sorhagen, N.S. (2013). Early teacher expectations disproportionately affect poor children's high school performance. *Journal of Educational Psychology*, 105(2), 465.

Spadafora, N., Farrell, A.H., Provenzano, D.A., Marini, Z.A., and Volk, A.A. (2016). Temperamental Differences and Classroom Incivility Exploring the Role of Individual Differences. *Canadian Journal of School Psychology*.

Spilt, J.L., Koomen, H.M., and Thijs, J.T. (2011). Teacher wellbeing: the importance of teacher–student relationships. *Educational Psychology Review*, 23(4), 457–477.

Stafford, A., Alberto, P., Frederick, L., Heflin, L., and Heller, K. (2002). Preference variability and the instruction of choice making with students with severe intellectual disabilities. *Education and Training in Mental Retardation and Developmental Disabilities*, 37, 70–88.

Stage, S.A., and Quiroz, D.R. (1997). A meta-analysis of interventions to decrease disruptive classroom behavior in public education settings. *School Psychology Review*, 26(3), 333–368.

Stansfeld, S.A., Head, J., and Marmot, M.G. (1997). Explaining social class differences in depression and well-being. *Social Psychiatry and Psychiatric Epidemiology*, 33(1), 1–9.

Staude-Müller, F., Bliesener, T., and Luthman, S. (2008). Hostile and hardened? An experimental study on (de-)sensitization to violence and suffering through playing video games. *Swiss Journal of Psychology*, 67(1), 41–50.

Steil, L.K. (1991). Listening training: the key to success in today's organizations. In: D. Borisoff and M. Purdy (eds.), *Listening in everyday life*. Lanham, MD: University Press of America.

Steinberg, L., Graham, S., O'Brien, L., Woolard, J., Cauffman, E., and Banich, M. (2009). Age differences in future orientation and delay discounting. *Child Development*, 80, 28–44.

Steinberg, M.S., and Dodge, K.A. (1983). Attributional bias in aggressive adolescent boys and girls. *Journal of Social and Clinical Psychology*, 1(4), 312–321.

Steptoe, A., and Appels, A. (eds.). (1989). *Stress, personal control and health*. Chichester: Wiley.

Stern, G.G. (1970). *People in context*. New York: Wiley.

Stipek, D., Recchia, S., and McClintic, S. (1992). Self-evaluation in young children. *Monographs of the Society for Research in Child Development*, 57, 1 (Serial No 226).

Stoll, L. (1996). Linking school effectiveness and school improvement: issues and possibilities. In: J. Gray, D. Reynolds, and C. Fitz-Gibbon (eds.), *Merging traditions: the future of research on school effectiveness and school improvement*. London: Cassell.

Sukhodolsky, D.G., Kassinove, H., and Gorman, B.S. (2004). Cognitive-behavioral therapy for anger in children and adolescents: a meta-analysis. *Aggression and Violent Behavior*, 9(3), 247–269.

Sukhodolsky, D.G., and Scahill, L. (2012). *Cognitive-behavioral therapy for anger and aggression in children and adolescents*. New York: Guilford Press.

Sutherland, V.J., and Cooper, C.L. (1991). *Understanding stress: a psychological perspective for health professionals*. London: Chapman and Hall.

Swann, W.B., Jr., Pelham, B.W., and Krull, D.S. (1989). Agreeable fancy or disagreeable truth? Reconciling self-enhancement and self-verification. *Journal of Personality and Social Psychology*, 57: 782–791.

Syrotuik, J., and D'Arcy, C. (1984). Social support and mental health: direct, protective and compensatory effects. *Social Science and Medicine*, 18, 229–236.

Taguiri, R. (1968). The concept of organizational climate. In: G. Taguiri and G. Litwin (eds.), *Organizational climate: explorations of a concept*. Cambridge, MA: Harvard University Press.

Tannenbaum, R., and Schmidt, W.H. (1958). How to choose a leadership pattern. *Harvard Business Review*, March–April.

Taylor, S.E., and Crocker, J. (1981). Schematic bases of social information processing. In: *Social cognition: the Ontario symposium* (vol. 1, pp. 89–134).

Teacher Training Agency/Department for Education and Skills. (2012). *Improving teacher training for behaviour*. London: TTA.

Tedeschi, J.T. (ed.). (2013). *Impression management theory and social psychological research*. New York: Academic Press.

Thoits, P.A. (2010). Stress and health major findings and policy implications. *Journal of Health and Social Behavior*, 51(1 suppl.), S41–S53.

Thompson, T. (1994). Self-worth protection: review and implications for the classroom. *Educational Review*, 46(3), 259–274.

Thompson, R.F. (2000). *The brain: a neuroscience primer* (3rd ed.). New York: Worth.

Toland, J., and Boyle, C. (2008). Applying cognitive behavioural methods to retrain children's attributions for success and failure in learning. *School Psychology International*, 29(3), 286–302.

Torrington, D., and Weightman, J. (1989). *The reality of school management*. Oxford: Blackwell.

Tottenham, N., Hare, T.A., and Casey, B.J. (2011). Behavioral assessment of emotion discrimination, emotion regulation, and cognitive control in childhood, adolescence, and adulthood. *Frontiers in Psychology*, 2, 39.

Townsend, T. (ed.). (2007). *International handbook of school effectiveness and improvement* (vol. 17). Dordrecht: Springer.

Travers, C.J., and Cooper, C.L. (1996). *Teachers under pressure: stress in the teaching profession*. Hove: Psychology Press.

Tremblay, R. (2007). The development of youth violence: an old story with new data. *European Journal of Criminal Policy Research*, 13, 161–170.

Tremblay, R.E., Nagin, D.S., Seguin, J.R., Zoccolillo, M., Zelazo, P.D., and Boivin, M. (2004). Physical aggression during early childhood: trajectories and predictors. *Pediatrics*, 114, 43–50.

Tschannen-Moran, M., and Woolfolk-Hoy, A. (2007). The differential antecedents of self-efficacy beliefs of novice and experienced teachers. *Teaching and Teacher Education*, 23(6), 944–956.

Tsouloupas, C.N., Carson, R.L., Matthews, R., Grawitch, M.J., and Barber, L.K. (2010). Exploring the association between teachers' perceived student misbehaviour and emotional exhaustion: the importance of teacher efficacy beliefs and emotion regulation. *Educational Psychology*, 30, 173–189.

Turati, C., Simion, F., Milani, I., and Umiltà, C. (2002). Newborns' preference for faces: what is crucial? *Journal of Developmental Psychology*, 38(6), 875–882.

United Nations. (1989). Convention on the rights of the child. *Geneva: Office of the High Commissioner of Human Rights*.

Van Leijenhorst, L., Zanolie, K., Van Meel, C.S., Westenberg, P.M., Rombouts, S.A., and Crone, E.A. (2010). What motivates the adolescent? Brain regions mediating reward sensitivity across adolescence. *Cerebral Cortex*, 20(1), 61–69.

Van Werkhoven, W. (1990). The attunement strategy and spelling problems. In: A. Van der Ley and K.J. Kappers (eds.), *Dyslexie '90*. Lisse: Swets and Zeitlinger.

Verquer, M.L., Beehr, T.A., and Wagner, S.H. (2003). A meta-analysis of relations between person–organization fit and work attitudes. *Journal of Vocational Behavior*, 63(3), 473–489.

Vine, I. (1973). The role of facial-visual signalling in early social development. In: M. von Cranach and I. Vine (eds.), *Social communication and movement*. New York: Academic Press.

Volkow, N.D., Wang, G.J., Newcorn, J., Telang, F., Solanto, M.V., Fowler, J.S., Logan, J., Ma, Y., Schulz, K., Pradhan, K., and Wong, C. (2007). Depressed dopamine activity in caudate and preliminary evidence of limbic involvement in adults with attention-deficit/hyperactivity disorder. *Archives of general psychiatry*, 64(8), 932–940.

Vygotsky, L.S. (1962). *Thought and language*. Cambridge: MIT Press.

Vygotsky, L.S. (1978). *Mind in society: the development of higher psychological processes*. Cambridge, MA: Harvard University Press.

Wahba, M.A., and Bridwell, L.G. (1976). Maslow reconsidered: a review of research on the need hierarchy theory. *Organizational Behavior and Human Performance*, 15(2), 212–240.

Wallace, G. (1996). Relating to teachers. In: J. Rudduck, R. Chaplain, and G. Wallace (eds.), *School improvement: what can pupils tell us?* London: David Fulton.

Wannarka, R., and Ruhl, K. (2008). Seating arrangements that promote positive academic and behavioural outcomes: a review of empirical research. *Support for Learning*, 23(2), 89–93.

Wargocki, P., and Wyon, D.P. (2007). The effects of outdoor air supply rate and supply air filter condition in classrooms on the performance of schoolwork by children (RP-1257). *HVACandR Research*, 13(2), 165–191.

Webb, J.M., Diana, E.M., Luft, P., Brooks, E.W., and Brennan, E.L. (1997). Influence of pedagogical expertise and feedback on assessing student comprehension from nonverbal behavior. *Journal of Educational Research*, 91(2), 89–97.

Wegner, D.M., and Bargh, J.A. (1998). Control and automaticity in social life. In: D. Gilbert, S. Fiske, and G. Lindzey (eds.), *Handbook of social psychology* (4th ed.). Boston, MA: McGraw-Hill.

Wehlage, G.G., Rutter, R.A., Gregory, A., Smith, N.L., and Fernandez, R.R. (1989). *Reducing the risk: schools as communities of support*. Lewes: Falmer Press.

Weick, K.E. (1976). Educational organisations as loosely coupled systems. *Administrative Science Quarterly*, 21, 1–19.

Weiner, B. (1992). *Human Motivation*. London: Sage.

Weinstein, C.S. (1988). Preservice teachers' expectations about the first year of teaching. *Teaching and Teacher Education*, 4(1), 31–40.

Weinstein, C.S., and David, T.G. (1987). *Spaces for children: the built environment and child development*. New York: Plenum Press.

Weinstein, R.S. (2002). *Reaching higher*. Cambridge, MA: Harvard University Press.

Weisz, J.R., and Kazdin, A.E. (eds.). (2010). *Evidence-based psychotherapies for children and adolescents*. New York: Guilford Press.

Whalen, P.J., Rauch, S.L., Etcoff, N.L., McInerney, S.C., Lee, M.B., and Jenike, M.A. (1998). Masked presentations of emotional facial expressions modulate amygdala activity without explicit knowledge. *The Journal of Neuroscience*, 18(1), 411–418.

Wheldall, K., and Lam, Y.Y. (1987). Rows versus tables II. The effects of classroom seating arrangements on classroom disruption rate, on task behaviour and teacher behaviour in three special school classes. *Educational Psychology*, 7(4), 303–312.

Wheldall, K., and Merrett, F. (1984). *Positive teaching: the behavioural approach.* London: Allen and Unwin.

Wilkinson, C., and Cave, E. (1987). *Teaching and managing: inseparable activities in schools.*

Willcutt, E.G., Doyle, A.E., Nigg, J.T., Faraone, S.V., and Pennington, B.F. (2005). Validity of the executive function theory of attention-deficit/hyperactivity disorder: a meta-analytic review. *Biological Psychiatry*, 57, 1336–1346.

Williams, L.E., and Bargh, J.A. (2008). Experiencing physical warmth promotes interpersonal warmth. *Science*, 322(5901), 606–607.

Wilshaw, M. (2015). *Lack of support puts young teachers off, Ofsted warns.* London: BBC. Available from: http://www.bbc.co.uk/news/education-34267369 [Accessed 20th January 2017].

Wilson, S.J., and Lipsey, M. W. (2007). School-based interventions for aggressive and disruptive behavior: Update of a meta-analysis. *American Journal of Preventive Medicine*, 33(2).

Winsler, A., Fernyhough, C., and Montero, I. (eds.). (2009). *Private speech, executive functioning, and the development of verbal self-regulation.* Cambridge: Cambridge University Press.

Wolery, M., Bailey, D., and Sugai, G. (1988). *Effective teaching: principles and procedures of applied behavior analysis with exceptional students.* Boston, MA: Allyn and Bacon.

Woolfolk Hoy, A., Hoy, W.K., and Davis, H.A. (2009). Teachers' self-efficacy beliefs. *Handbook of Motivation in School*, 627–653.

Wortman, C., Loftus, E., and Weaver, C. (1998). *Psychology* (5th ed.). New York: McGraw-Hill.

Zaleznik, A. (1977). Managers and leaders: are they different? *Harvard Business Review*, May–June, 47–60.

Zebrowski, J.A. (2007). *New research on social perception.* New York: Nova Publishers.

Zeidner, M. (1988). The relative severity of common classroom discipline techniques: the students' perspective. *British Journal of Educational Psychology*, 58, 69–77.

Zentner, M., and Bates, J.E. (2008). Child temperament: an integrative review of concepts, research programs, and measures. *European Journal of Developmental Science*, 2(1–2), 7–37.

Zillmann, D., Bryant, J., Comisky, P.W., and Medoff, N.J. (1981). Excitation and hedonic valence in the effect of erotica on motivated intermale aggression. *European Journal of Social Psychology*, 11(3), 233–252.

Zuckerman, M., DePaulo, B.M., and Rosenthal, R. (1981). Verbal and non-verbal communication of deception. In: L. Berkowitz (ed.), *Advances in experimental social psychology.* New York: Academic Press.

# Index

ABC model of behaviour 8
Abelson, R.P. 23, 177
Abramowitz, A.J. 190
Abrams, D. 63
academic achievement 62, 169, 187
action zone (teaching hub) 142, 152
adolescence: and stress 52; risk-taking in 52, 186, 204; socio-emotional development 3, 181, 185–7, 219; well-being 53–55
aggression: pupil 19, 22–4, 27, 149, 184–5, 189, 193–4, 196, 201, 216; teacher/adult 85, 89, 97, 99–100, 121
Alberto, P.A. 15, 17, 18, 205, 210
all about me questionnaire 13, 217–18
Allport, G.W. 66
Ambady, N. 66
American Psychiatric Association 188
amygdala 35, 65
Andersen, S.L. 186
Anderson, C. 23, 24
Anderson, C.M. 163
Anderson, N.H. 69
Anderson, P. 191
Angelo, T.A. 98
anger 24, 65, 90, 94, 100, 102–3, 110; proneness 81; pupil 98, 207, 231; teacher 32, 34–5, 41, 67, 75, 232
anger management 25, 208
anticipatory: behaviour strategies 122; coping 50
Antonucci, T. 45
anxiety 39, 46, 48, 52, 97, 206; pupil 53–4, 143, 166, 182; teacher 34, 82, 83
appraisal: cognitive 33, 43
Argyle, M. 83, 92–4
Asch, S.E. 67–9
Ashbrook, P.K. 166

Ashton, M.C. 187
Ashton, P.T. 46
assault: on self 34, 71; physical 118, 201, 231
assembly 177
assertive behaviour 96, 99–103
assertiveness 3, 4, 33, 46, 81, 88–9, 91, 210, 213, 215
assessment of: behaviour 65, 67–8, 98, 197–9; classroom climate 152, 162; self 83, 114, 213–14
Association of Teachers and Lecturers (ATL) 184
at-risk pupils 52, 60, 153, 159, 184
attachment 69, 183, 194
attention: difficulties 144, 194–5, 198, 235; getting pupils' 86, 93, 176–80, 223–5
attention deficit hyperactivity disorder (ADHD) 3, 144, 188–92; label 5, 78, 182; supporting 235–6
attribution 70; causal 70, 72; errors 71
attributional bias: self-serving 71, 74, 86, 128
Aussiker, A. 48
authority: conveying 91; establishing 3, 7, 79, 86, 103, 170, 172, 212, 221, 223; of headteachers 133, 135; of teachers 36, 51, 82–3, 91, 96, 99, 154, 168, 174, 184, 189, 192
automaticity 36, 65
Axelrod, S. 18

Babad, E. 63, 74–5
Backes, C. 175
Baddeley A. 191
Bahou, L. 54
Ball, C. 222

Bandura, A. 19–23, 27, 46–8
Bargh, J.A. 65, 67, 69
Barker, G.P. 159
Barkley, R.A. 190, 191
Baron-Cohen, S. 80
Bates, J.E. 81
Baumeister, R. 32, 169
Baxter, J.C 97
Beck, J.S. 19
Beck, R. 25
Becker, W.C. 175
behaviour: analysis 199, 201–3; causal explanations of 18, 70–4, 155, 157; modification 204–5
behaviour difficulties and disorders *see* emotional and behavioural difficulties
behaviour management: and emotions 75; and engagement 79; and pupil well-being 53, 186; effective 44–5, 47; efficacy 213–14; groupwork and 149; multilevel 1–2, 160; punishment and 18; research and 7; rules, routine and 163; senior staff role 3, 127–8, 140; skills 152, 221; support and 120; theories and research 6–7, 28; teacher training xiii, xiv, 6–7, 30, 184; whole-school 4, 105, 135
behaviour policy 1, 3, 54, 110, 116, 127, 135; consistency and 105–7; framework 107–8
behavioural: approaches 7–18, 199–205; expectations 107, 164, 168, 173, 223
belongingness 31, 113, 153, 167–9, 186
Berkowitz, L. 24
Berridge, K.C. 35, 190
Bettinger, E. 17
Blackwell, L.S. 6, 156
Blatchford, P. 148
Blum, K. 190
bobo doll 22–3
body language 36, 89, 96, 98; *see also* posture
Bohlin, G. 190
Botella, C. 92
Bower, G.H. 100
Bower, S.A. 100
Bowlby, J. 69
Braaten, E.B. 192
Bradshaw, C.P. 53
Braxton, J. 187
Brewer, M.B. 69
Brewin, C.R. 36

Bridwell, L.G. 169
Brock, L.L. 192
Bronfenbrenner, U. 46
Brooks, F. 53
Brophy, J.E. 13, 60, 75, 142, 146
Bryk, A.S. 117
bullying 105, 166, 220; cyberbullying 54, 166
Burnett, P. 11, 13, 14, 160
Bush, T. 126, 132
Bushman B.J. 23
Butcher, B. 52

Calder, B.J. 36
callous-unemotional trait 193–4, 209
Cameron, J. 16
Cameron, O. 15
Canter, L. 100, 173, 176
Canter, M. 100, 173
Carlson, S.M. 27
Carver, C.S. 46
Catalano, R.F. 53
Cave, E 117
Chadee, D. 84
challenging behaviour 1–2, 16, 75, 105, 184, 196, 209
Chan, D.W. 45
Chance, P. 16
Chanfreau, J. 53, 55
Chantrey-Wood, K. 148, 149, 222
Chaplain, R. 30, 33–4, 37, 49, 53–5, 110, 130–1, 136, 159, 171, 183–4, 198, 205, 208–9
character (personal quality) 80–1
Chatter, N. 24
Chazan, M 185
Choe, D.E. 27
Cicchetti, D. 52
circle time 111, 151
classroom climate 1, 3–4, 20, 77, 142; and inclusion 308; and motivation 153–6; and pupil engagement 151–3; and rewards 15; and rules 164; interruptions and 35, 118, 177, 189, 223, 241; negative 30, 48
classroom displays 114, 222, 235
classroom environment 5, 13, 30–1, 143, 160, 197, 211–12, 221
classroom layout 145–51, 170, 221–2
classroom management strategies: overlapping 229–230; proactive 18, 29, 44, 96, 139, 164, 172, 210–12, 216,

221–30, 235; reactive 211, 221, 229, 231–4; reorientation 174, 221, 230–1; ripple effect 230; scanning 88, 91, 152, 230; withitness 89, 91, 212, 229, 230
Coates, T.J. 33
cognitive (self) appraisal *see* appraisal
cognitive-behavioural approaches 4, 7, 18, 82, 190, 205, 234
Cohen, J. 112
Cohen, S. 45
Coie, J.D. 208
Cole, G.A. 119, 120
Cole, T. 183
communication 29, 45, 80–1, 85, 87, 108, 112, 117–19, 149–50, 152, 208; and feedback 83; eye contact 93–5; gesture 96; lack of 31; networks 119–20; nonverbal 89–90; posture 96; the face 92; under pressure 120–2
Compas, B.E. 52, 186
conditioning: classical 9–10; operant 11–18
conditions for learning 149, 171
conduct disorder 182–4, 187, 193–5, 209
conflict resolution 25, 81, 118, 213
contiguity 10
Cook, M. 93
Cooper, C.L. 34, 182
Cooper, J. 14
Cooper, L. 133
Cooper, P. 182
coping: levels of 35–43; model of 37–43; strategies 24, 31–3, 43; styles 50
Covington M.V. 16, 154, 158, 161
Cox, C. 133
Craske, M.L. 160
Creemers, B.P.M. 114
Crocker, J. 64
Croft, D.B. 114
Crone, E.A. 18, 186
Cross, K.P. 98
crowdedness 148–9
Cutrona, C.E. 46, 134

D'Arcy, C. 32
Dahl, R.E. 186
Dalgleish, T. 35, 166
data gathering 198, 203, 217–18; open recording 198–9; scales and checklists 198
Davis, K.E. 71
Dawson, P. 191

Deci, E. 16
decision making 22, 25–6, 54, 108, 110, 191–2 leadership and 126, 128, 131, 133–4
defiance 5, 37, 154, 188, 192–3
depression 34, 54, 76, 160, 182
detention 8, 17, 82, 106, 168, 233
Diagnostic and Statistical Manual of Mental Disorders (DSM V) criteria 189, 192
difficult/disruptive pupils 1, 3, 9, 21, 30, 32, 41, 45, 57, 65, 71, 77, 107, 110, 120, 122, 131, 135–6, 140, 148, 183
Dimmock, C. 126
discipline 30, 106, 108, 111, 116, 124, 134, 139–40, 171
disengaged pupils 15, 21, 54, 114, 154, 156, 159, 161, 166
dispositional characteristics 33, 74, 122, 127, 132, 159, 197
disruption: levels of xiii, 135, 145, 188, 196; reaction to 233
distractions 27, 99, 122, 137, 144, 166, 190, 192; reducing 235
Dobson, K. 205
Dodge, K.A. 194, 208
Doherty-Sneddon, G. 93
Doll, B. 142, 171
Donahoe, J. 15
dopamine: and ADHD 187, 190; and rewards 9, 186, 190
Dorsel, V. 15
Doyle, W. 148, 163
Dozois, D. 205
Driscoll, M.E. 117
Dryfoos, J.G. 53
DuBois, D.L 55
Dudley, P. 148
Dunham. J. 52
Dweck, C.S. 156, 159, 161

Eaton, A. 183
Eccles, J.S. 54
Education, Health and Care Plans (EHCs) 185
effective schools: characteristics of 105, 108–9, 111–12, 114, 126
efficacy: behaviour management 213–14; collective 47; pupil 21, 76, 143, 151, 153, 160, 170; self 21–2, 33, 42; teacher 31, 46–9, 122, 134–5, 173
Eisenberger, N.I. 35

either ... or consequences 174, 232
Ekman, P. 85, 89, 90, 92
Elashoff, J.D. 58
Ellis, A. 206
Ellis, H.C. 166
Ellis, I. 175
embarrassment 69, 82, 122, 177
Emmer, E.T. 48, 164, 176
emotion regulation 47, 80–1, 166, 184, 187, 191–2, 194–5, 219
emotional: objectivity 134, 174, 233; reactions 157–8, 178, 184–6, 192, 206; and failure 157
emotional and behavioural difficulties (EBD) 182; development of 194–5; effective interventions 199; negative thinking and 25; teacher-pupil relationships and 113; teaching strategies 235–6. *see also* SEMH difficulties
emotions 22, 75, 90, 92–4, 96, 101, 120, 143, 153, 166, 192–4, 206–8, 216; and stress 34–7; micro-expressions 85; negative 25, 32, 192–3
empathy 29, 69, 80, 192, 194, 207, 227
engagement with learning (pupils) 9, 13–14, 35, 79, 143, 148, 151, 153, 162, 164, 186, 190, 217, 221–2, 234, 236
Eron, L. 23
ethos *see* organisational climate
Evertson, C.M. 15, 75, 146, 174, 175, 176
evidence-based practice iii, 4, 6, 132, 146, 148–9, 160–1, 197, 199, 208, 210
exclusion 16, 114, 124, 134, 153, 233
executive functioning (self regulation) 27, 185, 191–2, 195, 232
expectations (teacher) 57; and social class 59–60; avoiding negative effects 76; communicating 63, 74–5, 211, 220; effects on pupils 59, 60–2; forming 63; high 77; process 62
extraversion 33
eye: contact 14, 37, 64, 74, 83, 85, 89–91, 93–95, 103, 152, 229–30, 233
Eysenck, M. 166

Fabiano, G.A. 18, 199
facial expression 35, 37–8, 83, 85, 89–92
Farber, I. 30
Farley, F. 52
fear 30, 67, 83, 85, 90, 93–4, 99–100, 103, 131, 216
fear of failure 153, 154–5, 158

feedback: emotional 92; from others 13, 32, 43, 45–6, 61–2, 64, 83, 86–7, 98, 101, 107, 115, 120, 170; to pupils 14, 21, 74–5, 78, 98, 103, 154, 160
Feinstein, L. 53, 110
Fernandez, E. 25
Fiske, S.T. 66, 69, 70
Folkman, S. 33, 50
Fosterling, F. 70
Freeman, Andrea. 33, 34, 37, 39, 49, 183, 184
Friedberg, R.D. 18
Friedman, I.A. 30
Friesen, W.V. 85, 92
Fuligni, A.J. 54

Gale C.R. 53
Galloway, D. 32
Galván, A. 9
Gansle, K.A. 205
Gavish, B. 30
gaze 93–4; types of 94–5
gesture 10, 25, 74, 83–6, 91, 96–7
Gettinger, M. 222
Gibson, S. 48
Glover, D. 126, 132
goals: mastery 156–7; organisational 108, 112, 114, 117, 123, 132; orientation 55, 153; performance 156, 158; personal 16, 20–1, 26, 27, 35, 57, 76–8, 99, 102, 123, 146, 157, 187, 191–2, 196, 225, 229, 235; setting 133
Goddard, R.D. 47
Goldstein, H. 109
Golem effect (negative expectations) 63
Gonzalez, J.E. 206
Good, C. 161
Good, T.L. 60, 142, 146
Goodman, R. 198
Gottfredson, D.C. 174
Graham, S. 66, 159
Gray, H. 130
Gray, J. 109, 110, 126
Greenspan, S. 80
Gronn, P. 132
groupwork 143, 148–51; problems with 148–9, 222
Gruder, C.L. 36
Guare, R. 191
guilt 35, 69, 156, 194
Gump, P. 146
Gutman, L. 53, 110

Halpin, A.W. 114
Hampson, P.J. 37
Hamre, B.K. 113
Hargie, O. 96
Hargreaves, D. 133
Hargreaves, D.H. 173
Harris, A. 132, 141
Harris, M.J. 59, 60, 74
Harrison, R.P. 92
Hastings, N. 148, 149, 222
Hattie, J.A.C. 60
Haydn, T. 152
Hazlett-Stevens, H. 48
head of year/faculty 82, 134, 136
headteacher 126; and behaviour policies 105, 106, 109; good leadership 132; management style 127, 129; support from 135, 138
Heider, F. 70, 71
Hesler, M.W. 85
Hess, E.H. 94
Hewstone, M. 35
Heywood, S. 97
Hiebert, B. 30
hierarchy of needs 167–9
Higgins, A.T. 144
Hirschy, A. 187
Hogg, M.A. 63
hopelessness 157, 159, 206
hostile attributional bias 194
Hoy, W.K. 113, 114
Huesmann, L.R. 23
humour 12, 33, 67, 117, 164, 174, 231
Hurley, S. 24
Hustler, D. 130
Hyland, F. 14
Hyland, K. 14
hyperactive impulsive 188, 189

immediacy 84
impression formation 67–69, 76
impulsive-aggressive pupils 27
impulsivity 25, 188, 193
inclusion 5, 184,
individual coping analysis (ICAN) 49–51
ineffective strategies 43
inner speech 25–7, 191–2
interpersonal relationships 31, 33, 63, 86, 92, 94, 112–13, 116–17, 142, 164, 173, 197
irrational thinking 206–7
Irwin, C.E. 185

Jacobson, L. 58
Jamal, F. 54, 110
Jarvis, M. 30
Jenson, W.R. 222
Jerusalem, M. 32
job satisfaction 31, 32, 42, 116, 122, 123
Johnson, B. 31
Jones, A. 129, 130
Jones, E.E. 71
Jones, L.S. 177
Jones, V.F. 177
Jordan, A. 47
Jussim, L. 57, 60

Kagan, J. 80, 81
Kahn, R. 45, 221
Kalker, P. 32
Kanwisher, N. 80
Kaplan, D.S. 201
Kaplan, J. 159
Kaplan, R.M. 160
Katz, R.L. 132
Kauffman, J.M. 15, 188
Kelley, H.H. 71, 72
Kendall, P. 19, 25
Kessels, U. 14
Kihlstrom, J.F. 36
Kimonis, E. 193
Klassen, R. 31, 47
Kostic, A. 84
Kounin, J.S. 229
Kringelbach, M.L. 35
Kun, A. 158
Kunc, R. 30
Kutnick, P. 148, 149, 222
Kyriacou, C. 30, 31, 34, 52

Lackney, J. 148
Lalljee, M. 86
Lam, Y.Y. 147
Lambert, R.J. 32
Larson, J. 18
Lazarus, R.S. 34, 50
leadership styles 127
learned helplessness 158, 159–60
least restrictive approach 5, 199
Lee, K 187
Leinhardt, G. 10
Leithwood, K. 126
Lerner, R.M. 54, 187
Lewin, K. 133
Liang J. 166
Light, P. 148

limbic system 9, 35
listening skills 88, 89, 97–9
Lochman, J.E. 7, 18
Locke, E.A. 19
locus of control 33, 53, 80, 81, 155
Loeber, R. 193
loose and tight coupled schools 114
Louis, K. 109
Loveless, T. 14
Luria, A.R. 25–7
Lyubomirsky, S. 48

Maag, J. 12, 16, 17
MacBeath, J. 126
MacDonald, J.P. 19
Maier, S.F. 46
Malle, B.F. 71
Mandel, V. 13, 160
Manning, B. 25
Martella, R. 145
Marzano, R.J. 164
Maslow, A.H. 167, 169, 173, 178
mastery experiences 21, 47
Matsumoto, D 85
May, T. 54
McAteer-Early, T. 47
McClure, J.M. 18
McCormick, C.M. 186
McCroskey, J. 81, 84
McNamara, D. 148
Mehrabian, A. 84, 96
Meichnbaum, D. 25
memory: working 27, 191
mental health 3, 52–4, 110, 181, 182–4, 186–7, 193, 198
mentors 31, 141, 146
Merrett, F. 18, 30, 31
Merton, R.K. 58
Miles, M. 109
Miller, A. 47, 71
mindset: fixed 156, 158; growth (learning) 156–7
Mischel, W. 188
Miskel, C.G. 113
modelling behaviour 21, 22, 24–7, 177, 196, 204, 208, 212, 221, 230, 231
modifying behaviour 204–5
Moore, G. 148
Moos, R.H. 152
Morris, J.A. 32
Morris, P.E. 37
Mortimore, P. 109, 111, 112
Moses, L.J. 27

motivation: theories 153–6; extrinsic 16, 24; intrinsic 12, 16, 24
motivational styles 156–61
Müeller, K.J. 16
Mulford, B. 126
Murphy, J. 114
Murray-Harvey, R.T. 31, 32

Nadler, D. 114
National Institute for Health and Clinical Excellence (NICE) 183, 188, 193, 220
negative (behaviour) cycles 12, 44, 65, 66, 129, 174, 250
Nelson, J.R. 75
Neuberg, S.L. 69
neural alarm system 35
neurochemistry of ADHD 190
neuromyths xv
neuroscience xiv, xv, 9, 192
neurotransmitter 9, 195
Nias, J. 131
Nicholls, J.G. 160
Nolen-Hoeksema, S. 48
non-verbal behaviour (NVB) 62, 79, 84, 86, 87, 89
Norwich, B. 183
NUT (National Union of Teachers) 29

O'Leary, S.G. 190
Ofsted (Office for Standards in Education) xiii, xiv, 106, 108, 127, 134, 135, 139
Oosterlan, J. 192
Open Systems Group 114
oppositional defiant disorder (ODD) 3, 188 189, 192–3
organisational: climate 113–14, 117, 123, 134, 140, 141, 176; culture 1, 31, 113, 123; variables 44
Osterman, K.F. 53, 113, 186
overlearning 36, 52, 96, 178
Oxford, M. 194
Ozer, E.M. 185

Pajares, F. 21
parents: angry 121; contact with 59, 77, 106, 217, 233
Patterson, D. 25
Pavlov, I.P. 10, 26
Payne, R.L. 115
Pease, A. 93, 94, 95
Perret-Clermont, A.N. 148

personal strengths and concerns 3, 123, 212–13
personality: implicit theories 67, 68; traits 65, 68, 187, 194, 209
person-focused (centred) leaders 133, 134
person-organisation fit 122
Peterson, E.R. 77
Phelps, F.G. 93
Phillips, D. 22
physical assault 23, 118, 201, 231
Pianta, R.C. 113
Pickehain, L. 10
Pierce, W.D. 16
Piquero, A.R. 193
Plummer, G. 148
Poole, I.R. 176
Porter, L. 7
Porter, S. 85
posture 25, 74, 83–4, 89–91, 96, 103, 220, 230
Power, M. 35, 36
powerlessness 101
praise: problems with 13–14, 21, 48, 159, 160
procrastination 100, 154, 158, 190, 206
Proshansky, E. 146
proxemics (personal space) 96, 103, 230
psychological safety 166, 167
punishment (sanctions) 18, 19, 111, 112, 124; hierarchy 233; negative 17; positive 17
pupils: disengaged 15, 21, 54, 154, 159, 161, 166; grouping 77; normal distribution of 219; perspectives 109–11; rights of 54; school-fit 58, understanding your 217–18; voice (perspectives) 108–10
pupil referral units 111
Pygmalion effect 63

Quiroz, D.R. 18, 229

Rational Emotive Therapy (RET) 205–8
recuperative breaks 48
Reeslund, K.L. 52, 186
Reezigt, G.J. 114
refusal to work 198, 201
reinforcement 7, 11, 12, 16, 225, 229; continuous 14, 15; intermittent 14, 15, 225; negative 11, 13, 17; positive 11, 13; schedule 227, 228, 234, 236
Reivich, K. 160

relationships 75, 83, 137, 153, 207
resilience 3, 21, 29, 31, 42, 52, 53, 80, 81, 112, 156, 170, 186
restraining pupils 105–6, 201, 216
rewards: cloakroom tickets 226; stickers 13, 174, 204, 234; see also reinforcement
Reyna, V.F. 52
Rhode, G 15
Richmond, V.P. 81, 84, 92
risk-taking 52, 186, 219
Rist, R.G. 59, 60
Ritalin 190
rituals 163, 175–8
Robertson, J. 16
Robinson, T.E. 190
Rodrigues, A. 190
Rogers, C. 61, 63, 69, 148
role: ambiguity 31, 221; conflict 31; play 208
Romi, S. 100
Rosen, L.A. 192
Rosenthal, R. 58–60, 74, 77
Rosenthal, R.H. 48
Rosenthal, T.L. 48
routines: classroom 3, 10, 170, 175–9, 223; evaluating 179–80, 225; schoolwide 106
Rubie-Davis, C. 57, 59, 63, 77
Rudduck, J. 54, 110, 171
rudeness 12, 22, 187
Rudolph, U. 70
Ruhl, K. 146, 147
rules 163; breaking 189, 193, 201; classroom 163, 164–166; establishing 3, 171, 223–4; functions 163; limit setting approach 172; and psychological safety 167; rules about 175; school (core) 164, 171; teaching 211, 216; types of 173
Russell, D.W. 46, 134
Russell, J. 191
Rutter, M. 52, 108, 112

safety: internet 166–7; physical 166; psychological 166
Sammons, P. 111, 126, 128
sanctions 8, 12, 16, 44, 77, 100, 105, 106, 116, 135, 163, 165, 174, 231, 233; see punishments
Sandberg, S. 52
Santrock, J.W. 185
Sarason, B.R. 31

# Index

Sarason, I.G. 31
Savage, T. 164
Saxe, R. 80
scaffolding 88, 149, 208, 212
Scahill, L. 7
scanning 9, 88, 91, 170, 230
Scheier, M.F. 46
schema 64, 66, 69; causal 71, 72; event 64
Schimmel, D. 101
Schmidt, W.H. 133
Schmuck, P.A. 61
Schmuck, R.A. 61
Schneider, M. 144
school furniture design 145
school improvement/effectiveness 108–9
Schraml, K. 55
Schunk, D.H. 153, 160
Schwarzer, R. 33
Scott, S. 192
seating arrangements (classroom) 143, 145, 146; groups 148; rows 146
Séguin, J. 27
self professional 35, 128
self- actualisation 167; awareness 28, 192, 212, 220; control 163, 170, 171, 219, 221, 225, 227, 231, 234; determination 153; esteem 21, 33, 169, 194, 214; regulation 19, 20, 22, 25, 26, 27, 46, 79, 81, 142, 158, 163, 170, 186, 190, 192, 199, 208, 210, 211, 219, 232, 235
self-fulfilling prophecy 30, 58, 60, 76
self-instruction training 25, 26, 27, 208, 234
self-worth protection 158, 159, 160
SEN (special educational needs) 113, 182–3, 185
senior leadership team (SLT) 126
Shaw J.A 53
Shonkoff, J. 22
Sibrava, N.J. 48
Silins, H. 126
Skinner, B.F. 11
Skowronski, J.J. 15, 17, 18, 205, 210
Slonim, R. 17
Smilansky, J. 33
Smiley, P.A. 159
Smith, S. 205, 208
Snow, R.E. 58, 59
Snyder, M. 76
social awareness 79–81, 98
social categorisation 66
social cognition 63, 65, 66, 185
social cognitive theory 19

social competence 25, 31, 79–80, 103, 149, 170, 172, 192, 205, 208, 210–12
social development 27, 28, 111, 113, 162, 186, 212, 218, 222
Social Emotional Mental Health difficulties (SEMH) 182–3
social identity 44, 54, 65, 76, 115, 133, 169, 170, 178
social information processing 25, 27, 64
social perception 57, 66, 68, 72
social problem solving 25, 170, 205, 208, 212, 234
social script 64, 77
social skills 42; hierarchy of 89, 91; professional 3, 79
social support 3, 31, 32, 44, 45, 49, 55, 117, 134, 136, 211, 213; evaluating 214
socio-emotional development 185–187
Sonuga-Barke, E.J. 27, 188
Sorhagen, N.S. 59
Spauding, S.A. 163
Spillane, J. 132
Spilt, J.L. 32
Stage, S.A. 18, 229
Stanovich, P. 47
Stansfeld, S.A. 45
Staude-Müller, F. 24
Steinberg, L. 17
Steinberg, M.S. 194
Stern, G.G. 113, 115
Stipek, D. 172
Strengths and Difficulties Questionnaire (SDQ) 198
stress 3, 29; definition of 34; pupils 52–55; teacher 29–33
stressors 49–51, 53; life events 55
Sukhodolsky, D.G. 7, 19
Sutherland, V.J. 34
Swann, W.B. Jnr 83
Swant, S.G. 160
swearing 50, 121, 173, 202
Syrotuik, J. 32

Taguiri, R. 113
talking out of turn (TOOT) 5, 204, 214, 230
Tannenbaum, R. 133
task-focused leaders 133
Taylor, C. xiii, 30, 210
Taylor, S.E. 64, 66, 70
teacher expectancy *see* expectations
teacher training xiii, xiv, 184; *see also* behaviour management
Teicher, M.H. 186

temperament 80–1, 187, 188, 195
Theory of Mind (ToM) 80
Thompson, R.F. 9
Thompson, T. 158, 160
Thorensen, C.E. 33
Toth, S.L. 52
Tottenham, N. 192
Tremblay, R. 23, 185
Troutman, A.C. 15, 17, 18, 205, 210
trust: mutual 117, 170; trustworthiness 65
Tschannen-Moran, M. 47
Turnure, J.E. 144
Tushman, M. 114

underachievement 57, 158, 169, 184
understanding: pupils 217; school 111; yourself 212
unintended outcomes 60
Urban, T. 21

Van Werkhoven, W. 96
verbal: abuse 201; persuasion 21
Verquer, M.L. 122
vicarious reinforcement *see* modelling
vindictiveness 189, 193
violence 23, 24, 52, 112, 166, 193, 201
voice: pupil 108; teacher 83, 84, 86, 91
Volkow, N.D. 190
Vygotsky, L.S. 25, 26, 27, 148

Wahba, M.A. 169
Wallace, G. 140, 171
Wannarka, R. 146, 147
warmth (psychological) 63, 67–69, 74, 153, 207
Waugh, D. 148

Webb, J.M. 98
Webb, R.B. 46
Wegner, D.M. 65
Wehlage, G.G. 142
Weick, K.E. 114
Weiner, B. 154, 155
Weinstein, C.S. 48, 142
Weinstein, R.S. 63
well-being 29; pupil 3, 52, 53, 54, 55, 108, 110, 115, 143, 156, 166, 178, 182, 184, 217, 220; teacher 30, 31, 32, 33, 35, 47, 49, 52, 56, 115, 116, 124
Whalen, P.J. 65
Wheldall, K. 18, 30, 31, 147
whole-school approaches 3, 51, 53, 105, 133, 161, 164, 165, 181, 208, 210, 211, 216, 224
Wilcox, B. 109
Wilkinson, C. 117
Williams, L.E. 67, 69
Wills, T. 45
Wilshaw, M. 30, 139
Winsler, A. 26
Wolery, M. 203
Wolfe, M. 146
Woolfolk Hoy, A. 47, 57
workload 31, 47, 55
Wortman, C. 23

Zaleznik, A. 132
Zentner, M. 81
Zhike, L. 166
Zillmann, D. 24
zone of potential development 26
Zuckerman, M 94
Zupan, B. 25

Printed in Great Britain
by Amazon